LITIGATION
AND
TRIAL PRACTICE
FOR THE
LEGAL PARAPROFESSIONAL

SECOND EDITION

By

RODERICK D. BLANCHARD
Meagher, Geer, Markham & Anderson
Member of the Minnesota Bar

Paralegal Series

WEST PUBLISHING COMPANY
St. Paul   New York   Los Angeles   San Francisco

Copy Editor: Peggy O'Mara
Compositor: Metro Graphic Arts
Typeface: Century Schoolbook

Library of Congress Cataloging in Publication Data
Blanchard, Roderick D.
  Litigation and trial practice for the legal
  paraprofessional.

  (Paralegal series)
  Includes index.
  1. Civil procedure — United States. 2. Trial
  practice — United States. I. Title. II. Series.

KF8840.B53 1982   347.73'7   81-19817
ISBN 0-314-63160-7   347.3077   AACR2

2nd Reprint—1983

To my wife, Mary

CONTENTS ▬▬▬▬▬▬▬▬▬▬

4. Affirmative Defenses   55

5. Jurisdiction   59

6. Introduction to Federal Procedure   69

7. Pleadings   81

8. Additional Parties   97

9. Gathering The Evidence   103

10. Investigation   109

Preface ▬▬▬▬▬▬▬▬▬▬▬▬▬▬▬▬▬▬▬

Several years ago I started teaching a course in civil litigation for paralegal students. It was a new course in a new college program. There were no textbooks available, not even an established format for the course. After a good deal of thought and discussion with other lawyers, I concluded that the course should have the purpose of informing paralegal students about the objectives of civil litigation, lawyers' role in handling civil cases, the means by which lawyers' objectives may be achieved, and, just as important, the limitations on lawyers' authority and the courts' powers. This book is predicated upon the belief that the more understanding a paralegal has about the legal system and lawyers' functions, the more competent assistance a paralegal can provide the client and the lawyers with whom he or she works. I do not think that a paraprofessional course in civil litigation should be limited to a study of law office procedures and legal forms. These skills can be quickly learned on the job if a paralegal has a good understanding of the legal system and procedures.

All law offices and all lawyers must follow the same rules of law, the same rules of court procedure, adhere to the same professional and moral standards and strive for the same objectives for their clients. To be an effective professional a paralegal must have an understanding about the reasons for assignments and an appreciation of how his or her efforts fit into the overall representation of the client. A paralegal's education in the profession does not end upon completion of school.

Lawyers should be able to assign numerous responsiblities to paralegals without lowering the high quality of service for which nearly all lawyers strive. I have come to believe that if a lawyer has the assistance of one or more paralegals, there is a good probability that the clients' problems will receive more prompt attention, better and more thorough handling. What's more, the paralegal services may permit lower legal fees with the improved service. The entire legal system will benefit from the help of competent paralegals.

Paralegal assistance is an interesting, even exciting, occupation. Each case is a new challenge. There is a great opportunity for personal pride and satisfaction in doing an important job well. Paralegals should be able to take a major role in gathering the evidence necessary to prove a claim or defense. Paralegals are becoming increasingly involved in phases of trial preparation such as interviewing clients, locating and interviewing witnesses, analyzing and preserving evidence and preparing litigation documents. The variety of problems, their complexity, the personalities of the litigants and witnesses contribute to make civil litigation a fascinating area of the law. But paralegalism is not a short cut to a license to practice law. There are a few necessary limits imposed upon the scope of a paralegal's activities.

Controversies that become the subject of civil litigation must be solved, and they can be solved through the courts. No type of tribunal has worked so well for so long as the English courts, after which our American courts are patterned. It is interesting, therefore, that so many laymen have only a vague understanding of how civil litigation works. Most judges and lawyers who serve the judicial system are convinced of its irreplaceable value. The lack of *informed* criticism of the system is cogent evidence that the system does work well. The increasing work load imposed upon the system by government and society is indicative of the judicial system's ever increasing importance.

I hope that this book will contribute toward a greater appreciation of the judicial system and the legal profession that helps it to work so well.

There are a few dissident voices who urge abandonment of the jury system for some more efficient method of ferreting out the truth in civil lawsuits. The few who would undertake such a drastic change would do so not because the present system does not work well, but for the purpose of obtaining "substantial" justice more economically. "Substantial justice" is something less than *justice*. "Substantial justice" is a term used to describe administrative hearings and arbitration procedures which seek compromise solutions rather than determine who is correct in fact or what law actually is determinative. The advocates of "substantial justice" see it as an acceptable compromise to obtain economies — as long as it is someone else's rights that are in controversy. I strongly believe in the present system and the traditional adversary method of handling civil litigation. I believe that it is imperative that the jury system continue in civil litigation. The checks and balances in our judicial system should not be forsaken for economy or expediency. There are ways in which the present system could be improved to make litigation more economical and speedy. But the basic premises upon which the present system is founded are sound.

Unfortunately, I have found it difficult to convey, in a textbook, the full drama and excitement of civil litigation. I wish that each principle of jurisprudence, each rule of procedure, and each rule of evidence could be illustrated by examples — especially actual experiences. I have tried in this second edition to provide more examples to illustrate legal principles and the operation of the rules of law and procedure. It is my hope that the student's professors can supply more examples and expand upon the matters that are covered.

Introduction

societys mechanism for providing an orderly, just (fairness) predictability, effeciency - role of civil litigation in legal system.

Civil litigation is the method by which private controversies are resolved through judicial means. Through litigation the courts are able to determine and declare parties' legal rights and obligations. A study of civil litigation necessarily involves many facets of the law. A lawyer must call upon all his education and experience for competent handling of litigation. Knowledge of the substantive law must be applied in various categories such as property, contracts, torts, and agency. Substantive law establishes the parties' rights and obligations. After a lawyer has determined what the client's rights and duties are, and whether there is a controversy about them, he must determine how to establish or prove those rights in court.

The determination of legal rights and obligations often depends upon a party's ability to prove certain controverted facts. If there is no dispute on the facts, the controversy can be resolved as a *matter of law* of the judge. A jury does not resolve issues of law — only issues of fact. Questions of law and procedure are decided by judges.

Preparing a case for trial and trying the case require a thorough knowledge of the rules of civil procedure and the rules of evidence. Litigation involves the whole field of law — substantive law, procedural law and the law of evidence. That is why law schools do not teach civil litigation as a separate course. Each case is a unique challenge and must be given individual handling.

In most legal controversies, there is a dispute on the facts which must be resolved before the rules of law can be applied to determine the parties' rights under the law. The facts are established in a trial by the jury's verdict — "verdict" literally means "to speak the truth." The ultimate determination of the parties' respective rights and obligations is the court's decree or judgment. The final step in handling civil litigation is the enforcement of the judgment for the benefit of the prevailing party.

In England the legal profession is divided into two branches. One branch is composed of solicitors who act as the client's agent in the preparation of documents and handling of transactions. The other branch is composed of barristers who prepare and present cases in court. Only barristers may become judges. Lawyers are not similarly categorized in the United States. However, as a practical matter, lawyers are tending to become more and more specialized. As in England, litigation is becoming a field of specialization. Indeed, many lawyers are becoming so specialized in litigation that they handle only certain types of cases. For example, some very able trial lawyers choose to handle only business litigation. They do not feel comfortable handling personal injury cases with all of the medical problems and human emotions that are involved. And some lawyers who handle personal injury cases prefer not to handle litigation involving complicated accounting, business and tax problems. It is a matter of personal preference and aptitude.

Ordinarily, a judge cannot select the types of cases he or she must try. They have a right to expect the lawyers who appear before them to provide the necessary background information on the law and subject matter to enable them to effectively preside over the trial.

The terms "lawyer" and "attorney" are often used synonymously, and that will be true in this book. However, we might just note in passing that "attorney" simply means agent — one who can act for another. Sometimes the term is enlarged to "attorney-at-law." The term "lawyer," however, always refers to a person who is educated and trained in the law; one who may advise clients and represent them in court.

Litigation presupposes a trial even though a large majority of the cases are either settled or dismissed before reaching that final stage. We are principally concerned with the lawyers' preparation for trial, with an emphasis on those areas where paralegals can assume major responsibility. It is important for paralegals to have a good understanding of lawyers' complete role in litigation. A paralegal should know and have an appreciation for the procedures lawyers must follow; the methods by which a client's legitimate objectives may be accomplished; and the standards and ethics which govern lawyers' conduct. With such knowledge, a paralegal can understand how his or her efforts fit into the whole picture; can initiate action for the benefit of the client; and can avoid engaging in any improper conduct which would embarrass the client or expose the client to costs and penalties.

Many of the procedures and activities described herein, historically performed by lawyers, can be done by paralegals who have a good basic understanding of the judicial system. The purpose of this book is to outline and analyze the structure of civil lawsuits and to explain the procedures used in civil litigation. The emphasis is upon litigation as it is conducted in the Federal District Courts. A vast majority of the states have similar, if not identical, rules of civil procedures. We will analyze a lawyer's relationship to the client and with the courts that are served. It is hoped that students will become more familiar with the language of the profession and thus be able to communicate more effectively with lawyers and other paralegals. Students may even gain an appreciation for *legal analysis* which is one of the primary objectives of an education in the law.

Criminal procedures differ substantially from the procedures used in civil litigation. The two branches of the law are quite distinct, so do not assume that the rules and procedures discussed herein necessarily carry over into the field of criminal law.

The student must have access to a current publication of the *Federal Rules of Civil Procedure For The United States District Courts*. Most of the forms and documents contained herein are from actual court files. However, the names, dates and places have been changed even though the matters are of public record. The forms in the Appendix are supplemental to the official forms found in *Federal Rules* and are intended to be illustrative of documents used in litigation. They should be referred to while studying the text. The glossary contained in this book should be helpful, but frequent use of a good law dictionary, such as *Black's Law Dictionary,* will be even greater help.

Most of the examples used in the text come from accident cases. However, the rules and principles apply equally to cases arising out of business dealings, real estate transactions, and other kinds of transactions. Accident cases have been chosen to illustrate problems and solutions primarily because most of us can readily relate to the situations involved.

Throughout the book there are references to *The Federal Rules of Civil Procedure.* These are Rules 1 to 86. There are also references to the *Federal Rules of Evidence* which are numbered 101 to 1103.

There is some repetition in the text. For example, some of the discussion concerning preparation of a client for his or her deposition is also relevant to, and discussed in, the preparation of a client to testify at trial. Discussions of evidentiary problems and procedures appear in the sections on evidence, discovery and trial. Repetition may not excite the imagination, but it does assist learning and helps to show the interrelationship of rules and procedures.

Principles of Litigation ============

Our judicial system and court procedures evolved gradually out of centuries of experience. The procedures and principles have proven effective for peaceably resolving controversies. The judicial system is based upon logic and reason, but its success is largely due to the fact that it takes into consideration the strengths and weaknesses of human nature. It contains inherent checks and balances and numerous safeguards to insure that justice is accomplished according to law. The system may not work perfectly, but it does work exceedingly well.

When a person's legal rights have been violated, causing injury or loss, litigation provides a means for identifying the rights, proving the alleged violations, establishing the nature and extent of the loss, and providing a remedy — usually in the form of money compensation. Compensation is usually referred to by lawyers as "money damages" or simply **damages.**

There should be no reason for people to feel forced to resort to violence or self-help to obtain justice. If the judicial system were too complicated, too expensive, or unpredictable in the dispensation of justice, parties would avoid using courts and resort to self-help. Therefore, the procedures for instituting a lawsuit and prosecuting it have been kept relatively simple. The cost of litigation to the parties is only a fraction of its actual total cost. For example, the current filing fee for the plaintiff in a federal district court is only twenty dollars. There is no filing fee for the defendant. If parties were forced to bear the entire cost of their litigation, such as the cost of the courtroom and court personnel, the parties might be forced to forego valuable rights, or consent to obligations which, in justice, they do not owe. Courts ought to be available to everyone who needs them, and, generally, they are.

Considering the number of courts and the enormous amount of important litigation they handle, it is amazing that they work so well. Most lawyers who regularly appear in court have the utmost respect for the system and confidence in the ability of courts to make just determinations. Hardly any other organ of government enjoys the same degree of respect.

CAUSE OF ACTION

When should a person resort to litigation as means of resolving a controversy? Obviously, not every dispute is a proper subject for litigation. Nor can the courts always provide the ideal remedy or even a satisfactory remedy. Anyone who has a claim that can be formulated into a *cause of action* may put that claim into suit — usually with the help of a lawyer. A cause of action arises only when one party has acted contrary to law and the wrongful act or omission causes some harm, injury, or loss to another. The wrongful act may be the breach of a contractual duty, a statutory duty, or a duty established by common law. But ordinarily, no cause of action will lie unless a real loss or injury is directly caused by the unlawful act or omission.

A party cannot "split" a cause of action. If a party has several items of loss all arising of the same transaction or occurrence, all claims must be included in one lawsuit. For example, an automobile accident may cause a party to suffer automobile damage, personal injuries, a loss of income, medical expenses, and a loss of personal property such as clothing. All of the party's losses must be included in one lawsuit. If any item is omitted, even inadvertently, the party is precluded from recovering damages for the loss in another suit. Likewise, if a plaintiff has a claim in negligence and a claim for breach of warranty against a defendant — both arising out of one occurrence — he or she must sue on both theories in the one lawsuit. Any claims not asserted are waived. Any defense not duly asserted is waived. A defendant cannot obtain a new trial or a second trial on the grounds that he or she inadvertently overlooked a defense that might have been available if duly asserted.

STARE DECISIS

The law must be consistent and predictable. Otherwise, parties would never *know* what their legal rights and obligations are, and lawyers would be unable to advise their clients. Therefore, once a rule of law has been propounded, that rule is adhered to by all courts in that jurisdiction until the precedent of that rule is overruled by a higher court. The principle requiring courts to follow established precedent is called **stare decisis.** *Once decided, lower courts bound by decesion of higher courts in that jurisdiction*

JURISDICTION

A court which undertakes to determine a controversy must have jurisdiction over the parties and the subject matter of the case otherwise its judgment is

Important

unenforceable — a nullity. Jurisdiction over the plaintiff is hardly ever a problem. The plaintiff files a complaint, and thereby submits to the court's jurisdiction. Jurisdiction over the defendant can be obtained only if he or she is within the territorial limits of the court and if service of process (summons and complaint) is accomplished according to law. But once the defendant accedes to the court's jurisdiction — even if inadvertently — it cannot be escaped.

A court's jurisdiction over the subject matter depends upon the powers granted to the court by the authority which created it. The parties cannot give the court jurisdiction over the subject matter. As soon as a court becomes aware of a jurisdictional defect, the case must be dismissed.

A judgment obtained in one jurisdiction is readily enforceable in another jurisdiction. The procedure is quite simple. The foreign judgment is made the subject of a lawsuit in the new jurisdiction. An allegation is made that the judgment was duly obtained in the other court and an authenticated or exemplified copy of the judgment is filed with the new court. The only basis for the defendant (judgment debtor) to avoid the judgment is to prove that the court which rendered the judgment lacked jurisdiction over the defendant or lacked jurisdiction over the subject matter. Upon establishing the foreign judgment, the local court issues its own judgment which may be enforced like any other judgment within its jurisdiction.

MULTIPLICITY OF SUITS · efficiency

The plaintiff cannot sue the defendant in two or more courts on the same claim; courts will not allow multiplicity of litigation. If a case is sued in two courts, the defendant has the right to make a motion for dismissal of one of the cases. Multiplicity of litigation wastes the courts' time and imposes an economic hardship on the parties.

One might wonder why the plaintiff's lawyer would ever start more than one suit. The answer is that, on occasion, the plaintiff may experience difficulty obtaining jurisdiction over one or more of the defendants in one jurisdiction, so he starts as many lawsuits as is necessary, wherever necessary. Also, the plaintiff may start a lawsuit in one jurisdiction to keep the statute of limitations from running out while trying to obtain service on defendants in another jurisdiction.

RES JUDICATA · efficiency (same issue different people / issues)

A controversy may be litigated only once. When the parties have had their controversy determined by a court of competent jurisdiction, they cannot relitigate the matter. If the loser attempts to raise the same issues in a new case, the prevailing party has a complete defense by merely showing that the issues were already determined. The second court will not litigate the same issues a second time. The second court won't even litigate issues which should have been determined in the first trial, but were not. The principle is referred to as *res judicata,* which means the subject matter has been adjudicated.

Neither party may go to another court and contend that the first court reached the wrong result, except through established appellate procedures. If, however, the first determination was made by a court that lacked jurisdiction, that court's **judgment** or decree is a nullity. For a court's judgment to be effective and binding, the court must have jurisdiction over the parties and the subject matter.

COLLATERAL ESTOPPEL (same issue different people)

An accident may give rise to a cause of action in favor of the plaintiff against two or more persons. If the plaintiff sues only one person and the court determines that the plaintiff did not sustain a loss, or that the loss was caused solely by his or her own wrongful conduct, that determination is a bar to any claim the plaintiff may have against other persons not sued in the first case. The principle is called *collateral estoppel* or *estoppel by verdict*. The rationale is that the plaintiff presumbaly tried his case as well as he or she could and presented all of the available evidence; adverse result would be the same in a second trial against a different defendant. Courts should not be bothered by piecemeal litigation. The plaintiff should join in one action all persons who are liable to him or her.

REAL CONTROVERSY

There are fundamental limitations on the kinds of controversies which courts can handle. A controversy must be real, as opposed to hypothetical: It must arise out of an actual transaction or occurrence. Parties could conjure up all kinds of interesting fact situations for which they would like a court's "advisory opinion." But people are not permitted to use the courts to resolve their hypothetical questions. This principle of jurisprudence has some very practical applications. For example, if one party to a contract believes that the other party is going to breach the contract, it might be nice to have the issue litigated before the breach actually occurs. However, there is no controversy between them yet which will permit either party to invoke the power of the courts. For another illustration, suppose that during the course of a trial the parties are able to reach a settlement so that their controversy is, in fact, resolved; it would be considered a fraud upon the court for the parties to continue with the case just to see how it would have been decided.

REAL PARTY IN INTEREST

A lawsuit must be brought in the name of the person who *owns* the cause of action. As stated in Rule 17: "Every action shall be prosecuted in the name of the real party in interest." The defendant has an absolute right to deal with the party who owns the cause of action. If it appears that the plaintiff is not the real party in interest, the action must be dismissed by the court.

Suppose that Johnson loans Smith $500.00 on a promissory note and Smith defaults. Johnson considers the note as almost worthless because

Smith has no ability to pay at the present time. But Jones decides to buy the promissory note from Johnson for $50.00 on the basis that someday Smith will pay or can be compelled to pay in the future. Who owns the cause of action? Jones is the real party in interest in an action on the note. As a general rule, contract claims are assignable. The point with which we are concerned is that the lawsuit must be prosecuted in the name of the real party in interest. As a general rule, personal injury claims cannot be assigned or transferred. This principle tends to discourage intermeddlers from fomenting personal injury litigation.

NECESSARY PARTIES

If a plaintiff fails to include a person who ought to be a party in the lawsuit, either as a plaintiff or defendant, the action is subject to dismissal for failure to include a necessary party. Rule 19. However, the defendant may elect to sue such other person and make him an "involuntary" plaintiff or a third-party defendant. Court procedures encourage, and even require, joinders of all claims into one lawsuit to facilitate the ends of justice and to minimize the number of cases and trials.

For example: Suppose that Smith and Jones are co-owners of a parcel of real estate they claim was damaged by a trespasser. The action against the trespasser must be brought in the names of both Smith and Jones so that the entire claim can be resolved in one action and one trial. The action could not be maintained by only one of them.

JUDGES AND JURIES

A trial judge determines all questions of law and procedure that arise during the course of a trial. He controls the courtroom and the people in it. Lawyers, witnesses, parties and even spectators may be held in contempt of court for disruptive conduct and be summarily punished. This plenary authority is necessary for judges to insure respect for their courts.

The physical features of the typical courtroom promote the dignity and solemnity of the court. Invariably, the judge's bench is raised above the witnesses and spectators. The judge's robes set him or her apart from everyone else and provide an air of classic dignity. The robes are always black, emphasizing the solemnity of the proceedings. Professional ethics require lawyers to underscore the dignity of the court by always being respectful even in moments of acute disagreement. All of these factors help to make federal and state courts unique institutions. They have extensive power which is limited, primarily, by self discipline.

With experience, a judge acquires knowledge and understanding helpful to the handling of his or her responsiblities. But experience may also cause a judge to acquire prejudices for or against certain lawyers, parties, and types of litigation. Even though judges consciously endeavor to keep their personal feelings from affecting their decisions, the potential for problems exists. The real danger of prejudice lies in the subjective determination of controverted facts, the evaluation of witnesses and of their testimony. Since jurors are exposed to only a few cases during their term of service, it is unlikely that they will develop strong, fixed attitudes about a lawyer or a party or certain types of cases. Trial by jury provides one of the important checks to help balance our judicial system.

APPELLATE COURTS

Appellate courts, such as the United States Supreme Court, are primarily concerned with determining questions of law. Only after a controversy has been fully presented to a trial court and a determination made by the trial court does an appellate court become involved. Appellate courts depend upon the trial courts to resolve disputed issues of fact, so that the law can be applied to established facts. Appellate courts are concerned with both matters of substantive law, which determines the parties rights, and procedural law, which determines how the case must be prosecuted.

Appellate courts have inherent power to change court-made rules of law. On occasion, an appellate court determines that an old, established rule of law must be set aside. This is done by issuing a decision and written opinion that expressly *overrules* all prior decisions which are inconsistent with the new holding. Usually the new rule is made effective prospectively only. In that event, all causes of action arising out of transactions or occurrences before the date of the new decision are governed by the old rule of law. But all causes of action arising thereafter are governed by the new rule of law. If an appellate decision does not expressly state that the new rule is to be given prospective effect only, its effect is retroactive as well. Then the new rule applies even to pending cases, but not to cases already adjudicated or settled.

THE AUTHORITY
OF THE COURTS

When a controversy is put into suit, the parties call upon the government to use its personnel, facilities, and power to bring about a resolution of the problem. A court provides the forum in which parties state their claims and present their evidence in an orderly manner. Through the court's subpoena power, parties can require witnesses to appear in court to testify and produce any tangible evidence in their possession. Parties to a pending lawsuit can be compelled to comply with court orders and procedures through the court's power to impose sanctions and penalties. The prevailing party is awarded a judgment in his or her favor which is enforceable against the losing party through the power of the executive branch of the government. Courts have power to litigate controversies between individuals, corporations, governmental agencies, and other legal entities.

Courts Are Neutral
In An Adversary System

Litigation is an *adversary* proceeding. Each party is required to gather and present his or her own evidence. The court remains entirely neutral. Judges are permitted to ask clarifying questions of witnesses during the course of a trial, but, when this is done, the judge usually explains to the jury that they should not give any greater or lesser weight to the testimony elicited through those questions. In federal courts, a trial judge may comment on the evidence after instructing the jury concerning the applicable law. When a judge elects to do this, he should remind the jurors that they are the exclusive judges of the facts. They must determine the truth solely from the evidence presented during the course of the trial. They should not be influenced by what they think the judge wants the verdict to be. A judge usually instructs the jury that his or her comments are not intended to indicate what he or she thinks the outcome of the case ought to be. The judge usually tells the jury that if he or she has said anything or done anything which would seem to indicate such an opinion, the jury is to disregard it.

In some situations courts do intercede on behalf of minors and other incompetent persons to make sure that their rights are protected. Courts always make sure that a guardian is appointed to represent minors who are involved in civil litigation. If the plaintiff is a minor and desires to settle a claim, the settlement cannot be binding on him or her unless the settlement is approved by a court. In determining whether or not to approve a proposed minor's settlement, a court inquires into the circumstances of the occurrence or transaction upon which the defendant's liability is based.

Determining whether a settlement is prudent requires an analysis of the facts on which liability is predicated and an evaluation of the nature and extent of the loss sustained by the minor plaintiff. The defendant's ability to pay may be a factor. If the court feels that the proposed settlement is not adequate for the minor in light of all these factors, the settlement will be disallowed. This is one of the few instances in which judges take a role other than that of a neutral. If a judge refuses to approve a proposed minor's settlement and the defendant is unwilling to pay more, the case must go to trial. If the jury finds in favor of the defendant, the minor plaintiff has no recourse against the judge for not approving the proposed settlement. He must abide by the judgement.

Representatives

In cases involving a person who is incompetent to manage his or her own matters, such as a minor, the court must see to it that a guardian is or has been appointed for the purpose of protecting that person's interests in the litigation. This is true whether the incompetent is a plaintiff or a defendant. A guardian who is specially appointed to represent a litigant is called a **guardian ad litem.** The guardian will be discharged by the court upon conclusion of the litigation. His or her duty in the litigation is to protect the incompetent's interests and carry out the court's orders. If a guardian has already been appointed by a probate court, ordinarily that person is a proper representative to handle the incompetent's litigation. Then, a guardian ad litem is not necessary.

The parties' status in the case is indicated in the title of the action:

John Jones, as guardian ad litem of
Mary Jones, a minor,
                                        plaintiff
        vs.
Robert M. Smith
                                        defendant

The complaint usually contains a separate paragraph alleging that the representative was duly appointed to act in a representative capacity. Rule 9(a) specifically states, however, that such an allegation is not essential.

ASSIGNMENT OF CLAIMS

There are good reasons why personal injury claims cannot be assigned. If Jones sustains injuries due to the tortious conduct of the defendant, Jones is the only person who is permitted to sue the defendant to recover money damages for those injuries. If the law were otherwise, Jones might be inclined to sell his cause of action to another person. It is not too difficult to imagine some well-to-do individual or company speculating in personal injury lawsuits. Some injured parties would be willing to sell their claims for an inadequate sum of money to obtain payment immediately; the buyer might be able to turn a handsome profit on a subsequent **settlement** or jury verdict. Profit making is contrary to the objectives of civil litigation. Also, such dealings tend to shortchange injury victims who are in need. The plaintiff's lawyer must not permit the plaintiff to become a party to such a scheme.

Indemnification for a loss by the plaintiff's own insurer may complicate ownership of the claim. For example, if an automobile is damaged by the defendant in an accidental collision, the automobile owner may elect to receive payment for the loss under the collision coverage of his or her own automobile insurance policy. The insurance company has a right to an assignment of the automobile owner's claim against the tortfeasor. Most automobile insurance policies provide that the insured must bear the first one hundred dollars of the loss. If the insured retains a partial interest in the claim because of a deductible clause, he or she remains owner of the cause of action and is the real party in interest to bring the claim. If the insured succeeds in making a recovery against the tortfeasor, the insured's contract with his or her insurer requires a reimbursement to the insurer out of the recovery. The insured holds the funds in trust for the insurer.

If an insurer pays the full amount of its insured's loss pursuant to the terms of direct loss (not liability) insurance policy, the insurer becomes the real party in interest to bring an action agains the tortfeasor who caused the loss. The insurer owns the cause of action; the action must be brought in the insurer's name. For example, suppose that the insured's automobile was destroyed by a fire caused by the defendant's negligence. The insured may elect to obtain payment for the loss under the automobile policy. The loss comes under the "comprehensive" coverage which does not require the insured to pay any portion of the loss — no deductibles. In that event, when the insurer pays its own insured for the loss the insurer is **subrogated** to the claim against the defendant. The insurer becomes the owner of the cause of the action and is the real party in interest. Suits against the defendant tortfeasor must be brought in the name of the insurance company. The insured has no right to control the litigation. The insured's contract with the insurance company requires the insured to cooperate in the prosecution of the lawsuit.

Whenever a cause of action is properly assigned, it must be prosecuted in the name of the assignee. The maximum amount of money damages that the assignee can recover is, ordinarily, the amount paid for the assignment. Proof that the assignment was duly consummated is part of the cause of action.

COMMENCEMENT OF LAWSUIT

A lawsuit is very easy to start. The first step is preparation of a *complaint* which sets forth the plaintiff's claim against the defendant(s). In federal court the action is *commenced* by filing the complaint with the clerk of court. The clerk then prepares a summons directed to the defendant(s). A United States marshal serves the summons and complaint on each defendant. The summons directs the defendant to serve an *answer* upon the plaintiff's lawyer within twenty days from the date of service of the complaint. The defendant's lawyer prepares an answer in which the defendant must admit those allegations made in the complaint which are true, *deny* the allegations which are not true and allege **affirmative defenses.** The answer must be served upon the plaintiff's lawyer by mailing it or otherwise delivering it to him or her.

Counterclaims and Cross-Claims

The defendant is required to assert, by way of counterclaim, all claims that he or she has against the plaintiff arising out of the same transaction or occurrence. If the defendant fails to assert his claims against the plaintiff, the defendant waives his or her claims. The defendant is barred from bringing the claims in another lawsuit at another time. The entire controversy should be determined once and only once. It is more economical for the parties and the court to resolve the entire matter in one trial. Where there is more than one defendant they may also resolve claims between them by serving **cross-claims.** However, cross-claims are not compulsory.

REMEDIES

Sometimes courts are able to restore to a party the very thing which he or she lost through the wrongful conduct of another person. Included in such things may be real estate, personal property, documents, and, to a certain extent, intangibles such as a job or a reputation. Where restoration is not feasible, the law attempts to provide fair compensation for injury, damage, and losses through an award of "money damages." Money seems to be the best common denominator.

Through a civil suit, a party may be able to prevent (enjoin) an individual or corporation from pursuing a course of conduct that is harmful to persons or property. Courts have the power to issue restraining orders and injunctions to prohibit wrongful conduct. However, courts seldom are able to compel a party to perform activities. Regardless of the specific remedy sought, the procedures used for preparing and presenting a claim or defense are much the same.

DECLARATORY JUDGMENT ACTIONS

Courts may determine controversies which involve the interpretation of documents. A lawsuit brought for this purpose is called a declaratory judgment action. The court judgment determines the meaning and effect of the documents in dispute. For example, if the parties have a disagreement over the meaning of their contract, it is possible for either party to start a *declaratory judgment action* to have a court interpret the contract for them even though the contract has not been breached and no loss has been sustained. The court declares the parties' rights and obligations. The controversy must be real or the action will be dismissed. Declaratory judgment actions are given special treatment by Rule 57. Through declaratory judgments, parties are also able to establish legal status concerning employment, marriage, property ownership, and right to government benefits.

CIVIL PENALTIES

Rarely is civil litigation concerned with penalizing a wrongdoer. An award of money damages is for the purpose of making the plaintiff whole. The financial obligation imposed on the defendant, if found liable, is merely incidental to the objective of providing compensation. Courts do not concern themselves with whether or not the defendant can afford to pay or whether the plaintiff can afford to absorb the loss. There are a few exceptions, however. Many states have legislation imposing a civil penalty recoverable by a plaintiff employee if a dedendant employer wrongfully withholds the employee's wages. The employee may be awarded treble the amount wrongfully withheld. In addition, the employee is allowed interest from the date the wages were due. Similarly, in some states a trespasser who takes crops or lumber from land of another is subject to paying three times the value of the property taken. Obviously, the purpose of treble damages is to deter the wrongful conduct.

One other area of civil penalties deserves mention here. Most jurisdictions allow plaintiffs to recover punitive damages — a penalty assessed against the defendant in addition to compensatory damages — in cases where the defendant intentionally inflicted injury. For example, an intentional battery with a knife, gun or even a fist may be the basis for imposing punitive damages. Punitive damages are recoverable regardless of the degree of injury or other harm — as long as there is some harm. The measure of punitive damages depends upon the character of the wrongful conduct and the financial worth of the defendant.* If the monetary penalty is actually going to penalize the defendant, the size of it must be in proportion to the defendant's ability to pay — at least that is the rationale.

There is considerable and growing opposition to allowing punitive damages in civil actions. Its opponents argue that it subjects the defendant to double jeopardy. They argue that only the state should impose fines for criminal conduct. Where more than one claim may result from a tortious act, the imposition of multiple penalties could have ruinous consequences for the defendant. A claim of punitive damages injects the defendant's financial worth into the case which could adversely influence the jury on other issues. The merits and future of punitive damages are not a subject for this book, but it is a matter of concern to anyone interested in jurisprudence.

EXPENSE OF LITIGATION

Each party to a civil lawsuit must bear most of his own expenses, including investigation costs, most witness fees and lawyers' fees. There are a few exceptions to the general rule. Exceptions generally involve special remedies provided by statute where the monetary loss may be relatively small, but the principle at issue is important. Such legislation makes the courts more readily available to those who have been the victims of some form of official harrassment or discrimination. The prevailing parties in such lawsuits are usually allowed to recover all their expenses, including lawyers' fees. In most cases, however, taxable costs are limited to the filing fee, subpoena fees, United States marshal's fees and some small portion of expert witness fees.

SETTLEMENTS

When parties negotiate a settlement of a claim, they may take into consideration many factors which have no actual relevancy to their legal rights and obligations — such as the effect of the dispute on friends, business associates or relatives. A defendant's lack of insurance or lack of financial responsibility may be an important factor inducing the plaintiff to accept a compromise or reduced settlement. A party might be constrained to settle because of the cost of litigation or the unavailability of witnesses. But legal rights and duties do not turn on the availability or unavailability of insurance or the effect of litigation on personal relationships. If the parties are unable to reach a settlement, they have to set aside all collateral considerations and rely solely upon the factors that are material to an action at law. The parties must evaluate the strengths and weaknesses of their

*The term "exemplary damages" is sometimes used because the award is held out as an example to others and to discourage wrongful conduct.

respective positions in light of rules of law and the procedures by which courts apply those rules of law.

In various ways, the judicial system encourages parties to settle their own disputes. But when the parties cannot reach an accord or agree upon a settlement, the person who wants to force a determination may obtain a judicial determination and a judicial remedy through litigation. It is necessary, however, that the controversy be one which creates a cause of action. This is another way of saying that the controversy must be one over which courts have jurisdiction, one that can be determined by law, and one for which the law provides a remedy.

2

Lawyer and Client Relationships

A lawyer or attorney-at-law is an individual who has been granted the privilege of practicing law within one or more states upon meeting the requirements established by the highest courts of those states. No one has a constitutional right to practice law. An applicant for a license must demonstrate that he or she meets established minimum requirements of knowledge and ability. In some states the requirements are established by the legislature. Most states require an applicant to be a graduate of an accredited law school and to pass the state bar examination. Also, each applicant is screened to determine whether there is any evidence of poor moral character which is a basis for withholding and revoking a license. No one may practice law in any state without a license. Any individual who attempts to practice law without a license is subject to disciplinary proceedings by the courts as though he or she were a lawyer and is subject to criminal prosecution. Paralegals are not authorized to practice law — just as paramedics may not practice medicine. They may work with and assist lawyers. But a lawyer must assume ultimate responsibility for advice given and representation of the client in legal proceedings.

Only after having been authorized by the state's highest court to practice law in the courts of a state is an individual allowed to apply for admission to practice in the federal district courts in that state. A petition for admission to a federal district court must be supported by affidavits of two other lawyers who are admitted to practice in the court. The affidavits must affirm that the petitioner is a competent lawyer and has good moral character. No additional examination in the law is required. In a similar manner, lawyers are admitted to practice in the federal circuit courts of appeals and the United States Supreme Court.

A lawyer must be disbarred for any conduct which constitutes moral turpitude. Of course, this does not mean that misdemeanors or ordinance violations would necessarily result in disbarment. The privilege of practicing law is valuable and cannot be taken away at the "pleasure" of the court. A lawyer is entitled to have a hearing to controvert any charges which may affect his or her privilege to practice law.

Some states have *integrated bars* which means that membership in the bar association is a prerequisite to obtaining a license to practice law. The bar association is clothed with an official status, and given the initial responsibility for determining whether an applicant may be admitted to practice. An integrated bar association also has responsibility for conducting disciplinary proceedings against lawyers who are guilty of unethical conduct. In those states which do not have integrated bars, the highest court in the state has the authority to discipline and disbar delinquent lawyers. The court ordinarily performs the investigation and prosecution functions through personnel appointed by the court. Nevertheless, the authority remains with the court, and it must make the final decision on admissions, disciplinary action and disbarment.

Lawyers may represent clients in state courts, federal courts and other official bodies which conduct hearings affecting legal rights. They are authorized to advise laymen concerning legal problems and may prepare legal documents and instruments for clients such as contracts, wills, deeds, mortgages, patent applications and, of course, legal processes used in civil litigation. Such documents may be prepared by anyone for his own use, but laymen are not allowed to prepare legal documents for another person or for a company. That would constitute an unauthorized practice of law. Sometimes there is a fine line between the functions of lawyers and the activities of real estate brokers, tax advisers and certified public accountants. Indeed, certain accountants are authorized to appear on behalf of clients in tax courts. Just what activities are reserved exclusively to lawyers as part of the practice of law is far from clear. But the law makes a very important distinction between the communications between a client and his or her lawyer and the communications which clients have with other professional business advisers. Only the communications with lawyers are privileged.

The lawyer-client relationship is established whenever a lawyer permits a client to seek his or her professional advice. If the client discloses information, believing it to be under the protection of the attorney-client privilege, that is sufficient to establish the relationship. A lawyer is forever precluded from using such information to the detriment of the client and from disclosing it to others. The communications are privileged whether written or oral.

Fees are a matter of negotiation between a lawyer and client. A lawyer's compensation for services may be for an agreed sum for a particular undertaking, or the fee may be based upon an hourly rate, or, in matters of litigation and collections, the fee may be based upon a percentage of the monies recovered for the client. A lawyer's hourly rate is usually based upon his or her experience and the complexity of the presented problems. In the event a fee is based upon a percentage of monies recovered, the fee is contingent upon an actual recovery, which means the lawyer receives payment only in the event that he or she succeeds in collecting money for the client. Contingent fee percentages range between twenty percent and fifty percent. The percentage ordinarily depends upon the size of the case, the possibilities of an appeal and the likelihood of making a recovery. When a lawyer undertakes to represent a client, he may thereby preclude himself from securing certain other business and is another factor taken into consideration in setting a fee. There is no ethical limitation on the amount of lawyers' fees. But see Disciplinary Rule 2-106 which prohibits "clearly excessive" fees. In some types of cases the amount of the fee or percentage may be limited by statute or court rule. For example, court rules may prohibit a lawyer from charging over a certain percentage when representing a minor. A client is always free to choose another lawyer if the proposed fee arrangement is unacceptable.

A lawyer is considered a **fiduciary** of the client's properties and monies. As a fiduciary he or she must exercise the *highest degree of care* in handling a client's monies, properties, papers and confidential communications. The fiduciary relationship is similar to that of a trustee and the beneficiary of a trust. The fiduciary relationship does not terminate upon the conclusion of the client's business. It lasts forever! For that reason, a lawyer is precluded from representing new clients against a former client unless, of course, the former client gives express consent.

A lawyer is considered to be an agent of a client in handling that client's legal matters. Other parties may deal with the lawyer on the basis that he or she has authority to act for and bind the client. Notices directed to a lawyer as a representative of a client are binding upon the client. However, a lawyer's authority is limited to the particular matter for which he or she has been retained.

There are some very important limitations on a lawyer's authority in handling a client's litigation. A lawyer must not start a lawsuit for the client without the client's permission; nor dismiss a lawsuit without the client's express authority and direction to do so. Settlement negotiations may be conducted for the client, but he or she is not allowed to accept or reject a settlement without securing authority to do so — even if the settlement is known to be in the client's best interest.

A lawyer's authority and responsibility to a client goes beyond an ordinary agency. He or she has implicit authority to do whatever is reasonably necessary for the preparation and conduct of a trial. A lawyer may prepare interrogatories, schedule depositions, attend calendar calls, attend pretrial conferences and make representations to the court about state of readiness of the case. He or she may enter into stipulations with opposing parties concerning the evidence and trial procedures as well as agree or object to the admissibility of evidence. Of course, he or she may consult the client about such matters, but is not required to do so. A lawyer has the ultimate responsibility for handling the litigation, but is always subject to the client's ultimate authority.

Lawyers have dual roles in the judicial system. They are officers of the courts in which they practice. But they are also representatives of their clients. Lawyers are required to act in their clients' best interests and give them advice which will benefit the client in the conduct of their legal matters. But lawyers are also required to protect the courts from frauds and abuse. The success of the judicial system is absolutely dependent upon the ability of lawyers to serve their clients' needs *and* the courts' interests without compromise. Consequently, a very stringent code of professional ethics has been established to guide lawyers. Any violation of the code of ethics hurts the legal profession and contaminates the entire judicial system.

The *Code of Professional Responsibility* was adopted by the American Bar Association in 1969. The Code provides guidelines for resolution of various ethical problems. Many states have adopted the Code and the Disciplinary Rules as established standards of conduct which, if violated, provide the basis for imposing sanctions — including disbarment.

The Preamble to the *Code of Professional Responsibility* well states the importance of the ethical considerations.

Preamble.   The continued existence of a free and democratic society depends upon recognition of the concept that justice is based upon the rule of law grounded in respect for the dignity of the individual and his capacity through reason for enlightened self-government. Law so grounded makes justice possible, for only through such law does the dignity of the individual attain respect and protection. Without it, individual rights become subject to unrestrained power, respect for law is destroyed, and rational self-government is impossible.

In fulfilling his professional responsibilities, a lawyer necessarily assumes various roles that require the performance of many difficult tasks. Not every situation which he may encounter can be foreseen, but fundamental ethical principles are always present to guide him. Within the framework of these principles, a lawyer must with courage and foresight be able and ready to shape the body of the law to the ever-changing relationships of society.

Lawyers, as guardians of the law, play a vital role in the preservation of society. The fulfillment of this role requires an understanding by lawyers of their relationship with and function in our legal system. A consequent obligation of lawyers is to maintain the highest standards of ethical conduct.

The Code of Professional Responsibility points the way to the aspiring and provides standards by which to judge the transgressor. Each lawyer must find within his own conscience the touchstone against which to test the extent to which his actions should rise above minimum standards. But in the last analysis it is the desire for the respect and confidence of the members of his profession and of the society which he serves that should provide to a lawyer the incentive for the highest possible degree of ethical conduct. The possible loss of that respect and confidence is the ultimate sanction. So long as its practitioners are guided by these principles, the law will continue to be a noble profession. This is its greatness and its strength, which permit of no compromise.

Although the Code is directed at lawyers, it applies, at least by implication, to any person who assists lawyers, whether as an investigator, secretary or a certified paralegal.

The Disciplinary Rules were formulated out of ethical considerations. The disciplinary rules help to define ethical considerations and specify their application to problem areas. If accused of a violation of professional ethics, a lawyer is entitled to a hearing which meets all of the requirements of due process of law; has a right to know the charges against him or her; to present evidence in defense and to be heard by an impartial tribunal.

A lawyer must not direct or encourage a client to engage in conduct that is unethical for the lawyer. He or she must not let the client violate the lawyer's oath by making false answers to interrogatories, or testify falsely, or procure the absence of witnesses, or suborn perjury. Whatever is forbidden to the lawyer is forbidden to the client as well. If a lawyer discovers that a client is guilty of some such impropriety, he or she must take affirmative action to correct the wrong. Some of the considerations and alternatives are discussed below.

Lawyers are forbidden to engage in activities that foment litigation. It is not difficult to imagine a situation where a lawyer finds that business is a little slow, so is tempted to examine public records to find a problem with the title to some real estate for the purpose of obtaining a client — and some business. Similarly, unscrupulous lawyers could research newspapers and magazines for articles to find potential libel suits. In such cases, the lawyers create problems solely for their own financial gain. Similarly, lawyers are in a good position to encourage accident victims to pursue litigation rather than drop a claim or settle out of court. Such practices are degrading to the profession and could flood the courts with a lot of petty, unnecessary and unwanted litigation. Any lawyer who creates that kind of business should not be practicing law. Society's interests should be served — not damaged — by lawyers and litigation.

A lawyer who incites litigation is subject to disciplinary proceedings and possible disbarment. Paralegals, too, must avoid instigating litigation. That is not to say that a paralegal must avoid recommending a good lawyer when and where one is needed, but should not create a controversy where none exists.

Historically, lawyers were forbidden to advertise their services. They could not even permit others to advertise on their behalf. The profession is currently in a dilemma over advertising. Advertising is considered to be degrading, but perhaps necessary if the public is going to be fully informed about the availability of services and the charges for services. There are many people who are not personally acquainted with any lawyer and who are unaware of the various services that lawyers do provide. Lawyers may permit their names to be listed in professional directories. These directories are particularly useful to lawyers who need to refer clients to other lawyers or who otherwise need to obtain professional assistance in another community. The principal such directory is *Martindale-Hubbell* which is published in several large volumes each year.

CHAMPERTY

A lawyer is not permitted to provide financial support for a client by paying his or her living expenses during the pendency of litigation. Certainly it would be considerate and even charitable for a lawyer to provide a means of support for a client until the case is concluded, especially if the client is disabled and unable to work due to injuries. But if such a practice were undertaken, a lawyer would soon find him or herself personally inolved in the client's financial affairs and personally interested in the outcome of the case. The danger is much too great that his or her professional judgments could be affected by personal interest in the litigation. The inclination might be to recommend for or against a settlement in light of his or her own needs rather than those of the client. Rarely is good advice rendered by a person who is personally involved in the matter. There is also the problem that financing clients could become an expected practice; and most lawyers would find that to be an impossible burden. The lending of money is better left to banks and other financial institutions. The practice of advancing monies to a litigant on the basis that the "loan" will be paid out of the verdict or settlement is known as *champerty,* and it is unethical.

If a lawyer becomes financially involved in the client's case, there is the possibility that before the case is over, the client may end up "assigning" the claim to the lawyer. Assignment of personal injury claims is contrary to public policy. It is persmissible to assign causes of action arising out of transactions such as contract matters. But in the personal injury field, there is, again, a real danger of *maintenance* through the device of assignments. A lawyer must not pay a client's litigation costs or support the client — "maintain" him — during the pendency of the litigation. A lawyer is permitted to advance, on behalf of the client, various expenses incurred in connection with the litigation. But this may be done only on the basis that ultimately the expenses will be paid by the client regardless of the outcome of the case.

SOLICITATION AND ADVERTISING

Lawyers are forbidden to solicit business. Solicitation of litigation inconveniences the public and degrades the profession. The term "ambulance chasing" is probably a good one as being descriptive of one form of solicitation of legal business. It suggests that the first lawyer to the accident or to the victim's bedside is going to get the case. Certainly, if solicitation were permitted, there would be a tendency amongst lawyers to try to be the first one to get to the victim, or the lawyers might hire "runners" to find and sign up clients. People who have just been injured or who have sustained some grievous loss through an accident should not be hounded by lawyers wanting business. A decedent's relatives should not be pursued by lawyers anxious to probate the estate. The criminal courts should not be crowded with lawyers waiting to sell their services to persons just charged with a criminal offense. One can imagine lawyers lined up like taxi cabs waiting for business. The dignity of the profession and its self-esteem must be maintained. Professional standards and conduct must reflect the needs of the community and society. Those needs take precedence over an individual lawyer's need to earn a living in the practice of law.

LAWYER-CLIENT PRIVILEGE

Communications between a lawyer and client are privileged. The privilege belongs to the client, not to the lawyer. The client may waive his or her privilege either intentionally or inadvertently. All that is needed is for a client to relate to some third person the substance of the otherwise privileged communications. The privilege applies to written communications as well as oral. A lawyer's records prepared from those communications are similarly privileged.

There is a substantial difference between confidential communications and privileged communications. A matter which is kept secret between two or more persons would be considered confidential. Most businesses are desirous of keeping their customers' matters confidential. Banks, lending institutions, credit card companies, department stores strive to keep their records from getting into the hands of the curious. They avoid publicizing information in their possession about their customers. Nevertheless, a court of law could compel a company to produce its records if the records were relevant to a controversy in suit. But if a communication is *privileged,* no person and no court can legally compel a disclosure of the communication for *any* purpose.

The reason a client's statements to his or her lawyer are privileged, is that the client is able to obtain good, competent legal advice only by "telling all" to the lawyer. If laboring under the fear that his or her statements to the lawyer may be used as an admission or confession against them later on, he or she might be inclined to hold back information which is vital. The privilege applies whether the client discusses marital problems, business problems, criminal matters, preparation of tax returns, etc. It does not matter what the subject is as long as the client is seeking professional legal help or advice.

The law makes an important distinction between advice sought by the client in order to determine legal rights, and advice sought for the purpose of evading law in some current or future activity. For example, if a client should consult a lawyer for the purpose of working out a plan to illegally evade taxes, the communications would not come within the privilege. Indeed, under those circumstances, a lawyer would be duty bound to try to persuade the client to comply with the law. If that fails, he could be required to inform the proper authorities of the client's scheme. The lawyer could even be compelled to testify against the would-be client concerning the client's scheme.

For a long time, it was the rule that the privileged status of a communication was lost if the subject matter was voluntarily disclosed to any third person, even the lawyer's private secretary. Most courts, however, now recognize that lawyers must act through others — such as a private secretary — and in some jurisdictions the privilege has been extended to include them. Perhaps courts will determine that the privilege extends to communications with paralegals who work with lawyers on behalf of clients. Courts should recognize that it is desirable and necessary for lawyers to impart privileged information to paralegals assisting them. Of course, if the privilege is enlarged in this manner, it will be necessary for paralegals to be subject to the same close controls which courts have over lawyers and subject to the same rigid professional ethics.

Recently, there have been several cases in which news reporters have attempted to establish a rule that their "confidential" news sources have, or should have, a privileged status. In the past, a reporter could be punished through a contempt of court citation for failure to disclose the identity of witnesses who provided him or her with information. The issue presented to the courts in these cases is whether the need for privileged news sources outweighs the need for identification of witnesses who have important evidence relevant to criminal and civil suits. The question also arises whether any news items is newsworthy if the name of the source of this information is not subject to disclosure. Some reporters who have challenged the law and who have attempted to bring about a change have been forced to spend time in jail for refusal to comply with court orders directing them to testify. Their incarcerations were punishment for being in contempt of court, i.e., failing to comply with court orders.

If a client makes derogatory statements against his or her lawyer or commences suit for malpractice, the client cannot assert the privilege in an effort to keep the former lawyer from defending him or herself. The privilege is intended to be used as a shield and never as a sword. A lawyer may use all of the client's records and communications, whether written or oral, to defend himself.

Though a lawyer owes to a client duties of complete fidelity and ordinary care, the highest obligation is to the courts. Therefore, he or she must not perpetrate a fraud upon a court by producing false testimony or otherwise abuse the judicial process for any purpose. If a lawyer should learn that a client has attempted to bribe a witness or juror, or the like, his or her first effort should be to urge the client to confess the wrongdoing to the other party in the action with the hope that the matter can be resolved. If the client refuses to do so, the lawyer's only recourse may be to inform the court of the wrongful act. Some authorities argue that, under those circumstances, a lawyer may withdraw from further representation of the client, and should make no disclosure to the court. This position is based on the theory that the criminal act — the fraud — has already been perpetrated without the lawyer's knowledge. At this point, the client is in need of legal advice because of the problem the client created, just as for any other crime. Most courts, if not all, have rejected this argument.

If a lawyer handles a client's legal matters in such a way as to realize a profit, aside from a proper legal fee for services, there is a presumption that the profit was obtained by undue influence or fraud. The possibility of this happening is particularly real in the field of estate planning, business planning and real estate transactions. If the client or client's representative (such as a guardian or administrator) brings a claim against the lawyer, the lawyer has the burden of showing that the transaction was fair and otherwise proper. For example: if a lawyer prepared a will for a client and included him or herself as a beneficiary, the heirs would be in a good position to challenge the bequest. The lawyer would have the burden of proving that the bequest was in accord with the testator's wishes, that the testator was competent, and that the testator was not subjected to any undue influence.

A lawyer, of course, is required to exercise due diligence and ordinary skill in handling a client's legal matters. If negligent — that is, failing to measure up to the standards of ordinary care exercised by the profession in that state — he or she is liable to the client for any loss proximately caused by the negligence. Negligence in rendering professional service is commonly called legal malpractice. Due care does not mean that lawyers handling litigation must win their client's cases. Theoretically, lawyers are going to "lose" half of the cases they try. The standard of ordinary care or due care does mean that trial lawyers must possess the knowledge and skill ordinarily possessed by lawyers handling civil litigation. Lawyers must use due care in gathering the evidence. They must exercise ordinary ability in trying cases. The same skill and knowledge must be applied in the preparation of legal documents and in giving legal advice. Lawyers seem to have the most problems in lack of due diligence. It is very easy to wait too long before giving necessary notices, commencing an action, or otherwise *actively* pursuing matters — especially if the matter seems to lack substance or merit. With the added help of paralegals lawyers may do better at keeping current.

A client may discharge his or her lawyer at will. The relationshp is considered to be so personal and so dependent upon the client's trust, that a client cannot be compelled to continue using a lawyer whom he or she does not want. A client does not even have to have a good reason for terminating the relationship. A lawyer, on the other hand, may have a little more difficulty terminating the relationship. For example, if the lawyer is handling a case that is very near trial, withdrawal from the case could impose a hardship not only on the client but also upon the court. Some courts have special rules and procedures which lawyers must follow to be able to withdraw from a case. Some courts have determined that a client's inability to pay a fee for legal services is not grounds for a lawyer to withdraw. This is especially true in criminal cases. Consequently, lawyers may feel constrained to obtain a substantial retainer at the outset.

If a lawyer does withdraw from a case, a letter should be written to the client confirming the withdrawal. Proof of delivery of the letter should be established through some third person or the post office, i.e., registered mail. Otherwise, if problems develop at a later date, the client might try to excuse him or herself on the basis that the lawyer was still acting on his or her behalf. It would appear then that the lawyer was not doing his job. A letter or formal notice of withdrawal helps to protect against such problems. If a lawyer is handling litigation which is actually pending in court, a formal notice of withdrawal must be filed with the court along with the other requirements established by local practice or rules. In some states a lawyer may have to obtain permission from the court to withdraw.

Occasionally, a would-be client discusses the merits of a possible claim with a lawyer and wants the lawyer to handle the case, but the lawyer advises that the claim has no merit, or for other reasons, refuses to take the case; but before the would-be client gets around to talking to another lawyer, the statutue of limitations* runs against the claim. Before hand, the lawyer should make sure that the client knows: (1) he or she is not going to handle the case; and (2) the date on which the statute of limitations will run against the alleged cause of action. The best procedure is to put this information in a letter to the would-be client so that the possibility of a misunderstanding is reduced. It is also a good idea to establish proof of delivery of the letter.

If discharged, a lawyer is entitled to be paid for services rendered. Payment may be based on the value of the services *received* by the client. He or she may not necessarily be entitled to recover attorney's fees on the basis of the original retainer agreement. Of course, one indicator of the value of such services is the original retainer agreement. If the client refuses to pay, the lawyer may file a lien with the court in which the action is pending. The lien gives the lawyer a claim upon any recovery of money obtained by the client in the particular case. This puts the new lawyer and adverse party on notice of the first lawyer's claim. The amount of the lien is subject to determination by litigation if the parties are unable to agree upon it. A lawyer always has the right to bring an action in court for payment of a fee. Otherwise, lawyers would be at the mercy of unscrupulous clients.

If a party undertakes self-representation in litigation, he or she is referred to as an "attorney pro se". Usually judges try to discourage laymen from representing themselves. They can easily become lost in the procedural maze and substantive law. It is not unusual that when undertaking self-representation a layman does so principally out of spite or desire to fight the system. He or she has probably consulted with several lawyers who advise that the claim is not valid or that his or her purposes are misguided. If the claim is too large for the small claims court, it probably warrants the expense of a lawyer's help.

A lawyer is an officer of the court and must conduct him or herself in a professional manner at all times, showing respect to the court even when seriously disagreeing with the presiding judge. A lawyer's zeal and desire to serve a client must not provoke misuse or abuse of the court. His or her highest duty is always to the court. If believing that a judge has acted improperly in any matter, a lawyer has the right and duty to bring that fact to the attention of the proper authorities. He or she must not insult or cast aspersions on the court in public.

There should never be a direct conflict between a lawyer's duties to a client and his other obligation to the court. The Canons of Professional Ethics help lawyers to determine where their obligations lie and how to avoid or resolve apparent conficts.

*The term "limitations" means the time at the end of which no action at law or suit in equity can be maintained.

3

Causes of Action, Remedies, and Defenses

The law strives to afford a suitable remedy to every person who has suffered an actual loss caused by another's illegal conduct. However, there seems to be no limit to the types of controversies that evolve between people. Courts cannot undo every wrong, nor can they provide a remedy for every loss and inconvenience. After centuries of cogitation and experience the courts have concluded that only certain types of wrongful conduct which causes injuries or losses should be redressed through the courts. A claim for which relief may be granted by the courts is called a *cause of action*. Hence, a civil lawsuit is often referred to as an **action at law** or simply an *action*.

When a lawyer begins handling a case, whether for the plaintiff or defendant, he or she must determine whether the facts giving rise to the dispute established a cause of action. If one or more of the necessary elements to a cause of action is missing, the claim must fail. The lawsuit will be dismissed. Time, effort and money used to prove a claim that cannot be formulated into a cause of action is simply wasted. If the plaintiff does not have a cause of action, he or she should be told so as soon as possible.

The course of a lawyer's investigation, discovery procedures and trial preparation is dictated by the legal issues, and the legal issues are largely determined by the elements of the cause of action. If the claim is to be based on common law negligence, the plaintiff's lawyer must obtain evidence showing (1) that the defendent failed to exercise reasonable care in light of the foreseeability of harm to others, or acted contrary to a statute; (2) that the negligent act or omission was a breach of a legal duty owed to the plaintiff; (3)

that the negligent act or omission caused the accident (occurrence) in question; (4) that the negligent act was a direct or proximate cause of the injury or loss sustained by the plaintiff. If any one of the these elements is missing, the plaintiff's claim does not meet the requirements of a cause of action in negligence. If the claim is based on a contract, the plaintiff's lawyer must obtain evidence to prove (1) that the parties were legally competent to enter into a contractual relationship; (2) that a contract was made through a valid offer and acceptance; (3) that a consideration was exchanged between the parties; (4) that if the alleged contract is of the type that must be in writing and signed, that the formalities were met; (5) that the defendant's alleged breach caused the plaintiff to suffer an actual loss. If any one of these elements is missing, the claim cannot be a cause of action for breach of contract.

The defendant can defeat the claim, whether in tort or contract, by disproving any one of the elements necessary to the plaintiff's claim. But the burden of proof is upon the plaintiff to establish the elements of the claim. The burden is not on the defendant to disprove the claim.

A client may feel that he or she has a claim for breach of contract, but on analysis, the lawyer may determine that the only possible cause of action is for fraud which involves different elements and a different measure of damages. Similarly, a client may want to sue for an alleged trespass to recover money damages, but upon reducing the facts to their basic elements, a lawyer may determine that the proper claim — or only claim — is for an injunction to abate a nuisance* created by the defendant's conduct.

Every cause of action requires the plaintiff to prove (1) that the defendant breached a legal duty owned to plaintiff; (2) that the plaintiff sustained a compensible injury or loss for which the law provides a remedy; (3) that the defendant's breach of duty was the proximate cause of plaintiff's injury or loss. Each cause of action is predicted upon a particular legal duty protecting certain kinds of interests of a person or his or her property, and provides a particular remedy for a proven wrong. Much of a lawyer's education and training is devoted to obtaining an understanding of causes of actions, their elements and application.

For each cause of action, certain **affirmative defenses** are available. An affirmative defense usually arises out of some wrongful conduct on the part of the plaintiff — but not always. Each affirmative defense has certain elements which the defendant must prove. Proof of an affirmative defense by a preponderance of the evidence totally defeats the plaintiff's cause of action, or, in certain cases, reduces the amount of plaintiff's recovery of money damages. The defendant must prove affirmative defenses or the defenses are disallowed.

A paralegal is not ordinarily expected to know all about all causes of action and all affirmative defenses. But when working on a particular case, a paralegal should familiarize him or herself with the elements applicable to

---

*A nuisance, in this context, is any wrongful conduct that substantially interferes with or disturbs the occupant's use and enjoyment of his or her real property. *Nuisance* is a cause of action for which the courts provide a remedy at law.

the particular cause of action and the affirmative defenses raised. Any lawyer should be happy to have paralegals indicate an interest in the technical aspects of the case. As stated earlier, the more knowledgeable a paralegal is about the law and legal procedures, the more effectively he or she can handle litigation. But it is beyond the scope of this book to discuss causes of actions and affirmative defenses in depth.

Some of the more common types of causes of action are discussed below. The purpose of the analysis is to show that a cause of action *always* has certain elements which must be established. If the claim does not include the elements necessary to a cause of action, or they cannot be proved, the claim is not a matter for the courts.

BREACH OF CONTRACT

K - means contract

In its most simple form, a contract is merely a legally enforceable promise. If the defendant has breached a contract, he or she is subject to an *action for breach of contract* by which the plaintiff is able to recover money damages compensating for the losses resulting from the breach. The parties ordinarily enter into a contract expecting that each will benefit from it. The benefits may be monetary profit or the acquisition of something desired, such as land, personalty or even an idea. The type of remedy afforded by law depends, in part, on the purpose of the contract and the parties' objectives and reasonable expectations.

When undertaking a case involving an alleged breach of contract, a lawyer's first effort must be to determine whether there is a contract. An action for breach of contract presupposes a valid, enforceable contract. Contracts may take many forms and may come about in numerous ways. Some contracts are in writing, signed by both parties; some contracts are entirely oral; some are implied by the parties' conduct; and some are implied by operation of law. Notwithstanding the variety of types of contracts, there are certain elements that are essential to all contracts. An enforcible contract requires: (1) parties legally capable of entering into a contract; (2) an offer to contract; (3) an acceptance of the offer; (4) the exchange of legal consideration; (5) a meeting of the parties' minds concerning the subject of the contract; (6) compliance with particular formalities imposed by statute for some types of contracts. A purported contract is not enforcible if the object of the contract is unlawful.

The parties must have the capacity to contract. Otherwise, the contract is void or voidable at the election of the party who lacked capacity. A person is not capable of making an enforcible contract if a minor, insane, or intoxicated at the time of the making. A company that is not incorporated has no separate legal standing and cannot contract for itself. An unincorporated company can contract only through its owners as individuals. Partnerships are legal entities that may contract through one or more authorized partners.

The plaintiff who sues on the contract, has the burden of proving that the contract was made and that he or she has performed all conditions precedent or that all conditions precedent have occurred.* The plaintiff must prove that the defendant breached the contract, and the nature and extent of the loss resulting from the defendant's breach of the contract. The proof must be by a fair preponderance of the evidence.

The contract offer ordinarily contains the substance and terms and conditions of the contract. Acceptance of the offer must be effectively communicated to the offeror in compliance with any conditions imposed by the offeror. If the acceptance is qualified, or changes one or more of the essential terms of the offer, the acceptance may actually be a counter-offer which does not create a contract unless duly accepted by the original offeror.

A contract is made only if the parties reach a meeting of the minds concerning the subject matter. For example, if the seller offers to sell an automobile to the buyer, it is essential that they have in mind the same vehicle or a valid contract cannot result from their negotiations. There is a fine line between this requirement for all contracts and another concept referred to as **unilateral mistake** which does not invalidate an otherwise good contract. A unilateral mistake is any misunderstanding that one party to the contract has.

A contract requires the exchange of consideration. A simple promise — even if made under oath — is not a contract and cannot be enforced at law. Unless a consideration is given for the promise, there is no contract. The most common consideration is the payment of money. However, a mere promise exchanged for another promise may be legal consideration which will support a contract. If a contract recites that a consideration has been paid but, in fact, it was not, the alleged contract is defective and unenforceable.

Complaint Alleging
Action in Breach of Contract

Comes now plaintiff and for its complaint against defendant alleges:

1. [Jurisdictional Allegations]

Establish contract

2. On August 2, 1982, defendant contracted to sell to plaintiff and deliver to plaintiff ten tons of newsprint quality rolled paper.

3. That the terms and conditions of said contract between the parties was reduced to writing, a copy of which is attached hereto and incorporated by reference.

4. That said written contract was duly signed by defendant's representative at the time and place specified therein.

Conditions Precedent

5. That plaintiff paid to defendant the sum of $3,000.00 as the initial partial payment as recited in the written contract.

6. That all conditions precedent of said contract have been performed or have occurred.

Breach of Contract

7. That defendant did not deliver said newsprint paper to plaintiff as required by the terms of said contract, and defendant is in default.

*A condition precedent must occur before the contract becomes effective even though all the terms and conditions have been agreed upon. A common example of a condition precedent is where the buyer agrees to purchase a new house on condition that he can sell his present house.

8. That plaintiff has necessarily sought and obtained other newsprint paper to meet its needs and requirements.

Loss due to Brief

9. That as a direct consequence of defendant's failure to perform on said contract plaintiff has suffered damages as follows:

a. plaintiff is entitled to recover the $3,000.00 initially paid to defendant as a down payment, together with interest at the rate specified in the written contract [or the legal rate provided by law].

b. plaintiff's printing business was necessarily interrupted for a period of ten working days causing plaintiff to suffer a loss of profits in the amount of $10,000.00.

c. plaintiff was required to purchase similiar newsprint from another supplier at an additional cost of $6,000.00.

Wherefore, plaintiff prays for judgment against defendant in the sum of $19,000.00 together with plaintiff's costs and disbursements herein.

(date)

_____

Attorneys for plaintiff

Answer

Comes now defendant, and for its answer to plaintiff's complaint:

1. Denies each and every allegation, statement, and matter in the complaint contained, except as hereinafter expressly admitted or alleged.

2. Admits the allegations of paragraphs one (1) through eight (8) of the complaint.

3. Admits that defendant is liable to plaintiff in the amount of $3,000.00 for money had and received, but denies defendant is liable for interest thereon.

First Defense

Alleges that paragraph nine b (9b) fails to state a claim upon which relieve can be granted.

Second Defense

Alleges that on August 7, 1982, defendants entire plant and warehouse was destroyed by fire through no fault of defendant, and that the loss of the plant and warehouse made impossible defendant's performance of the contract.

Wherefore, defendant prays that plaintiff take nothing by its alleged cause of action, and that defendant have judgment for its costs and disbursements.

(date)

_____

Attorneys for defendant

Certain contracts must be in writing and signed to be enforceable. The state statute which identifies contracts that must be written and signed is commonly referred to as the Statute of Frauds. The statute specifies the necessary elements to each written contract.

There are other bases upon which the defendant may properly seek to avoid a contract that was duly made. If the plaintiff breached the contract, his or her breach provides the defendant with a complete defense. But the defendant has the burden of proving that plaintiff also breached the contract. If the contract was obtained through fraud by the plaintiff, the contract is **voidable** by the defendant, but the defendant must allege and prove the fraud. If the parties made a new agreement to replace the old one and fully performed the new agreement, the old one is a nullity and unenforceable. The new agreement and its performance are called an *accord and satisfaction*. An accord and satisfaction is a complete defense. The defendant has the burden of proving the defense. A plaintiff's failure to sue within the time provided by the state's *statute of limitations* is also a defense. The defendant must plead the statute of limitations in his or her answer. The defendant must prove the facts making the statute applicable. Once in a while, after a contract is made, circumstances develop making performance of the contract impossible. *Impossibility* is a defense which the defendant must plead and prove. It is a complete defense.

In most instances, contracts are mutually beneficial. When a breach occurs concerning one facet of the contract, the parties may elect to continue performance of the rest of the contract. That may be the only realistic choice in some cases. If a party elects to proceed with the contract knowing the other party has breached one of its terms or conditions, the election to proceed may constitute a *waiver* of the breach. It would be unfair for the plaintiff to sue on the contract after waiving a breach. Therefore, *waiver* is a complete defense which the defendant must prove.

There are other affirmative defenses which may be available in contract actions. A partial list of them appears in Rule 8 (c).

SPECIFIC PERFORMANCE

In some breach of contract actions, the award of money damages is clearly an insufficient remedy. In those cases, a court of **general jurisdiction** has the authority to require a party to perform the contract. The remedy is called *specific performance*. Courts are frequently asked to decree specific performance of contracts involving the sale of land. The law views each parcel of land as unique. Therefore, money damages are not necessarily adequate. That is not to say that every breached contract for the sale of land is enforced by an action for specific performance. Another example is a contract for the sale of a piece of art which is unique. The buyer may force the seller to deliver the art work and title by an action for specific performance. One type of contract for which specific performance is not allowed is a contract for personal services. Courts cannot compel an individual to work. However, a court may order a person *not* to work or not to perform certain services or activities. A party who is ordered not to do something is *enjoined* from performing the specified activity.

Complaint Alleging Action for Specific Performance

Comes now plaintiff and for his cause of action against defendant alleges:

1. [Jurisdictional Allegations]
2. That on or about August 3, 1981, plaintiff and defendant, through his duly appointed agent, entered into a written contract by which defendant agreed to sell and plaintiff agreed to buy certain specific real estate. A copy of Said contract is attached hereto as Exhibit A.
3. That as provided by said written contract plaintiff duly tendered to defendant the purchase price of the land specified in Exhibit A.
4. That defendant wrongfully refused to accept the tender.
5. That defendant wrongfully refused to convey title of said land to plaintiff.
6. That plaintiff is ready, willing and able to perform on the contract and hereby offers the full purchase price to defendant.
7. That plaintiff cannot obtain similar land similarly situated which would meet plaintiff's requirements.
8. That all conditions precedent have been performed or have occurred.

Wherefore, plaintiff prays that defendant be ordered to specifically perform the contract by providing plaintiff with a warranty deed to said land.

If specific performance is not granted, plaintiff prays for judgment against defendant in the sum of $50,000.00 as damages for defendant's breach of contract.

Plaintiff further prays for his costs and disbursement herein.

(date)

_____

Attorney for plaintiff

Answer

Comes now defendant and for his answer to plaintiff's complaint:

1. Denies each and every allegation, statement and matter in said complaint contained, except as hereinafter expressly admitted or alleged.
2. Admits that he is the owner of the land described in Exhibit A.
3. Denies that he executed the contract identified as Exhibit A attached to the complaint.
4. Denies that any person had authority to sign said contract for him or to act on his behalf concerning said land.
5. Denies that he received any consideration for the alleged contract.

Wherefore, defendant prays that plaintiff take nothing by reason of his pretended cause of action and that defendant have judgment for his costs and disbursements herein.

(date)

_____

Attorney for defendant

FRAUD AND DECEIT

A misrepresentation may become the basis for an action in *fraud*. The law recognizes that many people make many statements, both written and oral, that are not true or only half true, but no legal liability should result. If a person regularly tells people that he or she is five years younger than is reality, should that misrepresentation create a cause of action? Of course not. But if a person misrepresents his or her age in an application for a life insurance policy and the insurer relies upon the misrepresentation to its detriment, the misrepresentation may be actionable as a fraud. If the owner of an automobile claims that an automobile gives thirty miles per gallon of gasoline, but it actually delivers only fifteen miles per gallon, the misrepresentation is reprehensible but it is not actionable. However, if the seller of an automobile makes a similar misrepresentation to a buyer, a cause of action for *fraud* may accrue in favor of the buyer. Suppose the seller of a house misrepresents to his buyer that the neighbors are really nice people when he or she knows that the neighbors are cantankerous, difficult people. Does the misrepresentation create a cause of action for fraud? Suppose the seller of a residential lot tells the purchaser that the area is quiet, but a month later an airplane flight pattern is established directly above the property. Is there a fraud? Suppose an art dealer misrepresents a certain painting to be an original and the painting is purchased by a knowledgable collector who knows that it is not an original. Does the collector have a claim for fraud? Does it make a difference whether the misrepresentation is made in good faith?

Fraud is a **tort,** and is not based upon principles of contract. A tort is conduct that violates another person's rights which are created by law and for which the law provides a remedy if injury or other loss is caused by the wrongful conduct. The objective of the law of torts is to compensate a party for loss without providing profit. Whereas in contract law, the parties voluntarily enter into an agreement for the purpose of profit. If one party breaches the contract, the loss of the anticipated profit flows naturally from the breach. The law allows a recovery of lost profits in contract actions.

At common law certain factors must be present before a misrepresentation becomes tortious, and, therefore, actionable as a *fraud*. The misrepresentation must be (1) of a present or past fact; (2) the defendant must intend or expect the plaintiff to rely upon the misrepresentation; (3) the plaintiff must rely upon it; (4) the plaintiff must suffer a loss because of the reliance. Therefore, the statement of a mere opinion is not usually actionable. However, if the opinion is rendered by an expert concerning a matter within the scope of his or her expertise, an erroneous opinion may be actionable on the basis of fraud or negligence. If the seller of a parcel of land knows that an aircraft flight pattern is going to be established over the land in the near future, representation to the contrary may constitute a fraud even though the event is to take place in the future. The fraud occurs because of the defendant's present knowledge of established plans for action. Otherwise, prognostication is similar to rendering a mere opinion — not actionable as a fraud.

The defendant must intend or expect that the plaintiff will *rely* upon the misrepresentation, and the plaintiff must, in fact, rely upon it. If the vendor of a parcel of land represents that the parcel is two hundred feet deep but before the sale, the buyer measures the length and determines it is only one hundred ninety feet deep, the buyer cannot later sue for fraud, because he or she did not rely upon the misrepresentation. Reliance is an essential element.

The plaintiff must prove that the misrepresentation which was relied upon caused him or her to suffer damage or a loss. Suppose that the seller of a used automobile misrepresents that it is a 1981 model knowing that it is a 1980 model; suppose that 1981 models have an average value of $300.00 more than comparable 1980 models; suppose further that the buyer ends up paying no more for the automobile than would have been paid for a 1980 model. In other words, suppose the buyer received full value for what was paid, but believed he or she was getting a better bragain than what was received. Was a loss suffered due to the misrepresentation? Certainly there was a breach of contract and maybe a breach of warranty. The answer to whether or not a *loss* occurred depends upon whether the parties are in a state which follows the *loss-of-the-bargain* rule of damages or the *out-of-pocket* rule of damages. In the example, the buyer is not out-of-pocket any money. He has not actually lost anything. He merely lost an expectation. If the state allows damages for a loss-of-the bargain, the buyer's damages are $300.00.

In most states an action for fraud now lies if a person makes a statement as a positive assertion, not knowing whether it is true, and, nevertheless, intends the statement to be relied upon. For example, suppose a real estate agent shows a house he or she is selling for the owner and a prospective buyer asks the agent whether the basement has a water problem, and the agent — without knowing — says "no". If the basement does have a water problem and the buyer relied upon the statement, an action for *negligent misrepresentation* may be brought against the agent.

Rule 9(b) requires that the plaintiff plead with particularity his or her cause of action for fraud. In other words, unlike most causes of action, the specific facts supporting each element of the cause of action must be set forth in the complaint. The following is an example.

Complaint
Alleging Action in Fraud

> Comes now the plaintiff above named and for his cause of action against defendant, alleges:
> [Allege facts showing jurisdiction.]

1. That on or about June 1, 1981, plaintiff and defendant entered into an agreement by which defendant agreed to sell to plaintiff a certain 1980 Buick automobile, and plaintiff agreed to buy said automobile.

2. That the parties' agreement was reduced to a writing, and copy thereof is attached hereto as Exhibit A and is incorporated herein by reference.

3. That defendant represented to plaintiff that said automobile had a "new" engine, as appears more fully in Exhibit A.

4. That defendant intended plaintiff to rely upon said representation, and plaintiff did so rely.

5. That plaintiff's said representation was false; the engine is now new, and the original engine was never replaced or overhauled before the sale.

6. That plaintiff paid to defendant the sum of Seven Thousand Five Hundred ($7,500.00) Dollars for said automobile in reliance upon defendant's false representation.

7. That the cost of a new engine for said automobile is Five Hundred ($500.00) Dollars, and the fair market value of the automobile without a new engine is not more than Seven Thousand ($7,000.00) Dollars.

8. That plaintiff has sustained a loss due to defendant's fraudulent misrepresentations in the amount of Five Hundred ($500.00) Dollars.

Wherefore, plaintiff prays for judgment against defendant in the sum of Five Hundred ($500.00) Dollars, together with his costs and disbursements herein.

_____
                                              Attorney for Plaintiff

TRESPASS

A person who is in possession of real property has a right to the quiet, peaceful possession of the property. The right to possession may be based upon ownership or lease or easement rights or through adverse possession.* Any unauthorized entry on the premises constitutes a trespass. The occupant may sue for damages resulting from the wrongful entry. For example, suppose that a tenant of a farm has remained in possession of the property after the lease expired. If a stranger enters upon the land without permission, the stranger is a trespasser, and the tenant may bring an action in *trespass* against the stranger for any damage the trespasser caused. If the trespasser did not cause any discernible damage he or she is still liable for nominal money damages and, possibly, punitive damages — depending upon the purpose for which he or she entered upon the premises. The law presumes some damage (such as a bending of the grass). In this way, the law is able to affirm the possessor's right to exclusive, peaceful occupancy.

*A person may acquire ownership and title to real estate by occupying it for a statutorily specified number of years such as ten or fifteen. The occupancy must be open, notorious and contrary to the rights of anyone else in the property. A tenant cannot acquire title from the landlord by mere occupancy.

A trespass occurs whenever the entry is made without consent of the possesor or without legal authority. In the above example, even though the farmer is in possession, his or her possessory rights are subject to the higher or superior right of the owner to recover possession upon expiration of the lease. The hold-over tenant cannot sue the landlord who enters the land to take back possession in accordance with the requirements of local law. Historically, the common law permitted the landlord to use reasonable force to eject the hold-over tenant. Many states have enacted laws against self-help and require the landlord to use the services of the state by bringing an action for *unlawful detainer* or action in *ejectment* against the hold-over tenant. Such actions enable the landlord to obtain possession within thirty days or less.

The trespasser is liable for the damage caused by his or her entry. The wrongful entrance upon the premises may be intentional for the purpose of using the property or removing material from the premises such as water, cutting trees, seizing crops or mining minerals. A trespass may be involuntary as where a ship is driven ashore or into a dock by a storm or where an airplane crashed on the land. Or a trespass may result from negligent conduct on the part of the defendant. For example, suppose a drunken person drives a car off the road and runs into the plaintiff's house. The unpermitted entry is a trespass.

However, the defendant's involuntary entry caused by the wrongful conduct of another person is not a trespass. For example, if the alleged trespasser was driving an automobile which was struck by another vehicle forcing it off the road on to the plaintiff's property, the entrant is not a trespasser. However, the negligent motorist who caused the accident and entrance may be treated as a trespasser. A trespass may be committed by throwing articles upon plaintiff's land or across the land. Wrongful placement of utility lines over the property may be a trespass.

If the trespasser enters for the purpose of stealing crops, trees or minerals, he or she is liable either for the value of the materials taken or for the diminution in the value of the real estate. For example, if a trespasser cuts down an ornamental tree for the wood or as a matter of spite, the damage to the land (diminution in value) may exceed the worth of the tree or cost of a similar tree. On the other hand, the trespasser may wrongfully remove a mineral such as gravel, and the value of the gravel is worth more than the land has been diminshed in value. The occupant may elect to recover the value of the gravel. In many states the occupant is allowed by statute to recover three times the value of the property wrongfully damaged or taken by the trespasser. Treble damages in such cases is a civil penalty for the benefit of the victim.

If an entry upon real estate is without legal right or without the occupant's consent, the entry is wrongful and is a trespass. The trespasser is absolutely liable for any damage he or she causes — even if the entry was unavoidable. Suppose that an airplane crashed upon the land causing damage. The airplane's entry is a trespass. The pilot is liable in trespass even though he or she was not negligent and could not have prevented the accident. However, the pilot, in such circumstances, is liable only for the actual damage caused.

At common law the occupant of property could use such force as is reasonably necessary to eject a trespasser from the premises. The occupant owes the trespasser a duty not to intentionally injure or kill him or her. The law places a higher value on "life and limb" than on the protection of real estate. Therefore, a trespasser does not subject him or herself to being intentionally shot or injured. Nor may the occupant set a "trap" for trespassers without being liable for compensation for the trespasser's injuries. Of course, the occupant of land does have a common law right to self-defense. The occupant's best alternative, when practicable, is to call upon the local authorities to remove trespassers.

Consent to an entry upon the premises or authority to enter implied by law is a complete defense to an action in trespass. The defendant has the burden of proving consent or authority. They are defenses which must be pleaded in the answer. Consent may be expressed orally or in writing or implied by the circumstances. Authority is implied by law when the entrant has a legal duty to enter. A police officer or fireman who enters upon the property in the line of official duty has implied authority. They are not trespassers.

Complaint Alleging Action in Trespass

Comes now plaintiff and for his cause of action against defendant alleges:

1. [Jurisdictional Allegations]

2. That at all times material herein plaintiff was and is the owner and in possession of Lots 1-5, Block 4, Townsend Addition, Clay County, State of Iowa.

3. That on August 4, 1981, defendant wrongfully entered and trespassed upon said premises and damaged plaintiff's buildings, removed gravel from the premises and destroyed three trees all to plaintiff's damage in the sum of $26,000.00.

Wherefore, plaintiff prays for judgment against defendant in the sum of $26,000.00 together with his costs and disbursements herein.

(date)

_____

Attorney for plaintiff

Answer

Comes now defendant and for his answer to plaintiff's complaint:

1. Denies each and every allegation, statement and matter in said complaint contained except as herein after expressly admitted or alleged.

2. Admits the allegations of paragraph two (2) of the complaint.

3. Admits that defendant entered upon said premises on August 4, 1981, but specifically denies that the entry was wrongful or a trespass.

4. Denies that defendant caused any damage to plaintiff's buildings, and put plaintiff to his strict proof of same.

5. Admits that defendant cut down three trees which had been located upon the premises, but denies that said trees had any value.

6. Alleges that he entered the premises with consent of the owner and or possessor of the premises and that he was duly authorized and directed to remove the trees from the premises.

Wherefore, defendant prays that plaintiff take nothing by reason of his pretended cause of action, and that defendant have judgment for his costs and disbursements herein.

(date)

_____
Attorney for defendant

ASSAULT AND BATTERY

An *assault* is any intentional threat of bodily harm or death. An assault gives rise to an action for compensatory damages in favor of the person who has been put in fear of bodily harm or death. The threat of injury or death may come from a mere gesture with or without words. The wrongful conduct must cause the plaintiff to be fearful or there is no assault.

A *battery* is any impermissible contact intentionally inflicted upon another person. The defendant commits a battery upon the plaintiff by intentionally striking or otherwise contacting him or her in an impermissible manner. Battery may occur from any unpermitted contacts that inflict physical discomfort or emotional distress. Even a kiss may be a battery if undesired by the recipient. The cause of action requires proof of a contact; that the contact was without actual or apparent consent; and the contact was intentional. Intent to make contact may be implied from the nature of the contact and surrounding circumstances. Compensatory money damages are allowed for any physical injury and emotional distress resulting from a battery. Punitive damages are allowed in many states where the battery is malicious, i.e., where there is an intent to cause harm as a result of the impermissible contact.

Complaint Alleging Action for Assault and Battery

Comes now plaintiff and for his cause of action against defendant alleges:

1. [Jurisdictional Allegations]

2. That on August 6, 1981, in the City of Smithville, Ohio, defendant

assaulted plaintiff by pointing a rifle (weapon) at plaintiff and threatened to shoot plaintiff.

3. That plaintiff was put in great fear for his life and was fearful of severe bodily harm.

4. That defendant struck plaintiff with a blunt portion of his rifle thereby breaking plaintiff's jaw and rendering plaintiff unconscious.

5. That as a direct consequence of the battery, plaintiff suffered severe and painful injuries which may be permanent in nature.

6. That plaintiff incurred medical expenses, will incur future medical expenses, has suffered a loss of income and will suffer a loss of earning capacity as a direct consequence of the battery.

7. The assault and battery perpetrated by defendant upon plaintiff was intentional and malicious.

8. That plaintiff is entitled to recover punitive (exemplary) damages from defendant.

Wherefore, plaintiff demands judgment against defendant in the sum of $50,000.00 for compesnatory damages and $10,000.00 as punitive damages, together with plaintiff's costs and disbursements herein.

(date)

_____

Attorney for plaintiff

Answer

Comes now defendant, and for his answers to plaintiff's complaint:

1. Denies each and every allegation, statement, and matter in the complaint, except as hereinafter expressly admitted or alleged.

2. Admits the allegations of paragraphs 1, 2, 3 and 4 of the complaint.

3. Alleges that defendant is without sufficient knowledge or information upon which to form a belief concerning plaintiff's claims of injuries and damages and, therefore, puts plaintiff to his strict proof of same.

4. Alleges that plaintiff trespassed upon defendant's premises and entered defendant's dwelling for the purpose of burglarizing the dwelling.

5. Alleges that when defendant discovered plaintiff in defendant's home, plaintiff was armed with a knife and carrying off personal property belonging to defendant.

6. Alleges that defendant then and there arrested plaintiff and held plaintiff until the police could be summoned.

7. Specifically denies that defendant used more force than appeared necessary to protect himself, his property and to effectuate the arrest.

Wherefore, defendant prays that plaintiff take nothing by reason of his pretended cause of action, and that defendant have judgment for his costs and disbursements herein.

(date)

_____

Attorneys for defendant

NEGLIGENCE

Negligence is failure to use reasonable care. Reasonable care is that care which a reasonable person would use under like circumstances. Negligence is the doing of some act which a reasonable person would not do, or the failure to do something which a reasonable person would do, under like circumstances. In the case of a child, reasonable care is that care which a reasonable child of the same age, intelligence, training and experience would have used under like circumstances. A cause of action in *negligence* lies against a person who causes damage or destruction of property or injury to a person through negligent conduct.

To understand the basis for a negligence action, it is necessary to understand the underlying *duty* of "due" or "reasonable" care. Every person owes a duty of reasonable care not to injure others or damage others' property. The duty is to act reasonably considering the foreseeability of harm to others. The law does not demand perfection. What is reasonable care depends upon existing circumstances which *are* known or *should be known*. The test is what risks of harm are foreseeable and is the act or omission in question reasonable in light of the foreseeable dangers. A person's conduct is not judged on the basis of hindsight. Adults are charged with knowledge ordinarily possessed by members of the community, and knowledge of natural laws such as gravity. A higher duty is imposed upon common carriers such as airlines, railroads and bus companies. They must exercise the highest degree of care for the protection of their passengers.

Some states recognize degrees of negligence such as ordinary, gross, willful and wanton. But these characterizations of negligence have lost their original significance in most states.

The relationship between persons may be critical in determining whether a duty of care exists at all. Some examples may be helpful to understand the concept of a *duty* and the bases for a *duty*.

1. Suppose a person sees a neighbor using a metal ladder very near an uninsulated electric power line and recognizes that the neighbor is in danger of being electrocuted. Does he have a legal duty to warn or stop the neighbor? No. Failure to warn or stop the neighbor would not result in legal liability to that person if injury did occur. The law does not require ordinary individuals to act to protect members of the public, whether they are neighbors or not, from injuring themselves. But if a home owner has an acquaintance on the premises helping with some house painting and sees him on a metal ladder near a power line, the home owner has a duty to stop the dangerous activity, or is negligent for violating the duty. The duty arises out of the relationship.
2. Suppose a person comes upon a trench in the road and realizes that motorists may not be so fortunate to discover and avoid it; that if a vehicle were to run into the trench, it would be damaged and its occupants injured. Does the person have a duty to warn motorists of the danger or to stop motorists, or to fill the trench? Is there negligence toward the motoring public for a failure to take these precautions? No. The person has no duty to the public under the circumstances even though morally some protective action may be called for. However, the person who made the trench and endangered

the public did violate his duty of reasonable care. Suppose that the trench exists in an area of highway which is under the control of a construction contractor. He *may* have a duty to protect the public from the trench, even though not created by the contractor, arising from the contractual relationship with the government to protect the public in the construction zone. The State may be negligent for failing to discover the danger and eliminate it.

3. Suppose a person invites people to her home for a social gathering. She knows that most of the guests will use the front sidewalk but unknown is that several bricks in the sidewalk are dangerously loose. One of the guests trips on a loose brick, falls and is injured. A negligence action may lie against the host as the occupant of the premises. She owes a duty of reasonable care to make the premises reasonably safe. The duty includes an obligation to conduct reasonable inspections to discover potential hazards and to take preventive action such as to give warnings or correct the danger. However, the laws of some states provide that the occupant owes no duty of inspection to mere social guests; that there is no duty to prepare the premises for them. His or her only duty is to correct known defects or hazardous conditions or effectively warn the social guests. So, if this host was unaware of the loose bricks, she is not liable in negligence to the injured social guest. In those states a duty to prepare the premises applies only to business invitees.

4. Suppose that a man dug a hole in his backyard for planting a tree. Suppose that during the night a thief entered the premises to steal a boat engine and was in the process of leaving when he fell in the hole and sustained injuries. Is the property owner liable to the thief for negligently leaving the hole unguarded? Does the thief's malevolent purpose insulate the property owner from liability? In most states, thieves are treated as trespassers. They have no right to be on the premises; the property owner owes them no duty of care. However, the property owner must not use more force than is reasonably necessary to eject the trespasser. Nor may traps be set for the purpose of injuring trespassers.

So-called malpractice cases are really just actions in negligence. They are claims against professional people based upon their alleged failure to measure up to the standards of their profession. Of course, the substandard performance or conduct must have caused some harm to the plaintiff for an action to lie. Malpractice actions may be brought against physicians, lawyers, nurses, accountants, pharmacists, engineers, architects, etc. The gravamen of the claim is that the professional failed to adhere to, or comply with, the standards of his or her profession. Presumably, laymen are not familiar with the professional duties and standards. Consequently, the law requires other professionals, who are familiar with the professional standards, to establish the standards in court. Expert testimony may also be necessary to determine whether the standards have been violated. An untoward or disappointing result from the professional's services is not, in itself, a sufficient basis for maintaining a malpractice action in court. It is for this reason that a patient who sues his or her physician usually must find another physician who will testify that the treating physician's conduct deviated from acceptable professional standards. Otherwise, the patient's case must be dismissed for failure to prove a **prima facie** case.

The above examples illustrate that though the concept of negligence is simple enough, its application is difficult. To make the whole subject more difficult, the law of negligence is constantly changing. The study of *tort negligence* involves a study of the interrelationships between people, the public, institutions and governments. Each relationship creates a different duty. For example, a bus driver must exercise the highest degree of care for the benefit of passengers and only reasonable care for the protection of other motorists or pedestrians.

Many legal duties are established by statute. A violation of a statutory duty is negligence. There can be no excuse or justification for noncompliance with a statute enacted to protect particular people or properties. A violation of a statute is referred to as **negligence per se** which means that the violation is, in itself, negligence. Example: a statute forbids merchants to sell guns to minors. A gun is sold to a minor who accidentally shoots another person. The vendor's illegal sale is negligence per se — the statute was enacted to prevent that very occurrence from happening.

Some statutes, by their terms, expressly provide that a violation is not negligence per se, but merely *prima facie negligence* which means that a violation is merely evidence of negligence. The application of such a statute is illustrated in the following typical jury instruction:

> If the statute was violated, the violation is negligence unless the jury finds evidence tending to show reasonable excuse or justification or evidence from which a reasonable person, under the circumstances, could believe that the violation would not endanger any person entitled to the protection of the statute.

If the statutory violation were not limited to prima facie negligence, the violator would not be permitted to show excuse or justification.

Most state highway codes provide that traffic violations are merely prima facie negligence and not negligence per se. A technical violation may be excused or justified. A violation is to be judged on the basis of all the circumstances, including the known risks and those which reasonably should have been anticipated. A jury has the task of weighing the excuse against the gravity of the violation and the foreseeability of harm resulting from the violation. In the absence of any reasonable excuse or justification, a judge would have to determine that the violation was a negligent act or omission. Would a jury be justified in excusing a father's unlawful speed if he is driving his seriously injured child to a hospital to obtain medical care? Perhaps. Suppose he collides with a car which violated a stop sign — the father being on a through street.

In a negligence action, the plaintiff must prove that the defendant's conduct was negligent *and* that the negligence was a proximate cause of the occurrence or accident. If the defendant's negligence is not a proximate cause of the accident, the defendant is not liable for the accident. The term *direct cause* is sometimes used in place of proximate cause. The subject of causation is just as esoteric as the concept of negligence. A proximate cause is a cause that has a substantial part in bringing about the accident either immediately or through happenings which naturally follow one after another. For example, suppose a motorist parks an automobile two feet from the curb when local law requires him to park within one foot, and another motorist runs into the back of the parked automobile. It is unlikely that the technical violation (of parking two feet from the curb) was the actual cause of the accident. Suppose that a motorist is traveling ten miles over the posted speed limit and is struck by another vehicle which went through a stop sign. The excessive speed is merely coincidental and not a proximate cause. The cause of the accident was the stop sign violation because the violation would have caused an accident even if the motorist on the through street had been traveling within the speed limit. Speed did not, in this illustration, cause the accident or induce negligence on the part of the other driver. Usually the issue of proximate cause is a question of fact for a jury to decide.

There may be more than one proximate cause of an accident. When the effects of negligent conduct of two or more persons actively work at substantially the same time to cause the accident, the conduct of each may be a proximate cause of the accident. If two defendants contribute toward a plaintiff's loss, they are **jointly and severally liable** for the entire loss. For example, if two motorists collide in an intersection because both failed to keep a proper lookout, their concurrent negligence makes both of them liable for their passengers' injuries.

Another facet of the law of causation is the concept of the *efficient intervening cause* or *superceding cause*. A superceding cause relieves all prior negligent conduct of any liability for an accident. But the requirements of a superceding cause are very specific. For a cause to be a superceding cause, its harmful effects must have occurred after the original negligence and the superceding cause must not have been brought about by the original negligence. For example, if the driver of an automobile sees a truck unlawfully stopped upon the highway ahead and has sufficient time in which to avoid a collision but negligently fails to do so, the automobile driver's negligence is a superceding cause of the collision. The superceding negligence of the driver insulates the owner of the stopped truck from legal liability for the collision though he created the dangerous condition.

A party who claims another was negligent must prove negligence by a fair preponderance of the evidence; or, said another way, negligence must be established by the greater weight of the evidence. The mere fact that an accident occurs does not, in itself, necessarily mean that someone was negligent. If there is a deficiency in the evidence, so that negligence is not proved, the court must direct a verdict against the party who has the burden of proof. A **directed verdict** means that the claim or defense is disallowed by the judge because there are insufficient facts to support a contrary result.

Historically, there were two affirmative defenses frequently asserted in negligence actions: *contributory negligence* and *assumption of risk*. Contributory negligence is not a special kind or quality of negligence. It simply designates the negligence as being on the party who is making the claim, i.e., the plaintiff. If the defendant was able to prove by a fair preponderance of the evidence that the plaintiff was contributorily negligent or that he or she assumed the risk, the plaintiff's claim was defeated. The defendant prevailed even though the plaintiff was able to show that the defendant was negligent. Historically, the law was not at all concerned with degrees of fault. Negligence and causation were considered absolutes. Any causal negligence was sufficient to create a claim or a defense. Similarly, the plaintiff's assumption of the risk provided the defendant with a complete defense. The plaintiff assumed the risk if he or she voluntarily placed him or herself in a position to chance a known hazard. The defendant must prove that the plaintiff had actual knowledge of the specific risk; that the risk was appreciated; that a choice or opportunity to avoid the risk was available but he or she voluntarily chose to incur the risk.

As an example of an assumption or risk, suppose that a cook in a restaurant negligently permits the sink to overflow and a lot of soapy water spills on the floor making it slippery. Suppose the janitor is summoned to clean up the water. He begins the task but then slips and falls on the floor because of the soap. He knew the risk, and appreciated the danger of the slippery floor. But it is his job to deal with such conditions. By proceeding with the clean up work he voluntarily chose to incur the risk. He has no claim against the cook or cook's employer, because of the assumed risk.

The law of contributory negligence and assumption of risk has evolved in most states into the law of *comparative negligence*. The law of comparative negligence is a so-called equitable approach to tort litigation. The doctrine is justified by its proponents as more fair. The objective is to secure some compensation for the plaintiff even though he or she was also negligent and contributed to the loss. The jury is required to evaluate each parties' casual negligence and apportion their negligence on a percentage basis.

There are two forms of comparative negligence. In those states adopting pure comparative negligence, the plaintiff's recovery of money damages is reduced by the amount or percentage of his or her causal negligence. For example, if the plaintiff is found to be 20 percent causally negligent, his or her damages award is reduced by that amount. If 75 percent causally negligent, the damages award is reduced by that amount. Other states having *ordinary comparative negligence* similarly reduce the plaintiff's award by his or her percentage of causal negligence, but any recovery against a defendant who is less negligent than he or she is not permitted. Where ordinary comparative negligence applies, a plaintiff who is 51 percent at fault cannot recover any compensation. In states having comparative negligence, the defense of assumption of risk is treated as a form of comparative negligence.

In states that apply the law of contributory negligence, each defendant who is liable for plaintiff's injury or loss is liable jointly and individually for the whole as well as equally liable between themselves for the whole. In states having comparative negligence, the codefendants are also jointly and individually liable for the amount of damages recoverable by plaintiff. But as between the co-defendants each is liable only for his or her percentage of causal negligence. For example, if the jury determines that the plaintiff was 20 percent at fault, defendant A was 10 percent at fault, defendant B was 30 percent at fault and defendant C was 40 percent at fault, and the amount of damages was $10,000.00, the plaintiff's recovery will be $8,000.00. The plaintiff can recover no damages from defendant A who was less negligent than he or she was. Defendants B and C are liable to the plaintiff for the entire $8,000.00. As between defendants B (30%) and C (40%), their obligation for the $8,000.00 award is in proportion. Defendant B would be obligated for $3,428.57 and defendant C would be obligated for $4,571.43. The proportionate amounts are easily calculated by converting the 30% to 30/70 or 3/7 and converting the 40% to 40/70 or 4/7. 3/7 x $8,000 = $3,428.57 and 4/7 x $8,000 = $4,571.43.

Complaint Alleging
Action for Negligence

Come now the plaintiffs above named, and for their cause of action against defendants, allege:

1. That plaintiffs are and at all times material herein have been husband and wife, and they reside in the State of Wisconsin.

2. That defendant Shawn And Associates, Inc. is and at all times material herein was a Wisconsin corporation having its office and principal place of business in Spencer, Wisconsin.

3. That the defendant Drake Apartments, Inc. is and at all times material herein was a Wisconsin corporation having its office and principal place of business in Spencer, Wisconsin.

4. That the defendant Barton & Associates, Inc. is and at all times material herein was a Minnesota corporation having its office and principal place of business in Madison, Minnesota.

5. That on or about July 19, 1977, Shawn And Associates, Inc. contracted with Drake Apartments, the owner of premises located at 724 South 5th Street, Spencer, Wisconsin (hereinafter the job site), to act as general contractor for the construction of an addition to said premises, and in connection therewith Shawn And Associates, Inc. agreed to assume responsibility for providing a safe place to work for all persons working at the job site, including all subcontractors and their employees.

6. That on or about October 26, 1976, Drake Apartments entered into a contract with Barton & Associates whereby Barton & Associates agreed to provide certain services, including architectural services, to Drake Apartments.

On or about the 28th day of July, 1977, Shawn And Associates, as general contractor, entered into a contract, attached as Exhibit A, with the Johnson Construction Company, a subcontractor, for the erection by Johnson Construction of the structural steel frame for the addition to said premises. In connection therewith Shawn And Associates agreed to assume responsibility for providing a safe place to work for Johnson Construction and all Johnson Construction employees working at the job site, and Johnson Construction agreed to indemnify Shawn And Associates from all claims for damages and injury in connection with the work.

7. That plaintiff John Doe at all times material herein was employed by Johnson Construction as a steel worker.

8. That Drake Apartments negligently and in violation of its legal obligations failed to employ a competent and careful contractor to do the work and to perform the duties which Drake Apartments owed to third persons, including the plaintiffs, and to take precautions against risk of physical harm to persons on the premises.

9. That prior to and on February 7, 1978, defendants negligently and in violation of federal and state OSHA standards and in breach of their contractual obligations, failed to provide plaintiff John Doe with a safe place to work at the job site, failed to use proper construction procedures and to properly supervise the work at the job site, failed to properly inspect the job site and to correct unsafe conditions, failed to erect proper barricading to protect plaintiff at the job site, failed to adequately warn plaintiff of unsafe conditions and hazards existing at the job site, and failed to fulfill its non-delegable contractual and legal responsiblities with respect to working conditions at the job site.

10. That defendant Barton & Associates negligently and in breach of its contractual duties to plaintiff failed to provide general administration of the construction contract, failed to properly represent the owner, failed to determine in general if the work was proceeding properly and in accordance with the contract documents, and failed to advise and consult with Drake Apartments regarding safety on the job site.

11. That on February 7, 1978 as a direct consequence of the negligence of the Defendants, and each of them, plaintiff John Doe, while working at the job site, fell in a stairwell at the job site and suffered permanent injuries and permanent disability.

12. That because of his injuries plaintiff John Doe has been prevented from transacting his business and has lost wages in the approximate amount of Fifty Thousand Dollars ($50,000.00); he has incurred expenses and obligations for medical attention, hospitalization and related care, and miscellaneous items in the approximate amount of One Hundred Thousand Dollars ($100,000.00); he has been and will in the future be totally physically disabled and totally dependent upon others for his care; he has lost all future earning capacity and will lose all future wages; he will incur substantial medical, additional living and miscellaneous expenses in the future; and he has suffered and will in the future suffer great pain of body and mind.

13. That due to the injuries sustained by John Doe, plaintiff Jane Doe has been and in the future will be required to provide care for her husband; she has permanently lost the services of her husband; her comfort and happiness in his society and companionship have been permanently impaired.

Wherefore, the plaintiffs, and each of them, demand judgment in their favor and against the Defendants, and each of them, jointly and severally, as follows:

1. Money damages for plaintiff John Doe in the sum of One Hundred Fifty Thousand Dollars ($150,000.00).

2. Money damages for plaintiff Jane Doe in the sum of Fifty Thousand Dollars ($50,000.00).

3. Reimbursement for plaintiff's costs and disbursements herein.

(date)

_____

Attorneys for plaintiff

PRODUCTS LIABILITY

Manufacturers, distributors, wholesalers and retailers may be held liable for injuries caused by defects in the products they sell. The liability extends to the purchaser and, in many instances, to users who were not purchasers, and even bystanders. The plaintiff's claim may be based upon *negligence* or *breach of warranty* or *strict liability in tort*. Sometimes the facts permit plaintiff to recover damages on all three theories. In other cases, the recovery may be limited to one legal theory. The theory upon which recovery is allowed may affect the *measure* of damages and the total amount of damages recoverable. Defenses applicable to a negligence action may not apply to a warranty action or to a strict liability action. Therefore, the plaintiff's lawyer chooses the action or actions carefully. In most cases, however, all three causes of action will be pleaded against the vendor.

As to negligence actions, manufacturers owe to purchasers and users a duty of reasonable care to make their products reasonably safe or to not make them unreasonably dangerous. A product may be unreasonably dangerous because of its design, materials used, poor assembly, or failure to provide adequate instructions or warnings about the product. If the manufacturer exercises reasonable care, he is not liable in negligence even though the product is defective. For example, if the defendant manufacturer builds an automobile that has a defective axle and the defect could not have been prevented or discovered by the exercise of reasonable care, the manufacturer is not liable to the purchaser or occupants who are injured in an accident caused by the broken axle. The retail vendor of the automobile would not be liable either.

The purchaser of a product may be able to recover damages for a breach of warranty. A warranty may be express or implied by law. An expressed warranty may be written or oral. The law implies certain warranties with the sale of any *new* product when sold by a manufacturer or other vendor who is in the business of handling those products. Implied warranties include a warranty that the product is of merchantable quality; reasonably fit to be used for the purpose for which it is sold. An automobile with a defective axle is not of merchantable quality and is not fit for use as a motor vehicle. So, in the above example, a recovery may be possible under a breach of warranty theory. But the warranty arises out of the sale and is subject to the contract of sale because the law permits the vendor to qualify and limit the warranties. Indeed, the contract of sale may exclude all warranties by making the sale "with all faults" or "sold as is". Furthermore, contracts often limit the time during which a warranty may be claimed. Assume for purposes of the above example, the axle broke 25 months after it was purchased and the contract eliminated all warranties after 24 months. The result is verdict for the defendant. Also, the affirmative defense of contributory negligence or comparative negligence is available to the defendant in warranty claims. (Note, a claim for breach of warranty may be used to recover damages for repairing or replacing the product and for consequential injuries caused by the defect.)

In recent decades, all states have adopted the theory of *strict liability in tort* as a basis for recovering money damages for *injuries* caused by a product defect. In many states strict liability in tort does not apply to property damage claims — only injuries. Strict liability is imposed upon all business vendors of *new* products in favor of any user of the product who is injured because of a defect in the product. The plaintiff need not be the purchaser. The plaintiff must prove that the defendant was a vendor in the chain of sale of the defective product — whether manufacturer, wholesaler or retailer — and that the product was defective when it left the vendor's possession. A product is considered to be defective if it is unreasonably dangerous for use in the ordinary manner. A defect may be due to errors in fabrication, poor materials, inadequate design, inadequate instructions for the product's use or inadequate warnings against risks inherent in the product or its use. The plaintiff must prove that the alleged defect caused his or her injury. Proof of product misuse is an affirmative defense. That is, the defendant must prove that the product was not being used for its intended purpose or being used in a dangerous manner which could not reasonably have been foreseen by the vendor. However, ordinary negligence is not a defense to an action based upon strict liability in tort. If the plaintiff contributed to the defect by altering the product, his or her fault may bar a recovery against the vendor.

Remedies: money damages.

If the plaintiff elects to sue only the retailer, the retailer may assert a claim against the manufacturer for **indemnity** — provided that the defect was in the product when it left the manufacturer's possession. The retailer is just another purchaser or user as far as the manufacturer is concerned. But they are each liable to the plaintiff consumer for the full amount of compensation awarded to him.

One might wonder why a negligence action is ever pursued in a products case. Obviously, a case based upon strict liability in tort is easier to prove. But there are cases in which a jury has determined that the product in question was not defective but that the vendor's negligence caused the accident in question. See *Bigham v. J. C. Penney Company,* 268 N.W. 2d 892 (Minn., 1978).

Complaint Alleging Action for Strict Liability In Tort

Plaintiff for her Complaint against Defendant alleges as follows:
[Jurisdictional Allegations]

FIRST COUNT

1. At the times herein mentioned, defendant Dawn Co. Inc. was engaged in the manufacture of a chemical oven cleaner called "Sparkel". Said cleaner was sold for the general use of the public.

2. During the latter part of 1979, plaintiff purchased a can of defendant's oven cleaner identified by the marking "5M142D", which was manufactured and sold by defendant for retail sales to the general public.

3. At all times following the purchase of the oven cleaner, plaintiff reasonably and properly handled the product.

4. Defendant supplied said oven cleaner to retailers knowing that in the regular course of business it would be resold to a customer for use as an oven cleaner.

5. Defendant failed to provide plaintiff with a warning concerning the hazards of using said oven cleaner.

6. Said oven cleaner was negligently designed, manufactured, tested, and inspected by defendant; and the oven cleaner was dangerous to the physical health of users when the product left the defendant's control or possession.

7. Defendant was negligent in failing to provide adequate instructions for its use and failing to warn of the product's dangers.

8. On March 12, 1979, plaintiff used said oven cleaner for the first time in accordance with the printed instructions on the can when attempting to clean her oven at her home located at 5606 Lawndale Lane, Spencer, Illinois.

9. Defendant's negligence directly caused plaintiff to suffer severe itching, swelling, dizziness, restricted breathing, and suffered an anaphlactic reaction to plaintiff's general damage in the sum of $30,000.00

10. Plaintiff incurred expenses for medical attention, hospital and medicines in the sum of $500.00.

SECOND COUNT

11. Plaintiff realleges Paragraphs 1 through 10 of Count One as if allegations herein were set forth in full.

12. In marketing the oven cleaner product, defendant impliedly warranted that the product was of merchantable quality and fit for the purpose for which it was intended.

13. In fact, the product was not of merchantable quality and was unsafe and unfit for the purpose intended.

14. Defendant's breach of implied warranties caused plaintiff to suffer serious bodily injuries.

THIRD COUNT

15. Plaintiff realleges Paragraphs 1 through 14 of Count One and Count Two as if allegations herein were set forth in full.

16. Defendant expressly warranted that the oven cleaner contained no caustic or choking fumes or chemicals to irritate eyes or nose.

17. Said oven cleaner did not conform to the express warranties made by defendant and printed on the product container.

18. As a result of defendant's breach of the express warranties, plaintiff suffered serious bodily injuries.

FOURTH COUNT

19. Plaintiff realleges Paragraphs 1 through 18 of Count One through Count Three as if allegations were set forth in full.

20. The oven cleaner manufactured and sold by defendant was unreasonably dangerous for use in the ordinary manner and, therefore, was a defective product.

21. Plaintiff used the product in the intended manner.

22. As a result of the defective character of the oven cleaner, plaintiff suffered injuries as described above.

23. As a result of the defective condition of the oven cleaner, defendant is strictly liable in tort to plaintiff for the injuries she sustained and losses suffered as described above.

Wherefore, plaintiff prays for judgment against defendant in the sum of $25,000.00 and her costs and disbursements herein.

(date)

_____
Attorney for plaintiff

Answer

Comes now defendant and for its answer to plaintiff's complaint:

1. Denies each and every allegation, statement, matter and thing in said complaint contained, except as herein after expressly admitted or alleged.

2. Admits the allegations of paragraphs one and two of the complaint.

3. Alleges that defendant is without sufficient knowledge or information upon which to form a belief concerning plaintiff's claims of injuries and damages, and therefore puts plaintiff to her strict proof of same.

4. Alleges that if plaintiff sustained injuries and damages as alleged in the complaint, they were caused by the negligence of plaintiff.

5. Alleges that plaintiff did not serve defendant with notice of breach of warranty as required by law.

6. Alleges that plaintiff assumed the risk of injury.

[It is not necessary to allege that plaintiff misused the product, and that was the cause of injury because "misuse" is not an affirmative defense even though misuse by plaintiff would prevent plaintiff from recovering money damages. The plaintiff has the burden of proving that the plaintiff used the product in the ordinary intended manner.]

Wherefore, defendant prays that plaintiff take nothing by reason of her pretended cause of action, and that defendant have judgment for its costs and disbursements herein.

(date)

_____
Attorney for defendant

LIQUOR VENDORS' LIABILITY

It is a well known and accepted fact that the use of intoxicating liquors often causes or contributes significantly to accidental injuries and property damage. The liquor industry is closely controlled through the police power of the states. A form of strict liability is now imposed upon liquor vendors who make illegal sales or illegally barter intoxicants when the sale or bartering contributes to the occurrence of an accident. Note, the illegal sale or bartering does not have to be a proximate cause of the accident. The law only requires that the illegal sale contribute toward the accident in some way. For example, it was determined in one case that an illegal sale of intoxicants contributed to a man's suicide, so the vendor was liable to the man's surviving spouse and children for loss of support. The court acknowledged that the man's intoxication probably did not cause him to commit suicide but the jury could properly find that the intoxication contributed to the suicide.

The plaintiff must prove that the defendant vendor made an illegal sale. The two most common types of illegal sales resulting in liability are sales to minors and sales to persons who are already obviously intoxicated. Such sales are prohibited by law. In addition to the illegal sale, the plaintiff must prove that the intoxication contributed to the wrongful conduct and that the intoxicated person caused a loss or injury.

The alleged intoxicated person (A.I.P.) does not have any claim against the vendor for injuring him or herself. However, if the intoxicated person is injured and becomes disabled for a period of time, the spouse and children have a claim against the vendor for *loss of support*. Of course, if the intoxicated person dies, the claim for loss of support may be very substantial.

Most states recognize *complicity* as an affirmative defense. If the defendant is able to prove that the plaintiff was complicit in the illegal sale, the plaintiff is barred from recovering money damages from the defendant vendor. For example, if two men spend several hours in a liquor establishment buying each other intoxicants, and they become *obviously* intoxicated; and an illegal sale of liquor is made to them; and one of the intoxicated persons attempts to drive his car with his fellow drunkard as a passenger; and they have an accident which was contributed to by intoxication; the plaintiff passenger's complicity in the illegal sale is a bar to his claim against the liquor vendor who illegally sold liquor to the driver. Similarly, if the plaintiff is complicit in the sale of intoxicants to a minor and is injured as a result of the minor's intoxication, he or she cannot recover compensation from the liquor vendor who made the illegal sale. The defendant must plead *complicity* in his or her answer as an affirmative defense, and has the burden of proving complicity by a preponderance of the evidence.

Dram shop statutes require the plaintiff to give notice of the illegal sale, the occurrence, loss, and intent to make a claim. The notice must be given to the liquor vendor within a specified number of days after the occurrence. A typical period for giving notice is 120 days. Failure to give the notice bars any action against the vendor. The reason for the notice requirement is to give the vendor an opportunity to investigate and evaluate the claim before the evidence disappears. If a notice is required by state law, the plaintiff must allege in the complaint that he or she complied with the notice requirement. If the allegation is denied, the burden is on plaintiff to prove that he duly gave or served notice. Usually the notice is given in writing and proof of delivery of the notice is made and preserved.

A liquor vendor's liability is, in most states, created by statute. Unless specified in the statue, negligence on the part of the plaintiff is not a defense. However, the law of comparative negligence or comparative fault seems to be moving toward application in these cases. If comparative negligence is applicable, the plaintiff's recovery of money damages is reduced by his or her percentage of causal negligence.

Complaint Alleging Dram Shop Statutory Actions

Come now the plaintiffs above named and for their claim and cause of action against defendants, and each of them, herein complain and allege as follows:

[Jurisdictional Allegations]

COUNT ONE

1. Joy Peterson is the administratrix for the Estate of James William Peterson.

2. That on June 1, 1980, defendant Kenneth Roberts was operating his motor vehicle on Constance Boulevard at or near the intersection of Highway 65 in Tampa, Florida.

3. That at the above date and time, James Richard Anderson was operating his motor vehicle on Highway 65 at or near the intersection with Constance Boulevard in Tampa, Florida.

4. That plaintiffs Christine Peterson and James William Peterson were passengers in the automobile owned and operated by James Peterson.

5. That at the above time and place the defendant Kenneth Roberts and the intestate James Anderson, operated their respective vehicles in such a negligent, careless and unlawful manner that they caused their vehicles to come into violent collision.

6. That as a direct result of said collision Christine Peterson and James Peterson suffered serious and permanent injuries and were prevented from transacting their business, sustained great pain of body and mind and have incurred and will in the future incur expenses for medical attention and hospitalization in the sum not presently known but believed to exceed Fifty Thousand ($50,000.00) Dollars.

7. That as a direct and proximate result of defendants' negligence plaintiffs Christine Peterson and James Peterson have each sustained and will sustain in the future a loss of earnings and loss of earning capacity in a sum not presently capable of determination.

COUNT TWO

Reallege all paragraphs set out in Count One.

8. That on May 31 and June 1, 1980, defendant The Happy Hour Tavern illegally sold, furnished and/or bartered intoxicating liquors to Kenneth Roberts in violation of [Statute] and by this violation of statute and by the illegal sale, furnishing or bartering, caused and/or contributed to the intoxication of Kenneth Roberts.

9. That on May 31 and June 1, 1980, defendant The Happy Hour Tavern negligently supplied, furnished or gave alcoholic beverages to defendant Kenneth Roberts, thereby causing or adding to the intoxication of said Kenneth Roberts.

[In most states an allegation of a negligent sale of intoxicants would *not* state a cause of action.]

10. That as a direct and proximate result of the illegal selling, furnishing, bartering [or negligence in supplying] on May 31 and June 1, 1980, Kenneth Roberts collided with a motor vehicle owned and negligently operated by James Anderson in which plaintiffs Christine Peterson and James Peterson were passengers, thereby causing severe and permanent injuries to Christine Peterson and James Peterson as alleged above.

11. That as a direct and proximate consequence of said collision, plaintiffs Christine Peterson and James Peterson suffered injuries of which they herein complain.

12. That as a further, direct and proximate consequence of said collision plaintiffs Christine Peterson and James Peterson have incurred hospital expenses and medical expenses and they will require medical attention in the future.

13. That plaintiffs Christine Peterson and James Peterson have been damaged in their ability to earn income and will suffer said inability into the future.

Wherefore, plaintiffs, and each of them pray for judgment against the defendants, and each of them, in the sum of Fifty Thousand ($50,000.00) Dollars, plus their costs and disbursements herein.

(date)

_____

Attorney for plaintiffs

Answer

Comes now defendant, Happy Hour Tavern, and for its separate answer to plaintiff's complaint:

1. Denies each and every allegation, statement, matter and thing in said complaint contained, except as hereinafter expressly admitted or alleged.

2. Alleges defendant is without sufficient knowledge or information upon which to form a belief concerning plaintiff's claims of injuries and damages and, therefore, puts plaintiffs to their strict proof of same.

3. Alleges that plaintiffs failed to serve notice of claim upon defendant as required by law.

Wherefore, defendant prays that plaintiffs take nothing by reason of their pretended cause of action, and that it have judgment for its costs and disbursements herein.

(date)

_____

Attorney for defendant

["Complicity" is an affirmative defense which must be averred if it is going to be claimed as a defense to the dram shop claim.]

NUISANCE

The owner of real estate and the occupants of real estate are entitled to use and enjoy the property without being subjected to disturbing odors, noises or activities that are of a continuing nature. The law protects them against the loss of use and enjoyment of their property by allowing money damages as compensation for wrongful conduct that significantly disturbs the use and enjoyment of property. In addition, if the *nuisance* is likely to continue, courts have the power to enjoin a nuisance, i.e., order that the nuisance be abated.

The court must weigh the value of the activity complained of and the character of the area, against the effects on plaintiff's use of his or her premises. For example, if the defendant establishes a creosote plant near an established residential area, the smell and fumes may be too much for the residents. They may have an action for damages and an injunction to abate operation of the plant. But suppose the plaintiff buys a house which is near a commercial or government airport and in the path of aircraft landing and taking off. Noise may constitute a nuisance that is actionable. But the necessity of having the airport where it is and the utility of the activity justify the impairment of plaintiff's use and enjoyment of property. Of course, there is also a tendency on the part of the courts to protect the existing character of the area, so if the defendant's airport or railroad or sanitary landfill or paint factory was in the area first, fairness suggests that the newcomer should expect that he or she may have to put up with the status quo. However, being there first is no guaranty of prevailing in a nuisance action.

An action to recover damages caused by a nuisance does not require proof of fault or wrongful conduct. The plaintiff must prove that the alleged nuisance has created a substantial interference in the use and enjoyment of his or her property; that the utility of the nuisance does not justify its continuance and interference with plaintiff's property.

Complaint Alleging Action for Creating a Nuisance

Comes now plaintiff and for his cause of action against defendant alleges:

1. [Jurisdictional Allegations]

2. That at all times material herein plaintiff was the owner and in possession of the premises commonly known as 3908 East Ninth Street, Bakersville, Ohio.

3. That plaintiff occupied said premises as his homestead with his family.

4. That during the period of June 1, 1981, to the date of the commencement of the above entitled action defendant has occupied and used the premises at 4000 East Ninth Street, Bakersville, Ohio, as a meat cutting plant and the preparation of various meats for sale in commerce.

5. That during said period of time defendant has allowed meat products, meat by-products and various chemicals to create toxic and offensive smelling fumes and odors.

6. That said fumes and odors significantly reduce the plaintiff's use, comfort, enjoyment and value of plaintiff's said property.

7. That prior to commencement of this action, plaintiff notified defendant of the adverse effect that defendant's activities have had on plaintiff's premises.

8. That defendant's activities could be conducted in a manner so as not to endanger and impair the use of other properties in the area.

9. That defendant's present activities create and permit the noxious and toxic odors and fumes that damage plaintiff's property and impair its use.

10. That plaintiff has suffered damages in the amount of $15,000.00 for the loss of enjoyment and impaired use of his property.

11. That unless defendant is enjoined from continuing to create the noxious fumes and odors, plaintiff's property will continue to suffer damage.

Wherefore, plaintiff prays for judgment against defendant permanently enjoining defendant from creating toxic and noxious fumes and odors which escape from defendant's premises to adjoining properties, and further prays for damages in the sum of $15,000.00 together with plaintiff's costs and disbursements herein.

(date)

_____

Attorney for plaintiff

Answer

Comes now defendant and for its answer to plaintiff's complaint:

1. Denies each and every allegation, statement and matter in the complaint contained, except as herein after expressly admitted or alleged.

2. Admits the allegations of paragraphs 1, 2, 3, 4 and 7.

3. Specifically denies that defendant's use of defendant's land has created a nuisance.

4. Alleges that defendant is without sufficient knowledge and information upon which to form a belief concerning plaintiff's alleged damages, and puts plaintiff to his strict proof of same.

5. Alleges that plaintiff's plant and operations have been conducted in essentially the same manner for twenty-five years and that the plaintiffs acquired their premises knowing of the existence of defendant's facilities.

6. Alleges that defendant purchased an easement from plaintiff's predecessors in interest which easement and covenant runs with the land and which binds plaintiff precluding plaintiff from suing defendant.

7. Alleges that plaintiff's pretended cause of action is barred by laches.

8. Alleges that plaintiff's pretended cause of action is barred by the easement and covenant not to sue which is attached hereto as Exhibit A and incorporated by reference.

9. That plaintiff's pretended cause of action is barred by the applicable Ohio statute of limitations.

Wherefore, defendant prays that plaintiff take nothing by reason of its pretended cause of action, and that defendant have judgment for its costs and disbursement herein.

(date)

_____

Attorney for defendant

MISCELLANEOUS CAUSES OF ACTION

A person who engages in *ultra hazardous activity* is strictly liable for damage caused by the activity. An activity is ultra hazardous if it is incapable of being conducted without a significant likelihood of damage to property or injury to persons. A person engaged in an ultra hazardous activity is liable even though he or she conducts the activity with great care. Fault is not an issue. Nor is the utility necessity of the conduct an issue. The only real question is whether the activity is appropriate for the area in which the activity is conducted.

Some examples of ultra hazardous activity should be helpful. Very often heavy construction work requires pile driving in urban areas where the vibrations in the earth may cause substantial damage to nearby existing structures. Even though the pile driving is necessary, the contractor is liable for its consequential effects. Dynamiting is a similar ultra hazardous activity.

Some less obviously dangerous activities may be ultra hazardous. For example, creation of a dam that stores water may be an ultra hazardous activity due to percolation of water through surrounding soil. The owner of the dam is absolutely liable for damage caused by the percolation and for harm caused to persons and property in the event the dam bursts. Keeping of a wild animal that gets loose and causes injury is an ultra hazardous activity.

Spraying crops with a chemical that is detrimental to other foliage on adjacent properties *may* be an ultra hazardous activity. In each of these examples, the defendant has acted reasonably to promote his or her own business or other interest for a proper purpose, but because the activity is ultra hazardous, the actor is strictly liable for any harm caused to others.

REPLEVIN

If a person wrongfully obtains possession of personal property or wrongfully retains possession of personal property, the rightful owner may bring an action in *replevin* to recover possession of the property. The courts use their power to restore the property to its rightful owner or custodian. The gravamen of the action is the right to immediate possession.

Sometimes the plaintiff can obtain possession with commencement of the action through use of an *order to show cause* which requires the former possessor to show cause, if he or she can, why the property should not be turned over to the plaintiff or kept by the court while the action is pending. The plaintiff may be required to post a bond protecting the defendant in the event the case is decided in favor of the defendant. The bond is intended to compensate the defendant for his or her loss of use of the property and even for the value of the property.

A party obtains an order to show cause by presenting the court with a motion and affidavits which tend to establish the moving parties' right to immediate possession of the property. Upon such a showing the court *may* issue an order compeling the possessor to appear before the court and show good cause why the property should not be turned over to the moving party.

There are many, many other causes of action providing various forms of relief. Just to mention a few: actions for dissolution of marriage, actions for dissolution of a partnership, actions for damages caused by domestic animals, actions for damages for United States patent infringements, actions for damages for unfair competition, actions for violation of civil rights. Each action has its own specific requirements or elements and is subject to certain affirmative defenses. A paralegal may wish to increase his or her understanding of the law by studying causes of action. *Corpus Juris Secundum* and *American Jurisprudence Second* are treatises on the law which provide concise statements about the causes of action, their application and limitations.

Affirmative Defenses ⎯⎯⎯⎯⎯ **4**

A defendant will win a lawsuit if the plaintiff cannot prove his or her case, i.e., prove all of the elements necessary to the cause of action. The burden is on the plaintiff to establish each element by a fair preponderance of the evidence. The defendant will also prevail if he or she can prove that the claim is barred by one or more *affirmative defenses*. A list of affirmative defenses appears in Rule 8(c). The list is not all inclusive. Any circumstance or set of facts or legal theory which has the effect of avoiding or defeating a plaintiff's claim, even though the claim is basically true and proven, is considered an affirmative defense.

The defendant has the burden of proving the facts which establish an affirmative defense. Again, the burden of proof is met if the facts are proved by a fair preponderance of the evidence. In some few matters, a higher degree of proof may be required. For example, proof of a mutual mistake by the parties as grounds for reforming a written contract must be established by evidence that is *clear and convincing*. Even then, the burden of proof is somewhat less than "beyond a reasonable doubt" which is the government's burden of proof in a criminal prosecution action.

Affirmative defenses must be pleaded by the defendant in his or her answer or they are waived. Usually it is sufficient to allege the affirmative defense by its name without any detailed statement of facts. Each affirmative defense should be set forth in a separate paragraph for clarity and convenience of the parties.

ACCORD AND SATISFACTION

The first affirmative defense listed in Rule 8(c) is *accord and satisfaction*. This defense may be available where a controversy arises out of a transaction. If the parties, in recognition of their dispute, enter into a new agreement, called an *accord,* and proceed to fulfill the terms of that agreement, a *satisfaction,* the new undertaking is a complete defense to any claim on the original transaction. The defense requires evidence that both parties recognized that a bona fide dispute existed and that the new agreement was entered into as a compromise on both sides. Proof of the payment and acceptance of payment is necessary to the defense. If the promisor has defaulted on both the old agreement and the new undertaking, the plaintiff may elect to sue on either.

When a dispute arises out of a transaction, it is not uncommon for a person to tender a check in a reduced amount as "payment in full". If it is made clear that the check is offered to resolve a disputed claim — not in recognition of a just obligation — and that if accepted by the payee, the disputed obligation is fully discharged, the acceptance and negotiation of the check constitutes an accord and satisfaction. The object of the tender must be manifest. The payee must accept the tender according to the stated terms or return the check uncashed.

ARBITRATION AND AWARD

If the parties to a dispute agree to submit their controversy to a third party or tribunal for determination, and the matter is resolved accordingly, the disappointed party cannot subsequently litigate the controversy in court. The prior determination is binding as an *arbitration and award.* Only if there was fraud or some other defect in the arbitration procedure may the losing party contest the award. Arbitration is frequently provided as the primary means for settling disputes under insurance policies, construction contracts and labor agreements. The arbitration procedure may be specified by the agreement in question or the parties may adopt the provisions of the Uniform Arbitration Act which is part of the laws of most states.

STATUTES OF LIMITATIONS

Any cause of action is subject to being barred by a *statute of limitations.* The purpose of a statute of limitations is to bar old, stale claims. For example, if two motorists had been involved in what seemed to be a minor accident, it would be unfair for one to sue the other ten years later claiming the accident actually caused grievous bodily harm. The defendant would probably be hindered in gathering evidence with which to defend himself or herself at that late date. The same is true for contract actions. So the legislatures have established time periods in which claims must be sued or the claims are barred. Each state has statutes of limitations with varying time periods depending upon the type of cause of action and remedy claimed.

In some states, the applicable statute may be as short as one year for a particular type of action. In other states, the statutory period may be as long as six years or even more for the same action. Various kinds of professional malpractice actions may be given special treatment by having a particularly short statute of limitations. Such cases often present unique problems in preserving evidence, so there is good reason for treating them separately.

The statute of limitations does not run out against a minor during his or her minority. A minor plaintiff is always allowed the time designated by the statute. If that time runs out during his minority, he is still allowed another year after reaching legal age. For example, if a six year statute of limitations applies to a particular cause of action and the plaintiff is sixteen years of age at the time the cause of action accrues and the plaintiff attains legal majority at age eighteen, the statute runs against his or her claim when the six year period expires. But if the minor plaintiff is only ten years old when the cause of action accrues, the action will not be barred until one year after he reaches legal age.

If the plaintiff's cause of action is based upon fraud, the cause of action does not accrue until the fraud is discovered or should have been discovered. If the defendant conceals the fact that the plaintiff has a claim against him or her, the statute does not begin to run until the plaintiff discovers that he or she has a claim. In medical malpractice cases, the cause of action accrues at the time of the negligence *and* injury. However, the statute of limitations does not begin to run on medical malpractice cases until the patient or physician terminates the treatment. In some states the statute does not begin to run until the patient discovers the malpractice and consequential injury.

ASSUMPTION OF RISK

Assumption of risk is a defense that applies to actions in negligence and breach of warranty claims. The defendant must prove that the plaintiff's loss (injury or property damage) was the result of a danger or risk which was apparent to the plaintiff — known and appreciated; that he or she voluntarily chose to incur the risk; and that the injury resulted from the risk assumed. A typical application of the defense is where the plaintiff knowingly proceeds to walk on a sidewalk or floor which is obviously slippery. But if the defenant's slippery sidewalk is the only practicable means that the plaintiff has of going to his or her destination, can it be said that the risk was *voluntarily* incurred? Most likely not.

If a patron at a professional baseball game has the opportunity of sitting in a protected area but voluntarily chooses to sit in an open area, he can hardly complain about getting hit by a "home-run" ball. He chose to be where the action is. The ball park is not liable for negligently failing to provide protection.

If a person voluntarily chooses to ride with a drunk driver, he or she must know that there is a risk that they will have an accident. The same is true if someone elects to ride in an automobile which is driven by another in a race on the public streets. The assumed risk of injury arises from a danger that is apprehended and voluntarily incurred.

One more example may be instructive. Suppose that the plaintiff purchased a new electric appliance. After using it a couple times, he discovers that it has an apparent short. If he nevertheless continues to use the appliance, he assumes the risk of injury or loss which results from the electrical short. He would also be contributorily negligent. Often the two defenses overlap.

CONTRIBUTORY NEGLIGENCE

Contributory negligence is a term given to negligence on the part of the claimant (usually the plaintiff) which bars his or her claim against another party. For example, in a negligence action where the plaintiff and the defendant have sued each other, the parties' contributory negligence would prevent both from recovering against the other. Contributory negligence is not a defense to an action based upon strict liability in tort; nor is it a defense to a claim under the Dram Shop Act against a liquor vendor.

The defense of contributory negligence has been abolished by those states which have adopted the law of comparative negligence or comparative fault.

DISCHARGE IN BANKRUPTCY

Federal laws provide that individuals and corporations may voluntarily declare bankruptcy if they cannot meet their current obligations. Three creditors can force an individual or corporation into involuntary bankruptcy. The effect of the court's determination that the petitioner is bankrupt is to discharge him or her from all declared debts as of the date of the petition. The creditors must be given notice of the petition for bankruptcy so that they have an opportunity to challenge the petition and to share in the debtor's existing assets. Defects in the proceedings such as a failure to give a creditor notice precludes the debtor from being discharged.

Certain kinds of debts are not dischargeable in bankruptcy. Such debts are those created by the petitioner's fraud, willful conversion (theft) of property, and intentional tortious acts causing injury to persons or damage to property.

DURESS

A promise which is otherwise legally enforceable is not binding if it was exacted from the promisor by duress. Duress is the threat of death, bodily harm, or damage to property.

5

Jurisdiction

A court's authority over people, corporations and property is limited to the court's jurisdiction. Indeed, in this context, the terms "authority" and "jurisdiction" are essentially synonymous. In other words, if a court acts outside of or beyond its jurisdiction, it acts beyond its authority — beyond its power. The government that creates a court establishes the court's jurisdiction. We ordinarily think of the courts as one of the three separate branches of governement — necessary to the marvelous system of checks and balances built into the United States' system of government. In the federal government, however, only the United States Supreme Court is entirely separate. It was created by the Constitution, and the Constitution establishes its authority. Its powers cannot be abridged or expanded by Congress. But the lower courts (federal district courts and circuit courts of appeals) were created by acts of Congress. Congress determined their organization, function and the scope of their jurisdiction. Though separate and independent, the branches of government must work together. A healthy spirit of cooperation was manifested by the Congress when it recognized that the lower courts should operate pursuant to rules established by the Supreme Court and enacted enabling legislation authorizing the Supreme Court to promulgate the Federal Rules of Civil Procedure, an important part of our study in this book.

The power, structure, rules of procedure and function of a court created by a legislature can be changed at will by the legislature. As an example, the United States Congress enacted the Federal Rules of Evidence to be used by the federal district courts. The codification of the rules of evidence replaced a system of common law rules of evidence follwed by the federal courts for two centuries. Federal judges must follow and apply the new rules even if they happen to prefer the old common law rules. It is necessary to look to the authority by which each court was created to determine the scope of the court's jurisdiction. Similarly, state legislatures may change the structure and functions of the state courts through legislation. For example, more judges may be added, or courts may be merged, or an intermediate court for appeals may be created by legislative action.

When a lawyer obtains a new case, one of the first considerations is to determine which court or courts have jurisdiction in the matter. For purposes of this book, jurisdiction may be divided into three basic categories: (1) jurisdiction over persons;* (2) jurisdiction over the subject matter of the litigation; and (3) geographical or territorial jurisdiction. Jurisdiction over a case exists only if *all* three jurisdictional requirements are met.

There are numerous ways in which a court's jurisdiction may be limited. Probably the most obvious limitation is the geographical or territorial limit on a court's power. With some few exceptions, a court has no authority beyond its territorial limits. The limitation is a very practical one. For example, if the judgment debtor and subject matter of a lawsuit are within the territorial limits of the court, enforcement of the judgment by the prevailing party is usually no problem. However, one can imagine the difficulty that a court in Massachusetts would have in determining title to real estate located in Texas, let alone enforcing a judgment affecting title to that land. Jurisdiction may be further limited by the types of cases which certain courts may hear, the size of the money judgments which they can award, and the types of remedies they may provide. There is no way that the parties can confer jurisdiction upon the court if the statutory requirements have not been met. However, jurisdiction over the defendant may be conferred upon the court by his or her consent or by failure to object to the lack of jurisdiction in a seasonable manner by making a motion for dismissal or by raising the objection in the defendant's answer.

When the plaintiff commences a civil action in a particular court, he or she thereby submits to the court's jurisdiction — at least insofar as the particular transaction or occurrence is concerned. The court obtains jurisdiction over the defendant through service of a summons upon the defendant in the manner provided by law and the court's rules of civil procedure. If the summons or service of the summons is defective for any reason, the court fails to obtain jurisdiction over the person of the defendant. (Service of process is discussed in greater detail in Chapter 6.) The jurisdictional defect created by an insufficiency in service of process may be waived by the defendant. The waiver may be intentional or inadvertent. However, the *parties* cannot confer jurisdiction upon the court over the subject matter.

---

*Jurisdiction of the person refers to jurisdiction over parties who are individuals, corporations, and other legal entities.

Another factor that may affect jurisdiction is the identity of the parties. For example, state courts do not have jurisdiction over the United States Government or any of its agencies. All civil actions involving the United States must be brought in Federal district courts. A state court does not have jurisdiction over claims against another state. Jurisdiction could be obtained over a state only in a federal court.

The territorial limitation on a court's jurisdiction becomes a little vague in accident cases. For example, suppose two acquaintances from California are traveling in an automobile through Minnesota when they are involved in a collision, and the passenger desires to bring a negligence action against the driver to recover money damages for personal injuries. Must the lawsuit be brought in Minnesota? Suppose the driver and passenger return to their native California? Do they have to return to Minnesota to litigate their dispute? Causes of action arising out of occurrences (torts) usually are "transitory". This means that the cause of action accrues in the territory where the accident occurred, but also follows the parties (at least, it follows the defendant). Generally speaking, a cause of action may be brought in any jurisdiction where the defendant can be found. In the above hypothetical situation, the cause of action could be sued in any state where the defendant can be found. The action could be brought in Minnesota, whether or not the defendant driver is in Minnesota at the time the action is commenced. The Minnesota court's authority exists under the state's nonresident motorist statute which provides that a non-resident motorist impliedly appoints the Secretary of State or Commissioner of Highways as an agent to receive service of process relating to any motor vehicle accident occurring within the state. All states have such statutes. The plaintiff passenger could have a summons and complaint served upon the Minnesota Commissioner of Highways but he or she must also mail a copy of the summons and complaint to the nonresident motorist at that person's last known address pursuant to the statute. Through this procedure, the Minnesota courts can obtain jurisdiction over the driver.

If a manufacturer produces a defective product which is shipped into another state for resale and use, and the product causes injury to the retail purchaser, the latter has a cause of action against the manufacturer. A few decades ago, it would have been necessary for the consumer to bring the lawsuit in the state where the manufacturer was incorporated or where it conducted its business. However, in recent years, the concept of due process of law has been broadened to permit states to enact so-called long-arm statutes for protection of their citizens in cases such as this. The cause of action is considered to have its origin in the state where the injury occurred. Service of process may be made upon the foreign corporation by serving the Secretary of State of the state where the injury occurred. The plaintiff must promptly mail copies of the summons and complaint to the foreign corporation at its registered office or principle place of business. The foreign corporation will have to defend itself in the state where the consumer's injury occurred. If the plaintiff consumer moves to another state, the cause of action does not follow him or her. The suit must be brought in the state where the injury occurred or where the defendant manufacturer conducts its business as of the time of service. A corporation can always be sued in the state where it was incorporated. A cause of action in tort or for breach of contract "follows" the defendant, whether a natural person or a corporation. It does not "follow" the plaintiff. But if the plaintiff follows the defendant to another state and brings the action there, the defendant can **counterclaim** against the plaintiff. Whenever the plaintiff elects to sue in a particular court, he submits to the jurisdiction of that court during the pendency of the suit.

The amount of money damages claimed in the complaint determines whether certain courts have jurisdiction to handle the case. Small claims courts cannot award damages over a few hundred dollars. The exact amount varies from state to state. If a plaintiff has a claim for $350, but the jurisdictional limit is only $300, he must give up fifty dollars of the claim in order to use the small claims court. On the other hand, the Federal District Courts require that the amount in controversy, in so-called diversity suits*, *exceed* $10,000. The court does not have jurisdiction to handle cases involving lesser amounts. There is no way in which the parties can bestow jurisdiction on the court by agreement or otherwise, if the amount in controversy is $10,000 or less. It would be a fraud on the court to feign an amount in excess of $10,000 for the purpose of trying to give the court jurisdiction.

A court of general jurisdiction can render all forms of remedies available at law and equity. In addition to awarding money damages in unlimited amounts, they can issue decrees for adoption, divorce, injunctions, specific performance, change of name, and judgments determining title to real estate. (Some of these remedies are discussed in Chapter 5.) Courts of limited jurisdiction are unable to provide some of these remedies to parties.

FEDERAL COURT ORGANIZATION

The United States Supreme Court was established by the United States Constitution. It is an independent, separate branch of our federal government. The Constitution also authorized Congress to establish such inferior courts as the Congress deems appropriate. Through that power, Congress has created a United States federal district court for each state and for certain United States territories. Federal lawsuits begin in these courts and go to trial in them. Congress also created eleven Circuit Courts of Appeals. If believing that the district court committed prejudicial error in the trial of his or her case, a party may appeal to the circuit court in his or her area. The jurisdiction of the district courts and the circuit courts are established and limited by the statutes creating them. So there are three principle levels of courts in the federal system. The jurisdiction of each district court is limited to the geographical boundaries of the state or territory it serves. Each state's district courts have been subdivided into divisions for ease of administration. The jurisdiction of the court in each division, however, is statewide.

---

*Diversity suits authorize a citizen of one state to sue in Federal court if the defendant is a resident of a different state.

The federal district courts are courts of original jurisdiction. This means that a case originates in a district court — there it is decided for the first time. The federal district courts are also courts of limited jurisdiction. They are limited in the types of cases that they may handle, the amount of damages they may award, and only certain persons may use the courts.

Federal law provides that certain types of cases must be brought in a federal court, such as cases involving United States patent infringements — regardless of the amount of money in controversy. The same is true of any action against the United States government or any of its agencies. Federal district courts provide forums for litigants who have claims against the United States Government, against a foreign state, against a foreign corporation, or against an individual who is a resident of another state.

A corporation is considered to be a resident of the state of its incorporation. When an action is against a private person or corporation of another state, the claim must involve a sum of money greater than $10,000 to give the federal court jurisdiction. In other words, even though a diversity of residency exists, if the claim is for the sum of $10,000 or less, a federal district court does not have jurisdiction. This is a limitation imposed by federal statute, not the Constitution. A large body of law has developed concerning the question of whether or not a diversity of residency (or diversity of citizenship) exists determining whether cases can be brought in federal court. If the case is not subject to federal jurisdiction, the plaintiff must resort to the state courts — an unsatisfactory alternative to some litigants.

Usually there is no great problem in determining whether or not a controversy involves more than $10,000 in cases arising out of transaction, such as an action on a contract or promissory note. Cases involving personal injury claims however, are often very difficult to evaluate for determining whether the jurisdictional requirement has been met. As a rule of thumb, courts and parties look to the amount of special damages* and the seriousness of any injury. If there is medical evidence of a significant permanent disability, federal district courts usually accept jurisdiction. However, federal district judges may differ on how stringently they apply this limitation. If a case goes through trial and the jury determines that full compensation should be less than $10,000, the court will allow entry of judgment for the lesser amount. The monetary limitation does not cause the court to lose jurisdiction retroactively.

Each state has one federal district court. Each district court is subdivided into a number of divisions (various locations or branches) for the convenient administration of the court's business. There are times when two or more federal district courts (each in a separate state or territory) has jurisdiction, but one is the proper **venue.** There are a number of rules which determine where cases should be venued. When a lawyer refers to venue, with regard to federal courts, he or she may be referring to the district as a whole or to a particular division within a district. Generally speaking, the proper venue is the one most convenient to all the parties and witnesses.

---

*Special damages are out-of-pocket expenses which the claimant has incurred because of the alleged wrongful conduct of the defendant.

Federal district courts are **courts of record** which means that a complete record is made of the court's proceedings. A complete or partial transcript can be obtained by a party or even a nonparty, for various purposes. The record is available to an appellate court for review of any aspect of the case. However, a transcript is not made unless it is specifically ordered, and the person who orders it must pay for it.

If a party believes that errors occurred in the trial which require a new trial or reversal, he or she may appeal the district court judgment to the appropriate circuit court of appeals. Cases do not originate in the appelate courts. There are twelve circuit courts of appeals. Their territorial jurisdiction is outlined in the map on page 404.

The court of last resort in the federal judicial system is the United States Supreme Court. Relatively few cases are appealed to the Supreme Court. Most cases that do reach it are appealed on a petition for a writ of **certiorari.** This is a procedure by which the appellant requests the Supreme Court to issue an order allowing him or her to appeal. If the Supreme Court feels that the issue to be appealed is significant, it may grant the application by ordering the lower court to "send up" its file for review.

Each state has a system of courts which have general jurisdiction, usually described as district courts. Each district court has power to hear almost any kind of case involving any sum of money and to grant all forms of judicial remedies. Each district court has statewide jurisdiction, that is, their subpoenas, orders and decrees may be enforced anywhere within the state and even against its citizens who are outside the state. Each district court operates within a specified territory — usually a county or group of counties. As a general rule, a cause of action which accrues within a county *should* be filed with the court in that county as the proper venue. But, as mentioned above, a district court's jurisdiction is statewide.

In a tort action, the cause of action accrues in the county where the loss or injury occurred. In a contract case, the cause of action accrues in the county where the contract was to be performed which is usually where the breach occurred. In a real estate case, the cause of action accrues in the county where the real estate is located. Usually the proper venue is the most convenient place for the case to be tried. Venue also refers to the territory from which the jury is selected. Factors affecting venue and jurisdiction may be the same, but the two terms involve quite different concepts.

The plaintiff selects a venue when he or she commences the action by designating the court at the top of the complaint. If the defendant believes the plaintiff selected the wrong venue, he or she must make a demand for a change of venue within the time specified by law — usually before the answer is due. Otherwise, the defendant waives the right to have the case heard in the proper venue. The right to a change of venue is waived by a failure to seasonably object. If for some reason the preferred venue is not convenient, the action is ordinarily brought in the venue where most of the defendants reside.

Each state has various other courts of limited jurisdiction. Most cities have small claims courts. These courts exist for the speedy, inexpensive handling of small claims which involve nothing more than the award of money damages. They handle a tremendous volume of property damage claims, claims for wages, claims for breached contracts, collection of rent, collection of delinquent accounts and even small personal injury cases.

The jurisdiction of small claims courts may be as large as $1000, or even more, depending upon the needs of the community. Lawyers are allowed to appear on behalf of clients, but the system tends to discourage lawyers' participation. The amount in controversy usually does not warrant the expense of legal representation. The procedures are kept informal so that a lawyer's guidance is not necessary. The rules of evidence are not followed closely. The parties are encouraged to simply tell their stories in their own words with as few interruptions as possible. The judge or referee asks such questions as he or she deems necessary. Of course, companies and corporations cannot appear in person, so they usually send lawyers to appear on their behalf along with the necessary witnesses. These courts have subpoena power but it is seldom used.

Service of process in small claims courts is kept very simple and inexpensive. The usual procedure is to have the plaintiff prepare a sworn complaint in the clerk of court's office. The complaint contains a short, narrative statement of the plaintiff's version of the facts. Usually the clerk of court tries to help the plaintiff frame the allegations. The filing fee is nominal, generally one to ten dollars. A copy of the complaint is mailed by the clerk of court to the defendant at his or her last known address. A notice accompanies the complaint directing the defendant to appear in court at a specified time to defend against the allegations, and if the defendant fails to do so, a default judgment may be taken against him or her. If the last known address proves to be incorrect, that would be grounds for setting aside any default judgment obtained against the defendant. The defendant is not required to prepare and serve an answer to the complaint.

The cases are usually heard within six weeks from the date of filing. Twenty or more cases may be scheduled for hearing in the course of a morning or afternoon session. After the judge has heard the narrative testimony of the parties and their witnesses, he or she takes the matter under advisement. Obviously, he or she must make a decision right away because it would not be possible to keep all the cases in mind for very long, but rendering a decision in open court might lead to a courtroom altercation. Also, it might upset the other parties who are waiting for their cases to be heard and cause them to change their "stories" to fit the presider's pronouncements.

Notwithstanding the informality of the small claims courts, their decision should be rendered according to the law rather than the judges' personal sense of equity. For example, if the plaintiff has sued on an oral contract which is unenforceable because it comes within the statute of frauds and should have been in writing, the decision should be for the defendant. The judge should inform the plaintiff during the hearing that the law requires some contracts like this to be in writing to be enforceable. This can be done without pronouncing the court's decision. Using this approach, the court helps the party to understand why he or she lost. The party may not be quite as angry against the system when receiving the formal notice of decision. Of course, this example does not apply where the only controversy is over the facts giving rise to the claim and the only problem is to determine which witnesses are telling the truth. The judge never comments on the credibility of the witnesses. That would only cause problems.

Small claims courts are not courts of record. The only documentation of the trial is the court's order for judgment. If a litigant is disappointed in the outcome, he or she cannot appeal directly to an appellate court. Usually, the procedure is to appeal to the next higher court of original jurisdiction — probably a municipal court or a county court. There the parties receive a new trial — "trial de novo". This time the case is tried with all of the usual court formalities. Of course, the appeal must be taken within the designated period of time and in the manner prescribed by the small claims court's rules. Notice of the decision and judgment usually contains the information necessary for the losing party to appeal and obtain a trial de novo.

In some communities certain "smaller" civil cases are tried by a local justice of the peace. A justice of the peace is usually not a lawyer, and may not have formal training in the law. His or her income probably depends directly upon the litigation he handles. "Justice courts" lack some of the safeguards which characterize courts of law. Consequently, the "justice courts" seem to be disappearing.

Municipal courts and county courts handle a large volume of litigation even though they are courts of limited jurisdiction. They cannot render judgments in excess of a specified amount, such as ten thousand dollars. They are courts of original jurisdiction. They are courts of record, so a transcript of the proceedings and evidence received during the course of the trial is available. An appeal may be taken directly to an appellate court from a municipal or county court. The parties have a right to trial by jury just as if the matter were brought in a court of general jurisdiction. Usually, the rules of procedure for municipal and county courts are very similar to the district court's rules. There is considerable value in keeping the rules of procedures uniform in all courts throughout the state. For the same reason, many states have adopted rules similar to the federal district court Rules of Civil Procedure. The limitations on a municipal court's jurisdiction prevent it from handling suits for divorce, or for determining title to real estate, or for granting injunctions, or rendering other types of "equitable" relief.

Courts of general jurisdiction can handle any type of civil lawsuit. There is no maximum amount of money damages that they can award; there is no minimum amount required for jurisdiction. Their judgments and decrees may be enforced anywhere within the territorial limits of the state. They are always courts of record. The losing party may appeal directly from the court to the appropriate appellate court. A court of general jurisdiction has authority and powers through the state supreme court which the legislature cannot take away. For example, the legislature could not provide in a statute that the district courts shall not have jurisdiction to determine that a particular statute is unconstitutional. Some district court rules provide that if the plaintiff is the prevailing party but recovers a judgment for an amount of money within the monetary jurisdiction of a lower court, the losing party may "tax" his or her costs against the prevailing party. The purpose of such rules is to encourage parties to use the lower courts if at all possible, and to save the courts of general jurisdiction for the more significant cases. Taxable costs may include the filing fee, witness fees and the cost of service of process.

Appellate courts do not have original jurisdiction of lawsuits. That is, cases are not commenced in the appellate courts. Their function is to supervise the trial courts and make sure that trial courts act within the law, follow prescribed procedures, and do not abuse their discretionary powers. Appellate courts make the final determination of all questions of law. The trial courts still have primary responsiblity for resolving disputed facts.

Appellate courts reverse trial judges for abuses of discretion only when the abuse is manifest. For example, trial judges have broad discretion in determing whether a person qualifies as an expert witness. If the trial court's ruling is challenged on appeal, it is not uncommon for the appellate court to state in its published decision that the appellate court might have ruled differently than the trial court, but the holding is affirmed because the trial court's ruling was not clearly wrong. The same is true where an appellate court is asked to pass judgment on a trial court's order that affirms or disallows the amount of money damages awarded by a jury.

Appellate courts never take testimony to resolve issues before them; i.e., witnesses are never allowed to testify. An appellate court's rules may or may not provide for oral argument by lawyers concerning issues of law that have been appealed. Motions to the appellate courts are always made in writing, not orally. The established procedures are quite technical and discourage laymen from attempting to prosecute their own appeals. Appellate court decisions are published so that other litigants may obtain guidance by the precedent established by such decisions. The fact that the appellate court decisions (opinions) are published is another check within the judicial system to keep courts responsible to the citizens.

6

Introduction to Federal Procedure

The structure of a civil lawsuit is largely established by the Federal Rules of Civil Procedure. The Rules prescribe the methods for commencing lawsuits, conducting discovery procedures, presenting motions, conducting the trial and perfecting appeals. An understanding of the purposes, applications and interrelationship of these Rules is essential to competent handling of civil litigation. If a paralegal is going to understand what lawyers do in the handling of civil litigation and how they do it, a good understanding of the Rules is essential.

COMMENCEMENT OF A LAWSUIT

A lawsuit is easy to start and it should be. Parties who have valid claims should not be discouraged from using the courts to resolve those claims. If a person has a meritorious claim, his or her first step should be to consult with a lawyer to determine whether or not the claim is one which can be formulated into a cause of action. If a lawyer concludes that the claim has probable merit, he or she prepares a complaint which sets out the necessary allegations to establish the client's cause of action. Rule 11 provides that the complaint must be signed by a lawyer; or if no lawyer has been retained, the complaint must be signed by the plaintiff. The complaint is not a verified document, i.e., it is not notarized. The lawyer's signature at the bottom of the complaint is his or her personal certification that there is apparent good ground to support the claim and that the action has not been brought for the purpose of harrassment, embarrassment or delay. A lawyer does not have to browbeat the client to determine whether or not the claim has merit, but for the client's sake, and the lawyer's own protection, he or she ought to comply with the spirit of Rule 11.

Before the Federal Rules of Civil Procedure were adopted in 1938, the complaint had to set forth, at length, all the facts which gave rise to the claim. The form and language of the complaint were as important as the substance. If the complaint failed to state sufficient facts to establish a cause of action, the complaint was subject to being summarily dismissed upon a demurrer (motion) filed by the defendant. The importance placed upon the complaint is indicated by the fact that it supposedly provided the defendant with all of the information about the plaintiff's claim that the defendant needed to either admit his or her liability or to defend against the suit. The Rules have substantially reduced the technical requirements of the complaint, but it still has the function of informing the court and defendant of the basic facts which give the court jurisdiction, and informs the defendant of the nature of the claim against him or her and the amount of plaintiff's claim.

Conciseness has become one of the hallmarks of a well drafted complaint. As provided in Rule 8: "A complaint shall contain a short and plain statement of the claim showing the pleader is entitled to relief." The Complaint must allege the legal basis for the court's jurisdiction; the names of the persons involved; the date and place of the transaction or occurrence; and the nature of the legal wrong allegedly perpetrated by the defendant; the nature and extent of the losses/injuries sustained by plaintiff; and, finally, the type and amount of the relief or compensation demanded by plaintiff. The Rules do not require the allegations to be stated in a particular, legalistic manner. However, the elements of a cause of action must be set forth or the complaint is subject to dismissal, and the lawsuit is terminated.

If plaintiff wants to assert a claim for breach of contract, the allegations of the complaint may be similar to the following.

Complaint Alleging
Action in Breach of Contract

For his cause of action against defendant, plaintiff alleges:

1. That plaintiff is a resident of the State of New York, and defendant is a resident of the State of New Jersey; the amount in controversy exceeds Ten Thousand ($10,000.00) Dollars, not including costs and interest.

2. That on May 10, 1981, plaintiff and defendant entered into a written contract in which plaintiff agreed to purchase from defendant and defendant agreed to sell a certain XYZ electronic computer bearing the manufacturer's serial no. _____ , and then located at defendant's plant at *(street address),* Newark, New Jersey.

3. That the agreed purchase price for the computer to be delivered at defendant's said plant was Thirty Thousand ($30,000.00) Dollars.

4. That a copy of said contract is attached hereto as Exhibit A and incorporated herein by reference.

5. That defendant promised to deliver said computer to plaintiff at defendant's plant in Newark, New Jersey on June 15, 1981.

6. That defendant failed to deliver said computer to plaintiff at said time and place, although plaintiff has made demand upon defendant to do so.

7. That plaintiff tendered to defendant the agreed purchase price of Thirty Thousand ($30,000.00) Dollars, and all other conditions precedent have occurred or have been performed by plaintiff.

8. That by reason of defendant's breach of contract, plaintiff has been required to purchase another electronic computer, similar in type, at a cost of Fifty Thousand ($50,000.00) Dollars; therefore, defendant's breach of contract has caused plaintiff to sustain a loss in the amount of Twenty Thousand ($20,000.00) Dollars, plus interest thereon at the legal rate of 8% per annum.

Wherefore, plaintiff prays for judgment against defendant in the sum of Twenty Thousand ($20,000.00) Dollars, together with interest thereon at the legal rate of 8% per annum from the date of defendant's breach, together with plaintiff's costs and disbursements herein.

Plaintiff demands trial by jury.

(date)

_____

Attorney for Plaintiff

In the above form, the complaint has identified the contract, the place of its performance, the time and place of the breach and the nature of the cause of action, namely "breach of contract". The document used to formalize the transaction has been fully identified by attaching a photocopy to the original complaint and to each copy of the complaint served. Photocopying of exhibits reduces the possibility of error in critical wording. Clearly, the defendant has been provided with enough information to decide whether to deny the claim or admit liability. A responsive pleading is an *answer* which the defendant serves upon the plaintiff's lawyer.

Whether a transaction or an occurrence is the basis for a lawsuit, the time and place must be specified in the complaint. The complaint must describe the legal wrong committed by the defendant: assault and battery, negligence, trespass, slander, etc. Time factors are very important not only to identify the occurrence, but also to determine whether the statute of limitations has run against the claim and whether the parties have complied with notice requirements. The place of the occurrence may determine which court has jurisdiction. The place of the occurrence may determine which state's laws are to be applied in determining the parties' substantive rights.

The complaint must describe, in general terms, the types of loss or injury and the extent of the loss plaintiff sustained. The loss may take various forms such as a loss of profits, expenses, pain and suffering, disfigurement, embarrassment, disability, loss of good reputation, loss of use of money, loss of support, the loss of property. The losses may relate to the past and/or the future. An amount of money damages is often specified for each item of loss.

Fundamental to all tort litigation is the requirement that the alleged occurrence must be a direct (proximate) cause of the loss sustained by the plaintiff. If there is a lack of causation, if the wrongful conduct of the defendant did not actually cause plaintiff's loss, the plaintiff is not entitled to compensation from the defendant. Therefore, the complaint must specifically allege that the tort committed by the defendant was the proximate or direct cause of plaintiff's loss.

Finally, the complaint must contain an ad damnum clause — the "Wherefore" clause — in which plaintiff specifies the relief or recovery which he or she wants from the defendant. The ad damnum clause puts the defendant on notice just how much money damages plaintiff is demanding. Nothing but a sense of professional responsiblity prevents plaintiff's counsel from asking for an excessively large amount of money. Litigants and newspapers often seem unduly impressed by large demands stated in complaints.

The amount stated in the ad damnum is particularly important in those courts where jurisdiction is affected by the amount in controversy. If it is too much, a county or municipal court cannot have jurisdiction over the case. Such courts usually have jurisdictional limits of a few thousand dollars. Other courts, such as a United States Federal District Court, may not have jurisdiction in certain types of cases unless plaintiff, in good faith, is able to demand judgment for an amount *in excess* of $10,000, exclusive of costs and interest.

If the defendant fails to serve an answer to the complaint within the specified time, he or she is considered to be in default. The plaintiff is able to obtain judgment against the defendant by application to the court. Rule 55. However, plaintiff's recovery is limited to the amount of the ad damnum — even though he or she is able to show more damages when "proving up" the default judgment. It can happen that by duly appearing and defending against the claim the defendant's obligation may be determined to be more than the amount demanded in the complaint. If he or she had defaulted, plaintiff's recovery would have been limited to the amount in the ad damnum clause.

Occasionally, a case seems to be minor when sued, but develops into a very serious one commanding a much higher award than originally presumed. Plaintiff's counsel may move the court for an order allowing him or her to increase the ad damnum as soon as the real value becomes known. The motion should be supported by affidavits setting forth the change in circumstances. The plaintiff must be prepared to show the court that the amendment will not prejudice the defendant's preparation for trial. For example, if a defendant has let her liability insurance company defend the case for her, but the amendment permits a recovery in excess of the insurance policy limits, sufficient time must be given for the defendant to consult with her own personal lawyer about her personal exposure. And the lawyer should have enough time to become acquainted with the case.

Ordinarily, the plaintiff is not allowed to increase the ad damnum clause to an amount in excess of the defendant's liability insurance policy limits once the case reaches trial. When the ad damnum exceeds the coverage provided by the defendant's insurance policy, a substantial conflict may exist between the defendant and the liability insurance company. Advice and services may be needed of a lawyer whom the defendant must retain at his or her own expense. The basic problem is whether the insurance company should pay the full amount of its policy to settle the case where there is an opportunity to do so, given the possibility of a recovery against the insured defendant for an amount in excess of the insurance policy limits if the case is not settled. If there is time for everyone to further evaluate the case and prepare for trial, the plaintiff is usually allowed to increase the ad damnum — assuming he or she is able to convince the court that there is good cause for the increase.

SERVICE OF PROCESS

A civil action is *commenced* in federal district court when the plaintiff files his or her complaint with the clerk of court. Rule 3. In state courts, the action is usually *commenced* when the summons and complaint or petition are served upon the defendant. The exact time at which an action is commenced may be critical to the lawsuit. For example, a question may arise whether the action was commenced before the statute of limitations ran against the cause of action. Some contracts, especially insurance policies, provide that an action on the contract must be brought within a specified period of time after the occurrence in question. Failure to comply constitutes a breach of a condition which bars an action on the contract. A single day can and has made the difference.

Due process of law requires that the procedure for commencing an action effectively notify the defendant that he or she has been sued, giving the defendant an opportunity to appear in the action and defend him or herself. This is accomplished by *service of process,* pursuant to Rule 4. In federal district courts the clerk of court prepares and issues the summons. The papers are then given to the United States marshal who has the responsibility for serving the summons and complaint upon the defendant. The court may appoint some person, other than the marshal, to serve the summons and complaint. A person appointed must be at least eighteen years of age. Rule 4(i). A party to the action is forbidden to serve the summons and complaint. The possibility of violence and fraud is greatly reduced by having a marshal or some other independent person serve the papers.

The summons notifies a defendant that he or she has twenty days after the date of service upon him in which to "appear and defend." Note that the twenty day period does not necessarily begin to run on the same day that the action is "commenced," because, in Federal Courts, action is commenced by filing the complaint. A defendant "appears" in the case by serving an answer to the complaint or by serving a motion pursuant to Rule 12, but is not required to present him or herself before a judge in court as in criminal arraignments.

It is not essential to service in person that the papers be handed to and accepted by the defendant, but the process server must be sure of the defendant's identity. If the defendant decides to be uncooperative and "turns his or her back" on the process server, the process server may simply leave the summons and complaint in the defendant's presence. There is no need to touch the defendant as if playing a game of tag. The marshal makes a record of the service of process in a document called the "Marshal's Return" which he or she files with the clerk of court before the time for answering expires. If for some reason, a person other than a United States marshal is appointed by the court to serve the summons and complaint, he or she must use an affidavit (sworn statement) establishing the fact of service. The Marshal's Return or process server's affidavit of service must show the date, time, manner and place of service; they must also identify the person upon whom service was made.

The law does not require that service be made at any particular time of the day. However, service must be made at a reasonable hour considering the circumstances. Service may be in the dead of the night if the defendant ordinarily works nights and sleeps days. There is no prohibition against service on Sundays or legal holidays.

There are several other ways in which the summons and complaint may be served upon the defendant. The methods are simple, fairly inexpensive and reasonably effective for putting the defendant on notice of the suit. Service of the summons and complaint may be accomplished by leaving them at the defendant's usual place of abode with a person who resides therein and who is of suitable age and discretion. The Rule purposely does not require that the papers be left with an adult. Historically, anyone fourteen years of age or older is presumed to meet the age requirements. A younger person may qualify, but if any question should later arise as to whether service was valid, the burden is upon the plaintiff to show that the person with whom the summons and complaint were left was of "suitable age and discretion". Almost any member of the defendant's family or other resident may be a proper person to receive service of process for the defendant. Suppose the defendant's adult sister is staying at the defendant's home for only a few days. Could the summons and complaint be effectively served upon the defendant by leaving the papers with her? No, she is not a resident of the household.

Some companies are frequently involved in litigation, so it is convenient for them to appoint a particular person or agent to receive service of process for them. Service may be made upon the company by delivering the summons and complaint to the agent. An agent may be appointed by law to receive service of process for certain defendants. Most, if not all, states provide for service of process on the Secretary of State as an agent for domestic and foreign corporations. By law the Commissioner of Highways is appointed an agent to receive service of process for nonresident motorists who have had motor accidents on public highways within the state. The Commissioner of Insurance is appointed by law to receive service of process on behalf of any insurance company doing business within the state. A copy of the summons and complaint are actually delivered to the official's office. The official stamps the original summons and complaint, thereby acknowledging receipt and admitting service of them. The law requires the plaintiff to provide the agent with at least one additional copy which the agent sends to the defendant at the last known address or registered address of the defendant. In addition, the plaintiff may be required to mail a copy of the summons and complaint to the defendant's last known address. Ordinary mail will suffice unless registered mail is specified by state law. The plaintiff or his or her lawyer must then file an *affidavit of compliance* showing that the mailing requirements have been complied with. The affidavit is prima facie evidence of compliance and must be filed with the clerk of court. There is nothing preventing an individual from appointing another person such as a lawyer to act as his or her personal agent to receive service of process. Believe it or not, this is a convenience for some entrepreneurs.

If the defendant is a minor, service must be made upon him or her in the manner prescribed by the laws of the state in which the defendant minor resides. Usually, service must be made upon one of the minor's parents or other legal guardian. The plaintiff may cause a guardian to be appointed for the child if he or she doesn't have one. A guardian who is appointed for the sole purpose of the lawsuit is called a "guardian ad litem." Some states authorize service directly upon a minor at least fourteen years of age. A guardian ad litem may be appointed for him or her later.

Age is only one type of legal disability which may affect service of process. If a defendant has been adjudged mentally incompetent to handle his or her own legal matters, the plaintiff must serve a copy of the summons and complaint on the guardian. The guardian must act to protect his or her ward's legal interests. Of course, the guardian will not actually conduct the litigation. His or her responsibility is to select and hire a lawyer to represent the ward and make decisions that are ordinarily reserved to the party such as whether or not to settle the claim. Some states require that a guardian be bonded so as to guaranty performance on behalf of the ward.

Service on a corporation may be made by delivering the summons and complaint to a managing agent or officer. Rule 4(d) (3). The corporation cannot restrict the method of service by limiting its officers' authority. But a corporation may appoint a non-officer, or even a nonemployee, to receive the papers.

Service on the United States Government requires at least two steps. The summons and complaint must be served upon the United States district attorney or assistant district attorney for the particular district in which the action is commenced. Copies must also be sent to the United States Attorney General at Washington, D.C. by registered mail or certified mail. Copies must be mailed to all United States offices or agencies affected by the litigation. Again, registered or certified mail must be used. Service is not complete (effective) until all the requirements are met. However, the action is *commenced* by filing the complaint with the clerk of court. The local United States district attorney may designate a non-lawyer to accept service for him or her at his or her office. When that is done, a letter or notice must be filed with the clerk of court naming the administrative employee who has been so designated. A plaintiff cannot sue the United States Government per se but only its agencies as authorized by law. The various statutes creating the agencies designate the manner for service of process and specify the proper person for receiving service within the agency.

When a municipality is a defendant, service can be made upon the chief executive officer or in any other manner established by local law.

The summons and complaint may be served by the United States marshal anywhere within the state of his or her jurisdiction, but not outside the state. If the defendant has left the state to *evade* service of process or is in the state but is hiding to avoid service, another method of service must be available to the plaintiff. In such cases, service may be made by publishing the summons in a newspaper having substantial circulation in the area. The methods prescribed are intended to give the defendant actual notice, especially if he or she is more or less expecting to be sued.

Most state laws require the summons to be published for a period of three weeks. As part of the publication procedure, the complaint must be filed with the clerk of court and be available for inspection.* The plaintiff is still required to mail a copy of the summons and complaint to the defendant's last known address. The plaintiff's lawyer or secretary must prepare and file an *affidavit of compliance* which shows that all steps required by law were followed. Usually, the newspaper publisher provides the plaintiff's lawyer with the publisher's affidavit proving the publication, and copies of the published notice are included for filing. If the defendant can be found in another state so that a copy of the summons and complaint may be delivered personally, that may constitute *service by publication* and give the court jurisdiction. In divorce actions, where the defendant is not a resident of the state, service of process may be accomplished by publication. (As noted elsewhere in this book, federal courts do not handle divorce actions or other domestic relations types of cases.)

On occasion, the subject of litigation is land or other tangible things within a state. In such cases the local court has jurisdiction over the subject matter, and anyone claiming an interest in the property, even nonresidents, can be compelled to submit to the court's jurisdiction or forfeit their interests in the property. A lawsuit against the property is called an *action in rem.*† Service of a summons and complaint must be made on each person known to claim an interest in the subject matter. Furthermore, the "world" must be given notice through publication of a notice of the action.

The defendant has twenty days in which to appear and defend. Rule 4 (b). He or she may appear in the action, within the meaning of the Rules, by serving and filing an answer or motion contesting the sufficiency of the complaint or contesting sufficiency of the service of process. Rule 12.

Once a party is represented by a lawyer, all pleadings, orders, motions, etc., must be served directly upon the lawyer. This is the most convenient arrangement for the parties and the lawyers. Service of the answer, motions,

---

*Almost without exception, documents filed with the clerk of court in civil litigation are public documents which anyone may examine.

†In such cases no person is designated as a defendant. However, anyone who claims an interest in the property must file an answer and assert his or her claim or their interest will be forfeited.

orders, etc., may be accomplished by simply mailing the documents to the lawyers at their last known address. Rule 5 (b). Service by mail is complete when the document is deposited at a post office or put in a U.S. mailbox. Whenever a pleading, motion, notice, etc., is served by mail, the addressee is given an extra three days in which to respond — three extra days from the date of mailing. Rule 6 (e). The date of mailing is the date of service.

Occasionally, it is desirable to personally serve papers upon the opposing lawyer. Personal service is complete when the papers are delivered to the lawyer wherever he or she may be. If the lawyer cannot be found, personal service can, nevertheless, be made by handing the papers to the lawyer's clerk or secretary at the office or other person in charge of the office. Otherwise, they may be left in a conspicuous place at his or her office. Personal service may be accomplished by leaving the papers at the lawyer's home with a resident, therein, who is of suitable age and discretion. Rule 5 (b). The person to whom the papers are given must be old enough to realize the importance of the matter and not inclined to forget to bring the papers to the lawyer's attention. Personal service on the lawyer may be ordered by the court whenever there is a shortage of time. The process server must make an affidavit stating the time and place where the document was left in the office or otherwise served.

If a party and his or her lawyer cannot be found so that service can be made upon them either by mail, in person, or through an office, service may be made by leaving the documents with the clerk of court. An affidavit must be prepared stating that the party and his or her lawyer could not be found. The affidavit should contain a brief description of the efforts made to locate them. Rule 5 (b).

When service is by mail, the lawyer making service or his or her secretary must make an affidavit of service by mail. The affidavit does not usually bear the title of the case. For example:

STATE OF ———————————

COUNTY OF ———————————
                                 AFFIDAVIT OF SERVICE
                                         BY MAIL

———————————————, being first duly sworn, deposes and says: That on the ——— day of ———, 19———, she served the attached ———, upon ———— , the attorney ——— representing the ——— , by depositing a true and correct copy thereof in the U.S. Mail in the City of ———, ——————— County, ———————, with postage prepaid, in an envelope directed and addressed to said attorney ——— at ———————————

———

/s/ —————————————————————

Subscribed and sworn to
before me this ——— day
of ———, 19———.

Notary Public

The original copy of the affidavit must be attached to the original document which is then filed with the court. It is highly desirable, if not essential, to attached a copy of the affidavit of mailing to the file copy for future reference. The preferred method of service depends upon the amount of time available and expense.

Once the complaint has been served upon the defendant, a time schedule automatically goes into effect to insure a steady progression of the case toward trial and ultimate disposition. The summons informs the defendant that he or she has twenty days in which to answer the complaint. Failure to answer within the designated time places the defendant in a default, and judgment may be taken against him or her as demanded for in the complaint. No specific provision is made in the Rules for an extension of the twenty day period by agreement of the parties; however, common practice has evolved whereby plaintiff's counsel agrees to accommodate the defendant or lawyer by granting a few extra days in which to serve the answer. For example, once a defendant's lawyer receives a complaint, he or she may need a few extra days to meet with the defendant, digest the factual information and analyze the case so that the answer will adquately state the issues. An informal extension of time for answering helps everyone.

If the defendant has liability insurance, he or she should deliver the complaint to his or her insurance agent promptly. Unfortunately they do not always do this. The insurance company may have difficulty in deciding whether or not to accept the defense of the claim and need extra time in which to make that corporate decision. More often than not, the plaintiff's lawyer informally agrees to grant additional time for answering. Both sides should try to avoid any unnecessary expenditure of time and money on motions by seeking extensions of time. An attitude of goodwill and cooperation benefits all parties and the court. Actually, it is amazing to many laymen just how much and how often "adverse" lawyers accommodate each other.

If the plaintiff wants a jury trial, he or she may demand it by "endorsing" the demand on the complaint. (See example page 71, supra.) This simply means that he or she may state on the complaint, in some conspicuous place, that "plaintiff demands trial by jury". If the plaintiff fails to make the demand in the complaint, he or she may still make the demand anytime within ten days after service of the last pleading directed to the issues to be tried. The demand may be made in a separate document. But the time requirements must be met. For example, in the typical case, the plaintiff could *serve* a demand for trial by jury during the ten day period following service of the defendant's answer. Of course, if the defendant demanded a jury trial in his or her answer, there is no need for the plaintiff to make a separate or additional demand. The defendant may make his or her demand for jury during the same ten day period. A third-party defendant may demand a jury trial by endorsing the demand on his or her third-party answer, or in a separate document served within ten days after the third-party answer was served. Failure to follow requirements of Rule 38(b) results in a waiver of a jury trial and the issues shall be tried to a judge without a jury. Rule 38(b).

In federal court, the case is automatically placed on the trial calendar when the summons and complaint are filed. But in many state courts, the case is not put on the trial calendar until one of the parties serves and files a *note of issue*. The note of issue informs the clerk of court that the case is ready for trial, at least the party filing is ready. It identifies all of the parties and their respective lawyers so that the clerk can send notices to the lawyers. If the first party to serve a note of issue demands a jury trial, there is no need for any other party to file a note of issue. A demand for a jury trial takes priority over the opposing party's preference for a trial by judge without a jury. If the first note of issue demands "trial by Court" without a jury, any other party who wants a jury trial must serve a counter note of issue — usually within ten days after the first note of issue — specifically demanding a jury trial. If the state court has terms of court, the rules of procedure usually require service of the note of issue at least thirty days before the opening of the term, or the case will have to wait until the next term. This is not a problem in those courts which have a continuous general term — that is, where jury cases are tried year round.

Note of Issue

STATE OF _____ , DISTRICT COURT,
County of _____ _____ Judicial District

John Jones	Plaintiff	
vs.		NOTE OF
Sally Smith	Defendant	ISSUE

To Defendant Sally Smith and _____ , her attorney, take notice that the above entitled action will be placed upon the Calendar for the next general term of the District Court to be held in and for said County at the Court House in the City of _____ , in said County, on the _____ day of _____ , 19 _____ , for the trial by Jury.

Yours respectfully,

_____

Attorney for Plaintiff

There are times when a case simply cannot be ready for trial at the time scheduled. Personal injury actions involving serious injuries or the probability of permanent disability, usually cannot be evaluated until twelve to eighteen months after the injury was sustained. It may take that long before the attending physicians can make a reasonably accurate prognosis. A trial at an earlier date might result in an unjust verdict for either party because of the difficulty in evaluating the claim. If a delay of the trial or a continuance is necessary, the parties may stipulate to a continuance or show the court good cause why the court should order a continuance. Time may be a natural healer, but the passage of time can only detract from a good cause of action or a good defense.

7

Pleadings

COMPLAINT

A civil action is commenced by filing a complaint with the clerk of district court. The complaint must describe the plaintiff's claim by stating a cause of action against the defendant(s). The defendant is allowed twenty days in which to serve an answer to the complaint. His or her answer must admit the allegations of the complaint which are true, deny the rest, and allege all the affirmative defenses that he has. Thus the complaint and answer establish the legal issues between the plaintiff and defendant. The legal issues determine what facts are material to the case. Civil litigation procedures center upon the use of pleadings. Each party's lawyer prepares the necessary pleadings to set forth his or her client's allegations and responses. By filing or serving a pleading, a party appears* in the case. Paralegals may prepare pleadings. But the lawyer handling the case must review his or her client's pleadings, approve them and certify that the pleading is proper by signing it. Rule 11.

The complaint has several important functions. Its caption identifies the court chosen by the plaintiff's lawyer. The clerk of court assigns to the case a file number which is part of the caption. The complaint's title identifies the intended defendant(s). However, a named defendant does not become a party

---

*"Appears" as used in civil litigation means that a person comes into the case as a party or comes before the court as a litigant. When a party appears in a case he or she submits to the court's jurisdiction unless specifically challenging jurisdiction at the outset.

until he or she is actually served* with a copy of the complaint. The complaint must contain allegations showing that the named court has jurisdiction over the subject matter and over the named defendant(s). The plaintiff automatically submits to the court's jurisdiction by filing the lawsuit.

A lawyer must have the substantive law in mind as he or she draws a complaint, making sure that the allegations establish a cause of action. Not every wrong or controversy gives rise to a claim that can be litigated. A man may call his neighbor "stupid" or say that he is a "jerk". As unflattering as these remarks are, they do not give rise to a cause of action for defamation. A salesman may spend many hours helping a customer with the selection of a house, a car or appliance, and then lose the sale to another salesman who spent only a few minutes with the customer. The first salesman may feel that he has been wronged, his time and help abused, but he does not have a cause of action for breach of contract. A complaint must state a cause of action, i.e., a claim for which a court can grant relief; otherwise, it is subject to being stricken on **motion.** Rule 12(b).

Before the Federal Rules of Civil Procedure were adopted, a complaint had to set forth fully all the facts constituting the plaintiff's cause of action. For example, in a trespass action, the plaintiff had to set forth in detail the facts which proved that he or she occupied the particular parcel of land as owner or lessee; that the defendant entered upon the land on a particular date in a particular manner; that the entry was without plaintiff's consent; that the defendant lacked authority to enter the land at the specified time and place; that the entry resulted in specified damage to the land. From these allegations, the defendant's lawyer knew that the plaintiff was claiming the defendant committed a trespass. Those were the facts which the plaintiff would have to prove at trial. The plaintiff could not attempt to prove different or additional facts. Also the defendant had no right to take the plaintiff's deposition. His or her only source of information about the plaintiff's claim came from the complaint. If the complaint failed to state sufficient facts to constitute a cause of action, it was subject to dismissal on motion by defendant. The motion was called a demurrer.

The defendant had only one means of *discovery* available.† That was to ask for a *bill of particulars* which is a request for a more detailed statement of the plaintiff's claim. A bill of particulars was not available as a matter of right, as interrogatories (written questions) may now be served upon another party as a matter of right. Each party secured the information and evidence for the claim and defense by conducting his or her own investigation.

Though still fundamental to the litigation process, pleadings have lost the informative function that they once had. Now the complaint may omit many of the factual details of the alleged wrong, but the complaint must still specify the legal wrong, i.e., the cause of action. The complaint merely puts the defendant on notice of the cause of action claimed and relates that cause of

---

*Under certain circumstances service may be by publication. Rule 4(e).

†Discovery refers to any procedure authorized by law which enables one party to obtain information from another party about the claims and defense and facts in the case.

action to a specific transaction or occurrence by identifying the time and place. Rule 9(f).

The complaint must identify the nature and extent of the loss which the plaintiff claims the defendant's wrongful conduct caused. The complaint ordinarily concludes by specifying the remedy and relief which the plaintiff wants the court to award.

The various allegations constituting the cause of action are separately stated in short paragraphs usually arranged in particular order. Each paragraph should be limited to a single set of circumstances or a single idea. Rule 8(a). If more than one transaction or occurrence is involved, each should be set forth in a separate *count*. If a document such as a contract or promissory note is the subject of the claim, a copy of the document may be attached to the complaint. The complaint gives a fairly good picture of the claims against the defendant so that he or she is able to admit the legal obligation or begin preparation of defenses against the claims. The complaint, then, establishes the scope of plaintiff's claims. Items of *special damages* must be stated specifically. Rule 9(g). Special damages are the "out-of-pocket" expenses that the plaintiff has incurred because of the defendant's wrongful conduct. In a personal injury action, the plaintiff's medical expenses, loss of past income, and property damage are items of special damages. They must be listed. A monetary value need not be given for each item — though that is frequently done. In a breach of contract action the amount of the lost profits and consequential expenses should be stated. This information is really necessary for the defendant to know at the outset. The other pertinent facts can be obtained by the defendant through discovery procedures.

If the complaint is vague or ambiguous so that the defendant's lawyer feels uncertain about the nature or scope of the claim being made, he or she may move the court for an order compelling the plaintiff to state the allegations with more particularity, more specifically, or more definitely. Rule 12(e).

The complaint must be filed for the purpose of making a claim through the courts and not for some ulterior or collateral purpose. All pleadings filed with the court are public records for anyone to read. Obviously, they are subject to engendering publicity — publicity that could be very harmful. Therefore, a pleading must be signed by a lawyer or by the party who acts as his or her own lawyer. The signature is a certification that the signator has read the pleading; that he or she believes there is good ground to support the allegations in the pleading; that the pleading has not been filed for the purpose of delaying a claim or for some other collateral purpose. (Note that a lawyer does not have to draft the complaint. Paralegals may be asked to prepare some pleadings.) Any allegation that is scandalous, impertinent or immaterial to the cause of action may be stricken by order of the court. Parties must not use a pleading as a vehicle with which to malign another party. Rules 11, 12(f). Any allegation that is redundant, incompetent or insufficient to state a claim or defense is subject to being stricken by court order. Rule 12(f).

The date the complaint is filed establishes the date on which the action is commenced. The clerk prepares a summons which is attached to the complaint. He or she directs a U.S. marshal to serve the summons and complaint upon the named defendant(s). The plaintiff's lawyer must advise the clerk or marshal of the defendant's last known addresses. It is helpful to give to the marshal the defendant's employment address, too. The summons is not considered to be a pleading.

The rules of civil procedure for many state courts provide that the plaintiff's lawyer shall prepare and sign the summons. He or she also arranges for service of the summons and complaint on the defendants *before* filing the documents with the court. In those states, the cause of action is *commenced* either (1) when the summons and complaint are delivered to the proper public officer, such as a sheriff, for service, or (2) when the summons and complaint are actually served upon the defendant. If the latter procedure is followed, the action may be commenced against multiple defendants on different days.

The summons directs each defendant to serve an answer to the complaint within twenty days after the date on which the summons and complaint were *served* upon him or her. The twenty day period begins to run on the next day after service. If the summons and complaint were served on Tuesday, the twenty day period begins to run on Wednesday. The answer may be prepared by the defendant, his or her lawyer, or someone on the lawyer's staff. However, it must be signed by the defendant or the lawyer — no one else. The answer uses the same title as the complaint, even if the defendant's name is misspelled or there is some other technical problem with the title. Later on the title may be amended by court order. The correct spelling of the parties' names may be set forth as a separate allegation in the answer, but the original title as set forth in the complaint is used until it is amended by court order. If there are two or more plaintiffs or two or more defendants, the answer and all subsequent pleadings may omit all names except the name of the first plaintiff and the name of the first defendant. The abbreviation "et al" is used to indicate the presence of the other parties.

The clerk of court assigns a file number to the action when the complaint is filed. The number may be similar to: "81 Civ. 532". The "81" means that the case was filed during the year 1981. "Civ." means it is a civil action. The last number indicates its chronology. All subsequent pleadings, motions, orders, affidavits, depositions must use that file number.

AMENDED COMPLAINT

The plaintiff may amend his or her complaint as a matter of right, and without leave of the court, if done before the defendant serves his or her answer. Rule 15(a). Otherwise, the plaintiff must secure leave of the court to serve and file an amended complaint. Of course, the defendant may agree (**stipulate**) to accept service of the amended complaint. Usually this is done by admitting service right on the original copy of the amended complaint.

Example:

Due and proper service of the Amended Complaint is admitted this _____ day of _____, 1975.

_____

Attorney for Defendant

An amended pleading is usually identified as "amended."

There are a number of reasons why a party might agree to accept an amended pleading without forcing the opponent to make a motion to the court. The amendment may simply correct a technical defect or clerical error which does not affect the parties' substantive rights. Or the amendment may contain corrections or allegations which the adverse party considers beneficial, or, at least, true. Generally, courts are very liberal permitting pleadings to be amended unless the opposing party is able to show actual prejudice resulting from a late amendment. Rule 15. With that fact in mind, lawyers know that opposition to a proposed amendment would probably be a waste of time and money. Ordinarily, the party seeking to amend volunteers to permit his or her opponent to conduct whatever additional discovery procedures are necessary for preparation on the new issues raised by the amendment.

The defendant has at least ten days in which to answer an amended complaint. But if the amended complaint was served within just a few days after the original complaint was served, then the defendant must answer within the same period of time as established by service of the original complaint. In other words, defendant's answer to the amended complaint is due at the same time as it would be to the original complaint; or within ten days after service of the amended complaint, whichever time period is longer.

Amendments relate back to the date of the original pleading. For example, suppose that in an action to recover compensation for damage to real estate, the original complaint alleged only a cause of action in negligence and after the suit was started the statute of limitations ran on all tort claims. If the plaintiff is allowed to amend his or her complaint to allege a cause of action in trespass, too, the amendment is deemed to relate back to the date on which the action was originally commended. By amending the original complaint the plaintiff has successfully avoided having the statute of limitations bar his claim.

If for some cogent reason, a party needs additional time to prepare and serve any pleading and the opposition will not agree to an extension of time, the party may apply to the court for an order granting an extension. Such an application (motion) may be made with or without notice to the opposing party if it is made before the prescribed time period expires. The moving party must show the court that he or she has good reason (grounds) for making the request. The reasons ordinarily are set forth in an affidavit of the party or his or her lawyer which is filed with the motion.

If the time allowed by the Rules has already expired, the party seeking an extension of time to correct a default must make a motion to the court with notice duly served upon opposing counsel. He or she must not only show the court good cause for extending the period of time, but must also show that the failure to act was the result of a justified mistake or excusable neglect. Just what circumstances may constitute excusable neglect is a matter left to the discretion of the court. The Rules do not attempt to detail circumstances which provide valid excuses. Judges consider not only the party's explanation or excuse, but the possibility of prejudice to the opposing party. A court may grant a motion extending the period of time, and avoiding the default, subject to payment of certain costs — including lawyer's fees — incurred by the opposing party as a consequence of the delay. A few time periods cannot be extended. Rule 6(b).

ANSWER

The next pleading used in civil litigation is the *answer*. The answer must be served within twenty days after the complaint was served upon the defendant. If more time is required, the defendant may request the plaintiff extend the time in which to answer.

The defendant determines the date the answer is due by counting twenty days beginning with the next day after the summons and complaint were served upon him or her. All of the time periods prescribed by the Rules exclude the day of the initial act or event. So it makes no difference to the defendant whether he or she was served at 10:00 a.m. or 8:00 p.m., the twenty day period begins to run the next day. The answer is due *on* the twentieth day, *not after* twenty days. If the twentieth day falls on a Saturday, Sunday or legal holiday, the time period is automatically extended to the next day which is not a Saturday, Sunday or legal holiday. Customarily, the defendant's lawyer simply telephones the plaintiff's lawyer and requests an additional few days in which to serve the answer. If an informal extension of time for answering has been secured, the extension should be confirmed by letter stating the date on which the answer, or other pleading, will be served. A formal stipulation is not essential but may be used. If the plaintiff won't or cannot voluntarily accommodate the defendant, the defendant may move the court for an order extending the time for answering. Rule 6(b).

Defendant's failure to answer the complaint within the time allowed by law or stipulation permits the plaintiff to secure a judgment by default. Rule 4(b). However, the defendant may *appear* in the case by serving a motion challenging jurisdiction or motion for an order striking the complaint, or a motion seeking judgment on the pleadings, or a motion for an order compelling a more definite statement of the allegations in the complaint. Rule 12(a). There is no need to serve an answer while a Rule 12 motion is pending. After the court rules on the motion, an answer is due within ten days of the ruling — unless the court dismisses the complaint or sets a different time for answering. Rule 12(a).

The defendant's answer must admit the truth of those allegations in the complaint that are known to be true. The formal admissions establish *conclusively* that the specified facts and allegations are not in controversy; are not at issue. The answer must deny the allegations that are not true. Any allegation in the complaint which is not denied is presumed to be admitted. Rule 8(d). Consequently, an answer usually begins with a general denial such as: "Defendant denies each and every allegation, statement, matter and thing in the complaint, except as hereinafter expressly admitted or alleged." If the defendant does not have sufficient knowledge upon which to form a belief concerning an allegation in the complaint, he or she may so state. The statement has the effect of a denial. A general denial, standing alone, is insufficient and contrary to the spirit of the Rules unless the defendant disputes that he or she was even involved in the transaction or occurrence in question. The language typically used is: "Alleges that defendant does not have sufficient knowledge or information upon which to form a belief concerning plaintiff's claims of [injuries or damages] and, therefore, puts plaintiff to his [or her] strict proof of same."

The answer uses numbered paragraphs, just like the complaint, to separate each set of circumstances and each affirmative defense. It is common practice to use one paragraph to lump admissions. For example:

> 2. Admits the allegations of paragraphs 1, 2 and 3 of the complaint, further admits that the motor vehicle accident occurred about the time and place specified in the complaint.

An admission that the accident occurred is not an admission of negligence or legal responsibility. Nevertheless, some lawyers seem constrained to add a statement such as: "Specifically denies that defendant was negligent", after admitting the occurrence. The plaintiff's lawyer should draft the complaint in a manner which enables the defendant to admit full paragraphs. But if the defendant's lawyer determines that he or she is able to admit only a portion of a paragraph, the admission should be made on that stated portion.

The admissions and denials in the answer do not have to be consistent with one another. For example, the answer may deny that the plaintiff and the defendant entered into a contract so that the plaintiff cannot maintain an action on the contract for breach of contract. In addition, the answer may allege that the plaintiff's claim is barred by affirmative defenses such as accord and satisfaction, release, fraud or waiver which are defenses that presume the contract was made. Rule 8(e) (2). (See Rules Appendix Forms 20 and 21 for examples of answers.)

The answer must allege all the affirmative defenses that the defendant has. Rule 8(c). Any affirmative defense not asserted in the answer is waived. An affirmative defense is a fact or set of circumstances which defeats the plaintiff's claim even though the plaintiff is able to prove his or her cause of action. A partial list of affirmative defenses appears in Rule 8(c). The defendant has the burden of proving his or her affirmative defenses. The plaintiff is not obligated to serve and file a responsive pleading to the answer for the purpose of admitting or denying defendant's affirmative defenses. The affirmative defenses are presumed to be denied. Each affirmative defense should be set forth in a separate, numbered paragraph for convenience of the parties and court. (See Rules Appendix Form No. 20.)

An answer also concludes with a "Wherefore" clause, in which the defendant states his or her request for relief. The following is a typical concluding paragraph in an answer:

Wherefore, defendant prays that plaintiff take nothing by reason of his alleged cause of action, and that defendant have judgment for his costs and disbursements herein.

The defendant must obtain permission from the court to amend his or her answer to allege any additional defense unless the plaintiff stipulates to an amendment. Rule 15(a). However, the answer may be amended, as a matter of right, without a court order if the amended pleading is served within twenty days after the original answer was served. Rule 15(a).

Most courts liberally permit amendments to pleadings, additional pleadings, and supplemental pleadings in the absence of *prejudice* to the party to be served. A party is prejudiced only if the delay adversely affects his or her ability to present a claim or defense on the merits. Rule 15(b). The merits of the case refers to the substance of the claim, i.e., the underlying facts. A determination on the merits means that the case is *not* decided on the basis of a procedural technicality.

COUNTERCLAIM

On occasion, a defendant may have a claim against the plaintiff that he or she wants to pursue. This is done by serving a *counterclaim* with his or her answer. The claim may arise out of the same transaction or occurrence as the plaintiff's claim. In that event, the countercalim is *compulsory* which means that the counterclaim *must* be asserted with the defendant's answer or it is waived. Rule 13(a). If the claim arises out of another transaction or occurrence, the defendant may elect whether or not to pursue it as a counterclaim. The counterclaim is permissive. Rule 13(b).

The counterclaim is, in effect, the defendant's complaint against the plaintiff. The requirements of a complaint apply to a counterclaim. However, many of the essential allegations are already set forth in the complaint and answer. Those allegations may be incorporated by reference. It is quite common for a counterclaim to contain a paragraph similar to the following:

Defendant hereby incorporates the allegations of paragraph 1 of the complaint and all of the defendant's answer as though fully set forth herein.

Of course, the counterclaim must concern a matter over which the court has jurisdiction. But the mere fact that the relief sought is more than the amount claimed in the complaint or different in kind is not a basis for avoiding the counterclaim in federal court. Rule 13(c). These factors may affect jurisdiction in state courts that have limited jurisdiction.

Obviously, it would be unfair to require the defendant to assert his or her cause of action in a counterclaim if it is already the subject of a pending suit, whether in the same or another court, therefore this is not required. Rule 13(a). For example, suppose that four motorists were involved in a single accident consisting of multiple "rear end collisions," and motorist A sued motorist B for damages, and motorist C sued motorist A in a separate action. If A decided to make a claim against motorist C, he could join C in the first action as a direct defendant or counterclaim in the action brought by C. If the cases were all in the same court, they would probably be consolidated for trial anyway. Rule 42. But if the two cases were in different courts, motorist A could have some difficulty deciding which procedure to follow.

A counterclaim based upon a cause of action that accrues after the answer was served may be made through a *supplemental counterclaim*. Rule 13(e). Supplemental pleadings are permitted only by order of the court upon a showing that the cause of action accrued after service of the original pleading. Rule 15(d). The court order allowing the supplemental pleading should specify whether or not a responsive pleading is necessary, i.e., an answer, answer to cross-claim, or reply to counterclaim.

If a countercalim requires the presence of a third person who is not subject to the court's jurisdiction, the counterclaim need not be asserted; it is not then compulsory. For example, a plaintiff sues a defendant for breach of contract. The defendant claims that the plaintiff and the plaintiff's partner caused the defendant to be defrauded in the same transaction, and that the partner is not subject to this court's jurisdiction. The defendant may assert his or her claim for fraud against both persons in another action in another court which does have jurisdiction over both persons.

The form of a counterclaim is similar to a complaint. If the counterclaim is added to the answer, the combined documents are usually identified as "Answer and Counterclaim". The counterclaim may be separately stated but, nevertheless, served with the answer. If the defendant inadvertently fails to serve a counterclaim with the answer, he or she may move the court for an order allowing the counterclaim. The grounds for the motion include oversight, inadvertence, and excusable neglect. Rule 13(f). A defendant must obtain permission to serve a counterclaim if not served with the answer since failure to assert the counterclaim in a timely manner may cause a delay in the normal progression of the case toward trial. Since it probably raises new issues, the parties may need additional time to investigate and conduct additional discovery procedures. Generally, the courts allow late pleadings and/or amendments to pleadings so as to avoid prejudicing a meritorious claim or defense. But courts often place a burden on the delinquent party to expedite the necessary discovery procedures and all other trial preparation. Costs and sanctions may be imposed as a condition precedent to allowing a late counterclaim. If the court refuses to allow the late counterclaim, the defendant is precluded from asserting the claim at a later date if the proposed counterclaim arose out of the same occurrence or transaction as the plaintiff's claim. Rule 13(a). Some lawyers are of the opinion that a counterclaim may be served anytime within twenty days of service of the answer because the answer may be amended without a court order during the first twenty days. Rule 15(a).

Most courts liberally permit amendments to pleadings, additional pleadings and supplemental pleadings in the absence of *prejudice* to the party to be served. A party is prejudiced only if the delay adversely affects his or her ability to present a claim or defense on the merits. Rule 15(b).

A counterclaim has obvious application where the defendant in an automobile accident case sues for his or her own injury and/or property damage — claiming the plaintiff is liable. A counterclaim may also be used by the defendant to make a claim against one plaintiff for **contribution** to the claim of another plaintiff. For example, suppose the two plaintiffs are husband and wife. They sustained injuries when their automobile was struck by the defendant's truck. If the plaintiff husband was driving and he was partially at fault, the defendant could counterclaim against the plaintiff husband for contribution to the wife's claim.*

As a general rule, the courts favor consolidating claims to be determined in a single trial. Consolidation usually leads to a speedier, more economical determination by avoiding duplicated effort. But if trial of the counterclaim with the "main action" would unduly complicate the trial, the court may order a severence of the claims for purpose of trial. Rules 13(i) and 42 (b).

REPLY TO COUNTERCLAIM

Since a counterclaim is for the purpose of stating a claim against the plaintiff, he or she must be given the opportunity to deny the allegations made and to plead his or her affirmative defenses. The plaintiff responds to the counterclaim by serving and filing a *reply to counterclaim*. Rule 7(a). The reply is tantamount to an answer, so the discussion applying to the defendant's answer applies to the requirements of a reply. A reply must be served within twenty days after service of the counterclaim. Since the counterclaim is usually served by mail, three days are added to the time period. Rules 12(a) and 6(e).

CROSS-CLAIM

When two or more plaintiffs have claims against a defendant arising out of the same transaction or occurrence, they may join as co-plaintiffs in a single action. Rule 20. Similarly, if two or more persons may be liable to the plaintiff for his or her loss, they may be included as joint defendants. Rule 20. The defendants may have claims to make against each other. The claims may be for injuries or losses that they sustained or the claims may be for contribution to the plaintiff's claim. A defendant may make a claim against a co-defendant by serving and filing a *cross-claim*. A cross-claim is, in effect, a complaint which states one or more causes of action against a co-defendant. The rules and guidelines for drafting complaints apply to cross-claims.

The following is typical of allegations found in cross-claims.

> Comes now defendant B and for his cross-claim against defendant C, alleges:
> 1. That plaintiff has commenced the above entitled action against each defendant above named and alleges that defendants are jointly and severally liable to plaintiff for money damages, as more fully set forth in the complaint, a copy of which has been duly served upon each defendant.

*The right to contribution in this example assumes that the lawsuit is brought in a state that does not recognize interspousal immunity.

2. That defendant B has denied liability to plaintiff as set forth more fully in his answer which has been served on all parties and filed with the court. [or . . . which is attached hereto as Exhibit A.]

3. That the accident described in the complaint was proximately caused by the negligence of defendant C.

4. That if defendant B is determined to be liable to plaintiff as alleged in the complaint, or otherwise, defendant B is entitled to contribution from defendant C on the grounds that C's negligence was a proximate cause of the accident and concurred with defendant B's alleged negligence to cause plaintiff's alleged loss.

Wherefore, defendant B prays for judgment of contribution from defendant C to any sums awarded in favor of plaintiff against defendant B, together with his costs and disbursements herein.

A cross-claim is usually served as a separate document. If the defendant upon whom a cross-claim is to be served has appeared in the case by serving an answer or Rule 12 motion, the cross-claim may be served upon his or her lawyer and may be served by mail. Rule 5(b). Usually the cross-claim cannot be served *with* the answer because the identity of the co-defendant's lawyer is not yet available. If a named co-defendant has not been served with the summons and complaint, a cross-claim must be served as provided by Rule 4 like an original summons and complaint.

The rules do not express a time limit for serving and filing cross-claims. Nevertheless, there is an inherent principle that service of a cross-claim shall not be so late as to unduly delay the trial of the main action, i.e., the plaintiff's case. A defendant who is served with a cross-claim must respond by serving and filing an *answer to cross-claim,* Rule 7(a). The answer to cross-claim is due twenty days after service of the cross-claim. Rule 12(a). If the cross-claim was served by mail, add three days to the date of service. The answer to cross-claim serves the same function as an answer, and the same general rules apply.

The identity of the lawyer representing a co-defendant can easily be obtained through the plaintiff's lawyer. In state courts, which use a *note of issue* to place the case on the trial calendar, all parties and their lawyers must be identified in the note of issue and the lawyers' addresses listed. A note of issue must be served upon all of the lawyers to be effective. Consequently, the note of issue serves as a convenient vehicle for notifying and informing the parties of the identity of the lawyers who have appeared in the case.

The use of cross-claims establishes technical *adversity* between the defendants. This may be important at trial in determining whether there is a right to cross-examination, whether the defendants have to share preemptory challenges in the jury selection, etc.

DEFAULTS

If a defendant defaults by failing to serve an answer or a Rule 12 motion within the twenty days allowed, the plaintiff may obtain judgment by default. Rule 55. The procedure is relatively simple and inexpensive. The first step is for the plaintiff's lawyer to prepare an affidavit showing that the defendant is in default. The fact of service of the summons and complaint is established through the *U.S. marshal's return* or the process server's *affidavit of service.* The plaintiff lawyer's affidavit avers that an answer was not duly served within the time allowed and that he or she has not granted an extension of time or that any extensions granted have expired. The *affidavit of default* is filed with the clerk.

If the claim involves a *sum certain,* the clerk of court is authorized to enter judgment without the necessity of a court order. The plaintiff only needs to show the clerk, by affidavit and appropriate documentation, what amount is due and owing. For example, the amount due on a promissory note can be calculated and established as a *sum certain.* Many contract actions involve a sum certain, such as a claim for rent. The clerk of court enters the judgment forthwith.

Whenever the amount of recovery is dependent upon a resolution of facts — even though not disputed by the defendant in default — the court must pass on the validity of the claim. Default matters are usually heard by a magistrate or by the judge at a special term. The plaintiff must be prepared to present evidence proving the transaction or occurrence, the wrongful conduct of the defendant that makes him or her liable, and the nature and extent of the damage sustained by the plaintiff. The court is not concerned with the form of the evidence at default hearings. If testimony is taken, the lawyer usually asks leading questions going to the very heart of the matter. **Hearsay** evidence is readily received and considered by the court. Plaintiff needs only to prove a *prima facie* case — not a persuasive case. The judge has no reason to doubt plaintiff's claim and right to the judgment. The presentation may take only a few minutes. If personal injuries are involved, the medical evidence may be submitted through a medical report filed with the court.

A default judgment cannot be taken against a minor or a person who is under a legal guardianship (ward) without some additional steps. If the minor does not have a guardian, the plaintiff must have one appointed. The legal guardian of a minor or incompetent must be served with a written notice of the plaintiff's application for a default judgment. Service upon the guardian may be made as provided in Rule 4. The notice of application for a default judgment must be served at least three days before the hearing. Rule 55(b) (2). The rule preserves the right to a jury trial, but the plaintiff almost never elects to present his or her default case to a jury. Whether right or wrong, trial judges are inclined to be very liberal in their allowance of damages in default proceedings. However, the amount of recovery cannot exceed the amount demanded in the complaint as originally served upon the defendant. The complaint ad damnum* cannot be increased by amendment without serving an amended complaint on the defendant. Of course, the defendant in default then has another opportunity to appear and defend against the claim.

---

*The complaint "ad damnum" is the same as the "wherefore clause" in which plaintiff specifies the relief he wants the court to award.

A judgment obtained by default may be set aside for good cause shown. Rule 55(c). The various grounds establishing good cause are listed in Rule 60(b). They are:

(1) mistake, inadvertence, surprise, or excusable neglect;

(2) newly discovered evidence which by due diligence could not have been discovered in time to move for a new trial under Rule 59(b);

(3) fraud (whether heretofore denominated intrinsic or extrinsic), misrepresentation, or other misconduct of an adverse party;

(4) the judgment is void;

(5) the judgment has been satisfied, released, or discharged, or a prior judgment upon which it is based has been reversed or otherwise vacated, or it is no longer equitable that the judgment should have prospective application;

(6) any other reason justifying relief from the operation of the judgment.

The motion shall be made within a reasonable time, and for reasons (1), (2), and (3) not more than one year after the judgment, order, or proceeding was entered or taken.

A judgment obtained by fraud can always be set aside. A judgment rendered by a court that does not have jurisdiction is always subject to attack. If a defendant seeks to have a default judgment set aside claiming "excusable neglect", the court may require him to show that he has a valid defense and has a reasonable expectation of prevailing. Also, as a condition to being allowed to serve and file an answer after being in default, the court may require the defendant to pay certain costs to the plaintiff.

SUPPLEMENTAL PLEADINGS

Upon motion the court may allow any party to serve a supplemental pleading. Supplemental pleadings pertain to new matters occurring since the original pleadings were served. No party has a right to serve a supplemental pleading. Leave of the court must be obtained. The alternative, of course, is for the complaining party to institute a new lawsuit which may or may not be consolidated with the pending action. For example, suppose a plaintiff commenced an action against the defendant for damming a stream, thereby depriving the plaintiff of his water rights. But subsequently, plaintiff suffered a loss of crops because of the unavailability of water. The original wrong resulted in two separate losses — separated in time. A supplemental complaint would be used to state the new additional claim.

ADVERSITY

The pleadings determine whether or not the parties are adversaries, i.e., whether or not there is *adversity* between them. Obviously, there is adversity between the plaintiff and defendant. But the presence of adversity is not so clear between co-defendants, and between the plaintiff and third-party defendants. As a general rule, there is no adversity unless one of them formally creates the adversity by serving a pleading raising issues between them. Codefendants may do this by serving cross-claims. A third-party defendant may do this by serving an answer to the original complaint. The plaintiff may establish adversity by amending his complaint to include a third-party defendant as a direct defendant. Some courts authorize a document called *notice of direct claim* which the plaintiff may serve upon the third-party defendant's lawyer.

There are some very important consequences that depend upon adversity between parties. Statements of an adverse party may be treated as admissions. The ultimate judgment or decree of the court may not be binding between codefendants in the absence of adversity between them, because, at least by inference, they have chosen not to litigate the matter as between them.

All pleadings and other papers served in a lawsuit must be filed with the clerk of court within a reasonable period of time and before any hearing involving the pleading. Of course, all documents must be filed with the clerk of court before the trial begins. In federal district court only the plaintiff has to pay a filing fee, and that is paid upon commencement of the action when the complaint is filed. So the parties have no reason to delay filing their papers. Failure to have them filed in good season may result in a delay of the proceedings and even result in sanctions imposed by the court against the delinquent party.

JURY DEMAND

If the plaintiff has a right to and wants trial by jury, he or she should state at a conspicuous place on the complaint: "Plaintiff demands trial by jury." The demand is usually stated at the end of the pleading. The defendant may assert his or her demand for a jury trial on the answer or in a separate document served within ten days after the answer was served. If a plaintiff chooses to file a separate document demanding a jury, the *jury demand* must be served and filed within ten days after service of the last pleading, answer or counterclaim, directed to the issues for which a jury is sought. If a jury trial is not demanded within the prescribed time, the parties waive their right to a jury trial. Rule 38(d).

NOTE OF ISSUE

In many state courts, the demand for a jury trial cannot be made in the pleading, but must be made in a "note of issue", which is filed by any party any time after the answer has been served. However, the local rules usually provide that the note of issue must be served and filed a certain number of days before the term of court opens, at least, in those courts which do not have a continuous term. A note of issue serves the function of placing the case on the "trial calendar" (docket) and apprises the clerk of court and each lawyer of the names and addresses of all the lawyers who have appeared in the case. If the first party to serve a note of issue does not demand trial by jury, an opposing lawyer may serve and file a counter note of issue demanding a jury trial. Usually, the counternote of issue must be served within a period of ten days after the first note of issue or not at all. A party's failure to demand a jury trial within the specified time results in a waiver of the right to a jury trial. Upon motion by either party, the court may order that the case be tried by a jury, but such a decision is left to the discretion of the judge and can be opposed on various grounds by the adverse party. Even if both parties agree that they want a jury trial, the court may deny their request.

8

Additional Parties

A plaintiff may include in one lawsuit all of the claims he or she has against the defendant even if some of the claims arose out of different transactions or different occurrences. Each separate claim should be stated in the complaint as a separate *count*. Rule 18(a) provides that:

> A party asserting a claim to relief as an original claim, counterclaim, cross-claim, or third-party claim may join, either as independent or as alternate claims, as many claims, legal, equitable, or maritime, as he has against an opposing party.

The possibility of one party having several claims against the defendant may seem very remote, but it is not. For example, suppose that the plaintiff company has been purchasing bolts of cloth from the defendant company for many years, but for the last three years the defendant's deliveries have been late, frequently causing plaintiff to experience "down time"; that the bolts of cloth are increasingly defective; that orders are being misplaced. Finally, the defendant company makes a major error which causes the plaintiff to suffer a large loss. Their business relationship is at an end. Once the plaintiff company has decided to sue, it might as well "go back" and sue for all of the breaches of contract and warranties that occurred over the past several years. This example involves a series of transactions between two parties.

A series of *occurrences* giving rise to multiple claims in favor of a plaintiff is a little more difficult to envision. But it can happen. Suppose that the defendant is a large contractor who has overall responsibility for construction of a large interstate freeway interchange next to a large shopping center owned by the plaintiff. The highway construction work may cause damage to the plaintiff's property at various times by use of explosives, pile driving and trespasses by large machinery. The contractor may have blocked access to the shopping center causing a loss in business. Dust and noise from the project might have created a legal *nuisance*. The plaintiff property owner could sue for all his or her losses in one lawsuit. Again each claim and/or each cause of action should be stated in the complaint in a separate *count*.

Even though the plaintiff may elect to join all of the claims in one lawsuit, the court may order that certain claims be tried separately. Rule 42(b). The severance may be requested by a party by making a *motion for severance,* or, the court may order a severance on its own motion. A severance is desirable when consolidated claims make a trial too complicated, too long or too cumbersome. If the determination of one of the claims may lead to a settlement, or other summary disposition of the other claims, a severance benefits everyone.

The right to join claims in one lawsuit is also available to a defendant in his or her counterclaim, cross-claim and in third-party actions. Rule 18(a).

Federal district courts have authority to consolidate cases for trial whenever cases involve *common questions of law* or *common questions of fact.* Rule 42(a). This is true even though the cases involve different parties. Cases are never consolidated for trial merely because they coincidentally involve common questions of fact or law. For example, the fact that two automobile accident cases happen to involve stop sign violations is no reason to consolidate those cases. There must be some underlying unifying factor which makes a consolidation convenient for the court without unduly complicating or prolonging the trial for the parties.

A few examples may be helpful to show when cases are likely to be consolidated. Suppose that five people sustain injuries in the crash of a small airplane. Each injured person decides to sue the pilot, manufacturer, and maintenance company. Suppose that legal responsibility is very unclear. The court may elect to consolidate the five cases for purposes of trial, at least for the purpose of determining liability — if any. The five cases may take twice as long as proving one case, but only two-fifths as long as trying each case separately. If the plaintiffs are able to establish liability, there is the possibility that some of the plaintiffs can settle the damages issue. The defendants gain by having to defend only once rather than five times. The basis for consolidation is the common question of facts, i.e., the accident.

Another example of cases involving common questions of fact is where the plaintiff has been injured in two separate accidents and has two separate claims. Of course, each defendant is likely to contend that the plaintiff's injuries occurred in "the other" accident. The parties may determine that they would prefer to consolidate both cases because they involve a common question of fact — injuries.

Consolidation is useful in business transaction cases as well as accident cases. Suppose that a corporation is engaged in the business of selling franchises for fast food stores. Suppose that a problem develops with ten of the franchisees. Their contracts with the franchisor are all the same. The parties may want to have the cases consolidated for one trial. Everyone saves time and expense.

Common questions of law is another important basis for consolidating cases. Now many cases have common questions of law but a consolidation of them would not be convenient or helpful. For example, assume that during the course of three months, five pedestrians fell on city sidewalks, sustained injuries and sued the city. Each of those cases involve common questions of law. *Could* they be consolidated? Perhaps. Should they be consolidated? No. The *questions* of law are not the major consideration. The points of law in question are pretty well settled. A consolidation of the cases is of no value if there is no genuine dispute about the application of legal principles common to the several cases. But, using the same example, suppose that in each of the five cases a legal question exists whether the plaintiffs gave due *notice of claim* to the defendant city within thirty days of the accident. The notice of claim is a condition precedent to maintenance of an action against the municipality. Suppose further that the plaintiffs *each* challenge the constitutionality of the statute or ordinance requiring the plaintiffs to file a notice of claim within thirty days of the accident. The legal issue is important and common to all. The cases may be consolidated for purposes of determining the issue. If the legal issue were resolved in the plaintiff's favor, the cases subsequently would be separated (severed) for individual jury trials. A judge would determine the legal issue without a jury.

Another example may be helpful. In a recent case property owners near an airport sued the airport commission, claiming that the noise from airplanes' landing and taking off constituted an involuntary partial condemnation or taking of their property for which they should be compensated. The legal theory was novel. Consolidation of those cases permitted the property owners to participate in a trial of the legal issue, i.e., whether there was a cause of action. If the legal issue were resolved in favor of the plaintiffs, clearing the way for a recovery, each plaintiff could prove his or her damage in a separate hearing. Rule 42.

In the above examples we discussed reasons for consolidating pending cases. Another procedure called *intervention* permits a person to *join* in a pending lawsuit by applying to the court for leave to become a party. Rule 24. He or she may apply to be a defendant or plaintiff. The criteria is the same as that for consolidating cases pursuant to Rule 42, i.e., common questions of law or fact. Using the above Rule 42 examples, any party who did not already have an action pending to consolidate with other cases could apply to intervene.

A motion for leave to intervene must show the court that the applicant's claim or defense does involve an *important* common question of law or fact and that his or her intervention in the case will conserve the court's time, save the parties' expense and cause prejudice to no one. Some statutes expressly encourage consolidation and direct the courts to order consolidations. Certain federal civil rights actions are typical of those encouraging consolidation and intervention. In those instances, a party may intervene as a *matter of right*. Rule 24(a). This means the party has an absolute right to intervene. He or she does not have to convince the court of the desirablity of the intervention.

A person may intervene as a matter of right if his or her interests in the subject matter may be affected by the outcome of the litigation. Rule 24(a). For example, suppose the defendant caused damage to real estate by creation of a nuisance, and the real estate is owned by three joint tenants, and two of the joint tenants sue for damages. The third joint tenant would be allowed to intervene in the case as a matter of right. Rule 24(a). If a trustee sues or is sued, the beneficiary may elect to intervene to protect his or her interest in the trust res.* If an agent is sued for a wrongful act committed in the course and scope of the agency, the principal, who is vicariously liable for the agent's acts, may intervene to make sure the defense is adequately presented. Rule 24. The right to intervene is granted whenever a person would be properly joined as a party or his or her claim or defense would properly be consolidated as involving common questions of law or fact.

The procedure for intervening is clearly described in Rule 24(c). A motion must be served upon all parties which states the grounds for the consolidation, i.e., the moving party's interest in the subject matter or his or her relationship to the parties or the common questions of law or fact which permits the matter to be joined with the pending actions. A copy of the proposed pleading, with a new title, must be attached to the motion. The pleading must fully set forth his or her claim or defense. Rule 24(c).

CLASS ACTIONS

The most ambitious consolidation of claims, defenses and parties is the use of class actions as authorized by Rule 23. The subject of class actions is beyond this book. The subject is complex; presenting problems that paralegals seldom are required to handle. It is enough for our purposes to understand that on occasion an entire class or group of persons may be the plaintiffs or defendants in an action in which the class or group is represented by one or just a few litigants. Class actions are not generally favored. The prerequisites for a class action are difficult to meet.

An example should be helpful to illustrate the use and prerequisites of class actions. Suppose that a large commercial bank contracted to pay interest on money it collects from mortgagors to hold in escrow to pay real estate taxes as they come due. Suppose further that a dispute arises whether the bank has calculated the interest properly or has made questionable charges against the escrow accounts. The number of mortgagors may be several thousand, but they can be easily identified. If an action is brought by one or several mortgagors to recover their alleged losses due to overcharging by the bank, it would be best for the class (all mortgagors) and the bank to have a resolution of the problem in one suit. The active participation of each and every mortgagor should not be necessary if the class is adequately represented. If liability exists, the damages for each mortgagor should be easy to determine. The bank avoids the expense of multiple suits. The amount to be recovered may not be large for each member of the class, so having a

---

*Res is a Latin word that means "a particular thing or matter." A trust res is the subject of the trust.

large total amount may be important to justify the cost of the litigation. If the case were not certified as a class action, the bank's successful defense against the initial plaintiffs would not be binding upon other plaintiff mortgagors. Theoretically, if the prerequisites of Rule 23 are met so that a class action is permissible, everyone tends to benefit. It is apparent, however, that a defendant may benefit if he or she or they can keep the court from certifying the case as a class action when the economics of the litigation preclude individual suits.

If a party wants to move the court for an order certifying a class action, he or she must show the court that all the following factors are present.

1. The class is so large it is not practical for them to sue or defend as individual parties in a consolidation of cases or joinder of parties in a single action.
2. There are common questions of law or fact affecting the right or obligations of all members of the class the same.
3. The party or parties applying for class certification are truly representative of the proposed class.
4. Separate suits by or against individual members of the proposed class might result in varying or inconsistent determinations for the members.
5. A class action can effectively dispose of all the legal and fact issues that exist between members of the proposed class and the adverse party.
6. The individual members of the proposed class do not have a superior interest in controlling the handling of the litigation.
7. There is no other pending litigation which would be adversely affected by certifying the class action.
8. Commencement of a class action would not unduly burden the court and would not cause prejudice to persons who might choose to have their case presented in another forum.

If a class action is allowed, the court exercises close control over the case to make sure that the class members receive notice of the case, and their rights and obligations in connection with the action. The class action cannot be compromised or dismissed without court approval. Rule 23(e).

One type of class action has been given special treatment: a shareholders' derivative action to enforce rights of their corporation against a party when the board of directors wronfully refuse or neglect to do so. Rule 23.1. Since the board of directors (not shareholders) is charged with the responsibility for running the business, the shareholders may institute actions only in extreme circumstances. The shareholders must show the court that an effort has been made to have the directors take the appropriate action and that they have refused. The shareholder who seeks to institute a derivative action must show that he or she was a shareholder at the time the transaction or occurrence in question took place and that he or she adequately represents the other shareholders. As in other class actions, a shareholders' derivative action cannot be compromised or dismissed without court approval.

SUBSTITUTION OF PARTIES

If a party dies while his or her lawsuit is pending, a representative party must be substituted. Any party may move the court for an order making the substitution. If a representative has been appointed in a probate proceeding, that representative may move the court for an order substituting him or herself for the decedent. If a party makes the motion for a substitution, and there is already a representative appointed by a probate court to handle the estate, that representative must be served with the motion and notice of hearing. The motion must be served in the manner provided in Rule 4 for service of a summons. The motion must not be served by mail upon a nonparty.

Once the parties and court are given formal notice of a party's death, served like an ordinary motion, the remaining parties have just ninety days in which to act to obtain a substitution for the duly appointed representative. Otherwise, the action against the decedent will be dismissed. Rule 25(a). The Rule implies that the court shall order the dismissal upon its own motion.

If a party becomes legally incompetent to handle his or her business, again, a representative party must be appointed and substituted. For example, if the party becomes senile, a guardian should be appointed by a probate court having jurisdiction. The guardian must replace the senile party in the manner discussed above.

If an action is brought by joint tenants to realty and one dies before a determination is reached, the action will continue in the name of the survivor. One of the characteristics of ownership of property as joint tenants is that title inures to the survivor. The title of the action may be amended by order of the court showing that the surviving joint tenant plaintiff is the only plaintiff. Rule 25(c).

THIRD-PARTY PRACTICE

For a detailed discussion of third-party practice, see Appendix IX (pages 402–403).

9

Gathering The Evidence

Each litigant has the responsibility of gathering and presenting the evidence necessary to establish his or her claim or defense. Ordinarily, the parties and lawyers begin gathering information by *investigating* the occurrence or transaction. The investigation does not require the help or cooperation of the other party or the assistance of the court. Lawyers ordinarily prefer to conduct the investigation as soon as possible and with as little involvement of the other side as possible. There are two profound jurisprudential principles that guide a lawyer in the investigation: (1) "the early bird catches the worm;" (2) "what your opponent doesn't know won't hurt you." Clearly, the more facts and information a party obtains, the better he or she can prepare a case for trial and the better he or she can evaluate the case.

Investigation involves interviewing witnesses and, perhaps, obtaining statements from them. The investigation includes on site inspections; obtaining or making photographs; obtaining documents such as medical, employment, production, business, court, and government agency records. Investigation also includes testing, obtaining diagrams, models, and plats. It includes locating expert witnesses and obtaining their analyses and opinions.

There are some significant limitations on the scope of any investigation. A lawyer and his or her staff must not interview a person who is represented by another lawyer. Professional ethics forbid a lawyer from interrogating the client of another lawyer. A lawyer may not trespass on the opponent's property. He or she has no right to demand documents in the possession of others and cannot force reluctant witnesses to talk with him or her. These limitations present a problem because the adversary system can work fairly only if the parties have equal *access* to the evidence. However, the legal system cannot and should not guaranty that each party will have the *same* evidence at trial.

The Federal Rules of Civil Procedure provide several *discovery* procedures which enable each party to have nearly equal access to all the witnesses, documents and other evidence. The discovery procedures have numerous safeguards protecting the litigants against abuses. Rule 26(a) specifies the methods for obtaining discovery:

> Parties may obtain discovery by one or more of the following methods: depositions upon oral examination or written questions; written interbogatories; production of documents or things or permission to enter upon land or other property, for inspection and other purposes; physical and mental examinations; and requests for admissions. Unless the court orders otherwise under subdivision (c) of this rule, the frequency of use of these methods is not limited.

The discovery procedures and investigation efforts should be coordinated so as to compliment each other. The objective of the investigation and discovery are basically the same: (1) to identify the known facts and their sources; (2) to find additional facts and possible sources of information; (3) to preserve evidence for presentation at trial; (4) to establish authoritative expert opinion evidence; and (5) to develop impeachment evidence countering the opponent's evidence. Incidentally, it is helpful to know what information the opponent has or does not have.

The discovery procedures help to carry out the Rule's objectives of making litigation just, speedy and inexpensive. By making all of the evidence and sources of evidence equally available to the parties, a just result is more likely. Enabling the parties to know all the relevant facts, allows them to evaluate their respective positions, increasing the likelihood that the parties will be able to arrive at a settlement. A settlement concludes the controversy earlier than it would be if a trial were necessary. In addition, if more cases are settled, the remaining cases can come to trial sooner. Parties minimize the expense of litigation through the judicious use of the discovery procedures thereby making litigation less expensive.

The discovery procedures should be viewed by each party as means for obtaining information through his or her own efforts. The discovery procedures should not be abused by placing unreasonable burdens on the opposition to do the work.

The rules of discovery facilitate settlement by enabling the parties to find out about the availability of liability insurance, medical insurance and other insurances that might affect the parties' decision to settle. The rules of discovery help lawyers to *reduce* the element of surprise that used to permeate trials. Surprises may come in various forms, such as surprise witnesses, surprise testimony and exhibits. Surprise does not promote justice. If a party has enough time to conduct a thorough investigation and analysis, he or she may be able to refute or explain surprise evidence. The rules of discovery are calculated to permit the investigation and analysis of the evidence in good season before trial.

The scope of discovery applicable to each of the discovery procedures is set forth in Rule 26(b) (1):

> Parties may obtain discovery regarding any matter, not privileged, which is relevant to the subject matter involved in the pending action, whether it relates to the claim or defense of the party seeking discovery or to the claim or defense of any other party, including the existence, description, nature, custody, condition and location of any books, documents, or other tangible things and the identity and location of persons having knowledge of any discoverable matter. It is not ground for objection that the information sought will be inadmissible at the trial if the information sought appears reasonably calculated to lead to the discovery of admissible evidence.

The scope of discovery is broad. Whenever a dispute arises concerning the scope or application of the rules of discovery, the courts are inclined toward an interpretation favoring discovery rather than limiting it.

The choice between unilateral investigation and discovery procedures, and the choice between the various discovery procedures depend upon the type of information needed, the amount of information needed, the time available to obtain the information, the anticipated use of the information, and the relative cost of the procedures. Each discovery procedure has its own value and limitations.

Lawyers are professional advisers, advocates and court officers. They are expected to scrupulously comply with the mandates of the discovery rules — to make full and accurate disclosures of information as provided by the rules when duly demanded. Lawyers must exercise control over their clients to make sure they, too, fully comply with the requirements of discovery procedures. Laymen might be surprised to know how well the system functions because of the professional reliability of lawyers and their staffs.

When a good faith dispute arises concerning the propriety of a discovery demand or the adequacy of a party's disclosure, any party may move the court to decide who is correct. If a party was wrong but "substantially justified" in demanding certain discovery (disclosures) or in refusing to make discovery, the court ordinarily requires each party to bear his or her own costs in connection with the motion to compel or quash discovery. Rule 37(a). A party is "substantially justified" if he or she took a position that was reasonable in light of the facts and law. However, if a party violates the discovery mandates without being "substantially justified", the court may impose sanctions of various kinds. Rule 37(b) (c) (d). The most severe sanctions are imprisonment — as a punishment for being in contempt of court — or a determination of the case in favor of the opponent. The least severe sanction is an award of costs to the opposing party.

Most discovery procedures are not available until after a lawsuit has been commenced. Nevertheless, because lawyers know that once an action is started most of the information they have is subject to discovery, there is a tendency to exchange information before suit. The parties' willingness to exchange information significantly increases the possibilities of settlement even without the necessity of a lawsuit.

More often than not, the parties begin their discovery by serving interrogators upon each other as provided by Rule 33. An interrogatory is merely a question propounded by one party to another. Interrogatories are usually served in sets. The plaintiff may serve interrogatories upon a defendant as soon as the summons and complaint have been served upon him or her — even at the same time. The defendant may serve interrogatories upon the plaintiff any time after the *action* is commenced, i.e., when the complaint is filed with the clerk of court. Therefore, it is theoretically possible for the defendant to serve interrogatories upon the plaintiff even before the U.S. marshal has served the summons and complaint on the defendant.

Interrogatories must be answered within 30 days from the date of service; but if service is by mail, the party upon whom they were served is granted another three days in which to answer. Rule 6(e). If interrogatories are served upon the defendant *along with* the summons and complaint, the defendant is allowed forty-five days in which to serve his or her answers to interrogatories. Rule 33(a). In other words, a defendant has at least forty-five days from the date the summons and complaint are served before he has to respond to interrogatories served upon him. These times periods may be shortened or lengthened by court order if there is a good reason for a change in a particular case. Rule 33(a). If a party needs more time for answering interrogatories than is allowed by the Rules, it is customary to ask the party who served the interrogatories for additional time. Usually such requests are granted. But if the request is not granted, the party needing more time may move the court for an order extending the time. Where need is shown and a party has been reasonably diligent in his or her efforts to comply, courts are prone to granting reasonable extensions.

Demands for discovery may be objectionable due to form or substance. If a party decides not to answer one or more interrogatories because he or she considers them objectionable, grounds or reasons must be stated for the objections. The next step is up to the party who propounded the interrogatories. He or she may acquiesce or take action to compel answers. Rules 33(a) and 37(a). If a party objects to a deposition scheduled by another party, he or she should move the court for an order quashing the notice of deposition.

A party must sign his or her own answers to interrogatories, and the signature must be notarized. However, if objections are made to one or more of the interrogatories, the party's lawyer must sign the objections. His or her signature does not have to be notarized since the lawyer is subject to the requirements of Rule 11.* If a party has answered some of the interrogatories and objected to others, the party and his or her lawyer sign at the bottom of the response which is entitled, "Answers To Interrogatories And Objections."

Interrogatories are usually the first discovery procedure used in a lawsuit. They are useful to obtain basic information and documents from the other parties such as a brief summary of the opponent's version of the

---

*The signature of a lawyer constitutes a certificate by him or her that he or she has read the pleading; that to the best of his or her knowledge, information, and belief, there is good ground to support it; and that it is not interposed for delay.

transaction or occurrence; whether the opponent knows of witnesses who have information about the parties or about the occurrence or transaction or losses; whether the opponent has obtained any witness statements; whether he or she has business records or other documents relevant to the case; or any relevant photographs, plats or diagrams. The answers to such interrogatories help to establish the framework for the rest of the investigation and to determine what other discovery procedures, if any, should be used.

When interrogatories are served upon a party corporation or other type of organization, the corporation must respond to the interrogatories with the information known to its employees and agents. Corporation personnel must work together to obtain the information with which to answer the interrogatories. An officer or managing agent must sign the answers for the corporation. If he or she does not have personal knowledge of the information set forth in the answers, his or her certification should state that the answers are made upon "information and belief." Technically, the opposing party does not have access to employees of another party — assuming that the employee's knowledge comes through his or her employment. But if a party corporation has an employee who coincidently witnessed an accident while acting *outside* the course of employment, the employee would be treated the same as any independent witness.

The Rules expressly provide that pendency of one party's discovery procedure may not be used as an excuse to postpone or delay the other parties' discovery efforts. For example, if the defendant has served interrogatories and they remain unanswered, the plaintiff may, nevertheless, schedule depositions or make a demand for production of documents. Rule 26(d). The delinquent party may be compelled by court order to respond to discovery demands. That is the proper remedy. Retaliation for delays by refusal to respond to the opponent's discovery demands is impermissible.

Frequently, interrogatories demand a disclosure of "categories of witnesses" such as (1) eyewitnesses to the occurrence; (2) all witnesses from whom statements have been obtained; (3) witnesses who have information about injuries; or (4) witnesses who took photographs. The Rules do not specifically authorize one party to require another to "categorize" witnesses, but the practice has become commonly accepted. Categorizing witnesses and evidence is consistent with the spirit and purposes of the discovery rules. However, a party is not allowed to use interrogatories or oral depositions to question *another party* about the knowledge or information that witnesses may have — even if the party questioned has interviewed and secured statements from the witnesses. Therefore, one party cannot propound an interrogatory requesting disclosure of the knowledge or information that specified witnesses have. Each party must gather his or her own evidence. The purpose of the Rules is to make the *sources* of evidence equally available to the parties. Litigation is still an adversary proceeding or contest. Each party must secure his or her own evidence and present it to the court.

Effective August 1, 1980, Rule 26(f) was added to establish a procedure for *discovery conferences*. Complicated cases involving extensive discovery may benefit from the new rule. Discovery conferences should have little value in the typical case. Indeed, the courts and parties should turn to discovery conferences only after a problem has arisen and some overall plan for discovery would help to expedite the parties' efforts. The new rule provides:

At any time after commencement of an action the court may direct the attorneys for the parties to appear before it for a conference on the subject of discovery. The court shall do so upon motion by the attorney for any party if the motion includes:

(1) A statement of the issues as they then appear;

(2) A proposed plan and schedule of discovery;

(3) Any limitations proposed to be placed on discovery;

(4) Any other proposed orders with respect to discovery; and

(5) A statement showing that the attorney making the motion has made a reasonable effort to reach agreement with opposing attorneys on the matters set forth in the motion. Each party and his attorney are under a duty to participate in good faith in the framing of a discovery plan if a plan is proposed by the attorney for any party. Notice of the motion shall be served on all parties. Objections or additions to matters set forth in the motion shall be served not later than 10 days after service of the motion.

Following the discovery conference, the court shall enter an order tentatively identifying the issues for discovery purposes, establishing a plan and schedule for discovery, setting limitations on discovery, if any; and determining such other matters, including the allocation of expenses, as are necessary for the proper management of discovery in the action. An order may be altered or amended whenever justice so requires.

Subject to the right of a party who properly moves for a discovery conference to prompt convening of the conference, the court may combine the discovery with a pretrial conference authorized by Rule 16.

10

Investigation

The facts surrounding the transaction or occurrence determine what the legal issues are; the legal issues determine what evidence is material to the case. Logic and the rules of evidence determine what evidence is relevant and admissible at trial.

A lawyer must locate and collect the evidence which bears upon a client's claim or defense. That means he or she must search out all the evidence — whether helpful or detrimental to the client's cause. A lawyer must try to be objective about a client's legal position. He or she cannot possibly give good, reliable advice unless all of the facts bearing on the problem are known. A lawyer's investigation is often the backbone of the pretrial preparation. Investigation usually begins upon his or her first meeting with the client or client's representative. The client, whether the plaintiff or defendant, ordinarily has a substantial part of the information concerning the transaction or occurrence in controversy. Usually, he or she is able to identify other persons who should be contacted and is aware of other sources of evidence such as documents and records.

A controversy that results in civil litigation always arises out of a set of facts. Rarely do the parties agree on all of the relevant facts. The trial of a civil action usually centers upon the facts in dispute. Lawyers operate on the assumption that the party who has done the best job of collecting, preserving and presenting evidence concerning the disputed facts will prevail at trial or secure the most advantageous settlement. This assumption is not inconsistent with the larger objective that the ultimate disposition is based upon the truth and law.

Investigation of the facts should begin as soon as possible. An investigator's objectives should be to (1) identify pertinent facts; (2) locate the evidence and sources of evidence; (3) preserve the evidence and (4) organize the evidence to make it useable at the trial. The investigation is an ongoing process that sometimes continues even after the trial has begun. An investigation is complete when the investigator *knows* what happened *and* has the means of proving to others what happened.

Basically a lawyer and his or her client want to know everything about the transaction or occurrence: when, where, why, how, who and by whom. There is no set formula for conducting the investigation. The nature of the occurrence, the type of claim and the possible defenses dictate how the investigation should be conducted. A good investigation depends upon common sense and objectivity. Experience should help an investigator to eliminate the irrelevant sooner. But an experienced investigator must be just as thorough as a novice.

An occurrence takes place somewhere. The character of the place may have a good deal to do with how and why it happened. As soon as possible, then, the site of an accident should be inspected, photographed, and perhaps diagrammed. Through an on site inspection an investigator is able to identify the important physical features and obtain an accurate perspective of the physical layout. In a typical intersection automobile accident case, the investigator should observe and record the widths of the roadways, location of traffic controls, signs and markings, and any obstructions to view. Even if photographs of the actual accident scene are available, an on site inspection is worthwhile. Having seen the place of the accident, the investigator is better prepared to talk with the witnesses and question the client. He or she is better equipped to ask the right questions, secure relevant details, and avoid being misled by witnesses who have imperfect memories.

The hallmarks of a good investigation are promptness and accuracy. Evidence tends to vanish like vapor with the passage of time. Physical evidence gets lost. Witnesses quickly forget the facts which they observed. Some witnesses try to forget. Some witnesses try not to be found. Therefore, the first order of business is to obtain the client's version of the occurrence, then to preserve it. Next, interview the witnesses. If evidence is in the custody of a nonparty, he or she should be impressed with the importance of preserving it for purposes of the litigation and should be given assistance with storing it. Photographs should be obtained not only for the purpose of showing the subject matter depicted but also as an aid to interviewing witnesses. Photographs may help witnesses to remember important details and to be more specific in their descriptions. There may be official records and reports which bear on the issues in the case. Copies should be obtained — again, as soon as possible. Such documents often provide the names and addresses of additional witnesses who will have to be contacted.

The optimum arrangement in accident cases is to meet the client, get acquainted and proceed to the accident location together. The client can demonstrate what happened. His or her explanations will be more meaningful. In automobile cases the client can drive through the occurrence again — noting relevant speeds, times and distance. Photographs should be obtained, especially if there is still some evidence of the accident such as debris, skidmarks, or gouge marks. Seldom is an investigator fortunate enough to be on the scene soon enough to preserve such evidence. But even if the skidmarks and debris are already gone, photographs may be used to show the areas in question and witnesses can draw the skidmarks and other evidence on the photographs when they testify at trial.

When the case is assigned to a paralegal for investigation he or she should begin by contacting the client and arrange for a personal interview. Many records cannot be obtained without signed authorizations, including tax returns, hospital records, medical records, personnel records, police accident reports, employment records, school records and official death records. The custodian of records may require a special form and the custodian's preference should be honored if possible. The paralegal should have the authorization documents available for the client to execute at the first meeting. Each law office has its own forms for this purpose. The client should sign the necessary authorizations at the first meeting. It might be desirable to leave the authorizations undated. Dates may be supplied when and as the authorizations are used. In that way if there happens to be some delay before the authorizations are used, they will still appear to be and *are* current.

Known witnesses should be interviewed immediately. Very often it is necessary to know something about the witness to be able to evaluate his or her evidence. The information to be obtained from a witness includes his or her identity, background, observations, contacts with the parties and any pertinent conclusions he or she may have. Has he or she been interviewed by anyone else or given a recorded statement to anyone else? The details are important. Accurate details make a witness's testimony authoritative. The details both test credibility and help to establish credibility. Details help a lawyer to present a sharper, clearer picture of the transaction or occurrence at trial. A lawyer is going to avoid unnecessary details when he or she presents the evidence to a jury, but when the investigation begins, no one can know which details are going to be uncontroverted or otherwise unimportant to the trial.

Often witnesses are reluctant to give statements because they do not understand the procedures and they want to avoid being involved in the controversy. A lawyer may have considerable difficulty convincing such witnesses to cooperate by giving a statement. Witnesses should be approached in a manner calculated to gain their confidence. The investigator should have no hesitancy or reluctance about identifying him or herself and explaining the purpose of the interview. The witness should be told and assured that there is nothing improper in talking to one side or the other or in giving statements. He or she may be encouraged to sign the statement, preferably on each page, by pointing out that the signature helps to guaranty that the statement is genuine and that the statement will be a convenient reference for him or her.

The witness will be more cooperative and responsive if he or she feels the interrogator is being straightforward and fair. A paralegal should begin by introducing him or herself and purpose, and should preview the matter with the witnesses so that there is a general understanding of the witness's version before he or she begins writing. By informing the witness of other information already obtained, the witness can see how his or her testimony fits into the case as a whole. Briefing the witness in this manner sometimes helps to catch the witness's interest and cooperation. Such a preview also helps the witness to recall additional facts which he or she might otherwise forget or feel are unimportant and not mention.

When a witness is interviewed, the investigator should obtain a handwritten, signed statement from him or her. The investigator almost always prepares the statement for the witness's signature because most witnesses simply would not make the effort to prepare a statement. A personal interview gives the investigator an opportunity to evaluate the witness. Recorded telephone statements are second best. As the interviewer proceeds with the questions, he or she should write down the information which is obtained. These notes will become the witness's statement. The witness's own words should be used insofar as possible. A statement ought to be single spaced to reduce the possibility of interpolation. When the interview is completed, the statement is done. The witness should be asked to read the statement to see if information recorded is correct. If it is agreed that the information has been accurately recorded, he or she may be willing to sign it. It is very important to have the statement signed. He or she cannot be *impeached* with the statement unless he or she has signed it. In some states and in some cases, the law requires that the witnesses be given a copy of the signed statement. See Rule (b) (3). The statement ought to conclude with an assertion showing that the witness has read it and received a copy. It is easy to make a carbon copy for the witness to keep.

[handwritten margin note: not true you can impeach]

The manner in which the witness is approached depends upon the interrogator's own personality, the witness's personality, his or her relation to the parties, his or her age and numerous other factors.

After developing the basic facts known by the witness, the paralegal should start writing out a statement for the witness to sign. The witness may or may not be told at the beginning of the interview that he or she will be asked to sign the statement. The written statement often begins with the date and place at the top:

(Date)

(Place)

"Statement of John D. Doe. I live at _____, _____. I am _____ years of age and employed at _____. My home telephone number is _____. My parents are _____, and they live at _____. They usually know where I am if I have to travel out of the state. On *(date)*, I was a witness to an accident at _____."   * * *

"I have read the above statement consisting of three pages. *Yes.*
The statement is true and correct. *Yes.*
I have received a copy. *Yes.*"

_____

Witness's Signature

It is not uncommon for the writer to make minor errors while writing the statement — sometimes on purpose. He or she should specifically point out the errors to the witness and ask him or her to initial the corrections. The initials in the body of the statement tend to corroborate the fact that the witness read the statement at the time it was prepared and, therefore, approved it.

A paralegal must use some common sense in determining what should go into the written statement and what, if anything, should be omitted. Remember, the whole statement might be received into evidence at trial to impeach the witness. Furthermore, many courts require parties to disclose witness statements to the other side. Rule 26 (b) (3). It might be nice to keep certain things out of the statement and out of evidence. But a witness certainly has a right to object to giving or signing a statement which omits facts that he or she considers important. The witness's sense of propriety must be respected even though there is no rule of law or professional ethic which requires all statements to be complete in every detail. A statement, though, must be accurate in every detail.

A reluctant witness may be a little more cooperative if he or she is told that it may be over a year before the case reaches trial and a written statement will help refresh his or her recollection. The assurance of its authenticity is his or her signature on it. If the witness is less than cooperative, the witness may be told that he or she is already involved, and a lack of cooperation will not help to avoid involvement. He or she can be advised that the alternative to an informal statement is a deposition which will require a response to a subpoena and testimony under oath: "The choice is yours!" If a witness will not give a signed statement or a court reporter's statement, consideration should be given to deposing (taking) the witness's deposition. An uncooperative witness may be subpoened for a deposition.

Sometimes it is not convenient to obtain a written, signed statement, but it is possible to obtain a *court reporter's statement*. The procedure involves interviewing the witness in the presence of a stenographer who makes a verbatim record and transcript of the questions and answers. The transcript can be very helpful to refresh the witness's recollection in preparation for trial. Also, the court reporter can be called upon to testify at trial to "prior statements" if the witness's testimony varies at trial from the statement. The transcript is not in itself used for impeachment. The court reporter can testify to what he or she heard during the interview, using the transcript notes to refresh and confirm his or her memory. The transcript will probably not be received into evidence as a signed statement would be.

A good statement, whether written and signed or a court reporter's transcript, should commit the witness to his or her version of the occurrence or transaction. It should clearly set forth the facts known by the witness and establish the basis and sources of his knowledge. For example, it is not enough to record the fact that the witness saw a vehicle traveling at X miles per hour. The statement must show when and where the witness first observed the vehicle, how long he or she observed it, and the direction of its travel. The statement must record where the witness was when he or she made the observations, the fact that he or she has adequate eye sight and is sufficiently experienced to make valid observations concerning speed.

A good statement should also record the witness's lack of knowledge of important facts. For example, a statement could properly note that the witness did not look for skidmarks; does not know of any other witness; did not talk to any of the parties; does not know any of the parties; did not hear a horn before the collision; did not see the traffic light, etc. Some signed statements are purely "negative" statements which are good insurance against having problems from those witnesses later on.

Having a signed statement from a witness, a lawyer pretty well knows where he or she stands with that witness so is better able to evaluate the client's claims or defenses. Signed statements are relatively easy to obtain and inexpensive to make. Unlike deposition, procurement of a statement does not expose the witness to the opposing side (But See Rule 26(b) (3).)

Some law firms have "witness statement forms" which they mail to witnesses with a request that the form be completed by the witness and mailed back. Such forms must be short and very specific. Consequently, they have limited value. I do not know what percentage of witnesses actually respond to the forms for I have never used them. Perhaps the primary value of such forms is to help a paralegal decide whether or not to interview certain witnesses. The forms may be particulary valuable where many witnesses must be contacted quickly. (See sample in Appendix.)

11

Interrogatories

Written interrogatories are the most simple and economical discovery procedure available in civil litigation. Written interrogatories are merely specific questions propounded to a party which the party must answer under oath. Each party usually serves interrogatories very soon after the action is commenced. Interrogatories are particularly useful for obtaining basic information about the opposing party, his or her version of the transaction or occurrence, and the existence of items of evidence.

Typical subjects for initial interrogatories include the opposing party's address, age, marital status, employment history, accident history, medical history, litigation history, any criminal convictions*, educational background, use of other names, and social security number. The interrogatories concerning a party's identity and background must be relevant to the subject matter of the litigation. Questions which are relevant to a divorce action may not be relevant to a tort action or to a contract action. Certain interrogatories are applicable to almost every action, such as interrogatories concerning the identity of witnesses, the existence of documents, existence of other tangible evidence and the opposing party's version of the transaction or occurrence. Most cases involve claims for money damages.

There are a number of factors which affect a claim for compensatory damages and which are proper subjects for interrogatories. Ordinarily, the

*Rule 609.

defendant serves interrogatories inquiring about the nature of the losses, the extent of the losses, the method of calculating damages, supporting documentation such as repair bills, invoices, and receipts. Interrogatories are used to obtain the identity of witnesses who have information about the claim of damages. The defendant is also entitled to know whether the plaintiff's loss was covered by the plaintiff's own direct loss insurance. Both the plaintiff and defendant are entitled to discover the existence and amount of insurance coverages applicable to the losses in question. The amount and availability of insurance may significantly affect their evaluations and attitude toward settlement possibilities. Insurance coverage is not a matter which is relevant to the trial. On occasion, however, a direct loss insurer that has made payments to the plaintiff as its insured may have an interest in the outcome of the litigation, and the insurer may even be the real party in interest. The defendant is entitled to know all the circumstances affecting an insurer's interests or lack of interest in the case, and such information is most conveniently obtained through interrogatories.

Paralegals should strive to develop a high degree of skill in preparing interrogatories. Drafting interrogatories requires an ability to use English clearly and properly. Well drafted interrogatories are concise. Each one should be calculated to obtain specific information. Form interrogatories are frequently used, but they must be directly applicable to the case. It is bad form to serve a set of interrogatories that were tailored for another type of case. A law office that is sloppy in its preparation and use of interrogatories loses the respect of other lawyers and the courts. It is also bad form for a lawyer or paralegal to use interrogatories that are not needed and merely impose a burden on the other side.

Interrogatories are used primarily to obtain information, but they have other uses as well. The answers may effectively establish that the opponent *lacks* certain evidence. For example, when the defendant serves interrogatories requiring the plaintiff to disclose the identity of witnesses to the accident and the identity of hired expert witnesses, a negative response by the plaintiff apprises the defendant that he or she does not have to spend time countering evidence by the plaintiff in those areas. Potential problems have been eliminated. If the responding party should try to produce a surprise witness at trial, after stating that he or she has no witnesses, the court, on motion, should preclude the witnesses from testifying. Or, the court may order a postponement of the trial allowing the defendant additional time in which to prepare. The court may order that the party who withheld information arrange for the surprise witness to submit to an oral deposition before testifying in court. Under those circumstances, the plaintiff may be required to pay all costs of the oral deposition. This procedure gives the "surprised party" an opportunity to determine whether he or she really needs more time to prepare for trial. A party's negative answers to interrogatories indicating he or she is not aware of any relevant documents, photographs, or other evidence, may, likewise, give the "surprised party" grounds for keeping any nondisclosed items out of evidence.

The answers to interrogatories are customarily drafted by a lawyer or paralegal for the client's signature based upon information which is available to each of them. In other words, the answers to interrogatories must be accurate in light of the information available to the party, his or her agents, employees, liability insurer (if any) and the lawyers.

The scope of inquiry by use of interrogatories is the same as in other discovery procedures, with the exception that use of interrogatories is the only prescribed means for obtaining information about the other parties' *hired* expert witnesses. Rule 26 (b) (4). Interrogatories may be used to obtain information about physical facts, opinions and even legal conclusions of the adverse party's lawyer. Rule 33 (b) provides: "An interrogatory otherwise proper is not necessarily objectionable merely because an answer to the interrogatory involves an opinion or contention that relates to fact or the application of law to fact. . . ." The purpose of the Rule is to give parties the means to obtain more specific, detailed information about another party's claims or defenses. For example, the complaint may assert a cause of action against the defendant by simply alleging that the defendant was negligent in the operation of his or her automobile so as to cause the automobile accident. Through interrogatories the defendant may require the plaintiff to specify all acts and omissions that the plaintiff claims were negligent. The plaintiff and his or her lawyer must respond with specific allegations such as unlawful speed, failure to yield right-of-way, driving on wrong side of roadway, failure to signal a turn, or failure to keep a proper lookout. The plaintiff's answers to interrogatories permit the defendant to concentrate his or her investigation and discovery in the areas of negligence claimed. If at trial, the plaintiff should attempt to prove that the defendant's vehicle was negligently maintained in a defective condition without disclosing such claim in his or her answers to interrogatories, the defendant may be able to exclude all evidence bearing on that issue, or be entitled to a postponement of the trial so that he or she can prepare on the "new" issue. Of course, the plaintiff may pose the same type of interrogatory to the defendant concerning affirmative defenses asserted in the answer. In this way, interrogatories are useful to help the parties to focus on specific fact issues and to fully prepare on the legal issues. Interrogatories may be used to obtain more detailed and specific information about any claim or defense whether contract, tort or statutory.

Interrogatories are often used to obtain specifics about conversations that a party had with another person or conversations between others that a party overheard. The interrogatories ask for the exact wording or request the *substance* of what was said by each person if the exact wording cannot be reiterated.

The Rules do not limit the number of interrogatories which may be served upon a party. However, each interrogatory must be relevant or calculated to lead to evidence admissible at trial. The Rule requiring interrogatories to be relevant helps to keep their use in reasonable proportion. If a party believes that interrogatories served upon him or her are excessively burdensome or constitute harassment, he or she may move the court for a protective order limiting the interrogatories in number, or in scope or subject matter. Rule 26 (c). The special rules of some federal district courts and the rules of practice in some state courts limit the number of interrogatories to fifty, including subpart questions. If a set of interrogatories exceeds the specified number, the responding party may refuse to answer any of them or choose the fifty interrogatories that he or she prefers to answer. Of course, the courts which limit the number of interrogatories also provide a means for obtaining a court order authorizing more interrogatories when reasonably necessary. The limitation tends to reduce the use of nuisance interrogatories.

The answers to interrogatories must be put into final form, signed, notarized and served within thirty days after the interrogatories were served. Objections to interrogatories must be served within the same time period. They are frequently served together. The following example should be helpful to an understanding of the rules affecting the time periods. If the defendant serves interrogatories upon the plaintiff by placing them in a United States mail box on June 1st, the thirty day period begins to run on June 2nd. Then add another three days because service was by mail. Rule 6 (e). Therefore, the answers to interrogatories must be served on or before July 5th. By adding three days for mailing, the time period actually ends on July 4th, but that is Independence Day, a legal holiday, so another day is added. If the legal holiday were not the last day of the time period, it would not expand the time for answering. Rule 6 (a). Parties frequently accommodate each other by voluntarily granting reasonable extensions of time. Parties may stipulate to modify the discovery rules in almost any manner that is convenient for them. However, the time limits prescribed by Rule 33 can be extended only by court order. Rule 29. The parties are generally encouraged to accommodate each other and avoid imposing upon the courts' time by making motions.

A party's answers to interrogatories may be used at trial "to the extent permitted by the rules of evidence." Rule 33 (b). The most common basis for receiving answers into evidence is that they constitute *admissions* by a party. For example, if a defendant in an automobile case admits in his answer to interrogatories that he did not stop for the stop sign, the answer is admissible in evidence to prove a stop sign violation. Answers to interrogatories may be used for impeachment purposes, i.e., to contradict a party's testimony at trial. For example, if the plaintiff answered that she was traveling forty miles per hour as she entered the intersection but at trial testified to going only thirty miles per hour, the inconsistency may be shown for its impeaching effect. Also, the admission of forty miles per hour constitutes **substantive evidence** as an admission of a party. Substantive evidence is any evidence that supports a verdict. Not all impeachment evidence is substantive evidence. Some impeachment evidence is heard by the jury only for the purpose of discrediting a witness but cannot be considered by the jury as proof of any facts in dispute between the parties.

Suppose that the plaintiff is asked through interrogatories to describe her personal injuries and that she describes only head and neck injuries in her answers. Then, at trial, she testifies that she has had low back pain ever since the accident. Her failure to refer to the low back pain in her answers to interrogatories may be used for impeachment and be substantive evidence tending to show that she did not have a low back injury. Answers to interrogatories are not considered to be judicial admissions in the sense that the answers conclusively establish the admitted facts. This is one of the important differences between Rule 33 answers to interrogatories and Rule 36 responses to requests for admissions.

Interrogatories are frequently used to obtain information from business records belonging to another party. The party receiving such interrogatories is given the option, under Rule 33 (c), to extrapolate the requested information or to make the records available to the opposing party so that he or she can conduct the review and make copies, compilations, abstracts or summaries. The primary consideration, obviously, is the time, expense and inconveniences involved.

The answers to interrogatories must be signed under oath by the responding party — not the party's lawyer. The lawyer may sign objections to interrogatories directed to his client. If the answers, or some of them, are not made upon personal knowledge, it is appropriate to state in the notary clause that the answers are "made upon information and belief." A corporate officer or managing agent may sign for a corporation. If specifically authorized by the corporate party, the lawyer handling the case may sign on behalf of the corporation.

Each interrogatory ought to be directed to a single subject. It should be short, specific and to the point. Carefully drawn interrogatories encourage responsive answers providing specific information. It is a common practice to divide an interrogatory into subparts, and there is no reason to avoid that form if it fits the need. For example:

1. For *each* witness statement obtained by defendant or his or her representatives state:
   a. the name and address of the person who interviewed the witness;
   b. the date on which the statement was obtained;
   c. the means by which the statement was recorded;
   d. the name and address of each person who was present when the statement was obtained;
   e. whether the witness has been given a copy of his or her statement.

Each subpart constitutes a separate interrogatory in those jurisdictions which limit a party to fifty interrogatories.

12

Expert Witnesses

Everything seems to be getting more complicated and civil litigation is no exception. Consequently, expert witnesses are being used more frequently in civil trials. Lawyers are finding new ways of using experts to develop claims and defenses. Certain types of litigation such as professional malpractice and defective product cases often require expert testimony. The areas or fields of expertise are limitless. Any subject which is beyond the experience and training of ordinary people may be a proper one for having expert testimony. Experts are allowed to use their education, experience and training to form expert *opinions* which may be expressed to the jury to help them determine the disputed facts. As a general rule, witnesses are not permitted to express opinions. Rule 701. So expert witnesses are given a very special status in the trial of a lawsuit.

A person must qualify to testify as an expert. This is done by showing the court that he or she has sufficient education, training and experience in the subject matter that his or her opinions would have some special value to the jury. Just how much education or experience in the field an expert is required to have is a matter which is left to the "sound discretion" of the trial judge. He or she has a great deal of latitude in such matters. Of course, the better the expert's qualifications, the more persuasive his or her testimony will be. There seems to be an increasing tendency toward the use of experts to prove matters that do not really require expert testimony. Leading this trend is the use of *accident reconstruction experts* who analyze the accident scene and vehicles to form opinions about how an accident was caused. In automobile accident cases the reconstruction experts determine the point of impact, angle of collision, speeds of the vehicles at impact and speeds when the brakes were applied, etc. Having seen a number of such experts testify, the author holds an "expert opinion" that many of these professional expert witnesses engage in a good deal of sophistry. The trend is not healthy for the legal system.

In theory the judge should not allow expert opinion evidence into the case unless such testimony is at least useful to the jury. Rule 702 states:

> If scientific, technical, or other specialized knowledge will assist the trier of fact to understand the evidence or to determine a fact in issue, a witness qualified as an expert by knowledge, skill, experience, training or education may testify thereto in the form of an opinion or otherwise.

It should be obvious that the involvement of an expert witness adds another dimension to the case. Once one side elects to hire an expert to testify on some aspect of the case, it almost becomes obligatory for the other side to get an expert to counteract the testimony of the first. In all probability, if one looks hard enough, he or she can find a professional expert to conjure up a theory helpful to the case.*

Good trial preparation requires each side to find out as much as possible about the other side's expert witnesses and their opinions. However, if the courts were to allow unbridled access to the adverse party's ired experts, the very heart of the adversary system would be threatened. These experts usually obtain most of their information, at least initially, from the lawyer and his or her file. They have to discuss the facts and theories of the case in detail. After a lawyer makes a full disclosure to the expert, the expert may decide, for one reason or another, he or she cannot help. Or, the lawyer might decide against that particular expert even if he or she is willing to help. If their communications were subject to discovery, the unsuccessful *attempts* to secure expert testimony could be devastating to the case.

Theories advanced and rejected in discussions might be used against a party. Statements of facts and assumptions of facts might be used in a detrimental way against a party. The Federal Rules of Civil Procedure have, with some difficulty, steered a course to preserve the adversary system and yet make available certain essential information about the experts who have been selected to testify at trial and their opinions. The information is obtainable only through written interrogatories unless, for good cause shown, a court orders that some other means of discovery, such as an oral deposition, may be used.

Rule 26(b) (4) specifies how and to what extent interrogatories may be used to discover expert opinions. Volumes have been written concerning the Rule's application. In substance, it provides that, unless otherwise stipulated by the parties, the only means of discovering information about the opponent's expert is through interrogatories directed to the party. Interrogatories directed to the expert are not allowed. The interrogatories may be used to obtain the expert's *identity* and a description of the *subject matter* to

---

*Please excuse the cynicism. But experience tells me that the courts have gone much too far in allowing quasi-experts to have questionable opinions of doubtful value.

which he or she will testify at trial. In addition, interrogatories may be propounded requiring the party to disclose each expert *opinion* the expert has about the subject matter. As to each opinion stated, the party may be required to disclose the *facts* upon which each opinion is predicated.

The following is a typical set of interrogatories used to obtain such information as provided by Rule 26(b) (4):

If you intend to call upon any expert witnesses including medical experts to testify at the trial:

(1) State name, age, address and employment of each such expert.

(2) Describe in detail the qualifications of each expert with particular reference to the issues about which the expert may be called upon to testify at trial.

(3) Describe in detail the subject matter on which each expert is expected to testify.

(4) State in detail all facts about which each expert is expected to testify.

(5) State fully the opinions to which each expert is expected to testify.

(6) State the substance of all facts upon which each opinion is based.

(7) Identify by author, title, publication date and publisher all writings which may be used as "learned treatises" by your expert at trial.

(8) Identify separately any documents you intend to call to the attention of any expert witness upon crossexamination.

An expert is hired to analyze the factual problem, render opinions within the areas of his or her expertise, advise concerning the need for additional facts, supply sources of information, and point out weaknesses in the case. It is customary for the expert to submit a written report to the party (lawyer) who hired him or her. A written report is desirable because it is important that everyone concerned know *exactly* what the expert is saying and what he or she is not saying. A written report reduces the possibilities of an error in communications. Rule 26 precludes discovery of the expert's report and precludes the adverse party from taking the expert's deposition. However, the court may order a party to produce the expert for a deposition if a need has been shown. The decision to make such a motion or to resist the motion must be made by a lawyer. A paralegal should be able to prepare the motion and supporting documentation for service and filing.

On rare occasion, a party may be entitled to discover the opinions of another party's expert who is *not* going to be called to testify as a witness at a trial. But to do so he or she must show the court that "exceptional circumstances" exist making it *impracticable* for him or her to obtain facts or opinions on the same subject matter by other means. An example may be helpful to understanding this limited but important exception. Suppose that a lady buys a bottle of a soft drink, consumes about half of it and becomes ill about an hour later. She assumes that the soft drink caused her illness. Her husband has the remainder analyzed by a local chemist. The chemist finds nothing unusual in the sample. Two months later the husband takes the remainder of the bottle to another chemist who finds a foreign chemical in the bottle. Assume further that the foreign substance is something not ordinarily found at the bottling plant but is common to households such as a pesticide.

An action is commenced months later. There is no more of the soft drink available to analyze. For obvious reasons, the plaintiffs may elect not to ask the first chemist to testify. Would it be fair to deny the defendant the right to have the information available through the first chemist? Of course not! The example is extreme for the purpose of showing the exception's operation. The exception can work in favor of plaintiffs just as well. Suppose that some of the soft drink is still available for an independent analysis for a chemist to be chosen by the defendant. Should the defendant, nevertheless, be entitled to the first expert's opinion, analysis, factual data, records? Probably yes. The soft drink may have been contaminated after the first chemist completed his or her analysis. Therefore, the *same subject* is not available for analysis.

Expert witnesses are expensive. They require payment for the time spent analyzing the problem, rendering their opinions and participating in legal proceedings. The Rules provide guidelines for determining who shall pay an expert for time spent in discovery proceedings. When an expert's opinion is sought through interrogatories, the party who hired the expert must pay his or her fees for the time spent answering interrogatories. If an oral deposition is ordered, the party who takes the deposition must pay the expert a *reasonable* fee for the time. The expert cannot extort an excessive fee from the opposing side. If the parties and expert cannot agree on what amount is reasonable, the issue may be submitted to the judge for determination.

If an expert is uncooperative after the court has authorized a deposition be taken, he or she may be compelled by subpoena to testify. Also, an expert may be compelled by subpoena to produce his or her records for inspection at the deposition. Violation of a subpoena subjects the expert to a contempt of court order. A party is presumed to be able to control his or her hired expert, so ordinarily subpoenas are not used. If a party cannot control an expert witness or obtain reasonable cooperation, he or she should notify the other side so that a subpoena can be obtained.

When a party seeks to use and benefit from the efforts of an expert originally hired by another party, he or she may be required to pay a "fair portion" of the expert's fees and expenses already incurred by the adverse party. Ordinarily, the parties or the court determines how the expenses should be assessed before the discovery is conducted. Rule 26(b) (C).

In an ordinary case, answers to interrogatories provide sufficient information about the opponent's experts to make additional means of discovery unnecessary. Not infrequently, lawyers agree to exchange experts' reports, like exchanging medical reports pursuant to Rule 35, as an alternative to interrogatories. Parties should use the most expeditious methods of discovery available to keep down the cost of litigation. However, the determining factor must be the adequacy of procedure to provide the information which is or should be available.

How should interrogatories be used in a typical case? Suppose that a plaintiff suffered an injury when a five year old metal extension ladder collapsed while he was on it; that he was carrying a heavy object and was near the top when the ladder's tread and siderail gave way; and that the ladder and the plaintiff fell to the ground at the same time. The plaintiff claims the ladder was defective and that the manufacturer is strictly liable because of an alleged defect. The complaint may or may not specify the type of defects claimed. There are countless possible defects, including defective materials, a defect in the metal creating a localized weakness, a defect in design such as making the treads too narrow or too thin or using inadequate fasteners, or failing to warn the user about foreseeable dangers such as the need to use the ladder at only certain angles or the danger of overextending or overloading it. The plaintiff discloses that he has an expert who will testify that the ladder is "defective." What information can be obtained through written interrogatories directed to the plaintiff?

The defendant can secure the expert's identity, including name, address, curriculum vitae, relationship to the plaintiff and a description of his or her areas of expertise.* Next, the defendant may inquire about the subject matter to which he or she will testify. The answers to the defendants interrogatories should specify the defect or defects claimed. For example, the ladder was defective because the metal in the siderail had fissures in it making the ladder too weak to support ordinary loads. The defendant is entitled to obtain a summary of the grounds for the plaintiff's experts' opinion. The interrogatories should demand disclosure of all tests conducted by the expert such as analysis of cross-sections of the siderail at the point where the siderail collapsed, any microscopic examinations and x-ray studies conducted to show the presence of fissures. The expert presumably determined the load strength by testing or calculations. He will have to disclose his load strength conclusions and the method by which the determination was obtained. Obviously, a lot of information can be obtained through interrogatories that are carefully drawn and properly answered.

What are the limitations when using interrogatories to obtain information about the adverse party's expert witnesses and their opinions? Quite a few. The answers to interrogatories do not give an adverse party the opportunity to evaluate the expert's personal appearance. Can he express himself orally? Does he appear authoritative? Does he recognize that other formulas or other methods of calculating the strength of the metal are accepted in the industry and give different results? Can he rule out the possibility that the alleged fissures developed at some time after the ladder was sold to the plaintiff? Have comparisons been made with other ladders? Can he rule out consumer misuse? How? What are the weaknesses in his theory about which he is aware?

The collapse of a roof on a large, new building is almost certain to engender litigation. Even if no one is injured, there will be a very large property damage claim. The owner will undoubtedly want someone to indemnify him for his loss. If the owner's loss is covered by his own insurance, the insurer will probably have subrogation rights against anyone who tortiously caused the collapse. It is not at all unusual for the building's owner or insurer to bring a negligence action against the architect, general contractor and selected subcontractors. The defendants usually serve cross-claims making everyone adverse parties. Each party in such litigation usually has its own "in house" experts on the business payroll. More often

*This analysis is not intended to be exhaustive.

than not, though, the parties hire independent (outside) experts to assist and advise concerning the litigation. A party who happens to be an expert is not protected by Rule 26(b) (4). Nor are expert employees protected. The adverse party may take their oral depositions and ask questions concerning the experts' background, education, training, connection with the project and opinions about the adequacy of the structure and cause of its collapse. The "work product" objection applies only to experts who are hired for the sole purpose of assisting with the particular litigation.

What if the plaintiff's lawyer notices the depositions of employee experts of the defendant who had nothing to do with the particular project? May the lawyer ask them questions about the structure and for opinions about the adequacy of design, materials, fabrication methods, etc.? The Rule does not seem to cover this situation. My guess is that a court would quash the notice for taking their depositions if the defendant showed by affidavits that they had no connection with the project. If they were deposed, they could probably *elect* to have no opinions concerning the subject matter. They should be compensated for their time by the party taking their depositions. Otherwise, courts would be encouraging "fishing" for expert opinions, trying to secure expert opinions through "admissions."

If a patient sues a physician for medical malpractice, the defendant physician will probably hire another physician to review the medical case for the purpose of determining whether he or she has been guilty of malpractice. The same hired physician may conduct a Rule 35 medical examination of the plaintiff. It is apparent that the one expert has two quite distinct roles. Each role must be handled separately. Rule 35 requires that the physician who conducts an independent medical examination must provide a complete report of his or her examination if requested by the plaintiff. The report is available through the party who requested the examination — not directly from the physician. The examining physician should report separately on his or her evaluation of the defendant physician's medical treatment of the plaintiff. That phase of the medical evaluation comes under Rule 26(b) (4) and is protected as part of the defendant attorney's work product.

13

Oral Depositions

The word "deposition" means sworn testimony. Rule 30 authorizes a party to require other parties and even nonparty witnesses to appear at a reasonably convenient time and place to give *oral* testimony about the case. Usually the deposition is conducted in an office of one of the lawyers. But it may be held almost anywhere such as the courthouse, a hotel or airport meeting room or a private home. The *deponent* is required to appear for the deposition and answer questions put to him or her by the lawyers. The deponent is entitled to have his or her own lawyer present — even if not a party to the suit. Interrogation of the deponent proceeds in a manner similar to the interrogation of a witness in court. A verbatim record of the entire proceedings is made by a stenographer who uses shorthand or stenographic notes to prepare a typed deposition transcript of each question, answer, statement and stipulation made during the course of the oral deposition. Rule 30 prescribes numerous safeguards for the benefit of the deponent, the parties and lawyers.

The discovery procedures are intended to provide parties with the means for obtaining access to testimony of any witness who has information about the case. The oral deposition procedure is probably the most important discovery tool and most valuable means of preserving evidence. An oral deposition allows a lawyer to have direct contact with the adverse parties. The procedure is relatively simple and very effective. It is moderately expensive but usually worth the cost. There is no other way of obtaining as much detailed information directly from the witnesses.

A paralegal is not permitted to take a witness's deposition. However, a paralegal's work often revolves around oral depositions, including scheduling, noticing, preparing for, observing, reviewing, correcting, digesting, consolidating, indexing, and utilizing the transcript for trial preparation. Therefore, a paralegal must have a good understanding of the oral deposition purposes, uses and procedures. One of the more important aspects of oral depositions for a paralegal is preparation of a client or nonparty witness for his or her deposition. A paralegal's ability to competently prepare a person for a deposition depends upon a good understanding of the entire process.

Scheduling a deposition is a simple procedure. A *Notice of Deposition* is prepared and served upon each party. Service is usually by mail. The notice states that the deposition of a specified person or party will be taken at a specified time and place before a person who is authorized to administer oaths. The notice must be in writing and signed by a lawyer. It must give everyone *reasonable time* in which to prepare. It may require the deponent to produce specified documents that are under his or her control. Rule 30(b) (1). If the identity of the person to be deposed is not known, he or she may be described by position or relationship to the parties. The notice of deposition is, in itself, a mandate to a party to appear at the time and place scheduled. If the time or place is a problem for the party whose oral deposition has been noticed, he or she has the responsibility of obtaining a cancellation or new time or a different place. Very seldom do lawyers find that they are unable to agree on a mutually convenient time and place. The practice is to proceed with the deposition at the time and place set forth in the notice of deposition if reasonably possible. Occasionally, a deposition has to be rescheduled several times due to conflicts. Professional courtesy requires lawyers to cooperate and accommodate each other.

The plaintiff is *not* permitted to take the defendant's deposition during the thirty day period following service of the summons and complaint upon the defendant. Otherwise, the defendant and his or her lawyer would have difficulty preparing for it. However, if the defendant elects to take the plaintiff's deposition within thirty days of service of the complaint, the plaintiff may obtain the defendant's deposition too. Rule 30(a). Also, a defendant may be required to give a deposition within thirty days after service of the summons and complaint by making a motion to the court showing special circumstances such as failing health. Rule 30(b) (2) specifies three situations (exceptions) which automatically give the plaintiff the right to take anyone's deposition during the first thirty days: (1) the deponent is about to leave the district and will be at least a hundred miles from the place where the trial is to be held; or (2) the deponent is about to leave the United States; or (3) the deponent is about to leave on a voyage to sea. No court order is necessary if any of these reasons are stated in the notice along with a brief explanation of the facts. Rule 30(a) appears to provide that any discovery procedure instituted by the defendant operates to permit the plaintiff to schedule the defendant's deposition within the first thirty days after service of the summons and complaint. Taken literally, it means that as soon as the defendant serves an interrogatory upon the plaintiff, the plaintiff may schedule the defendant's deposition at a reasonable time.

If a nonparty's deposition is noticed, the nonparty may be compelled to appear at the designated time and place by serving a subpoena upon him or her. The subpoena may require the witness to bring specified documents which are in his or her custody. The notice of deposition must also list the documents. Rule 30(b)(1). If he or she is willing to appear voluntarily without a subpoena, the expense and inconveniences of the subpoena process may be avoided. However, if the nonparty witness fails to appear at the scheduled time and place for his or her deposition, the party who scheduled it may be required to reimburse the other parties for expenses they incurred due to the aborted deposition, including lawyer's fees. If the nonparty witness had been served with a subpoena, and failed to comply with it, the party who scheduled the deposition cannot be blamed for the nonappearance, and costs cannot be assessed. Rule 30(g)(2). If the party who serves the notice fails to appear to take the deposition, he or she may be required to pay the costs incurred by all parties who did appear. Rule 30(g)(1).

A deposition should be scheduled to be taken at a *convenient* place. Of course, convenience is relative. If a nonparty is to be deposed, the deposition should be taken in his or her hometown or the town where he or she works. Otherwise, the deposition may be taken at the county seat of the county in which the deponent lives. If the deponent is a party, the primary consideration is the convenience of all the parties and their lawyers. If they all live in the same town, that is where the deposition should be taken, regardless of the fact the court is located in another city or county. If the parties and lawyers are located at various places around the state (federal district), the most convenient place may be the city in which the court is located. If the parties cannot agree on a convenient place, the judge may select it for them. Usually depositions are taken in a lawyer's office. The lawyer who schedules a deposition has the responsibility to arrange for the place and for a court reporter to record the testimony.

On occasion it is necessary for a party to obtain a deposition of an officer or employee of a corporation, partnership or government agency, but the party needing the deposition does not know the name of the person who should testify or even his or her position within the organization. If a lawyer is able to specify in the notice of deposition the subject matter for which the witness's testimony is needed, the organization's managers are required to determine, if possible, who within the organization should appear in response to the subpoena and/or notice of deposition. However, the subject matter must be specified with reasonable particularity. Rule 30(b)(6). If a nonparty corporation is subpoenaed, the subpoena must clearly inform the corporation of its duty to respond by designating someone to appear on its behalf at the deposition, and that the persons who do appear must be able to speak for the organization concerning the subject matter. The subpoena may cite and quote the rule.

If the organization is a party, there is no need to use a subpoena, and it is not necessary to inform the organization of its duty to designate someone to appear on its behalf. The organization's lawyer presumably knows the rule. In the event the organization selects the proper person to appear but he or she refuses, the organization should notify the lawyer who noticed the deposition.

He or she can then subpoena the individual to appear. An organization is expected to act in good faith and exercise its influence to facilitate the judicial process.

Everyone should make a real effort to be on time for the deposition. It is helpful to have an extra copy of the notice of deposition for the court reporter because he or she needs the caption of the case, the name of the deponent and the names and addresses of the lawyers. The notice contains all of this information. The court reporter records the lawyers' appearances, the presence of each party to the action and the time at which the deposition begins. On occasion, one of the lawyers may have a preliminary statement to make for the record. The deponent is placed under oath by the court reporter or other person authorized by law to administer oaths. Then the lawyer who noticed the deposition proceeds to question the deponent.

The first questions are usually directed at identifying the deponent. The lawyer continues the questioning until the facts with which he or she is concerned are covered. Then the other lawyers have the opportunity to ask questions. Seldom is there any argument or problem among the lawyers about the order in which they are to question the deponent. The deponent's own lawyer is always the last to ask questions, if any. His or her decision whether or not to ask questions usually depends upon the purpose of the deposition. If it is being taken by another party to obtain information (discovery), the deponent's own lawyer probably won't ask any questions except, perhaps, for the purpose of clarification. If, on the other hand, the deposition is taken for the purpose of preserving the deponent's testimony or there is a probability the deposition will be used in lieu of the witness's personal appearance in court, the examination will proceed the same as it would at trial.

The established procedure for taking oral depositions is intended to protect the parties from abuse and to insure the integrity of the proceedings. When a deposition is scheduled, *all* parties must be given notice. Rules 5(a), 30(b) (1). If a party is not served with a notice of the taking of a deposition *and* if his or her lawyer does not appear for the deposition, the deponent's deposition may not be used against that party for any purpose. As to that party, it is as though the deposition had never been taken. On the other hand, he or she is entitled to buy a copy of the deposition transcript and use it at trial for any proper purpose. Rule 32. If the deposition is scheduled at a time that is very inconvenient for a party or his or her lawyer, whether or not the party is the deponent, he or she has the right to move the court for an order setting a different time. Rule 30(b) (3). However, lawyers usually are able to agree on a mutually satisfactory time so that motions seldom are necessary.

If a person's deposition is taken within thirty days after service of the summons and complaint due to circumstances specified in Rule 30(b) (2) but a party was unable to obtain a lawyer to represent him or her at the deposition, the deposition may not be used against the party. Rule 30(b) (2). The Rule requires due diligence on the part of each party to obtain a lawyer, and the burden of persuading the court is on him or her to show diligence. An illustration may be helpful. Suppose that the plaintiff sued three defendants but the summons and complaint were served at two week intervals so that the last one was served four weeks after the first one. Suppose that within five days after the last complaint was served the plaintiff notices the deposition of a nonparty witness to be taken in the plaintiff lawyer's office in just seven days because the deponent is intending to move out of state permanently. The reason for taking the deposition early must be stated in the notice. Rule 30(b) (2). Assume that the first defendant served appeared in the case by service of an answer. The notice for deposition may be served upon him or her by mail, but personal service upon the lawyer would be preferable because of the shortness of time. Rule 5(b). Suppose that the second defendant has retained a lawyer but the lawyer has not yet interposed an answer. If the plaintiff's lawyer can, nevertheless, find out who the lawyer is that is representing the second defendant, service of the notice of deposition should be made upon that lawyer. Rule 5(b). Otherwise, service of the notice must be made upon that defendant by delivering it to him or her personally or by mail. Rule 5(b). Again, personal service is preferable because of the shortness of time. The third defendant has had the summons and complaint for only five days. Suppose he or she promptly delivered them and the notice of deposition to his or her insurance agent who, in turn, delivered them to the liability insurance company's claim department in another town for processing. There is a probability that the third defendant will not have a lawyer by the time the deposition is taken, notwithstanding due diligence on his or her part. Under the circumstances, the deposition could not be used *against* him or her at trial. But suppose through some "miracle" the liability insurer was able to provide a lawyer in time, then the lawyer's appearance at the deposition would result in a waiver of any defect in the notice and service of the notice. Rule 32(a).

Lawyers who have appeared in the case have a right to be present throughout the depositions. A lawyer may interpose objections to questions and object to any irregularity in the proceedings. The objections are recorded on the record for subsequent ruling by a judge if necessary. A party may obtain a ruling on an objection by making a motion at some convenient time after the deposition is concluded, or the party may elect to wait until the deposition is used at trial and then renew the objection. When an objection is made to evidence, whether to a question or an answer or an exhibit, the customary practice is to receive the evidence *subject* to the objection. Rule 30(c). For if the evidence were not received and the court were to determine that the objection was not valid, the witness's deposition would have to be taken again concerning the matters omitted. By receiving the evidence, subject to the objection, the evidence is available. If the evidence is not admissible at trial, the court can order it stricken. The jury will never hear it. Also, there is the possibility that the lawyer who made the objection may find that the answer is actually helpful to his or her theory and may decide to withdraw the objection. Or, he or she may decide that the answer is innocuous and not worth fighting about.

On occasion an evidential point may be so important to the deponent that his or her lawyer determines the deponent should not answer certain questions even if the answers were given "subject to objection." Questions that go to privileged communications and records and to attorneys' work product often fall into that category. In that event, two alternatives are open to the parties and their lawyers. They may elect to terminate the deposition at that point. The party seeking discovery may proceed to make a motion for an order compelling the deponent to answer the questions. Or, the lawyers may elect to proceed with other questions and finish the deposition concerning all other matters. The party seeking discovery may subsequently make a motion to compel answers to the questions which were objected to. If the court sustains the objections, there is no need to resume the deposition. If the objections are overruled, the deponent may be allowed to respond to the specific questions by answering written interrogatories. That would be more convenient and more economical than resuming the deposition. The court is authorized to award costs and attorneys' fees in favor of the party whose position at the deposition was correct. Rule 30(d) and 37(a) (4). The award is discretionary with the court.

The deposition testimony is recorded by stenographic means (shorthand or stenotype) unless the parties stipulate another means or unless the court orders that another method be used. Rules 29 and 30(b) (4). What other means are available? The deposition could be tape recorded, giving an audio record. If the deposition is to be used at trial, the tape would have to be played. Another means of recording a deposition is the use of video equipment. Video has the advantage of permitting the jury to see and hear the witness. The disadvantages are that video is expensive and somewhat cumbersome. It is necessary to have a technician to operate the equipment when the video tape is made and when it is played. It is difficult to edit a video tape presentation. Also, a video recording seems to magnify the problems witnesses have in speaking or articulating their answers. Witnesses tend to be even more nervous. Pauses between questions seem eternal. Discussions between the lawyers may seem more argumentative than intended. A video taped deposition requires experience and good planning to make it work well. If a law firm has its own video equipment, the firm may want its paralegals to obtain expertise operating the equipment. It should be noted that any party has a right to have a stenographic record and transcription made of the deposition even if some other means has been agreed to or ordered by the court. However, the party who wants the stenographic record must pay for it. Rule 30(b) (4). A typed transcript is clearly the most convenient form of record to work with in preparing for trial.

A party (lawyer) may elect to appear at the oral deposition by submitting written questions through the party who has scheduled and who takes the deposition. The written questions and the deponent's answers are incorporated into the reporter's stenographic notes and the deposition transcript. This is a little used, but potentially valuable, procedure. For example, suppose that a third-party plaintiff schedules the deposition of a witness to be taken half-way across the country, but the testimony is going to be relevant only to the third-party claim against the third-party defendant. The plaintiff's lawyer may avoid a substantial expense by not traveling to the deposition. He or she may be able to cover the few matters that are of interest by submitting a few simple questions. Written questions must be served upon the lawyer who noticed the deposition and who will be taking it. The written questions are placed in a sealed envelope which is not opened until the deposition begins. The lawyer gives the written questions to the deposition officer (court reporter) who presents the questions to the witness. The procedure obviously lacks flexibility and there is no opportunity for follow-up questions which may be useful for clarification or to develop a point that suddenly appears to be more important than previously believed.

Who can be excluded from the deposition? In the absence of objection, anyone may observe the deposition proceedings. However, one or more parties (lawyers) may object to the presence of certain persons. The reasons may be tactical or just because the room is crowded. The media does not have a right to be present — at least not yet! Otherwise, the taking of a deposition must be treated similar to a trial because, in fact, the deposition eventually may become part of the trial. The parties may agree to exclude certain persons from observing or agree to allow observers. Rule 29. If an objection is raised to the presence of certain persons, the party wishing to exclude persons from the deposition may move the court for an order sequestering witnesses pursuant to Rule 26(c) (5) and Rule 615. However, a party cannot be sequestered. If a public or private corporation is the party, it is entitled to have a designated representative attend all proceedings with the lawyer. The most common reason for a party to exclude persons from the deposition or trial is to keep one witness from hearing what other witnesses say. There is always the possibility that the testimony of one witness may cause another witness to change his or her testimony in some way.

Each party's lawyer has the right to ask the witness questions. The deponent's lawyer may ask questions even if the deponent is not a party. However, it is very seldom that a nonparty deponent is represented by a lawyer. There is no set limit on the number of questions, nor any time limit. A lawyer may ask additional questions following the interrogation by another lawyer. The questions must not become repetitious or irrelevant. The deposition ends when all of the lawyers have run out of questions to ask.

The deponent has a right to read and verify the deposition transcript before it is used for any purpose. The court reporter is required to submit the transcript to the deponent as it has been prepared. The deponent must read it for the purpose of correcting any errors whether in *substance* or *form*. The deponent is supposed to make a written statement giving reasons or an explanation for each change he or she makes in the transcript. The procedure usually followed is for the deponent and lawyer to review the transcript — not necessarily at the same time. Each notes the corrections and changes he or she thinks are appropriate. Then they discuss the matter. The lawyer then prepares an addendum or errata sheet which must be signed under oath by the deponent. The deponent must review the transcript and make his or her corrections within thirty days from the date it is received. The addendum is then sent to the court reporter who may or may not retype it for incorporation into the transcript. The deponent must sign a certification sheet verifying that he or she has read the deposition and that, as changed, it is correct. A paralegal should be able to provide considerable help in making sure that the client's transcript is correct.

A deponent may waive his right to make changes in the transcript if the parties agree. Rule 30(e). At the end of the deposition he simply states that he elects to waive his right to read and sign the transcript or that he waives his right to make changes in the transcript. The oral waiver is noted by the court reporter. If the deponent waives his right to review the transcript, he necessarily relies upon the accuracy of the stenographer (court reporter). In most cases, lawyers advise their clients to waive the right because usually there is no need to make substantive changes, the changes concerning form (such as spellings) are obvious and do not really affect anyone's legal rights. It is easier to simply rely upon the accuracy of the reporter.

A deponent automatically waives the right to review and correct the transcript if he or she delays signing it for more than thirty days after it is submitted to him or her. Day one of the thirty day period begins on the day after he or she receives the transcript. Rule 6(a). The court reporter is supposed to make a statement in the transcript explaining why the deponent was unable or unwilling to sign it. The transcript may then be used as though it has been signed by the deponent. A party may move the court for an order suppressing the use of the deposition, or any part of it, if there is some irregularity. But the burden rests upon the moving party to convince the court that the deposition is invalid or that its uses would cause prejudice outweighing its value to the court and jury. The motion to suppress must be made promptly after the error or irregularity in the proceedings has been discovered. Rule 32(d) (4).

The court reporter is obligated to promptly file the original copy of the deposition transcript. He or she must place it in a sealed envelope showing the title of the action and the name of the deponent and date of the deposition. If the reporter cannot deliver the transcript to the clerk for filing, he or she must send it by registered or certified mail for filing. Rule 30(f).

The party who noticed the deposition does not have a duty to order a transcript for the court or him or herself or for anyone else. The court reporter may sell copies of the transcript to anyone who wants them — whether or not a party to the action. It is not uncommon for a lawyer to search for and obtain copies of depositions given by an adverse party in other cases. He or she may be able to find out about a party's other litigation by examining the litigation indexes kept by the clerks of courts. The court files are available for public inspection. The clerk also keeps a list of all documents filed in connection with each case, so it is relatively easy to determine whether a person gave a deposition in the case. As part of the discovery procedures it is proper to inquire whether a party has given a deposition in any other case.

The original copy of a deposition transcript must be filed in a sealed envelope. The envelope may not be unsealed without a court order. Upon motion to the court, for good cause shown, it may be possible to review the original. However, an easier way of gaining access to the deposition is to contact one of the lawyers who was or is involved in the other case and review his or her copy of the transcript. Today it is an easy matter to photocopy transcripts. If for some reason, it is not desirable to contact one of the lawyers in the other case, the court reporter who took the deposition may be contacted. It is unlikely that he or she will have a copy of the deposition, but should have his or her stenographic notes. A new copy can be made from his or her notes. Obviously, it is cheaper and more convenient to try to find an existing copy.

Depositions are usually taken near the court where the action is pending, i.e., within the same city or within one hundred miles. But the Rules contemplate that many depositions will be taken out of the home district. If problems arise during the taking of a deposition away from the home district, the parties may apply for help or relief in the federal district court where the deposition is being taken. For example, if it appears to one or more of the parties that the deposition is being taken so as to embarrass or oppress the deponent, either he or she or a party may stop the deposition and move the court in that district for an order terminating the deposition or limiting the scope of the deposition or directing the manner of the taking of the deposition. Rule 26(c). It would be inconvenient for everyone to have to return to the home district court, obtain a ruling and then journey once again to the place where the deposition is being taken. Rule 30(c) appears to reserve to the home district court the obligation of ruling on evidential objections. If the deposition is terminated by order of a court other than the home district, the deposition cannot be resumed until ordered by the home district court, i.e., an order of the court in which the action is pending. The deponent or party has an absolute right to demand that the deposition be suspended until the court rules on his or her objection. The party or lawyer at fault may be required to pay expenses of the motion and deposition. Rules 30(d) and 37(a) (4).

If the deponent must be subpoenaed, the procedure is to prepare, serve and file a notice for taking the deposition. When the clerk of court receives the notice of deposition for filing, the clerk, on request, will issue a subpoena requiring the deponent to appear at the time and place scheduled. The subpoena may direct the deponent to produce specified documents and/or things for inspection and/or copying. Rule 45(b) (d). If the deponent finds the demand for documents or things too burdensome, he or she may serve and file an *objection to inspection*. Of course, the grounds for objecting must be stated. The objection must be delivered before the deposition. If more than ten days notice was given for taking the deposition, the objection must be served within ten days. If an objection is made, the party serving the subpoena has the right to move the court for an order compelling production. Rule 45(d). Otherwise, by electing to proceed with the deposition, he or she must assume the documents will not be available at that time.

A subpoena may be served by the United States marshal or by anyone at least eighteen years of age and not a party to the suit. The subpoena must be *delivered* to the deponent along with a witness fee for one day's attendance (currently $20.00) and a mileage fee (currently 20¢ per mile). Rule 45(c). Ordinarily, subpoenas are not used unless the deponent is a nonparty. So when a motion is noticed for the purpose of compelling the nonparty deponent to produce documents or things for inspection, a copy of the notice and motion must be served upon the deponent. He or she has a right to appear in opposition to the motion. Rule 45(d).

A deponent cannot be required to travel great distances to attend a deposition simply by serving a subpoena upon him or her. The rule is quite protective of people who are subpoenaed. If the deponent is a resident of the district (state), the deponent may be required to travel to any place within the county in which he or she resides or within the county in which he or she is regularly employed. A third alternative is a little more esoteric in its application; a deponent may be subpoenaed to appear for a deposition in the county in which he or she transacts business in person. Rule 45(d). By implication, he or she must regularly transact business in the county selected. If the deponent is not a resident of the district where the deposition is to be taken, the subpoena may direct him to appear for a deposition in the county in which the subpoena was served or within a forty mile radius of the place of service. If those two alternatives are not satisfactory, the party noticing the deposition has to obtain a court order setting another reasonably convenient place. Rule 45(d) (2). If a person fails to comply with a subpoena, he or she may be held in contempt of court and subject to penalties. Rule 45(f). The rules for subpoenaing a deponent for his or her deposition are not necessarily the same as those for subpoenaing a witness to testify at trial.

Almost no one wants to be subpoenaed for a deposition or for a hearing or a trial. Subpoenas tend to scare most people. A subpoena makes a person feel as though the whole weight of the court is upon his shoulders. Consequently, a lawyer runs a significant risk of alienating a witness by "dropping" a subpoena on him or her. It is a very good idea to personally explain to the witness before the subpoena is served why the subpoena procedure is being used. If a better reason cannot be found, tell him or her the Federal Rules of Civil Procedure require it! A witness may be more comfortable about receiving the subpoena if told that, in case of an emergency, he or she can be released from the subpoena. To obtain a release he or she should contact the lawyer who caused the subpoena to be served. The lawyer's name and address are on the subpoena. If the witness has a cogent reason for being unable to appear, he or she may be released and other arrangements made. It is never a good idea, however, to permit the person subpoenaed to believe that if he or she avoids the deposition this time, it will never be taken. In that event, the witness will "move heaven and earth" to find a reason to be unavailable at the time designated. Instead he or she should be counseled against trying to put off the inevitable. Get it over with. Of course, there are times when certain witnesses will purposely make themselves *unavailable* to be served with a subpoena if they have any advance warning. No advance warning should, therefore, be given to them.

When the court reporter files the original copy of the deposition transcript with the clerk of court, he or she must so advise the lawyer who took the deposition — specifying the date of filing. In turn the lawyer who took the deposition has the responsibility for notifying all other parties that the original transcript has been filed. Rule 31(c). This is done by serving a *notice of filing of deposition*. If this procedure is not followed, there is a very real danger that the original transcript may not be on file when the case is reached for trial. Nevertheless, a custom has developed among lawyers in many jurisdictions to stipulate on the record that they "waive notice of filing." If *notice of filing* is waived, the lawyer who took the deposition should still make sure that the original transcript is duly filed. Lawyers frequently waive notice of filing simply to lessen the amount of paper work.

There are two basic purposes for taking depositions: the preservation of testimony for use at trial, and the discovery of information available through the deponent. A deposition transcript may have various incidental uses and values. Once the deposition has been taken, regardless of the original purpose for which it was taken, the transcript may be used at trial in lieu of the witness's live testimony if he or she is *unavailable* for the trial. Or, it may be used to contradict and impeach the deponent at trial. Deposition transcriptions are regularly used to refresh the deponent's memory in preparation for trial. What is more, under certain circumstances a deposition taken in one case may be used in another case. Rule 804(b) (1).

Other witnesses may review the deponent's transcript to ascertain how their own testimony compares with the deponent's testimony. Lawyers study deposition transcriptions for the purpose of preparing their examination of the deponents and their examination of other witnesses who will be testifying on the same subject matter. A lawyer's decision whether or not to ask questions of the deponent and what questions not to ask depends upon how he or she expects the deposition to be used. For example, where one party takes the deposition of an adverse party, the deponent's lawyer seldom asks any questions. Obviously, the purpose of the deposition is to obtain information. There is no reason for the deponent's lawyer to ask the deponent additional questions and further educate the other parties. However, if there is reason to believe that the deponent is not going to be available for the trial, his or her lawyer should conduct a complete examination in the deposition.

Why should a party incur the expense and inconvenience of obtaining an oral deposition of another party or witness? The answer is that there are a number of good reasons for taking oral depositions. An oral deposition is the only means a lawyer has for compelling another party to appear and testify before the trial. The direct contact permits a lawyer to evaluate the deponent's "witness appeal." It is a fact of life that some people are more attractive witnesses than others. Appearance is only one factor, but an important one, affecting persuasiveness. Factors affecting appearance and persuasiveness are discussed in greater detail in Chapter 15. It should be noted here, however, that a good appearance depends to a large degree on adequate preparation. The hallmarks of a good witness are authority and sincerity.

An oral deposition allows a lawyer to obtain the witness's own statements, descriptions, and explanations, for he or she can put the questions directly to the deponent without going through the deponent's lawyer. The deponent must phrase his or her own answers. The strengths and weaknesses of the testimony may become visible in an oral deposition. Uncertainty may be indicated by his or her manner of answering. Or, the manner of answering may indicate dishonesty. A positive, strong attitude may be indicated toward the subject matter or other persons involved in the case.

The procedure for taking an oral deposition is quite informal. The participants must become acquainted by introducing themselves. The lawyer who scheduled the deposition ordinarily provides the court reporter with a copy of the notice of taking deposition. It provides the reporter with most information that he or she must have, including the title of the action, court file number, correct spelling of the deponent's name, the names of the lawyers who are appearing and the identity of their respective clients. The court reporter administers the oath to the deponent.

The lawyer who noticed the deposition may begin by stating some of the basic rules that are helpful to everyone if followed. These rules include advice to the witness not to answer before the question is completed; to ask for the question to be repeated or rephrased if he or she did not hear it or understand it; to speak loudly so that everyone can hear. The deponent's lawyer, if he or she has one, should have given these and additional instructions to their client when preparing for the deposition.

Usually the first questions concern the witness's identity and background: name, address, age, marital status, birthdate, birthplace, employment, social security number, criminal record. The other areas of questioning concern liability and damages. Each question should be singular and clearly stated. Double negatives should be avoided by the lawyers and deponent. Careful attention should be given to the use of words and their meanings. For example, consider the question: "Did you make a lefthand turn?" Answer: "Right." Does *right* mean a "right turn" or "correct"? It is the lawyer's responsibility to make sure that the questions are clearly stated and that the answers are meaningful, i.e., definitive and responsive. A deponent does not have the right to "go off the record." Only if the lawyers agree to an intermission may the court reporter stop recording the dialogue. No lawyer has a right to ask the "last question." A lawyer may ask leading questions and, otherwise, cross examine the deponent if he or she is an *adverse party* or a *hostile witness.* Rule 611(b) (c).

A lawyer does not necessarily object to every question that is "objectionable." That is true whether the testimony is given in a deposition or at trial. Rule 32(d) (3) (B) provides that the right to object at trial to questions or answers which are improper only because of the form of the question is waived unless the objections are made. For example, questions that are multiple in form or leading or argumentative are improper in form. In the absence of any objection during the deposition to such questions, no objection may be made to them when the transcript is used at trial. But Rule 32(d) (3) (A) preserves the right to make objections for the first time at trial if the objections concern the competency of the witness. Rule 601. (Competency of the testimony, Rules 602, 701, 702, 703; relevancy of the testimony, Rules 401-411.)

The deponent's testimony must be competent to be admissible in evidence at trial. In this regard, an expert witness's opinion evidence is not competent if it lacks sufficient **foundation.** The necessary foundation for an expert opinion requires evidence that the witness has special training and experience in the field and that he or she has sufficient knowledge and information about the subject matter in the particular case to have an opinion that will assist the jury to understand the case. Perhaps the largest worry a lawyer has when taking an expert's deposition for use at trial is that he or she may fail to show that the expert's testimony is competent. The court will not rule on the acceptability of the evidence until the trial.

Nonexpert witnesses are permitted to give opinion testimony concerning very few matters. But when they are allowed, there must be a showing that the witness had an opportunity to observe, understand and recall the events about which they are to give opinions. Failure to make the necessary showing makes the evidence subject to objection for lack of foundation. Again, presenting such testimony by deposition is worrisome and risky because of the danger that sufficient foundation will not be laid in the deposition. The lawyer taking the deposition will not have a final ruling on the admissibility of the evidence until trial, and a deficiency in foundation cannot be supplied then. For example, a nonexpert witness is asked for her opinion of the speed of a vehicle that she observed. But suppose she observed the automobile for two seconds or five seconds or fifteen seconds. Was the length of time sufficient to make a valid observation? The value judgment falls within the discretion of the trial judge. The fact is that fair-minded judges may differ on the ruling — hence, the lawyer's concern about the adequacy of foundation. In all probability, two seconds is not enough time in which to form a valid (competent) opinion of speed — especially if the view is head-on. Four or five seconds may be enough time to form an opinion and sufficient foundation then exists. Suppose the deponent is only ten years old, would she qualify to form an opinion of speed? Suppose she is fourteen years old. The decision will utlimately be made by the trial judge. The judge has a great deal of latitude in such matters.

Hypothetical questions are not common in depositions. Many lawyers contend that the ordinary hypothetical question is not a means of discovering facts and an improper means of trying to obtain an adverse party's expert opinions. A determination of whether or not hypothetical questions are proper in discovery proceedings is not a subject for this book. However, a client should be prepared to cope with them.

Hypothetical questions are primarily used as a means of obtaining opinion evidence from a witness who does not have sufficient *personal knowledge* of the facts to qualify to give an opinion. If the facts can be proved through other witnesses, an expert is permitted to assume the truth of those facts and, relying upon them, give an opinion concerning their effect. But when hypothetical questions are used in depositions, the most common purpose is to try to get the witness to establish a legal duty owed by one party to another. This is especially true in tort actions involving professional malpractice, construction accident cases, and product liability cases.

For example, suppose a question exists whether a general contractor on a construction project is responsible for erecting perimeter restraints around the floors of a multi-level building. One of the iron workers fell from the second structural level while the steel beams, columns and flooring were being installed. He was an employee of the steel erection company which had a subcontract for the work. No other subcontractors were on the job. No one but iron workers were allowed on the steel framework while being erected. A lawyer might ask the general contractor's superintendent whether he would take action to prevent an iron worker from engaging in an unsafe act. If so, what action would be taken? What is his authority to act? More specifically, if the superintendent saw an iron worker on the second floor who was repeatedly throwing down objects in a pedestrian area, would the superintendent speak directly with the iron worker to stop him? Could he cause the iron worker to be taken off the job? Does his authority to act come through the contract, subcontract union contract, or customs and practice? The probable answer is none. But if the general contractor's superintendent were to answer that he could stop the iron worker's misconduct, that answer in the deposition may be used to establish a legal duty to protect the iron workers from themselves. The deposition would be used at trial to try to establish that the general contractor has a legal duty to put up perimeter restraints for the steel workers.

The peculiarity of conducting discovery through the use of hypothetical questions is that if the superintendent denies any responsibility for supervising the iron workers, the opposing lawyer will contend that the superintendent's *opinions* lack foundation. But if the superintendent recognizes some authority or responsibility, the superintendent's statement will be used against the general contractor as an *admission* at trial. So the hypothetical question is frequently a "heads I win, tails you lose" effort to get admissions from another party.

The deponent's lawyer may try to avoid the problem by preparing the deponent to cope with the hypothetical by explaining the interrogator's objectives and going through some examples. The deponent's lawyer may try to object to the use of hypotheticals unless and until the examiner establishes that the witness has authority to give opinions and he or she *accepts* the witness's authority. Only then do his or her opinions have relevancy. The interrogator may then create a problem for him or herself. A paralegal should discuss the subject thoroughly with his or her employers to determine how they handle such matters. A paralegal may be assigned the task of preparing some hypothetical questions to be used in a deposition or trial. Beware, it is not an easy assignment. Many lawyers have great difficulty preparing intelligible, useful, and relevant hypothetical questions.

14

Uses of Oral Depositions at Trial

Depositions may be used at trial to present a person's testimony if he or she is unavailable for the trial. Rule 32(a) (3). Any part of a party's deposition may be presented by the adverse party as in the nature of admissions by the deponent. Rule 32(a) (2). A party's admissions in a deposition constitute substantive evidence as well as impeachment evidence when used against the party. The deposition of a nonparty witness who is *available* for trial may be used only for the purpose of impeachment. Rule 32(a) (1). If the deposition is used at trial, that means that a relevant portion or all of it may be read to the court and jury. The transcript is never made available to the jury to read. If the jury were given a copy of the transcript to read, there is a danger that more or less weight would be given to that particular evidence.

The deponent is considered *unavailable* for trial so that his or her deposition may be used in lieu of live testimony if he or she is (a) deceased, (b) more than 100 miles from the place of trial, (c) ill, (d) in prison, or (e) has not responded to a subpoena. Other reasons may be accepted by the court as establishing the witness's unavailability. Rule 32(a) (3).

The transcript may be used regardless of the purpose for which the deposition was originally taken. Therefore, if a lawyer elects not to ask a witness any questions in a discovery deposition, he or she is gambling on the witness's availability at trial. Frequently it is a gamble or risk worth taking.

The deposition may be presented to the jury in various ways. The manner chosen usually depends upon circumstances, the lawyer's preference and economics. The simplest, most economic method is for the lawyer to read the pertinent parts of the deposition to the jury. Depending upon the rules of the particular court, he may stand in front of the jury or sit in the witness stand and read the transcript. An introductory statement may be made telling the jury what he or she is going to do and why the deposition is being read in the absence of the witness. He or she should state when the deposition was taken and who was present when the deposition was taken; then indicate, for the court record, which pages and lines are being read. While he or she is reading, the other lawyers watch their transcripts to make sure that the reading is accurate. When he or she finishes reading those portions selected, the other lawyer may read any other parts which had been omitted — assuming that the testimony complies with the rules of evidence. This method is particularly useful when the deposition testimony is very short. But it tends to be boring and sometimes difficult for the jury to follow. These problems are compounded if the deposition is read rapidly. A deposition should *always* be read slowly, very slowly, with pauses between sentences. Otherwise, the jury has difficulty concentrating and assimilating the evidence. Jurors are supposed to look for conflicts in the evidence. They must have a moment to reflect on what they are hearing.

Another method of presenting deposition testimony is for someone, such as a paralegal, to sit in the witness stand, instead of the deponent, and read the deponent's part. Each lawyer reads his or her own part. Again, everyone should read slowly, using pauses. This method helps establish a dialogue which is easier for the jury to follow. The procedure is less boring. An effective reader can make him or herself appear to be the deponent. That can even be an advantage if the deponent did not make a particularly good appearance. Generally speaking, this procedure is much more desirable than having one person read all parts.

The deposition may be presented to a jury through a video tape which permits the jury to see and hear the witness. If the witness makes a particularly good appearance or the use of exhibits is particularly important to his or her testimony, the video presentation has obvious advantages over the other methods. There are, however, some significant disadvantages and problems using video. Video is expensive. In addition to the cost of the typed transcript, there is the cost of the video tape, video operator and the equipment for taking and presenting the testimony. Taking a video deposition is cumbersome. The room must be large enough to accommodate the lights, camera and other paraphernalia. The replay equipment has to be set up in the courtroom for the presentation of the evidence and arranged so that the judge, jury and lawyers are able to see the video picture. If an objection is made, the whole production has to be stopped until the court can rule on it. Usually a video picture is only of the deponent and his or her exhibits. After a while, a video picture of one person tends to become tedious. The witness may become quite uncomfortable being on camera for a long time. It is like having someone stare at you. Presentation of testimony by video certainly has its limitations and problems. Notwithstanding these problems, the trend is toward more and more use of video testimony.

If a witness makes statements in the deposition which are contrary to his or her sworn testimony at trial, the inconsistency may be shown for the purpose of impeachment. The jury is instructed at the end of a trial to consider any impeachment when evaluating a witness's credibility. Impeachment merely affects the weight or credibility of the testimony of nonparties. However, impeachment evidence of a party may be considered as substantive evidence which supports a verdict. The out of court statements by a nonparty cannot be considered as substantive evidence because the out of court statements are not always under oath or subject to cross-examination, and the jury was not able to hear and observe the person who made the alleged inconsistent statement. The jury's verdict should be based on the sworn testimony that they hear in court. Naturally, there are some exceptions to this rule, but we need not examine them here. Impeachment does not cause the witness to be disqualified from testifying or even subject him or her to penalties. Of course, if a witness is guilty of perjury, that would be basis for finding the witness in contempt of court and criminal charges could be made against him or her.

It is relatively easy for lawyers to use depositions, which are on file with the court, to show inconsistencies between the deposition testimony and the testimony at trial. For example, suppose that in a personal injury action the plaintiff testified at trial that her various aches and pains began immediately after the accident, and such testimony appears to be at variance with her deposition testimony in which she admitted that her low back discomfort did not begin until two months after the accident in question. Of course, a delay in the onset of pain by two months suggests that the accident did not cause the problem. The impeachment could be accomplished in the following manner on cross-examination:

Q. You will recall that on May 10, 1980, you appeared, with your attorney, at my office for your deposition?

A. Yes.

Q. At that time, you testified concerning your accident and the injuries you sustained?

A. Yes.

Q. Before testifying you took an oath to tell the truth, the whole truth, just as you did before testifying here in court?

A. Yes.

Q. Mrs. (witness), you will recall that during your deposition you were asked the following questions, and you gave the following answers.

A. Well, I don't know!

Q. Please listen. Beginning at page 24, line 10, the following testimony was given:

Q. Right after the collision occurred and the cars came to rest, how did you feel?

A. Shook up — kind of sick.

Q. Well, did you have any specific aches or pain?

A. Yes. My neck began hurting and I had a headache.

Q. Where was your headache located?

A. In the back of my head.

Q. When did the headache begin?

A. Right away.

Q. Did you have any other pains while at the accident scene?

A. No.

Q. Are you claiming any other injuries to your person besides your head and neck?

A. Yes.

Q. What?

A. My back hurts.

Q. Where does your back hurt?

A. In the lower part, here. (indicating)

Q. When did that begin to bother you?

A. It came on kind of gradual.

Q. Well, when did you first become aware of the problem; what were you doing?

A. I'm not too sure.

Q. So you can't say whether it was two months, six months or any particular time after the accident?

A. I know it wasn't six months — maybe two months.

Q. That's your best recollection?

A. Yes.

Q. Do you remember what you were doing when you first noticed that your low back was uncomfortable?

A. No.

Q. Now, just where in the low back do you have this pain?

A. Here. (indicating)

Q. Let the record show that the witness has pointed to an area just below the waistline, directly over the spine. Have I accurately described the location to which you were pointing?

A. Yes.

(End of Deposition)

Q. Now, that was your testimony when your deposition was taken, wasn't it?

A. Yes.

Q. And that was the truth — your testimony under oath?

A. Yes, but after the deposition I talked with my husband about it, and he said I complained about my back hurting the same day of the accident.

Attorney: Your Honor, I move that the witness's last answer be stricken as not responsive and on the grounds that it is hearsay.

Court: The last answer is stricken and the jury is instructed to disregard it.

Q. Certainly your memory about the accident and related events would have been better when your deposition was taken than now.

A. I don't know.

Q. You do not have any current recollection now as to when your back started hurting, do you? That is of your own memory.

A. Well, we talked about it and I'm just trying to remember — it's been so long, and I've seen so many doctors.

Attorney: I move that the last answer be stricken as not responsive.

Court: The last answer is stricken and the jury is instructed to disregard it.

It is hard to believe that the witness has lied, i.e., committed perjury in either her deposition or her court testimony. However, she was inconsistent; both answers could not be correct. She was quite satisfied to yield her recollection to that of her husband. But she cannot testify as to his recollection, because that is hearsay testimony. Perhaps her husband will be allowed to testify concerning his *observations* of her injuries, and such testimony would help to rehabilitate the witness. The jury will be instructed that impeachment of a witness or impeachment of the witness's testimony is a factor which they may and should consider when weighing the believability of the testimony.

It should be noted that a witness may be impeached in other ways, too. Anytime a witness has made a statement or conducted him or herself out of court in some manner inconsistent with testimony in court, the inconsistency may be shown for the purpose of impeachment. If, for example, a witness testifies that he saw that the traffic light was green for the plaintiff, another witness can testify that she heard the first witness state that he was not looking at the light at or before the collision. The impeaching witness must come to court and testify under oath as to what she heard. Whereas, a witness can be impeached by his or her deposition by simply reading the pertinent portions from the transcript. The safeguards against abuse are in the certification by the court reporter, the witness's right to read the transcript and verify its accuracy, and the fact that the original copy is on file with the clerk of court. As part of trial preparation, an attorney (paralegal) should make sure all deposition transcripts have been properly filed.

A witness may be impeached by any recorded statement he made or gave if the contents of the statement differ from his testimony in court. The necessary foundation for using a recorded statement to impeach a witness is more difficult than using a deposition transcript. See Rule 613. If the statement is in writing and signed by the witness, the cross-examination may be similar to the following:

Q. Do you recall that on (date) you were interviewed by a Ms. (paralegal) about this accident?

A. No. Well, maybe. I'm not sure. I've talked to so many people and it has been a long time. (Counsel has statement marked as Defendant's Exhibit #1 for identification.)

Q. I am now showing you a document marked as Defendant's Exhibit #1. Can you identify it?

A. No.

Q. Showing you the bottom of the second page, is that your signature?

A. It appears to be.

Q. Do you now recall that on the date shown here (date) you were interviewed at your home concerning this accident?

A. Could be.

Q. At that time, you were asked about your version of the accident as you saw it.

A. Perhaps.

Q. Please take the Exhibit now and read it to yourself.
(Witness examines the Exhibit)
A. Yes, I seem to recall it.
Q. This is your signature?
A. Yes.
Counsel: I offer Defendant's Exhibit #1 into evidence.
Court: For what purpose, Counsel? I don't see the connection yet.
Counsel: The Exhibit is being offered for impeachment purposes.
[At this point plaintiff's counsel would probably demand to see the statement as provided in Rule 613.]
Court to Witness: Is that your signature and your statement?
A. Yes.
Court to Plaintiff's Counsel: Is there any objection?
Counsel: Yes, there has been no foundation for the Exhibit, and it is not impeaching.
Court: Objections overruled. Exhibit received.
[Note that the contents of the document cannot be referred to until after the Exhibit is received into evidence.]
Q. You stated at the time you gave this statement that you did not see the traffic light before the collision.
A. I don't specifically remember saying that.
Q. Please read with me, now referring to Defendant's Exhibit #1: "I was standing at the southwest corner waiting for a bus which would be coming from the west. I was looking westerly when I heard the collision behind me. I turned around right away. The southbound car (white convertible) was stopped in the middle of the intersection. The eastbound car (Ford) slid sideways and came to rest at the northwest corner of the intersection. It was turned almost 180° around. I could see the driver of the Ford was slouched over. As soon as I was sure that no other cars were coming, I ran over to the Ford."
Q. Now, that is what your signed statement said, isn't it?
A. That's what it says.
Q. And when you gave that statement you were trying to be truthful — to give a truthful account of what you observed?
A. Yes.
Q. And to be truthful about what you didn't observe?
A. But the statement doesn't say everything I saw . . .
Q. When you signed it you considered it to be accurate, didn't you?
A. Yes.
Q. If an important point had been left out of the statement, you would have brought that to the attention of Ms. (paralegal) when she took the statement, wouldn't you?
A. Well, I didn't know what she thought was important.
Q. We're talking about what you think is important.
A. (No response)
Q. No further questions.

Re-direct Examination

Q. Is this written statement Defendant's Exhibit #1, in your handwriting?

A. No.

Q. But the signature is yours?

A. Yes.

Q. Did you choose the wording used in this statement?

A. No.

Q. Did you choose the things to be said or included in the statement?

A. No.

Q. Were you told when this statement was being written down that you would be asked to sign it?

A. No.

Q. Were you given a copy of the statement?

A. No.

Q. Did you read it before signing it?

A. Well, I just sort of glanced over it, and it looked O.K.; so I signed it. I think she told me I had to.

Q. Did you, in fact, look at the traffic light?

A. Yes, I did.

Q. What color was it?

Counsel Objection: The question is objected to for lack of foundation — there is no showing of just when the observation was made; and the witness has disqualified himself.

Court: Perhaps a little more foundation should be laid.

Councel: Yes, I was just about to do that, Your Honor.

Q. You say you did take notice of the traffic signal light?

A. Yes, sir.

Q. Just when did you make this observation of the light?

A. Soon as I heard the crash and turned around — when I looked to see if any other cars were coming; that's when I saw that the light was green for east west traffic.

Q. No further questions. Thank you.

Re-cross Examination

Q. Let's see now. On direct examination this morning, you said that you saw the light before the crash, but now you say you saw it after the crash. Is that right?

A. I guess the statement refreshed my memory.

Q. Are you familiar with the intersection? Do you catch a bus there every day?

A. No. I go that way to see my sister sometimes.

Q. Where is the traffic light located — the one you observed after the collision?

A. There is only one. It sort of hangs on a wire over the center. I saw the light that faces west, and it was definitely green.

Q. But you said that you saw the Ford sliding sideways and turning around and coming to rest at the northwest corner.

A. Yes.

Q. You saw all that, and then you saw the driver of the Ford slump over?

A. Yes.

Q. And you felt that you should get over to help him?

A. Yes.

Q. You realized that there might be an emergency right there in front of you?

A. I don't know if I . . . well, yea, sort of.

Q. As soon as you could see that no cars were coming, you dashed right over to the Ford?

A. Yes.

Q. Isn't it true that from the place of the bus stop where you were standing, you could not see the color of the light?

A. I don't know. I saw the light and it was green.

Q. But after hearing the crash, seeing the Ford slide to a stop and looking for other traffic in the area — about five or six seconds lapsed until you could have looked at the light.

A. I didn't time it. You don't have a stopwatch.

Q. It would have been at least five seconds, wouldn't it?

A. Four, maybe five. I suppose, something like that.

Q. You didn't tell Ms. (paralegal) when she interviewed you on (date) when this statement was given, that you saw the light, now did you?

A. No.

Q. Why not?

A. She didn't ask.

Q. And you didn't think she was interested or needed that information from you?

A. If she'd asked, I would have told her. I talked to a lot of people. And I was getting kind of tired of it all.

Q. You didn't tell the investigating police, either, that you saw the light, did you?

Counsel: Objection. That's irrelevant and calls for hearsay.

Court: Overruled.

Q. You may answer. Did you tell the police that you saw the light?

A. They were too busy. I gave them my name.

Q. I have no further questions of this witness.

Re-cross Examination.

Q. There is no doubt in your mind about it, is there? You did see the light?

Counsel: The question is objected to on the ground that it is repetitious, leading, and suggestive.

Court: Sustained.

Q. Thank you, Mr. (Witness). That will be all for now. You are excused.

The signed statement has almost the same value and effect for impeachment purposes as a deposition. But the statement is more difficult to use, because the statement must be identified and the witness must acknowledge that it is his or her statement. If, in the above example, the witness continued to deny that the signature was his, the person who took the statement would have to be called as a witness to identify the statement and relate the circumstances under which the statement was given by the witness. Then it becomes the paralegal's word against the word of the witness. If the statement had been secured by the attorney who was examining the witness, a further problem would be introduced. An attorney is forbidden by ethics to testify in a case which he or she is trying. It would be very difficult for him or her to put the statement into evidence if the witness remained adamant that he did not sign the statement.

15

Preparation of
Client for a Deposition

Paralegals can have a significant role in preparing a client for his or her oral deposition. While the attorney must assume ultimate responsibility for the client's preparation, much of the actual work can be done by a paralegal who understands the case, objectives, and procedures. Paralegals should not be disappointed if they are not assigned that responsibility until they have had considerable experience with the procedure through observation and discussions with the lawyers with whom they work. A client's deposition is an extremely important facet of civil litigation, with proper preparation being the key to its success.

There is no one method, procedure, or formula for preparing a client for a deposition. The various phases of preparation may be changed in their order and one or more phases omitted depending upon the particular case. However, unless there is a particular reason for changing, the following method and steps are usually beneficial. The client must be able to see and understand the big picture, so he or she can appreciate how and where his or her testimony fits into the case as a whole. Otherwise, there may not be full appreciation of the importance and effect of his or her testimony. The client will be much more comfortable throughout the deposition if he or she knows what is happening and why. For most of us, the unknown causes fear and nervousness. The more apprehensive or nervous the witness is, the more likely he or she is to make mistakes. It is important to preview the procedure to help minimize the likelihood of mistakes.

To begin with, the client should be informed about the present status of the case. He or she should be told how soon the case may reach trial and what information has been obtained through the ongoing investigation and discovery procedures. A reminder should be given as to what the legal issues are — described in terms that a layman can understand. He or she should be told how the fact issues relate to the legal issues. Particular care should be used to identify those facts which are undisputed and those facts which are contested. The theory of the claim or defense should be reviewed and explained. Finally, the mechanics of the deposition should be fully described, i.e., the oath, order of questioning, role of the court reporter, and the right to read the transcript.

An introduction in this manner enables a client to understand where his or her testimony fits, why certain questions will be put forth and the probable effect of his or her answers on the outcome of the case. The descriptions and explanations should come in the form of a dialogue with the client — not a lecture. Understanding and retention will be much better if he or she actively participates.

If the lawyer is going to ask a client certain questions, those questions and the answers should be previewed and discussed. More often than not the deponent's lawyer elects not to ask any questions in a *discovery* deposition. After all, why help the opposition? On occasion, however, clarifying questions may be helpful or even necessary to protect the deponent. A witness may think he said one thing, but it came out quite different. The point should be clarified before the deposition is concluded even if leading questions are necessary.

A lawyer cannot tell a client *what* to say, other than to tell the truth; but he or she can be very helpful by advising a client *how* to say it. There are certain guidelines to testifying in a deposition that are very helpful if not imperative for a witness to know and follow. The guidelines help a witness to avoid mistakes, facilitate the proceedings, and add authority and persuasiveness to his or her testimony. The guidelines are mostly common sense, but also take into consideration some of the peculiarities of the rules of evidence and court procedures.

Listen carefully to each question.   A witness should feel certain that he or she understands the question before giving an answer. The burden is on the lawyer to make each question clear and understandable. If the witness does not understand a question, it is not his or her fault or problem. The lawyer must repeat or rephrase the question if asked to do so. Knowing this makes a witness feel more self-assured and adequate when admitting that he or she did not hear or understand a question.

The witness should be encouraged to reflect on each question for a moment and silently phrase an answer before responding aloud. This procedure will help to avoid interruptions of the question. All too often witnesses are prone to answering before the question is completed. Not only are they in danger of making mistakes, but they cause the court reporter to have fits. It is difficult enough for the reporter to make shorthand notes of one person's testimony — but nearly impossible to record two people speaking at the same time. The usual consequence is that the reporter has to stop everyone, and the question has to be repeated. Obviously, the "too quick" answer serves only to complicate and delay the proceedings.

If the witness takes a moment to reflect on the question and to think through the answer, his or her lawyer will have the opportunity to interpose objections to improper questions. If the deponent answers too quickly he or she loses the protection provided by the rules of evidence. The witness should even be cautioned against permitting the lawyers to hurry him or her by showing impatience or irritation. Lawyers know that a thoughtful witness is less likely to be tripped up than one who rushes answers.

A witness can hardly be too thoughtful or deliberate when testifying in a deposition. Testimony at trial presents a little different situation. There, *excessive* hesitancy or delay may be interpreted, rightly or wrongly, as uncertainty, or a lack of authority or even a lack of candor. The correct pace may easily be determined and established by a little practicing in a mock examination before the trial begins. The pauses and little delays do not show up in deposition testimony — unless a video system is used.

Do not guess. If a witness does not know the answer to a question put to him or her, this should be admitted. Generally speaking, a wrong guess will do much more harm than a good guess can help. When a witness is merely guessing, it is usually evident, and if members of a jury conclude that the witness is prone to guessing, they will be inclined to discount the witness's testimony as a whole. His or her authority is severely diminished. What is even worse, a wrong guess may be interpreted as a lack of candor.

A witness does not create any trouble by admitting that he or she does not know the answer to a question. Indeed, he or she has a duty to admit a lack of knowledge or information. However, the rule against guessing does not mean that a witness should refrain from giving estimates or judgments or opinions or best recollections where properly called for. By way of example, a witness may not *know* the exact width of a street. Nevertheless, he may be able to give a reasonable estimate based upon familiarity with the street. The law usually does not require exactitude. Nor does the law require perfect recall. The law does require the witness to believe that his or her memory and judgment are reasonably accurate. To express some degree of uncertainty without guessing, witnesses often use expressions such as: "to the best of my memory," "as I recall," "I believe," or "I'm not certain, but . . . ." Whenever a witness is constrained to qualify an answer in this manner, he or she loses some authority and persuasiveness. These expressions should be avoided — or used only when necessary.

Once a witness realizes that he or she does not *have* to guess, and, consequently, does not have to answer every question, he or she may tend to believe that "not knowing" is an easy way out. This is especially true of nonparty witnesses. The deponents should be cautioned against evasion of their responsibility to the parties, court and community by claiming an imperfect memory. They should do the very best they can to remember and to be accurate.

A witness should be told that if he or she cannot remember a certain fact at the time, but believes the fact or information can be obtained within a few days, he or she should so indicate. In this way the door is kept open. Perhaps the information is available in records. By agreeing to try to obtain the requested information, he or she keeps from being discredited by mysteriously producing the information at trial.

Tell the truth.   Testimony is given under oath. A witness who testifies falsely is subject to the criminal penalties of perjury — a felony. Jurors are instructed that if they conclude that a witness has testified falsely, they may disregard everything a witness has said. False testimony by a witness is an abuse of the judicial process.

Very few people are capable and effective liars. A witness who takes the stand intending to lie looks anxious and uneasy or overcompensates in some other ways. He believes it can be done, but once on the stand and facing the jury, he is not so sure. If he took the stand in good faith but suddenly finds himself having lied, there is a sudden change in his demeanor. This seems to be human nature. It is one of the reasons why the adversary system for examining witnesses has proven to be valuable for getting at the truth. There is no surer way to lose a case than for a party to be caught in a lie. Telling the truth means testifying accurately — without exaggeration or minimization. A witness must not fabricate or twist the facts. His or her opinions must comport with intellectual honesty.

The nature of the adversary system assumes that each party will give him or herself the benefit of any actual, honest doubt concerning a disputed matter. For example, if a motorist honestly believes he was not exceeding a thirty mile per hour speed limit, but did not look at the speedometer to determine his actual speed, he should testify to what he believes. Further, he should be prepared to deny driving any faster than what he believes he was doing. He must candidly admit that his opinion of his speed is based upon his driving experience and not upon looking at the speedometer. But he should *refuse* to speculate that it is possible he was going faster than what he truly believes the speed was.

On occasion, a witness indicates a desire for the lawyer to tell him or her what to say. The witness must be told firmly that he or she is to tell the truth and nothing more, nothing less.

Short answers are best.   Short answers are desirable during the direct examination and mandatory during the crossexamination. Lawyers have the responsibility to bring out pertinent information through their questions. It is not the witness's duty to write the script.

A witness should strive to make answers responsive, direct and specific. Short answers help to make the witness appear polite, authoritative and nonargumentative. In other words, short answers usually aid in making the testimony more persuasive. Of course, there are times when a short answer cannot be used. But if there is a choice, the witness should opt for the short answer. When a narrative explanation is expressly called for, it must be given.

This guideline — to keep answers short — helps to reduce the likelihood that a witness will utter some statement which violates the rules of evidence or, worse, cause a mistrial. Long answers lead to exaggeration and misstatements.

Various factors increase the likelihood of an excessively long answer. These include when the witness (1) does not understand the question; (2) wants to explain how he or she happens to know the answer or remembers the facts; or (3) simply wants to emphasize his or her own importance. If an explanation or justification is truly called for, the lawyers will bring it out through proper questions, and they will keep the explanation within the framework of the rules of evidence.

Do not be suspicious or defensive.   A witness should have a positive attitude toward his or her role in a deposition or trial. If a party, he or she must appreciate the importance of the testimony. If an independent witness, he or she should recognize the value and importance of his or her contribution to the judicial system and the community. He or she should not presume that the lawyers will be abusive or ask trick questions. An attitude of hostility should not be assumed toward the side that did not call him or her. Any apparent hostility tends to mitigate against *his or her* objectivity and, therefore, against his or her persuasiveness. He or she will be helped by responding to *all* lawyers in the same direct, respectful manner.

Answer out loud.   We frequently communicate by signs and gestures, such as a nod of the head. But the court reporter may not see the gesture and is not required to record it. So each answer must be stated orally and loud enough for everyone in the room to hear.

Be sincere.   Sincerity is the hallmark of an effective witness. Second to sincerity is authority. A lawsuit is a serious matter for all concerned. Seldom, if ever, is there occasion for wise cracks or jokes. If there is an opportunity for the witness to poke fun at another person, the temptation should be resisted — even if he or she sees it as a means of "putting a lawyer in his place." As often as not, someone on the jury will be offended. The joke may well come back to the originator. If a duel of sharp-tongued wit develops, the forum favors the lawyer, because only he or she is authorized to initiate questions. Of course, a witness may ask questions for clarification.

Try not to show anger or impatience.   A witness must consciously strive to avoid losing his or her temper. A display of temper usually reflects adversely on the witness though the anger may be perfectly justified. He or she may even feel like the "star of the show" because of his or her self-righteous indignation. However, the risk of offending the court and jury is too great. A witness who loses his or her temper tends to lose perspective;

forgetting the big picture. He or she is much more subject to making avoidable errors in testimony. Anger is likely to cause him or her to forget the other guidelines for testifying. Once a feeling of anger takes over, it is likely to grow and grow. It usually does not go away spontaneously. A lawyer may try to obtain a court recess if he or she sees that the opponent has the witness angry and not thinking clearly. But it is not easy to get a recess for the benefit of a party who is undergoing a cross-examination. A witness should try to respond to each lawyer the same way, in a polite, courteous manner.

Sit erect or lean forward.   A witness's physical posture may affect his or her testimony and will certainly affect appearance. Obviously the witness looks best if sitting erect, but should lean forward a little, too. This helps him or her to appear interested and unafraid. This posture helps the witness to pay attention to the proceedings. It also adds to his or her appearance of authority. The witness should try to look at the lawyer who is asking the questions. At trial a witness should look at the jury about half the time. A conscious effort should be made to avoid looking at the floor or ceiling or out the window. A witness should approach the witness stand with the attitude that the jury has empathy for him or her and will appreciate his or her version of the matter. In this way, he or she may be able to avoid appearing defensive, which always detracts from the witness and the testimony.

Opinion evidence must be reasonable.   As a general rule, lay witnesses are not permitted to give opinions about facts — just the facts. But there are many conditions, situations and "facts" that, in ordinary human experience, can only be described as opinions. Courts recognize this. Some examples may be helpful. Witnesses seldom determine the speed of a motor vehicle in an accident by seeing the speedometer or obtaining a radar reading or clocking the vehicle. A witness who is reasonably familiar with motor vehicles and who observed the vehicle long enough to form an opinion of its speed in miles per hour is allowed to state an opinion or estimate of the automobile's speed in miles per hour. The witness is giving an estimate concerning factual data. However, a witness is not permitted to state a *conclusion* to the effect that it was going "fast" or "slow." A witness is allowed to give an opinion of a distance in some unit of measurement: feet, yards, miles, etc. Again, he or she may not state a *conclusion* that it was "close" or "far."

When a witness describes a street as "slippery" or the room as "fairly dark" or the rainfall as "heavy" or the street light as "dim", or an embankment as "steep" or elevator doors as "fast", he or she is giving an opinion. But how else can an ordinary person describe such conditions? There is no other practical way.

If opinion evidence is admissible, the witness should be sure that his or her opinion is reasonable in light of his or her own experience and in the experience of most people. His or her opinion should be tested against physical facts. The most common area of opinion evidence involves time and distance estimates. Remember, a witness must not guess. A witness may have the opportunity to revisit the accident scene to make comparison

observations to help him or her make an accurate estimate about a speed or
distance. If a moving object is involved, the correlation between time and
distance should be considered.

Estimating Speed

Mph	=	Feet per second
5		7
10		15
20		29
30		44
40		59
50		73
60		88

When a witness is questioned about a speed, distance, or time factor, the
witness should first determine whether or not he or she has a valid estimate
or judgment. If so, then he or she must decide whether or not to express an
opinion in terms of a range or a precise measurement. For example, a witness
could estimate skidmarks to be 40 to 50 feet in length, or 45 feet in length.
Either approach is legitimate and reasonable. Tactics or strategy may
determine, however, that one approach is preferable to the other in the
particular case. Next, the witness must be prepared to stay with the estimate
if challenged. The challenge usually begins by forcing him to "admit" that the
figure given is only an estimate — not a measured quantity. Next, the lawyer
may ask the witness to admit that it is *possible* that the estimate could be off
by one, two or three miles per hour and later suggest it could be off by even
five miles per hour (slower or faster). Again, the cross-examiner will resort to
the phrase: "Isn't it possible?" If the estimate could vary by five miles per hour
more or less, that creates a spread of 10 miles per hour. Pretty soon, it appears
that the estimate is of no value at all. Not only is the estimate likely to be
rejected as unreliable, but the witness's authority — if not credibility — has
been impaired. The solution is for the witness to refuse to speculate about a
possibility that the estimate could be slightly off. When asked if it is possible
that he was traveling one mile per hour slower or faster than estimated, the
witness should respond that his or her best estimate is as previously stated,
and he will not speculate about other possibilities. Even if the questioner
persists, the witness should continue in his refusal to go beyond the original
estimate. He thereby avoids weakening his testimony. The same principle
applies to almost any type of estimate involving measurements.

Memory and observations must comport with physical laws. Estimates and memory should be tested against natural law and physical or
scientific fact. For example, if a witness has the impression that a motor
vehicle collision occurred at 30 miles per hour, but the property damage is
slight, the witness's observation or memory is in error. The lawyer must
gently show the witness that his present recollection is not possible. Then

they must try to determine what the facts are and refresh his recollection. If, however, the witness's recollection cannot be refreshed; if, in fact, he has no valid estimate or recollection, he must not try to fabricate evidence.

Do not overemphasize honesty.   A witness should avoid using expressions such as "to be honest," "to tell the truth," "if I remember right," "to the best of my recollection," or "it seems to me." The expressions weaken the witness's authority and credibility. Testimony should be given without equivocation and without qualification unless absolutely necessary.

Avoid hypothetical questions.   Hypothetical questions relate to fact situations that are merely assumed to be true for the purpose of having the witness render an opinion or otherwise comment on the assumed facts. The facts used in the hypothetical question must be supplied by other testimony or exhibits. Hypothetical questions have a legitimate and important role in trials. However, it is questionable whether hypothetical questions may be properly used in discovery depositions. I advise my clients that we must answer questions about the facts of this case. He or she must tell what was done and what was not done. He or she must tell what he knows. A witness must admit a lack of knowledge when he or she really does not know. But I do not want speculations about what he or she would do or not do in hypothetical situations. The basic reason for this is that it is nearly impossible to prepare accurate responses for all the conceivable hypothetical situations that may be presented. Secondly, many hypothetical questions that are used to *test* a witness's knowledge, judgment or expertise are irrelevant to the case at hand. On occasion a question is phrased as a hypothetical but is actually based upon the facts of the present case. In that circumstance the witness should be prepared to answer.

A paralegal should not have to worry about helping and protecting the client from hypothetical questions in the deposition. That is the lawyer's job. But it is important to be aware of the problem and recognize the dangers. As an advocate, I would have to admit that, unless my opponent objects to such inquiry, I find that this type of questioning can be very productive in a discovery deposition.

Follow instructions.   If an objection is made, the witness should remain silent until the interrogator asks a new question or rephrases the question or until the witness's lawyer tells him or her that the question may be answered notwithstanding the objection. Whenever a difference of opinion occurs between the lawyers about the propriety of a question, they must decide what to do. The witness has no responsibility to do anything until directions are received from his or her lawyer. If the lawyer remains firm, the interrogator may terminate the deposition or go on to another line of questioning.

The witness's lawyer might object to a question but immediately follow up with a direction to the witness that the question may be answered "if he understands it." The usual purpose of such an objection and instruction is to warn the witness that the question is dangerous and possibly confusing. He or she should be particularly careful.

A deponent may elect to read the deposition transcript to make corrections in form and in substance. More often than not the deponent is advised to waive the right to review and sign the transcript. However, if either the deponent *or* lawyer thinks that the transcript should be reviewed, the right to review should not be waived. The witness should be told during the preparation about their right to read the transcript before it is certified and filed. If the lawyer decides at the end of the deposition that it is alright to waive the right to review, he or she will ask the deponent whether they wish to waive the right. That is a signal to the witness that the lawyer believes a waiver is acceptable. The witness may still indicate that he or she wants to review it. If the lawyer wants the witness to review the transcript, he or she will tell the reporter to make the transcript available for review.

A minimum of two hours should be allowed for deposition preparation with the client. The lawyer or paralegal should be fully prepared on the file before meeting the client or witness. After the witness has been instructed in the guidelines for testifying, the next step is to test him or her by interrogation as though the deposition were being taken. This gives the witness an opportunity to use the guidelines and practice phrasing answers. Either may stop the mock interrogation to discuss problems and how they are to be resolved.

16

Medical Examinations and Records

Lawsuits that involve a party's physical, mental or blood condition raise unique problems and receive special treatment by the rules of civil procedure. Most such cases are personal injury cases in which the plaintiff seeks compensation for injuries he or she claims were caused by the defendant. The problems arise from the fact that the subject matter of the claim is peculiarly under the plaintiff's control (his or her own mind and body). The subject matter may be very personal. Such cases always involve the plaintiff's medical privilege. These problems may exist even in noninjury cases where a party's medical condition is in controversy, including actions to determine paternity, actions to determine mental competency, actions to determine whether the plaintiff has a right to disability insurance benefits where either the cause of disability or the extent of disability is in issue. Medical questions may be raised in an action by or against an employee where the issue is whether or not he is physically or mentally able to perform the work required by his job. The point is that the need for medical information is not limited to personal injury cases. Our discussion, however, is concerned primarily with injury cases, because they are easy to relate to.

Only a party to the action can be required to submit to an independent medical examination.

A personal injury claim usually involves a number of separate but related medical questions. If there was an accident, what injuries were caused by the accident? What pain and suffering was caused by the injuries and for how long? What other symptoms and complaints are attributable to the injuries? What impairments or disabilities were caused by the injuries and for how long? What medical treatment was reasonably necessary for the injuries and for how long? Did the plaintiff use reasonable care in obtaining proper medical treatment? To answer these questions, it is necessary to know something about the plaintiff's pre-accident condition and medical history, the plaintiff's version of the effect of the accident on him or her, the plaintiff's symptomology, ability to function, the results of medical tests, response to treatment, etc. The plaintiff's communications with his or her own physicians are privileged. So are the medical and hospital records. So how is the defendant to evaluate the claim and prepare to defend against it? Rule 35 provides the answers.

Most states now provide that if the plaintiff commences an action to recover money damages for personal injuries, he or she thereby waives medical privilege. The extent of the waiver may vary from a total waiver to only a waiver of the privileged status of medical reports and/or records. The federal courts apply state law concerning medical privilege and its waiver. Therefore, the application of Rule 35 and its procedure may vary depending upon state law.

A physician who undertakes to provide medical care to an injury victim needs to have the patient's complete confidence. The physician is not part of the adversary system. Presumably, information is obtained from the patient for the purpose of providing appropriate treatment. A physician may be aware of the possibilities of litigation but is not charged with any responsibility for establishing the patient's claim. Indeed, the rules of evidence presume that the patient is candid with his or her physician and goes for medical treatment — not for the purpose of fabricating a claim. The physician is not expected to cross-examine the patient concerning the history or symptoms. A physician is expected only to obtain sufficient information to make an accurate diagnosis and to prescribe the proper treatment.

There are a number of reasons why the defendant's lawyer may feel that the treating physician's evaluation of the patient is inadequate or even in error. The medical or accident history may be erroneous or incomplete. The findings may be inconsistent with the symptoms. Sometimes the defendant's lawyer has more detailed information about the plaintiff's history and symptoms than the treating physician has. The symptoms may vary from time to time in an inexplicable way which creates doubt about their validity. Or, the treating physician may not have sufficient expertise in the various areas which must be considered. On rare occasion, collaboration may be suspected. As part of the checks and balances in the adversary nature of civil litigation, Rule 35 gives the defendant a right to have one or more independent medical examinations by qualified physicians of his or her choice.

An extreme, but true, case may serve as an example of how an independent medical examination works. The plaintiff was a forty-eight year old housewife who stopped her automobile in response to a traffic light. The defendant's semi-truck bumped the rear of her car. She told her treating physician that her car was struck forcefully and she was thrown about. She felt dazed and soon her neck, left arm and shoulder began to hurt. His diagnosis was that she suffered a musculoligamentous strain of the neck and shoulders. He undertook to treat her with medications and physical therapy for several years. At one point, the treating physician called in a psychiatrist for consultation who determined that the plaintiff was neurotic and a hypochondriac. These psychiatric problems were deep-seated and had existed long before the automobile accident. The defendant arranged for a Rule 35 medical examination by an orthopedic surgeon. The surgeon concluded that there was no objective evidence of injury or disability, but based upon the accident and medical history she gave and the continued symptom of pain in the neck and left shoulder, he concluded that she had a musculoligamentous strain without any apparent disability of the shoulder or neck. He had to assume the correctness of her subjective symptoms and medical history. After the defendant's physician testified in accordance with his report, the defendant's attorney asked the physician to assume as true certain additional facts contained in the testimony of the defendant truck driver: Namely, that the defendant was almost stopped at the moment of contact; that the contact merely resulted in a scratch to a chrome strip at the right rear fender of the plaintiff's automobile as shown by photographs; that the vehicles remained in contact after the initial contact; that the plaintiff's automobile was not moved at all by the contact; and that the plaintiff stepped out of her automobile immediately, without appearing injured and did not complain of injury while at the accident scene. The independent physician then testified that if the additional accident history was true, he would have to conclude that the plaintiff was not physically injured in the accident because there would have to be some movement of the plaintiff's automobile to move her inside of it to cause overstretching of her musculature. Her subjective complaints could not be attributed to any physical injury. Of course, the psychiatrist's diagnosis then provided the logical explanation for the plaintiff's overreaction to the accident and continued symptoms. The jury determined that she was not injured at all. The accident provided her with an opportunity to secure "secondary gains," including help with her housework, sympathy, and the opportunity to visit the doctors regularly. The possible recovery of money damages seemed to be of lesser importance in this case. The result would have been quite different if the defendant had not been able to have an independent medical evaluation and opinion.

Rule 35 authorizes the defendant to obtain a court order requiring the plaintiff to submit to an independent medical examination at a reasonable time and place. The defendant must show good cause (need) for the examination. He or she does this merely by showing that the plaintiff's physical, mental or blood condition is in controversy. The plaintiff cannot be compelled to submit to an independent medical examination. However, if he or she refuses to submit, the case may be dismissed. Rule 35.

A paralegal should be able to prepare, serve and file the motion and supporting documents necessary for compelling an adverse medical examination. He or she should be equally able to prepare affidavits and memorandums to oppose such motions. (See the Appendix for suggested forms.)

More often than not, the plaintiff's lawyer recognizes that the defendant is entitled to have an independent medical examination, so the lawyers schedule the examination without the necessity of a motion and court order. In fact, a court order is seldom sought except when a dispute arises about the number of examinations, the length of the examination, the scope of the examination, the competency of the examiner or place of the examination.

Whether the examination has been ordered or agreed to, the method of scheduling it is the same. The lawyer must find a physician who is willing and able to conduct the examination. A date and time is selected — usually through the physician's secretary. A letter is then sent to the plaintiff's lawyer confirming the arrangements. It is a good idea to request the plaintiff's lawyer to contact the plaintiff immediately to insure the plaintiff's availability. If the plaintiff fails to keep the appointment, he or she may be responsible for the physician's charges — assuming the charge is reasonable for the amount of time reserved by the physician for the examination.

Next, the lawyer who scheduled the independent medical examination should send a letter to the physician confirming the arrangements for the examination. The letter should fully inform the examiner about relevant details of the accident, the nature of all the plaintiff's complaints, type of treatment received, and the treating physician's diagnoses and prognoses. Copies of the treating physician's reports and records should be included with the letter with instructions that the enclosures may be used to direct his or examination and history taking. However, the doctor's report should be based upon the history obtained from the plaintiff, his or her examination and findings. The evaluation should be his or her own. It is not appropriate for the examiner to comment to the patient on findings or evaluation or treatment he or she has been receiving from other physicians. Nor should he or she suggest treatment to the patient. If he or she thinks additional or different treatment should be tried, this may be indicated in the report to the lawyer.

A good medical report has separate sections for the medical history, patient's symptoms and complaints listed in order of importance to the patient, examination, findings, diagnoses, evaluation and the prognosis including whether or not future treatment is necessary. These sections may be broken into appropriate subparagraphs. For example, the history section should contain paragraphs discussing the plaintiff's personal history, pre-accident condition, the accident and post-accident condition.

The independent medical report is the property and work product of the defendant's lawyer, i.e., the lawyer who requested the examination. The plaintiff's lawyer does not have a right to be present during the examination. He or she does not have a right to interview the physician, but does have a right to a copy of the report(s) which the examiner issues to the defendant's lawyer. The report(s) may be obtained only through the defendant's lawyer. When the plaintiff demands a copy, under federal rules, he or she becomes obligated to provide the defendant's lawyer with copies of all reports he or she has obtained from the treating physicians. Failure to comply would, at least, preclude the plaintiff from having the physician testify. In most jurisdictions, however, the plaintiff's medical records become available to the defendants as soon as the plaintiff commences the action.

The independent medical examination report provides the lawyers with information for evaluating the case and for preparing for trial. The plaintiff's lawyer ordinarily supplies the treating physicians with copies. The report serves another invaluable function. When the case reaches trial and the independent examiner testifies, his or her testimony is ordinarily based upon the report. He or she may not even remember the plaintiff and the examination at that time. It is quite common for the physician to read the report almost verbatim. A skilled defense lawyer knows how to establish a dialogue with the physician even though the physician is primarily reading from the report.

What is the defendant and the independent examiner looking for? They want to know to what extent the claims of injury and disability are corroborated by objective medical findings. Objective findings are distinguished from subjective complaints and subjective symptoms in that the examiner can observe them by sight, touch or sound. A condition is subjective when a determination of its existence depends solely upon the patient's response. A scar on the face is objective. An atrophied limb is objective. A headache is subjective. A limited range of motion in the body may be objective or subjective. When the claim is based exclusively or primarily on subjective complaints, the defendant lawyer and independent examiner are interested in knowing whether the plaintiff has been consistent with his or her complaints. A lack of consistency suggests that they are fabricated. Do the complaints comport with the type of injury diagnosed? If the symptoms come and go (recur), what causes them to relent and what causes them to begin? When do they recur? Is there a pattern? Is there evidence of normal progressive healing? If the diagnosis is based solely upon the patient's history and subjective complaints, there is no actual medical corroboration of the injury or disability.

There are numerous medical tests regularly used for the purpose of diagnosing injury. Some of the tests available include x-rays, computerized tomography, electromyograms, electroencephalograms, myelograms, angiograms, psychometric tests, discograms, and others. When the treating physician obtains such tests, the results ordinarily are available to the parties as part of the patient's medical-hospital records. The test results are quite objective and seldom need to be repeated. If physicians might differ in their interpretations of the tests, the raw data is usually available to both sides for review. The one significant exception is the interpretation of an electromyogram.*

If the plaintiff's own physician has not obtained the appropriate tests, the independent examiner may want to put the plaintiff through the tests. However, thers is a potential problem. Some of the tests are painful and some subject the patient to a significant medical risk. If the patient will not voluntarily submit to painful or risky tests, a court will not order him to

---

*Electromyography is a study of the electrical activity of nerves and muscle activity. The electrical activity is measured and evaluated by sound and reading an oscilloscope. No record is made during the testing. The testor simply records his or her interpretations.

submit.* The potential evidence is not available to either side. The defendant may not be permitted to cross-examine the plaintiff about his or her refusal to submit to the tests. On the other hand, the defendant's lawyer should be permitted to cross-examine the treating physicians about the availability of the tests to help make a definitive diagnosis. They will have to justify not obtaining the tests.

A paralegal should be able to help prepare the client for an independent medical examination. The client must be assured that the examination is routine for the type of case and perfectly proper. The client should be urged to be on time. He or she should not fear the examining physician, but should be relaxed and should treat the physician with respect and cooperation throughout the examination.

The client should be prepared to accurately relate his or her medical history. On occasion, a plaintiff takes a diary or notes to help in answering the questions. There is no law against it, but juries usually react negatively to the need for notes.

The client should be advised that he or she is not required to tell the examiner about conversations with his or her lawyer. Symptoms or other problems caused by his or her injuries should not be minimized, but neither should they be exaggerated. A lack of candor may seriously affect the case. He or she should realize that the examination really begins from the moment he or she enters the physician's office. At the very outset, the physician will observe how he or she walks, sits, and disrobes. Some of the tests may be repeated during the examination to determine whether responses are consistent. He or she must not let the physician or tests upset him or her. Submition to unusually painful testing or embarrassing procedures is not required.

On occasion, a party may receive treatment from a physician who does not want to be bothered by preparing a report summarizing his or her findings and conclusion. This creates a problem for both sides. The physician is not a party to the action and cannot be punished by the court. Under the circumstances, either party may be able to secure the physician's deposition. The physician can be required to attend the deposition by serving a subpoena upon him or her.

Many physicians insist upon being paid for their reports even before the report is prepared. The court has authority to require either party to pay the physician's bill for the report. If the plaintiff does not want the treating physician's report and does not intend to call that physician as his or her own witness at trial, the court may require the defendant to pay for the cost of preparing the report. Another problem is presented if the physician refuses to render a report until the bill for providing medical treatment has been paid. Occasionally, a plaintiff finds him or herself unable to pay for medical expenses until the litigation is concluded. If the reluctant physician is "required" to sit through a deposition in lieu of providing a report, he or she may be able to find a way of accommodating the parties.

Since a physician is considered to be an expert witness, the party

*Electromyograms and electroencephalograms are not considered too painful or too risky.

presenting him or her can be compelled under Rule 26 to disclose the substance of the expert's testimony. Rules 26 and 35 are not exclusive of each other. It should be noted that for the convenience of the parties they may agree to some other method of discovery of the medical reports, hospital records and medical opinions. In most cases, the procedures outlined by the rules work well and are followed by litigants without difficulty.

The Federal Rules provide that the adverse examination may be obtained wherever there is a controversy about a party's condition. Some state court rules of civil procedure provide that a Rule 35 medical examination may be obtained only if the medical condition was voluntarily put in issue by the party to be examined. Of course, when a plaintiff seeks compensation for injuries sustained in an accident, his or her physical condition has been put into issue. But suppose that the defendant wants to have the plaintiff's eyes examined because the defendant contends that the plaintiff's vision is defective and that is what caused the accident. Clearly, the eye condition is a physical condition which is in controversy, and the best way of determining whether there is a visual defect is to have a medical examination. However, it cannot be said that the plaintiff has placed his or her eye condition in issue, and under those state rules, a Rule 35 medical examination could not be obtained.

The following letter to a physician and physician's report on an independent neurological medical examination are illustrative of the use of Rule 35. The letter and report also illustrate the value and importance of an independent medical examination. Notice that the writers have carefully developed *relevant* details.

May 23, 1980

John A. Smith, M.D.
Room 527 Medical Arts Building
1000 5th Street
Dallas, Texas

Re: Diersen v. Machacek
    Our File: 37610

Dear Dr. Smith:

This letter will confirm the arrangements we have made for an independent neurological examination of Elizabeth Diersen to be conducted by you at your Medical Arts Office at 9:00 a.m. on July 14, 1980. Mrs. Diersen is represented by Attorney Thomas Tiger. His telephone number is 292-1555. The arrangements for this examination have been made through his office.

Mrs. Elizabeth Diersen is claiming neck and back injuries which she attributes to a rear-end type automobile accident. She is also claiming a problem with headaches, dizziness and pain in her right thigh.

Mrs. Diersen is 23 years of age having been born on January 21, 1957. She is married to Paul Diersen who is 33 years of age. They have one child. Mrs. Diersen completed high school. Her past gainful employments have been light assembly work. She worked with hand tools and worked with circuit boards. She states that she has not been involved in any other motor vehicle accidents. She broke a couple of ribs many years ago when she fell in a school parking lot. Otherwise, she has enjoyed good health.

The automobile accident in question occurred on Monday, March 6, 1978 about 7:00 a.m. on State Highway 5 in Eden, Texas. Mrs. Diersen stopped her Ford Mustang in a line of traffic that was backed up from a stop light. Without any previous warning she suddenly felt her car pushed ahead an undetermined distance. She did not contact the car in front of her. She did not hear a contact to her car. Her car seats had high backs. Her head struck the seatback. She did not strike anything else within the car when her car was pushed forward. She did not sustain any cuts, bumps, swelling or bruises.

What apparently happened was that my client, Mr. Robert Machacek, bumped the rear of an automobile driven by a Mr. Bellman and Mr. Bellman's car was pushed against the rear of Mrs. Diersen's automobile. Photographs show very minor damage to the back of the Diersen car. All three cars were drivable. Neither Mr. Bellman nor Mr. Machacek were injured. Mrs. Diersen did not feel injured at the accident scene. She continued on to work, called her husband, found herself feeling very upset about the accident and she started crying. Her husband was off work that day. He came to the plant, examined the car and drove it home. Mrs. Diersen left work early and drove their camper vehicle home. Upon her husband's suggestion she saw Dr. F. P. Ekrem that same afternoon. He is a general practitioner at the Spencer Clinic. Her complaints at that time included a headache and slight thigh tenderness. On examination he found that the reflexes in the upper and lower extremities were normal, she had an excellent range of motion in her neck with minimal tenderness at extremes. She had slight occipital tenderness at the left, minimal vertebral tenderness in the neck and no muscle spasm. No x-rays were taken. Tylenol and Valium were prescribed.

She returned on March 17th complaining of neck discomfort. He records:

> While working she has her head in one position looking downward, causing some neck strain. She also has to cut wire and there is associated bending. She has constant pain with bending down then straightening up.

He found a good range of motion in her neck with tenderness at the extremes of motion. His diagnosis was neck and low back strain and sprain. He felt she could return to work, gave her a booklet on back care and prescribed outpatient physical therapy. She returned April 12th complaining of more back pain, especially while doing household activities and picking up her child. She was having pain in her thigh and calf on the left side. These symptoms worsened toward evening. Dr. Ekrem found a full range of motion of the neck with no muscle spasm. The straight leg raising test was negative. Her back pain was identified as being at the insertion of the paraspinal muscles at the iliac crest posteriorly. He notes that *she* felt she could not go back to work. He last saw her on August 15, 1978, but in the meantime she started seeing Chiropractor John Zimmerman. His first examination was April 28, 1978. When she saw Dr. Ekrem in August she was complaining of dizziness and continued pain, the location of which is not specified. He felt she might benefit from physiotherapy. He suspected that the dizziness was due to postural hypotension.

Chiropractor Zimmerman treated Mrs. Diersen's neck and low back with chiropractic manipulation. Sometimes the adjustments were painful. He explained to her that her spine was out of alignment and that was causing her symptoms. He referred her to Chiropractor James Brant for a consultation. He last saw Mrs. Diersen in July of 1978. His services were discontinued because Mrs. Diersen was unable to pay his bill and because the Diersens moved from Eden to Crystal, Texas.

On July 28, 1978, Mrs. Diersen started treatment with Chiropractor Donald Wahlen. He felt she had myocytis of the cervical, dorsal and lumbar spine. She was treated with chiropractic adjustments, ultrasound, etc.

It appears that Chiropractor Wahlen referred Mrs. Diersen to D. L. Anderson and Dr. Allan Schut for evaluation. She was examined by one of them on September 6, 1978, at which time she was complaining of dizzy spells, neck pain and low back pain. He records that the low back pain did not begin until about a week after the accident. According to her history the physical therapy she had received at Methodist Hospital per Dr. Ekrem had not provided any help. The problem with dizziness began while she was under Chiropractor Zimmerman's care. The neurological examination was essentially normal. Specifically, testing of muscle strength and reflexes in the extremities was normal. Sensation was normal throughout the body. No Hoffman nor Babinski signs were present. Gait and leg swinging were negative. Romberg test was negative. However, she demonstrated some limitation in the range of motion of her neck. In this regard Dr. Anderson states:

> However, the patient has a long thin angular neck probably capable of more range of motion than is elicited at this time. She has palpable muscle spasms in the cervical muscles bilaterally as well as the upper trapezius muscles, particularly on the left side.

He found the motion in the dorsal and lumbar spine to be within normal limits. However, again, he describes "palpable muscle spasm bilaterally over the lumbo-sacral spine." Straight leg raising test was negative at 90°. The cause of her dizziness was not determined.

Dr. Anderson eventually had Mrs. Diersen admitted to the Eden Health Center for testing. She was also evaluated by Dr. Allan Schut. An electromyogram dated September 20, 1979 was negative for both lower extremities. Mr. Steven Rush, psychologist, conducted an evaluation. An MMPI [psychological test] showed Mrs. Diersen to be significantly neurotic. In addition he felt she sought secondary gain by obtaining financial benefits from her insurance coverage and other benefits which exceeded her wage loss. He also felt that she wanted to remain at home with her child rather than work. Though she states her home and family life is good and satisfying, the indications are to the contrary.

During the September 1979 hospitalization a myelogram was performed and interpreted by radiologist L. O. Campbell. His conclusion is:

> Congenital partial sacralization of L5. Bilateral small extra dural defects at L4-5 suggesting central bulging disc at this level.

Dr. David Olson was called in for consultation by Dr. D. L. Anderson. He concluded that surgery was not appropriate at the time, but he does not rule it out for the future.

More recently Mrs. Diersen has come under the care of a psychologist named Stanley Baker at Clifton Court in Dallas. He is putting her through various physical stress activities that cause her to shake. The purpose is to release her tensions. He massages her neck. They talk. So far she has gone through 7 such sessions at $50 per session. She thinks that Mr. Baker is helping her a lot. She intends to continue seeing him.

Mrs. Diersen's medical expenses now exceed $11,000. She continues to remain off work. She is apparently seeking Social Security disability benefits. She appears highly motivated to cling to her symptomology.

Please provide me with a narrative report on your examination and findings. Certainly psychiatric and psychological evaluations are necessary. Thank you for your very able assistance in this matter.

Very truly yours,

R. D. BLANCHARD

RE: Diersen, Elizabeth
7001 Lombardy Lane
Crystal, Texas
Your file #37610

Dear Mr. Blanchard:

On July 14th of 1980 I examined this 23 year old female whom you so kindly referred for a neurologic and psychiatric evaluation.

FAMILY HISTORY

The patient's mother is 45 and well. Her father is 51 years of age and well. She has two brothers and one sister. Her husband is 34 years of age and presently is unemployed. She has one boy age three. The patient graduated from Eden High School in 1975.

PERSONAL HISTORY

This patient denies any serious illnesses. She had a tonsillectomy at the age of five. Her appendix was removed in 1973. In December of 1979 the patient had a pyelonephritis and some bladder polyps removed by Dr. Walonick at the Eden Hospital.

PRESENT ILLNESS

The patient was involved in an automobile accident on March 6th of 1978. It occurred about 7:00 in the morning at Highway 5 and Mitchell Road. She was driving her car and was struck from the rear. At the time of the impact she said that her head hit the back of the seat, but that nothing happened to her. She was not knocked unconscious and actually did not feel very much. The police came and information was exchanged. She went on to work. She said she rested in the ladies room and after an hour went home.

At about 2:00 in the afternoon she saw her family physician Dr. Ekrem. He examined her, but did not take any x-rays. He gave her some Valium and told her to go home, rest and take a couple of days off work. At that time she said her left leg was aching.

The patient rested at home, and, according to the patient, her neck started to bother her later in the day. Two days later she attempted to go back to work and a few days after this she developed some soreness in her back. She went back to Dr. Ekrem who sent her for some physiotherapy on an outpatient basis at the Methodist Hospital. She went there two or three times a week for about five weeks and kept working off and on. Finally on March 21st, 1978 she was put on medical leave. According to the patient the physiotherapy did not help.

The patient then went to John Zimmerman, a Chiropractor in Eden, who took x-rays and did adjusting of her neck and back. He also gave her a neck and back brace. Later she moved to Crystal, Texas where she went to Dr. Donald Whalen, a Chiropractor. She took adjustments from him which started out three times a week and now she sees him as necessary. He sent her to a Dr. Brandt, a Chiropractor, for a consultation sometime in June of 1978.

The patient was having some dizzy spells so she went to a Dr. Malmoud who apparently is a partner of Dr. Ekrem. He felt that she was possibly having hypotension, but when he examined her her blood pressure was all right.

The patient was referred to Dr. Allan Schut and Dr. D. L. Anderson. They examined her, gave her physiotherapy in their office, and on two occasions she has been hospitalized. The first time was in April of 1979 where she was given in-hospital physiotherapy for two weeks, and rehabilitation for her neck and back. This was at the Eden Hospital. In September of 1979 Dr. Anderson put her back in the Eden Hospital where a spinogram was done. Dr. David Olson looked at the spinogram, said that she might possibly have a low midline ruptured disc. She was put on an exercise program and given a better back brace, but this did not cure her.

The patient has also been seen by Dr. Hammond for an insurance examination. She went to a doctor in Kellogg Square about a year ago who examined her, but she cannot remember his name. She had a Social Security examination at the University, but does not know the doctor's name. In addition, she has been to Dr. Walonick for her kidney problems at the request of Dr. Anderson. She is still seeing Dr. Anderson about once a month.

The patient was sent to a psychologist, Mr. Stanley Baker on Clifton Avenue. He has his wife, Sandy Baker, help him. They talk with her and, according to the patient, they talk about the lawsuit, the attorneys involved, letters that are coming to her, and try to get her to relax. They give her neck massage and put her in unusual positions. According to the patient, she will stand bent over for a long period of time or they may have her stand against the wall or even on her head. She has seen him about ten or twelve times and she thinks he might be helping her. According to the patient, they are giving her advice about what to do about the examinations.

The patient has been seen by the people from rehabilitation. Two names are Betty Johnson and Maddy Boll. They have given her advice and told her how to fill out the application blanks for rehabilitation. They have told her that she will continue to be paid as long as she is making less money than the job that she had when she was injured. They got her a job at the Spa Petite in Eden which she has been on for three days. She said she shows the members how to use the equipment and she is on a running and exercise program with the members of the club. The patient volunteered to me that she will continue to be paid by rehabilitation as long as her compensation from Spa Petite is less than she had when she was working for EMT Electronics.

The patient presently takes only Ampicillin for a strep throat, which was prescribed by Dr. Ekrem. If she has too bad a headache she takes Excedrin or Tylenol #3.

Prior to her employment with EMT Electronics she worked for Ross Shadow doing electronic soldering. After this she had a child and at one time worked for Kentucky Fried Chicken preparing food and waiting on tables.

According to the patient she has had a cortisone shot in her left hip at one time for bursitis. When she was in the hospital, as well as having a spinogram, she had an electromyogram of her left leg. According to the patient, she does not think she is getting much better. She said that all the therapy she has taken has really not helped very much as far as her neck, leg and back is concerned. She said that the doctors might think she is better, but she really is not.

PRESENT COMPLAINTS

1) Daily headaches. This is bioccipital and bifrontal. It lasts a couple of hours and is relieved by Excedrin. It is not associated with any nausea or vomiting and generally comes on about noon.
2) Dizzy spells. She gets them approximately once a day. It is a light-headedness rather than a vertigo.
3) Some stiffness and discomfort in her neck and shoulders (primarily left). It is brought on by anything and any type of paperwork or keeping her neck in one position bothers her.
4) Pain in the low back. This is a stiffness and soreness and is always present. She wears a brace from time to time, particularly when driving or if she is going to sit for a long time.
5) Aching in her left leg which is primarily in the thigh or hip region. It is worse in the evening. It is bothered by cold. Coughing and sneezing do not produce pain.

At this point the patient has no blurred vision or double vision. She does not have any complaints as far as her chest and abdomen are concerned. She has had no syncope or convulsions. She is sleeping better on a water bed. The patient's appetite is good. She does a lot of exercises and other than this does not play tennis, golf or any sports. She does walk a fair amount.

PHYSICAL EXAMINATION

The patient is 5'5" tall and weighs 123 pounds. She is well developed and well nourished. Blood pressure 100/70, pulse 66, respirations 18. Teeth and gums are normal. Eardrums are normal. Throat is negative. The chest is clear to auscultation and percussion and there are no cardiac irregularities or murmurs. The abdomen reveals no scars, masses or tenderness.

NEUROLOGICAL EXAMINATION

Cranial Nerves: The patient can smell test odors. The visual acuity is 20/20-2 bilaterally without correction. The visual fields were normal. The opthalmoscopic examination did not reveal any evidence of any increased intracranial pressure, hemorrhages or exudates. No optic atrophy. Good pulsation of the veins. The third, fourth and sixth cranial nerves were normal. The pupils were equal and react to light. No nystagmus. No facial asymmetry. No hypesthesia of the face or cornea. Hearing revealed to be normal.

Sensory Functions: The examination of the body to cotton, pin prick pain as well as vibration and position sense was normal.

Motor Functions: The patient has a good grip bilaterally and there is no atrophy, hypertrophy, twitching or tremor of the musculature.

Measurements:	Right	Left
Biceps	9¾"	9½"
Forearm	7½"	7¼"
Wrist	5¾"	5¾"
Hand	7"	7"
Thigh	14½"	14½"
Calf	12½"	12½"

Movements: The patient's neck goes through a full range of motion in all directions without any complaint of pain or evidence of spasm. The patient bends over to 90 degrees and comes about 1" from her toes. Straight leg raising tests go to 90 degrees. She is able to walk on her heels and toes and do a deep knee bend.

The patient has some tenderness over the left intertrocanteric bursa indicating a bursitis in this area.

Coordination: The patient's gait is normal. The finger to finger, finger to nose and heel to knee tests were done normally.

Reflexes: All of the reflexes were present and equal. The toe signs were negative. She does not have any bowel or bladder dysfunction and speech is normal.

X-RAYS

Roentgenograms were made of the cervical spine in the antero-posterior, lateral and both oblique directions.

Diagnosis: Negative for evidence of old or recent fracture or other bone or joint abnormality. A normal curvature is seen in flexion and extension.

Conclusion: Negative cervical spine study.

Roentgenograms were made of the lumbo-sacral spine in the antero-posterior and lateral directions.

Diagnosis: Negative for evidence of old or recent fracture. There are no productive or destructive changes and the disc spaces are maintained. The fifth lumbar vertebra is transitional. The sacro-iliac joints and hips appear normal.

A few droplets of contrast material are seen in the spinal canal as the result of a previous myelogram.

An IUD is identified and appears to be normal in location.

ELECTROENCEPHALOGRAM

Basic alpha rhythm 10 per second. This is an awake record with some eye blink artifact, movement and tension artifact. Some low voltage and low voltage fast activity. No evidence of any localized or diffuse spiking, slow waves or delta activity. No amplitude asymmetry. No seizure discharges of any sort. Photic stimulation did not produce any driving response. Hyperventilation did not produce any buildup or slowing.

Impression: Within normal limits.

ELECTROMYOGRAM

An electromyogram was done by Jane E. Wilson, M.D. on July 14th of 1980. She found the entire left leg to be normal. A copy of her entire report is included with this letter.

ECHOENCEPHALOGRAM

This echoencephalogram demonstrates a normal position for the midline echo complex.

MINNESOTA MULTIPHASIC PERSONALITY TEST

This was a valid test. There was a marked elevation on hysteria or conversion reaction. Some mild depression and hypochondriasis was noted. This profile indicated the patient had tension within herself that was being converted to the process of conversion to psychosomatic or psychophysiological symptoms. The symptoms undoubtedly have a secondary gain.

PSYCHOLOGICAL EXAMINATION

This patient was evaluated by Patrick Noble, Ph.D., Licensed Consulting Psychologist on July 14th of 1980. A copy of his entire report is included with this letter. His summary is as follows:

"The testing reveals an immature, dependent woman who has a basic personality that is in keeping with an individual who could easily siphon off her psychological conflicts into psychological manifestations. This type of personality develops over the years and is closely related to the fact that she apparently lived in a situation where she felt she was being controlled by a rather overpowering mother figure. Thus, her only out is to develop symptomatology to blame her psychological difficulties onto some medical problem."

CONCLUSIONS

If one considers the mechanism of the accident, it is very difficult to imagine that really very much did occur to this patient. She had no symptoms at the time of the accident and the back pain did not come on for several days. It is possible she could have had a very minimal strain of her neck, but one would expect that this would have disappeared with time. She has been over-examined, over-treated, and has had a tremendous number of chiropractic appointments. She has been going from doctor to doctor in an attempt to be cured, and this is not possible because 95% of her symptoms are psychological in nature. She has recently returned to work as a demonstrator at the Spa Petite.

The patient's present complaints are of headaches, light-headedness, pain in the neck and both shoulders, low back pain and aching in her left leg.

The physical examination is entirely normal for any abnormality as a result of this accident.

A complete neurological examination is negative. She does have bursitis in the left intertrocanteric bursa and this is probably producing discomfort in the left leg. This is a degenerative affair and not related to the accident. She has had an injection of hydrocortisone in this area in the past.

X-rays of the cervical spine were normal. An x-ray of the lumbosacral spine was negative. A few droplets of contrast material was seen in the spinal canal which was the result of a previous myelogram.

The electroencephalogram was normal.

The echoencephalogram is normal.

And electromyogram of the left leg is entirely normal.

The Minnesota Multiphasic Personality Test shows definite evidence of a conversion reaction with secondary gains. These secondary gains are obviously that the patient does not have to go to work, but can stay home and receive more compensation than she would get if she were working. In this respect there is a compensation neurosis present.

The psychological testing showed, "an immature, dependent woman who has a basic personality that is in keeping with an individual who could easily siphon off her psychological conflicts into psychological manifestations. This type of personality develops over the years and is closely related to the fact that she apparently lived in a situation where she felt she was being controlled by an overpowering mother figure. Thus, her only out is to develop symptomatology to blame her psychological difficulties onto some medical problem."

A great deal of the patient's symptoms are very close to consciousness. She has been told that a lot of her symptoms are on the basis of tension and that they are not organic in character. A lot of this is very close to being a conscious mechanism, particularly with her desire not to return to work and enjoy life at home as long as she can obtain financial rewards. The financial reward is paramount in her mind. This mechanism is so close to consciousness that it is really not far from malingering. These mechanisms have been investigated by psychologists who have treated her and have been documented, but seemingly disregarded by her physicians and chiropractors. I find no evidence from a clinical standpoint of a herniated lumbar intervertebral disc. There is no weakness, reflex disturbance, atrophy, and movements are excellent. The pain, I believe, is a result of the bursitis which is not attributable to the accident.

Sincerely yours,

John A. Smith, M.D.

ELECTROMYOGRAPHY REPORT

PATIENT: Mrs. Elizabeth Diersen

DATE: July 14, 1980

NERVE CONDUCTION STUDIES

nerve	motor conduction velocity Meters/Second	distal motor latency milliseconds	motor response amplitude millivolts
Left peroneal	46.5	5.0	5.0

LEFT LOWER EXTREMITY NEEDLE ELECTRODE STUDIES

muscle	insertional activity	motor unit activity
Iliopsoas	normal	normal
Rectus femoris	normal	normal
Vastus lateralis	normal	normal
Vastus medialis	normal	normal
Tibialis anterior	normal	normal
Extensor digitorum longus	normal	normal
Peroneus	normal	normal
Medial gastrocnemius	normal	normal for strength of contraction
Soleus	normal	normal
Gluteus maximus	normal	normal
Lumbar paraspinal	normal	normal

SUMMARY:

The motor conduction velocity, distal motor latency, and action potential are normal in the left peroneal nerve.

The needle electrode examinations reveal no significant variation from normal.

IMPRESSION:

The above electromyographic studies are within normal limits.

Jane E. Wilson, M.D.

PSYCHOLOGICAL EVALUATION

RE: Elizabeth Diersen

TESTS ADMINISTERED: HILLSIDE SHORT FORM OF THE WESCHLER BELLEVIEW EXAMINATION.
RORSCHACH
KAHN TEST OF SYMBOL ARRANGEMENT
SENTENCE COMPLETION

This lady indicates that she was in an accident 3-6-78. She states she was not unconscious and was not hospitalized and her only symptom is headache. At the present time she states her symptoms are, "headaches and dizziness, left leg aches, neck and lower backaches." Currently she is on no medication except Tylenol #3 for headaches. In the past she apparently has had various medications. She states she does not smoke, drinks occasionally and denies the use of drugs. She indicates that she started a job last week where she is working at a health club. In terms of social activity, she states they don't do much because it is too expensive and they tend to sit around home and watch T.V. although they do some camping.

The patient states that she comes from a family of four children where she is the oldest. Her father is a truck driver and her mother is a waitress. She has been married four years and her husband currently is unemployed and has worked for the Milwaukee Railroad in the past and has been laid off for about 8 or 9 weeks. There is one child of this marriage, a girl age 3. The patient states she completed high school. She indicates that she has had no serious illnesses except for an appendectomy. She has no history of any other serious accidents.

The patient is a rather stoic-faced individual who has very little expression on her facies. Speech is coherent, relevant, under good control and shows no loose associations. Affective responses are felt to be somewhat flat at this time and one gets the impression that she may have some feelings of depression. There are no evidences of psychotic ideation, the patient is considered to be of average intelligence, is oriented in contact, shows good comprehension, good attention span and no loss of recent or remote memory.

This patient has been tested previously and the evaluation done in March of 1979 indicated that she was a person who was immature, and had some self esteem problems with a diagnosis as immature woman in stress with self esteem issue, unexpressed anger and some sadness in relationship to her heterosexual life.

Testing at this time reveals a woman of average intelligence with a prorated IQ of 109. She continues to show the same type of immaturity and dependency that she apparently showed when she was tested previously. It would appear that she has been unsuccessful in separating from parental figures in the past and has more or less been living in a situation where the mother figure assumed a very domineering and controlling role. As a result of this the patient has developed a very passive, dependent and somewhat negativistic approach in dealing with her interpersonal life. She has problems also in attaining an adult heterosexual relationship and apparently would have some marital problems if this is not cleared up in the near future. The unresolved hostile feelings are still seen although it may very well relate to her resentments over how she has been treated in the past. The testing also indicates that she is a person who more than likely tends to siphon off her emotional problems into this accident as a way of attempting to resolve her psychological problems. It may also very well be even at present time that because of the financial conditions that this has intensified her symptomatology for she knows no other way of coping with the current changes except to maintain her symptomatology.

In summary, the testing continues to reveal an immature, dependent person who has a basic personality that is in keeping with an individual who could easily siphon off her psychological conflicts into physiological manifestations. This type of personality develops over the years and is closely related to the fact that she apparently lived in a situation where she felt she was being controlled by a rather overpowering mother figure. Thus, her only out is to develop symptomatology to blame her psychological difficulties onto some medical problem.

Patrick Noble, Ph.D.
Licensed Consulting Psychologist

17

Inspection and Copying of Documents and Things

A party needs to inspect all the relevant documents, land and things for the purpose of obtaining information and evidence for his or her case. Court rules establish a procedure by which any party may make a demand upon another party who has custody of such items to make them available for inspection, copying and even testing. Rule 34. Of course, it must appear that the items demanded are relevant or, at least, will lead to admissible evidence. Rule 26(b). The procedure is simple and inexpensive. It is initiated by serving a *demand for inspection* upon the party who has custody or control over the items in question. The demand for inspection does not have to be in any particular form, but see the Rules' Appendix of Forms, Form No. 24. A mere letter which sets forth the request in sufficient detail is adequate, and is commonly used in many states.

Rule 34 allows at least thirty days for a party to respond to a demand for inspection; forty-five days must be allowed if the demand is served upon the defendant along with the summons and complaint. Therefore, the defendant has at least fifteen more days in which to comply after his or her answer comes due. If the party making a demand needs production of the items sooner, he or she may move the court for an order shortening the time period. However, the preferable approach is to simply contact the party's lawyer and obtain his or her agreement to an earlier inspection. Lawyers should avoid imposing upon the court whenever possible.

The initial response to a demand for production may be a written statement indicating that the responding party will comply or he or she may submit a list of requirements for the production of the items. Rule 24(b). Any objection to the demand must be made in writing within thirty days. In most cases the parties are able to agree upon mutually satisfactory arrangements for the inspection, copying, and testing. If either party attempts to misuse the inspection procedure, he or she is subject to the sanctions provided by Rule 37(a).

A party's response to a demand for inspection could resemble the following:

Title of   Response to Request
Case   for Inspection

Defendant hereby responds to plaintiff's demand for inspection pursuant to Rule 34 of the Federal Rules of Civil Procedure:

1. Plaintiff's lawyer and designated experts may enter defendant's plant at Des Moines, Iowa, for the purpose of inspecting the conveyor system on Thursday, January 5, 1981, between the hours of 2:00 and 5:00 o'clock in the afternoon.

2. Plaintiff's representatives may take still pictures and motion pictures of the conveyor system in question.

3. Plaintiff's experts may make any measurements they need of the conveyor system and appurtenances.

4. Plaintiff's experts may not take samples of conveyor belt because that would seriously damage the conveyor system, and, presumably, samples of the belts are readily available from the B. F. Goodrich Company.

5. Defendant does not have any plans or specifications used for installation of the conveyor system. Therefore, they cannot be made available to plaintiff's experts at the time of the inspection.

                                                        _____
                                                        Attorney for Defendant

Depositions and interrogatories are the usual means for discovering the existence of documents and things and the identity of custodians. A demand for production should carefully specify the documents or things to be produced. Each item or category of items should be described with "reasonable particularity." Strict accuracy, however, is not required. The demand must specify a time, place and method of production. The parties may agree or stipulate to different terms and conditions than those specified in the demand. The *respondent* may object to all or part of the demand for inspection. The objections should be as specific and definitive as possible.

When documents are produced, they must be clearly identified or identifiable. Of course, a party should not attempt to evade the spirit of the Rule by burying important documents amongst reams of other documents.

Inspections ordinarily take place at a lawyer's office or at the home or office of the person who has custody. Nowadays photocopies of documents are easily made and cost is seldom a problem. Of course, the party who orders the copies must pay a reasonable cost for having copies made. If photographs are the articles to be copied, the custodian of the negatives usually decides who he or she wants to make the copies. The original photographs should be kept in his or her custody. New negatives can be made from those photographs if necessary, and new photographs can be made from the negatives. The custodian is fully protected by keeping one or the other.

A more difficult problem to handle is that of conducting tests on articles that are in the adversary's custody. There is a natural reluctance on the part of litigants to give up custody of important demonstrative evidence. There is always the danger of damage or loss. Some scientific tests require destruction of all or a portion of the subject matter being tested. For example, suppose that the controversy centers upon the flammability of an article of clothing, of which only a few small pieces remain, and that the necessary tests will destroy the remaining pieces. It may be necessary for the parties' experts to work together and jointly record the test results. It is not uncommon in such cases to have a motion picture made of the testing procedures. But even that Solomon-like solution is inadequate if the parties' experts cannot agree on which tests to conduct or the methods to use.

A party may need to go upon land or enter a building that belongs to his or her opponent. The reason for the entry may be to examine things upon the land or to examine and test the soil, or to test components of a structure. It may be necessary to obtain samples by taking borings in the soil or in concrete or in metal structures. The party who demands the inspection may want to photograph things or activities on the land such as the operation of a plant causing pollution. If the parties cannot agree on the proper procedures and limitations, the court must resolve the dispute for them. Judges try to weigh the importance of discovery against the hardships which may result. For example, a judge may allow the inspection and photographing of a manufacturing plant on condition that no secret processes be photographed and that none of the photographs be made available to the news media, or that the inspection be conducted on certain days during certain hours.

18

Requests for Admissions ━━━━━

Lawyers should strive to identify the areas of agreement as well as the areas of disagreement concerning the facts and the application of law to the relevant facts. After identifying the areas of agreement, steps may be taken to establish that there is no controversy concerning the particular matters. This approach to litigation promotes economy because the parties can avoid wasting time and money on unnecessary investigation and discovery procedures. Also, if a matter is taken out of controversy the lawyers have taken a major step toward reducing surprises at trial.

Of course, the pleadings (complaint and answer) are supposed to establish the legal issues through the allegations, admissions and denials made in them. But modern day pleadings are so generalized that they do not do a good job of particularizing the material facts or fact issues. And, when the action is commenced, the defendant usually is not in a position to admit much of anything. The defendant's lawyer needs time to gather information and assimilate the facts.

At some point before trial, usually after discovery is completed, the lawyers are able to make an objective determination about which facts are in controversy and which facts are undisputed. It is then that the party who has the burden of proving facts relevant to the cause of action or to the affirmative defense should consider establishing those facts by using *requests for admissions*. Through requests for admissions a party may demand that another party admit the truth of specified facts, the genuineness of specified documents, the truth of specified opinions, the stated application of law to particular facts. This is done by serving a set of written requests for admissions upon the party's lawyer just like serving interrogatories.

A request for admissions is not a means of discovery, because the party who propounds a request should *know* the facts he or she wants another party to admit, and should be sure that he or she wants the fact established. The effect of admitting a request is to take the specific matter out of issue. The matter becomes uncontrovertable in the case in which the admission is made. In other words, a party cannot change the admission at trial, and is bound by the admission unless he or she secures a court order, for good cause shown, allowing an amendment or revocation of the admission. A request for admissions may be directed to any matter that is within the scope of discovery as set forth in Rule 26(b). If the admission is to be used at trial, it must comport with the rules of evidence. Requests for admissions may be served only on parties to the suit.

Service of a request for admissions may be made with the summons and complaint or thereafter. The response may be signed by the responding party or by his or her lawyer. The response is due in 30 days after service of the request or within 45 days of the service of the summons and complaint. Failure to serve a response to the request for admissions within the allotted time operates as an admission. If more time is needed, the proponent of the request may give an extension. Otherwise, a court order is necessary. Though not provided for in the Rules, when a party fails to respond to a request for admissions, it is customary for the lawyer who served the request to prepare a *notice and affidavit of no response* which includes a statement that the admissions requested are deemed admitted for purposes of the pending action.

If an admission pertains to the application of law to facts, the court takes judicial notice of the admission. The admission becomes part of the law of the case. If the matter admitted is one of fact, the court informs the jury of the admitted facts at the appropriate time. A fact may be "admitted" in answers to interrogatories or in a deposition and, subsequently, denied or qualified at trial. The change may result in impeachment of the deponent's testimony. It is then up to the jury to determine the truth. But an admission of fact made in response to requests for admissions is conclusive and absolute. The admission may be withdrawn only by permission of the other parties or by leave of the court.

A party responding to requests for admissions has several alternatives: (1) deny the request, (2) admit the request, (3) assert an inability to admit or deny and explain his or her reasons, (4) make a qualified denial, (5) object to the request. An objection has the effect of a denial. Any denial must be carefully considered and truthful. As stated in Rule 36: "A denial shall fairly meet the substance of the requested admission, and when good faith requires that a party qualify his answer or deny only a part of the matter of which an admission is requested, he shall so specify so much of it as is true and qualify or deny the remainder."

The more specific and clearly drafted the requests, the more difficult it is for the responding party to avoid making the admissions desired by the proponent. Each request should be singular. But even then, a response may be to admit only a portion of the request. For example, a request to a defendant that he occupied certain real estate during the year 1981, may draw a response that he occupied the premises only during the month of January, 1981. But if he occupied the premises only in 1979, he would be safe to simply deny the request without any explanation. As mentioned above, requests for admissions should be made upon information *known* to the proponent for the purpose of taking a potentially disputed fact or opinion out of the case, not for the purpose of discovery. The burden is upon the proponent of the request to be accurate and specific. If he is not, the purposes of Rule 37 are not served. A misuse of requests for admissions increases the cost of litigation and creates friction between the parties. A request that is admitted is binding upon the proponent *and* responding party. Though not specifically stated in the Rules, an admission is not binding upon a party who did not propound the request or was not required to respond to the request for admissions. Therefore, if a request for admissions is served by the plaintiff on one defendant and admitted by that defendant, the admission does not affect any other defendant.

The use of requests for admissions should facilitate trial preparation and the trial by establishing the truth. Is there a duty to correct a response which was true when given but subsequently became incorrect? What if the response was believed to be correct when given but later found to be incorrect? What if a party erroneously makes an admission? Does it make any difference if the error was technical or inadvertent or now clearly demonstrable or always subject to some doubt? An admission duly made is not irrevocable. The party who mistakenly made the admission should first request the opponent for permission to withdraw or correct the admission. If the parties can resolve the problem by agreement, usually reduced to a formal stipulation, that is the quickest and easiest method of handling it. Otherwise, an admission may be withdrawn or modified only by permission of the court pursuant to a timely motion. The motion must (1) specifically request permission to withdraw or amend the admission, (2) state precisely how the proposed amended admission would read, (3) explain the reason for the amendment or withdrawal, (4) explain why the other parties will not be prejudiced by the correction. The motion should be supported by affidavits to establish facts relevant to the motion. Of course, withdrawal of an admission may adversely affect another party's claim or defense in a significant manner. That, however, does not mean the party has been prejudiced. The truth does not prejudice a party! However, if a party relied upon an admission to establish facts and the evidence which was available is no longer available to prove the facts, he or she has been prejudiced. Also, a party is prejudiced if he or she does not have a reasonable amount of time to investigate and gather available evidence concerning the issue or subject matter. A motion to withdraw or amend an admission ought to anticipate these *time* and *availability of evidence* problems.

A request for admissions may relate to specific facts. The following illustrative examples relate to specific facts of various kinds:

Please admit that:

1. Defendant entered the intersection in question without stopping for the stop sign.

[This request might be prompted by a notation in a police accident report that the party admitted a stop sign violation. Perhaps a follow-up request should be used as in No. 2 below.]

2. Defendant stated to Officer Burt Jones that defendant did not stop for the stop sign in question.

[This request involves the same subject matter but a different fact, i.e., the fact of a conversation. Admission that the conversation took place is not an admission that the stop sign violation occurred.]

3. Defendant was owner of the motor vehicle that struck the plaintiff pedestrian at the time and place specified in the complaint.

[Ownership of a vehicle is often critical to a claim and a disputed fact. The matter of ownership may also be a mixed question of law and fact.]

Defendant *delivered four* (4) *tons* of wheat to plaintiff *on September 5, 1980.*

[Though the request is a single, simple sentence, it contains a request for admission of five separate facts. Each fact is italicized. If the controversy centers only around the *value* of the wheat delivered, the plaintiff may be able to admit all five of the facts without any difficulty. But if there is a dispute over how many tons were delivered, all the facts but the quantity should be admitted by the plaintiff. This same request could be directed by the plaintiff to the defendant to establish that the defendant delivered *less* wheat than he or she contracted to deliver.]

5. Plaintiff was not wearing his eye glasses at the time of the accident referred to in the complaint.

6. The accident referred to in the complaint occurred at 6:04 p.m.

7. The signature that appears on the attached promissory note (copy) was made by defendant.

8. Plaintiff was familiar with the stairway on which she fell.

Or, Plaintiff used the stairway on ten (10) or more occasions before the accident in question.

9. On (date) defendant received written notice of a defect in the pipe in question.

10. The sidewalk on which plaintiff fell was:
     a. four feet wide:
     b. made of cement;
     c. dry;
     d. used by plaintiff at least three (3) times a month for one year before plaintiff's alleged accident.

Requests for admissions may relate to opinions; the following illustrative examples relate to various kinds of opinions. Theoretically, any opinion that a layman or expert may testify to is a proper subject for a request for admissions.

Please admit:

1. That when you observed defendant at the scene of the accident in question you observed that defendant was not intoxicated.

[Of course, the request could be phrased to establish the defendant was intoxicated. Either way, the matter of sobriety is an opinion.]

2. That while you were at the accident scene you did not form an opinion whether or not the plaintiff was intoxicated.

[Sometimes it is just as important to establish the absence of an opinion as the existence of an opinion.]

3. That the sidewalk on which plaintiff fell was slippery due to ice at the time she fell.

["Slippery" is an opinion. The presence of ice is a simple fact.]

4. That Dr. Stanley Smith's charges in the amount of $500.00 for services to plaintiff were reasonable.

[This type of request is being used frequently by plaintiffs in personal injury actions, especially if the lawyer does not intend to have the physician or hospital administrator appear at trial to testify. However, if the plaintiff refuses to permit the defendant's lawyer to *talk* with the physician, it is doubtful that the defendant has available the necessary information to confirm the truth of the request. The value of the services depends upon many factors including the physician's experience, time spent and skill. Such information usually is not available in the records. Therefore, unless the plaintiff will permit the defendant to interview the attending physician, the defendant properly denies the request on the basis that he or she lacks sufficient information upon which to make the admission.]

5. That the lumber delivered by defendant to plaintiff per the contract in question complied with the specified grades and qualities.

6. That the fair market value of plaintiff's automobile before the accident was $4,000.00.

7. That the ignition point for natural gas is 3300 degrees.

8. That rust caused the steel bar joists to fail.

All of the above matters involve opinions which would be relevant and admissible at trial.

Requests for admissions may relate to *mixed questions of law and fact,* or, otherwise stated, the application of law to facts. The following illustrative examples involve the application of law to facts:

Please admit:

1. That at the time the contract was signed by Joseph Smith, he was acting within the course and scope of his agency for plaintiff.

[The existence of an "agency" and the "scope" of the agency depend upon the existence of a legal relationship which may be created in various ways.]

2. That defendant was negligent in the operation of his airplane.

[The admission may be directed to the **ultimate question of fact** which requires the application of law to a collage of facts. If the admission is made and negligence is thereby established, there are still the issues of causation and damages to be established.]

    3. That on October 1, 1980, plaintiff was an employee of defendant who is entitled to benefits under the terms of defendant's contract with the teacher's union dated August 1, 1980.

    4. That at the time plaintiff was discharged from her employment by defendant, she was a "tenured" teacher within the meaning of the contract referred to in the complaint.

[If certain factors must be proved to establish "tenure", the admission may save considerable time and effort proving those factors.]

    5. That defendant's failure to stop for the stop sign was a proximate cause of the automobile accident in question.

[Proximate cause is probably the most subjective legal conclusion in tort law. Appellate courts are reluctant to hold, as a matter of law, that any set of facts establishes that an alleged cause is a proximate cause of an accident.]

    Requests for admissions may relate to the genuineness of documents. The usual procedure, as recommended by the rule, is to attach a good photocopy of the document to the request. However, that is not necessary. A request to admit the genuineness of a document may be made concerning documents that are in the possession of the party to whom the request is directed, or, if the documents are "furnished or made available for inspection," the request may simply identify the documents. A strict reading of Rule 36 places a burden on the *requestor* to provide the original or a suitable copy to the *respondent*. If a responding party admits that a document is *genuine,* he or she merely admits that it is what it purports to be. Rule 37 does not define "genuineness." There is some concern and controversy over its meaning. And it may be a word that, in this application, cannot be given a precise meaning. However, the lack of a clear definition does not seem to impair use of the request for admission procedure.

    The wording of each request for admission should make clear the scope of the request. Suppose that the lawsuit centers around a counterfeit document; that both parties know that the document is counterfeit; but a dispute exists over who prepared the document and who signed it. The above definition of "genuineness" would be difficult to use in this situation. Neither party would ask the other to admit that the document is what it purports to be. But a party may request the other to admit that *this* is a true copy of the counterfeit document; that the document is a counterfeit; that the opponent has possession of the original counterfeit; that the opponent knows or does not know who actually signed the counterfeit document. Of course, there is even less difficulty using a request that a document is genuine when the document is known to be valid. Then requests for admissions may be sought concerning the date of execution, identity of signatories, place of execution, and the consideration for it.

    If a party admits that a certain document is genuine, he or she does not thereby admit that it is also admissible in evidence. For example, a defendant may admit that a certain photograph of the plaintiff's decedent at the accident scene is genuine — as being that of the decedent and accurately showing his mutilated body. However, the photograph is still subject to the objection that it is inflammatory, and, therefore, its prejudicial effect outweighs its probative value. Or, a document that is admittedly genuine may, nevertheless, be excluded from evidence because it contains statements that are mere hearsay.

Requests for admissions may be used to help insure that a certain document will be received into evidence or, at least, the necessary foundation for the document exists. For example, the following requests may be directed to the plaintiff in a tort action where the defendant is claiming the plaintiff previously executed a release.

Please admit:

1. That the attached "Release of All Claims" is genuine.
2. That plaintiff signed the attached release on the date specified therein.
3. That plaintiff received the money described in the release as the consideration.
4. That the monies plaintiff received in exchange for the release have not been tendered or returned to defendant.

Affirmative responses to the above requests should greatly facilitate the defendant's trial preparation.

A response to a request for admissions is due in thirty days after service. If service was by mail, add three days. If service was made with the summons and complaint, responses are not due until forty-five days after service. If the responses cannot be prepared within the time provided by the rules, the respondent has the burden of securing an extension of time. If the proponent will not accommodate him or her, the respondent must obtain an extension by moving the court for an order granting more time. But the motion must be served before the time for answering expires. Rule 6(b).

If a party refuses to make admissions to requests for admissions duly made, the proponent of the requests must prove the facts or opinions or documents in the usual manner — with evidence — at trial. If he or she succeeds in establishing the truth of a matter covered in a request, there is an inference that the request should have been admitted. Having successfully proven the matter denied, the proponent may move the court (apply) for an order requiring the opponent to pay reasonable expenses necessarily incurred to establish the matter. Rule 37(c). Note, the proponent of the request for admissions does not have to be the prevailing party to take advantage of the Rule.

In most cases, it is difficult to know whether a specific fact or opinion was accepted by the jury as unqualifiedly true. The trial judge may submit interrogatories to a jury for answers to specific questions about the case. Rule 49(b). Otherwise, it is nearly impossible to know what the jury found. For example, suppose that the plaintiff in a personal injury action was treated by three physicians and the defendant is asked to admit that the treatment by each physician was necessary and the charges by each physician were reasonable. The requests for admissions are denied. The jury returns a verdict in the amount of $7,000.00. The verdict says nothing, implies nothing about the necessity or value of the medical treatment by each physician. The only permissible inference is that the plaintiff did sustain *an* injury and, probably, required *some* medical treatment. Of course, if the case is tried to a judge, he or she knows which facts in the determination were established.

Proving the truth of the matters requested is only the first step and requisite to recovering the costs of proving the matter. In addition, the proponent of the request for admissions must convince the court that the requests were proper in form and substance. Recovery of costs may still be disallowed if the court determines that the requests were "of no substantial importance" or that the respondent had good reason to believe that he or she would prevail on the matter. Obviously, these criteria are very subjective and give the trial judge a great deal of latitude. The wording implies that the judge should lean toward disallowance of costs unless the respondent acted in bad faith. However, bad faith is *not* the test or standard.

The following is a sample of a negative response to requests for admissions.

Response to
Request for Admissions

TO: Plaintiff _____ and _____ her attorney:

Come now defendants Dwight G. Hall and Willard Rosen and for their response to plaintiff's Request for Admissions, state:

REQUEST No. 1. That the reasonable value of the medical expenses incurred by plaintiff as a result of the injuries received by plaintiff in the accident of September 20, 1979, are as follows:

Dr. Jerome Cowan	9-15-78 thru 9-22-78	$ 92.00
Dr. Maynard Berwin	9-22-78 thru 2-5-79	308.00
Dr. Richard Copes	10-15-78 thru 10-31-79	125.00
Midwest Medical Center	9-21-78 thru 9-27-78	1,082.60
Metro. Medical Assoc.	1-19-79 thru 5-18-79	31.00
Drs. Peters and Elmer		
et al Dr. Hinkel	3-5-80	75.00
Prescriptions	10-3-77 thru 7-15-78	21.00
TOTAL		$1,734.70

RESPONSE: DENIED

Defendants Hall and Rosen object to the request for admissions for failing to provide adequate documentation and information concerning these requests for admissions seeking to impose upon defendants the burden of securing copies of records at defendants' expense and reviewing those records at defendants' expense. Defendants have been unable to make reasonable inquiry of the various physicians due to plaintiff's failure and/or refusal to provide authorizations permitting defendants' counsel to interview them. Therefore, the information known to defendants or information readily obtainable by the defendants is insufficient to enable them to admit the request for admissions.

As of this time, plaintiff has not authorized defedants' counsel to interview the attending physicians and hospital personnel. Therefore, defendants cannot verify the matters set forth in the various bills attached to plaintiff's request for admissions. Nor are the defendants able to determine the qualifications, experience, or expertise of the various providers of health care to determine whether or not their charges for medical services are reasonable. If plaintiff would specify the amount of time spent by each provider of health care for each service rendered, defendants would be in a better position to evaluate the truth of the requests. Also plaintiff should supply a copy of all hospital and medical records which are the bases for making the charges reflected in the bills attached to the request for admissions.

REQUEST No. 2. That if the proper parties were called to testify, they would testify that each of the aforementioned expenses for medical care and attention referred to in Request for Admission number one was reasonable.

RESPONSE: DENIED. Please refer to Response 1.

REQUEST No. 3. That in the event you deny either Request for Admission number one or Request for Admission number two, supra, state the name, address, age, occupation, and employer of every person whom you will call to testify to dispute the reasonableness of such medical expenses.

RESPONSE: DENIED. Please refer to Response 1.

Dated: November 10, 1980

_____
Attorney for Defendants

======19

Evidence ==========

Most civil litigation evolves out of disputes on the facts. A resolution of each controversy depends upon proving the relevant facts. Therefore, courts must provide and use a rational means for proving the facts. The procedure for proving facts must promote the truth, be founded in fairness and be practical. The common law developed exclusionary rules of evidence which were calculated to promote justice between the parties. The exclusionary rules are premised on the proposition that any sworn testimony is competent to prove a fact unless the testimony violates one of the exclusionary rules. The significance of this statement is that the burden rests upon the party desiring to exclude evidence to show that it should not be considered by the court or jury. Broadly speaking, the exclusionary rules are directed at the following matters —

1. The witness is *incompetent* or disqualified from testifying because he or she:
   a. has not taken the oath;
   b. is not mentally competent;
   c. lacks knowledge about the matter;
   d. cannot qualify as an expert.
2. The testimony lacks probative value and is, therefore, *irrelevant* because:
   a. it is logically too weak;
   b. it is too remote in time;
   c. it is too remote in location;

d. it is a collateral matter which could cause more confusion than assistance.

3. If testimony is not based upon what the witness observed but upon what someone else told him or her, the testimony is objectionable as *hearsay*. Documents containing unsworn statements, not being subject to cross-examination, contain hearsay, and are objectionable on that ground.

4. Testimony that contradicts or changes a legally enforcable written agreement is *parol* (oral) evidence which is objectionable because the validity of written agreements would otherwise be impaired.

5. Matters that are *privileged* are subject to exclusion if the privilege is duly asserted. The exclusion applies to oral and written communications and to documents. Matters that are subject to a privilege include:

a. communications between lawyer and client and related documents;

b. conversations between husband and wife;

c. conversations between a physician and patient about the patient's medical condition;

d. conversations between a person and his or her priest or minister for spiritual guidance;

e. statments that require a witness to incriminate him or herself.

6. Testimony is subject to objection because it lacks *foundation*. Before a witness may testify about a fact, it must be shown that the witness is competent to make observations, and did make observations concerning the matters to which he or she is to testify. If the witness is to testify as an expert, it must be shown that he or she has adequate training and experience to render opinions concerning the subject matter.

7. Testimony is subject to objection and exclusion because a statute forbids the court to allow the evidence. A legislature or other rule making body may establish a public policy against use of certain evidence.

These brief descriptions are not necessarily complete. But they are indicative of the areas and considerations leading to the exclusion of evidence. Fundamentally, all evidence is sworn testimony. If a document or thing is received in evidence, it is because a witness has been able to show that the document is genuine and contains reasonably reliable information. Some — very few — documents are self-authenticating.

The common law exclusionary rules of evidence were revised, modified and codified in the *Federal Rules of Evidence* which were promulgated by Congress on July 1, 1975. These Rules apply to all judicial proceedings in our federal courts. Many states have adopted codifications of rules of evidence based upon the federal example.

A party may have a legitimate claim or defense, but unless he or she can prove it, the claim or defense will fail. Most of a lawyer's time and effort spent preparing for trial involves gathering the evidence with which to prove his or her client's claims or defenses. Evidence is the testimony, exhibits and factual stipulations which a judge allows the jury to consider for the purpose of rendering a verdict. As a lawyer marshals the evidence for presentation at trial, he or she must consider, first, its admissibility and second, its persuasiveness. If there is a lack of evidence to prove a claim or defense, the judge must disallow the claim or defense for insufficiency of the evidence.

Many lawyers are inclined to risk the displeasure of the judge and irritation of the jury by presenting more evidence than necessary rather than risk the possibility of a directed verdict against a client or an adverse jury verdict due to the absence of some item of evidence. Needless to say, preparing for and handling a trial requires a lawyer to make important judgments about the evidence. He or she must decide how much time and money should be spent searching for evidence; what evidence should be disregarded; in what order the evidence should be presented; what means of presentation would be most effective. For example, should the operation of a machine be explained by using an expert witness, photographs, a model, drawings, or all four?

The judge must determine what evidence may be considered by the jury. However, evidence is seldom excluded unless one of the parties objects. There is an assumption that all the parties want the evidence unless objected to. If an objection is not seasonably made, it is waived. The jury must consider the evidence as a whole to determine the truth. Only after the truth has been ascertained is the jury able to apply the law to the facts for the purpose of reaching a verdict. The jury may draw inferences from established facts, but they cannot speculate about matters not proved by evidence. The jury cannot supply missing facts by guessing or even through the independent knowledge of the jurors. Jurors may use their knowledge only to evaluate the evidence presented in court.

After determining the facts and making appropriate inferences, the jury must resolve the *ultimate questions of fact*. In a negligence action, the *ultimate* facts are the answers to questions such as: (1) was the defendant negligent; (2) was the defendant's negligence a proximate cause of the accident; (3) was the plaintiff negligent; (4) was the plaintiff's negligence a proximate cause of the accident; if both were causally negligent, what are their percentages of causal negligence; (5) what sum of money would provide full and adequate compensation? In a contract case, the ultimate questions of fact are the answers to the questions: (1) did the parties have a valid contract; (2) did the defendant breach the contract; (3) did the plaintiff breach the contract; (4) what sum of money would fairly compensate the plaintiff?

CATEGORIES OF EVIDENCE

Evidence takes various forms and can be categorized in various ways. The law does not prefer one form of evidence over another. Application of the exclusionary rules of evidence does not turn or depend upon categories of evidence. Categorizing evidence is useful only for the purpose of gaining an understanding of the preparation and use of evidence in litigation.

Testimony

A witness may testify to almost anything that he or she has observed if able to comprehend and relate his or her observations. Even a child of tender years may qualify as a witness, but he or she must understand and appreciate the duty to tell the truth. The oath or affirmation required of witnesses emphasizes the court's commitment to the truth and the witness's duty to tell the whole truth. A witness must be mentally competent. He or she must not be under the influence of intoxicants or drugs. But a witness who was intoxicated at the time of an occurrence may, nevertheless, be permitted to testify concerning observations about the occurrence. State of intoxication relates to his or her believability, not to the admissibility. A lawyer is prohibited by legal ethics from testifying at a trial in which he or she appears as counsel.

The testimony is supposed to come from the witness, not from the lawyer who is questioning him or her. For that reason and others, leading questions are disfavored. Any question that contains its own answer or suggests the desired answer is a leading question. Leading questions are regularly used and frequently necessary during the cross-examination of a witness. Whenever cross-examination is allowed, there is a presumption that the witness, such as an adverse party, will not permit him or herself to be led around by the lawyer. Leading questions are routinely permitted during a direct examination for preliminary and background information where no controversy exists. Leading questions may be put to any witness at any time in the absence of objection by one of the parties. However, experienced trial lawyers know that leading questions used in the direct examination of a friendly witness tend to reduce the witness's authority. An important element of persuasiveness is lost.

Demonstrative and Illustrative Evidence

Any tangible or visual item is considered by most lawyers to be demonstrative evidence. Demonstrative evidence may involve the very heart of the controversy such as an allegedly defective product. For example, an allegedly defective tire may be the subject of the lawsuit. Or demonstrative evidence may be a pictorial presentation used merely to illustrate some aspect of the case. Tangible evidence that is directly related to the case is ordinarily received into evidence as an exhibit that the jury may take to the jury room and examine during their deliberation. It is, in itself, evidence upon which a verdict may be based. Suppose that the subject of the lawsuit is a large machine that is too big for the courtroom. Suppose the plaintiff claims that the machine is defective in design because it is top heavy and dangerously unstable. Photographs of the machine are evidence of what the machine looks like and may be helpful to show its operation. A model of the machine may be useful to show its physical characteristics, and, therefore, be received into evidence as an exhibit for the jury to examine.

Photographs may be used to show the facts in issue such as photographs of an accident scene showing the vehicles, parties, skidmarks, and vehicle damage. Motion pictures of an airplane crashing would be the most graphic kind of evidence of an event giving rise to a lawsuit. However, unless the motion picture tended to establish controverted facts, there is a danger that such a pictorial presentation would merely impassion the jury causing them to be prejudiced. In such cases, the judge must decide whether the photographs' prejudicial effect outweighs their probative value. The same is true of photographs made during the acute stages of an injury.

Some demonstrative evidence is presented to the jury during the trial as an aid to understanding a witness's testimony. The tangible evidence is used to illustrate the witness's observations or opinions. The evidence may or may not be marked as an exhibit. Very often illustrative evidence does not go to the jury for its use in its deliberations. For example, a witness may make a sketch on a blackboard to help explain his or her testimony and for the purpose of reinforcing the jurors' memories. Other examples of illustrative exhibits include photographs taken at an accident site *after* the instrumentalities involved have been removed. Photographs taken days or even months later may be helpful to illustrate conditions that existed at the time of the accident though those conditions are not depicted per se. In a product liability case, the manufacturer may have films showing destruction tests on similar products. Such films are used solely for illustrative purposes. A physician may use a model of the human spine to illustrate an injury to a vertebra or intervertebral disc, or to show how a nerve injury occurred in his or her opinion. The model would not necessarily be an exhibit to be used by the jury in their deliberations.

Engineers' scale drawings may be very helpful at trial to show sizes, relationships and even functions. Often the drawings are used by several different witnesses to illustrate each witness's observations. The jury could not possibly absorb and remember all the details shown in the drawing. Consequently, more often than not, such drawings become evidence that does go to the jury for consideration during their deliberations.

Another form of demonstrative evidence which is encouraged by courts as a time saver is use of summaries, charts and graphs for the purpose of reducing voluminous documents down to the essentials. Rule 1006.

Demonstrative evidence has the obvious value of psychological impact. Jurors are more likely to understand and remember the facts and a party's theory of the facts when demonstrative evidence is used. Lawyers are always looking for new ways and better ways of using demonstrative evidence.

Facts and Opinions

Generally courts require evidence to be factual rather than someone's opinion or belief about the facts. It is the jury's responsibility to draw conclusions from the facts observed by the witnesses. However, there are some very important exceptions.

Every day a person acts and reacts more on the basis of his or her opinions or conclusions than on the basis of established facts. Many situations and conditions cannot be described factually in a meaningful way. For example, an experienced driver observes that an automobile ahead of her has stopped, so she knows she must stop before she gets there. Most drivers are able to bring their automobile to a smooth complete stop at a reasonable distance behind the stopped vehicle without *knowing* the measured distance or the measured braking force. A driver stopping in an intersection to make a lefthand turn knows he must yield to oncoming traffic that is close enough to constitute a hazard if he were to proceed to make his turn. The left turning motorist must make a judgment concerning the oncoming vehicle's distance and speed. These judgments are usually quite reliable even though a motorist might not be able to estimate the number of feet or yards involved. How does one measure, factually, the slipperiness of a floor or the condition of lighting at a certain place at dusk? How can an eyewitness ever know, factually, the speed of a passing vehicle? At best, he or she can have an opinion about the facts. The law was established by people to deal with human situations and institutions. It must, therefore, deal with human problems on human terms. When a condition or situation is one which can best be described in the form of an opinion which is meaningful, opinion evidence is generally permitted. So, ordinarily, a witness who has personal knowledge about the condition of a floor or sidewalk or street is permitted to express an opinion that it was or was not slippery. A lay witness who admits to some "worldliness" usually qualifies to express an opinion whether a person he or she observed was or was not intoxicated. Lighting conditions may be described in commonly used terms such as "pitch black" or "fairly dark" or "easily visible" or "bright." These terms are probably more meaningful to a jury than scientific measurements.

EYEWITNESS VIEWS

Fact	Opinion
miles per hour	fast
1 mile	far or close
10,000 candle power	bright
specific color	dark or light
without variations	smooth
many variations	rough
inches, feet, yards, meters	"block" as unit of measurement
" "	wide or narrow
" "	high
100 decibels	loud or soft
crying	sad, depressed, unhappy, hurting
grimaced, muscle spasm	painful
weight lifted or moved	weak or strong
60 watt bulb	dim or bright
disfigured	ugly
in compliance	sufficient, adequate, correct
out of compliance	wrong, mistake

Of course, a witness cannot have a valid opinion unless he or she had an adequate opportunity to observe the occurrence, condition or person in question. Only after the witness has shown that he or she is capable of observing, did observe and is able to recall the observations, may he or she go on to render an opinion about what was observed. In other words, the opinion evidence requires a foundation. A witness would not qualify to give an opinion that a sidewalk was slippery due to ice if he or she merely observed it at a distance or had not used it for over a week. A witness would not qualify to give an opinion that another person was intoxicated unless he or she observed signs of intoxication such as slurred speech, unsteady gait, loud inappropriate conduct, loss of inhibitions, flushed appearance, odor of alcohol, or red eyes. A witness may express an opinion about the speed of a passing vehicle only if he or she observed it long enough and has sufficient experience to form a valid opinion about speed in miles per hour. In automobile accident cases, witnesses are *not* allowed to express opinions of speed in relative terms such as "fast", "slow" or "normal." Naturally, there has to be an exception! If a party *admits* to going "too fast", the admission would be received into evidence against him or her.

The following typical jury instructions contain guidelines for the jury for evaluating testimony.

> You are the sole judges of whether a witness is to be believed and of the weight to be given to his or her testimony. There are no hard and fast rules to guide you in this respect. In determining believability and weight you should take into consideration as to each witness the following:
>
> 1. Interest or lack of interest in the outcome of the case,
> 2. Relationship to the parties,
> 3. Ability and opportunity to know, remember, and relate the facts,
> 4. Manner and appearance,
> 5. Age and experience,
> 6. Frankness and sincerity, or lack thereof,
> 7. The reasonableness or unreasonableness of his or her testimony in the light of all the other evidence in the case,
> 8. Any impeachment of his or her testimony,
> 9. Any other factors that bear on believability and weight.
>
> You should in the last analysis rely upon your own experience, good judgment, and common sense.

Expert Witnesses

A person who has special education, training, knowledge and experience in a particular subject or field *may* qualify to give expert opinion testimony about the subject. A physician's diagnosis of an injury may be the determination of a fact, or, an opinion based upon apparent facts. The physician's determination of the cause of an injury or disability is almost always a matter of opinion. The preferred method of treatment is frequently a matter of opinion. A partial list of experts includes scientists, accountants, farmers, carpenters, electricians, engineers, architects, physicians, mechanics and machine operators. The author had the help of a professional baseball manager (Billy Martin) and baseball player in testifying as expert witnesses concerning batting in a particular case. So the fields and types of matters calling for experts are without limit. Again, the opinion evidence requires a foundation to establish that the witness has the necessary background and is sufficiently knowledgeable about the subject in question to have a reasonably reliable opinion.

The judge must decide in each case whether the foundation is adequate. It is not uncommon for competent expert witnesses to reach different conclusions. The fact that the experts' opinions differ is not a concern to the judge. If there is sufficient foundation for the opinions, the jury must consider and weigh the opinions along with all the other evidence and decide which, if any, of the experts are correct.

Cases involving claims of professional malpractice (whether or not medical) usually depend upon expert testimony in at least three or four areas. First, experts must determine the underlying facts concerning the *nature* of the injury, loss or failure. Second, experts must determine what *caused* the injury, loss or failure. Third, was the cause of the injury, loss or failure due to *negligence* on the part of the professional. The expert witness must be familiar with the customs and standards of the defendant's profession. Negligence is synonymous with malpractice in such cases. A professional person is liable for the harm proximately caused by his or her negligence.

In many cases it is necessary to go another step with the proof and show that a deviation from the applicable professional standards cannot be justified on the basis of professional judgment. When an expert gives such testimony, he or she is actually giving an opinion on the ultimate question of fact — telling the jury how he or she would decide the case based upon the information available to or assumed by him or her. Historically, a witness was not permitted to invade the province of the jury by testifying to the ultimate question of fact. However, the law has changed. Rule 704 expressly authorizes such opinion testimony — even by laymen. Perhaps a lay witness is now permitted to testify, not only that the sidewalk was "slippery" but that it was "too slippery to walk upon." The courts have not yet established the parameters of this relatively new and somewhat controversial rule.

The following is a typical jury instruction which contains guidelines for the jury on how to evaluate an expert witness and his or her testimony.

A witness who has special training, education or experience in a particular science, profession or calling, is an expert and, in addition to giving testimony as to facts, may be allowed to express an expert opinion. In determining the believability and the weight to be given such opinion evidence, you may consider, among other things:

1. The education, training, experience, knowledge, and ability of the expert.
2. The reasons given for his or her opinion.
3. The sources of information.
4. Factors already given for evaluating the testimony of a witness.

Direct and Circumstantial Evidence

A fact may be proved by either direct evidence or circumstantial evidence or both. The law does not prefer one form over the other. Direct evidence is the testimony from witnesses who observed the facts to which they testify. Direct evidence also includes the exhibits which, in themselves, establish facts. The testimony of a witness that he or she saw certain automobile skid marks is direct evidence proving the existence of the skidmarks. A photograph showing skidmarks is direct evidence proving the existence of the skidmarks.

Circumstantial evidence is *indirect* proof that depends upon principles of logic and common experience to prove a fact. The process depends upon deductive reasoning. By proving one or more facts through direct evidence it is *permissible* in law to infer from those established facts the existence of other facts. For example, by proving the existence of skidmarks by direct evidence a party may prove, by circumstantial evidence, the location of the vehicles before impact and at impact. The skidmarks also permit an inference that the driver applied her brakes at a certain point and, further, that the driver observed the danger at some point before applying her brakes. Or, suppose that a construction worker had spent two weeks working in close proximity to an electric powerline and then was burned upon contacting it. The circumstantial evidence permits an inference that he knew the wire was there and considered it to be dangerous having previously avoided it. The inference is permissible even though the witness denies that he was aware of it.

Substantive and Impeachment Evidence

Substantive evidence is *any* evidence the jury is allowed to consider that is capable of supporting a verdict. The form of the evidence makes no difference.

Impeachment evidence is considered for the purpose of testing the credibility of a witness. It is evidence that the witness has said something or written something or conducted him or herself in a manner inconsistent with what was testified to in court. For example, if a witness testified that he observed the defendant enter the intersection without stopping for the red light, he would be impeached by the testimony of another witness who heard the first witness say that he did not notice the color of the traffic lights at the time of the accident, or that he heard the first witness say, at the accident scene, that the *plaintiff* went through the red light. The reason that the second witness's testimony is not substantive evidence (but merely impeachment) is that the first witness's out of court statement is not sworn testimony subject to cross-examination. The second witness's testimony about what he heard the first witness say at the accident scene is sworn testimony subject to cross-examination, but not as to the truth of the first witness's observations — only about what the first witness said. If the jury chose to believe the sworn testimony of the first witness, they could determine that the defendant did violate the traffic light. But if the jury believed the second witness who heard the first witness say the plaintiff went through the red light, the jury would be left with no substantive evidence from these two witnesses about the color of the traffic light. More specifically, only the first witness claimed to see the color of the light, and he cannot be believed, so there is no evidence on the point through these two witnesses.

If impeachment evidence applies to a party, the impeachment evidence may also be substantive evidence. For example, if a witness heard the plaintiff admit that he went through the stop sign but the plaintiff testifies at trial that he stopped, the *party admission* would be received as impeachment and as substantive evidence that the plaintiff did go through the stop sign.

Hypothetical Questions

An expert witness must base an opinion on facts that he or she has observed or upon facts which have been proved through other witnesses and exhibits. "Proved" in this sense does not mean that the jury necessarily accepted those facts; it means that the facts have been received into evidence and the jury is allowed to consider them. Since an expert witness usually does not have personal knowledge about the occurrence and many other important facts, the problem arises: how can he or she qualify to render an opinion based upon those facts? The answer is: through the device of the hypothetical question. The hypothetical question permits the expert to *assume* that facts contained in the hypothetical question are true — just as though he or she had personally observed those facts. Sometimes the hypothetical questions are very long, involving many paragraphs. The longer the hypothetical question, the greater the risk that it might fail, either because it is technically defective or because it lacks persuasiveness. The jury is instructed at the end of the trial that the expert's opinion assumes and depends upon the truth of *all* the facts contained in the hypothetical questions. If the jury should determine that any one or more of the assumed facts is not true or not established, the expert's opinion based upon the hypothetical question should be rejected. The cross-examination of an expert who relies upon a hypothetical question is often directed at showing that the expert does not have knowledge of the facts and that he or she is assuming each fact to be true. Sometimes the cross-examiner is able to show that the hypothetical question contains facts that are contrary to the expert's own records or inconsistent with observations that the expert has made.

Hypothetical questions are almost always reduced to writing and previewed with the expert before he or she takes the stand. An experienced paralegal could help with preparation of the hypothetical question. Each lawyer develops his or her own form and approach. As a general rule, the shorter it is, the more reliable and effective it is.

Exhibits

Any tangible item that a party offers into evidence for the jury to consider must first become an exhibit and part of the record. It becomes an exhibit only after one or more witnesses have identified it and have shown that it is relevant to the case. Once it has been given an exhibit identification mark, the lawyers refer to it by the marking, usually a number or letter. The following dialogue is representative of the necessary foundation establishing identity, authenticity, and relevancy of an exhibit.

[Lawyer questioning personnel manager of a company laying foundation for admissibility of personnel records.]

Q. I am now showing you what has been marked as Plaintiff's Exhibit A. Can you identify that for us?

A. Yes, that is Mr. John Smith's personnel file with the XYZ Corporation.

Q. Who has custody of these records?

A. As personnel manager of the XYZ Corporation, I have custody of these records.

Q. How long have you been the personnel manager?

A. For the past ten years.

Q. Did you bring these records with you to court pursuant to a subpoena served upon you yesterday?

A. Yes.

Q. Have you brought with you all of Mr. Smith's personnel records that are kept in your custody and control?

A. Yes.

Q. Are these records kept in the ordinary course of the business of the XYZ Corporation?

A. They are.

Counsel to the Court: Plaintiff offers Plaintiff's Exhibit A into evidence.

Court: (To Defendant's counsel) Is there any objection to the Exhibit?

If the relevancy of the records is not apparent, relevancy must be shown by indicating how the documents tend to prove controverted facts. When a party offers a record into evidence, he or she must have the entire record available so that any portions omitted can be examined. Otherwise, there is danger of taking facts out of context. Once the original records are made available for examination, it is common for the parties to stipulate that photocopies may be received into evidence in lieu of the originals. The originals are then returned to their custodian.

[Plaintiff's lawyer questioning plaintiff laying foundation for a photograph that plaintiff took of his automobile after an accident.]

Q. I am now showing you a photograph marked as Plaintiff's Exhibit A. Can you identify it for us?

A. Yes, it is a photograph that I took of my automobile.

Q. When was the photograph taken?

A. On June 7, 1981.

Q. Where was it taken?

A. At the Anderson Chevrolet garage.

Q. What portion of your vehicle is depicted in the photograph?

A. The rear portion of my automobile.

Q. Does the picture fairly show the condition of your automobile as it appeared after the accident?

A. Yes.

Q. Is the damage that appears in the photograph entirely a result of the automobile accident on June 4, 1981?

A. No.

Q. What damage is shown in the photograph that, to your knowledge, did not occur in the accident?

A. The photograph shows the rear bumper pulled back on the right side. That happened at the garage — maybe when the car was towed in.

Q. Otherwise, does the photograph fairly show and represent the damage that the rear portion of the car sustained in the accident?

A. Yes.

Counsel to the Court: Plaintiff offers Plaintiff's Exhibit A into evidence.

Court to defendant's counsel: Is there any objection?

At this point, the defendant's lawyer is allowed to ask questions only about foundation for the exhibit, i.e., questions concerning admissibility of the exhibit. Any questions he or she has about its probative value will have to wait until the plaintiff's lawyer has finished his or her direct examination.

When a photograph is offered into evidence, it is desirable to have the photographer available to explain the method of making the photograph as well as its subject matter. It is well known that the type of lens used in a camera can significantly change the subject matter's appearance, especially its depth and apparent width. Distances between two points can be made to look quite different depending upon the type of lens used. However, it is often sufficient for purposes of laying foundation to have a witness or party to the suit who is acquainted with the subject matter testify that the photograph accurately portrays the subject. Note that the photograph does not establish itself. It is just an extension of the testimony of the witness. The extent of the foundation that is required depends upon the purpose for which the photograph is offered and whether there is any actual dispute over it. As often as not, both sides want the photograph in evidence.

Judicial Notice

A trial judge may take judicial notice of certain facts and those facts are binding upon the parties and the jury. As stated in Rule 201(b):

A judicially noticed fact must be one not subject to reasonable dispute in that it is either (1) generally known within the territorial jurisdiction of the trial court or (2) capable of accurate and ready determination by resorting to sources whose accuracy cannot reasonably be questioned.

For example, a judge may determine that December 25, 1981 fell on a Friday, or that there are 5,280 feet in a mile. When the judge takes judicial notice of a fact, the parties do not have to present evidence to establish the fact. The judge simply tells the jury that it is an established fact which they must accept as true.

Suppose that in an action for trespass it becomes material as to whether the trespass occurred within or outside the corporate limits of a municipality. If there were no controversy over the precise location of the alleged trespass, the trial judge could take judicial notice of the fact that the conduct occurred within or outside the corporate limits. However, a controversy over the location of the alleged trespass would have to be resolved by the jury from the evidence.

A court may take judicial notice of scientific fact. Examples: an object traveling at sixty miles per hour moves eighty-eight feet per second; December 25, 1981 falls on a Friday; water boils at 212 degrees Fahrenheit; Los Angeles is in the Pacific time zone. By statute in some states, a trial judge is authorized to take judicial notice of a person's normal life expectancy as established by approved actuarial tables.

According to Rule 201, the court may take judicial notice of such facts whether or not requested to do so by the parties. In civil litigation, which is our concern, judicially noticed facts are to be accepted by the jury as conclusive. The judge may conduct a hearing in the absence of the jury to determine whether or not the fact in question is true and whether he or she should take judicial notice of it.

Summaries

Occasionally litigation involves thousands of records and documents, the contents of which are essential to proving a claim or defense. More often than not, the parties do not have any real dispute about the contents in fact, but they do differ on the effect of the documents or conclusions to be drawn from them. The discovery rules provide a means for reviewing and copying the documents in advance of trial. Rule 1006 authorizes a party to prepare a summary of the records or charts that may be received into evidence in lieu of the original documents. The rule encourages the parties to conduct a thorough review of all the relevant documentation *before* the trial and thereby reduce the amount of time needed for presentation of the essential evidence from the documents. The rule authorizes that:

> The contents of voluminous writings, recordings, or photographs which cannot conveniently be examined in court may be presented in the form of a chart, summary, or calculation. The originals, or duplicates, shall be made available for examination or copying, or both, by other parties at reasonable time and place. The court may order that they be produced in court.

Summaries which are prepared for use as provided in Rule 1006 are not part of a lawyer's work product. They are discoverable and should be seasonably disclosed to all other parties to avoid unnecessary delay at trial. The original documents must be available for inspection and comparison.

Presumptions

Some facts may be established at trial by presumptions in law. The presumptions, unlike judicial noticed facts, are not binding upon the parties and jury. A jury may find for or against a presumed fact.

Suppose the plaintiff has the burden of proving that a certain written notice was delivered to the defendant. The plaintiff may prove it by showing that the notice was sent to the defendant by U.S. mail in an envelope that was properly addressed, had the proper postage and was deposited in a U.S. mailbox or delivered to a post office. By proving these facts and that the envelope was not returned, a presumption in law arises that the letter was delivered to the defendant addressee. This is true even though the defendant denies receiving the letter. The underlying facts concerning addressing and mailing the notice must be established by a witness who has personal knowledge or through business records. A post office receipt is not necessary but helpful. The jury must decide whether or not the presumption of delivery is more convincing or less convincing than the defendant's sworn denial. The presumption exists because of the necessity of such proof and the probability that it is true. As described by Rule 301:

> In all civil actions and proceedings not otherwise provided for by statute or by these rules, a presumption imposes on the party against whom it is directed the burden of going forward with evidence to rebut or meet the presumption, but does not shift to such party the burden of proof in the sense of the risk of nonpersuasion, which remains throughout the trial upon the party on whom it was originally cast.

In cases involving death, there is a presumption that the decedent did not commit suicide. In cases where the plaintiff delivers personal property to the defendant's custody and it is returned in a damaged condition, there is a presumption that the damage was caused by negligence on the part of the defendant. If the defendant fails to present any evidence explaining how the damage occurred, so as to negate any negligence on his part, the plaintiff is entitled to a verdict against the defendant. However, if the defendant does offer an explanation, it must be weighed by the jury against the presumption in law that the loss was caused by the defendant's negligence.

There are many other presumptions in law. Some have been created by the courts as part of the common law. Other presumptions have been created by statute. Their use and limitations are important in litigation. A comprehensive listing of presumptions and their applications is beyond the scope of this book.

Res Ipsa Loquitur

The plaintiff in a "negligence action" has the burden of proving that the defendant was negligent and that the defendant's negligence was a proximate cause of accident and the plaintiff's injury or other loss. Ordinarily the burden of proof is met by showing how the accident occurred and that the defendant violated some statute, contractual duty, custom, practice or other standard establishing a duty of reasonable care. But once in a while there is no evidence available to the plaintiff to show how or why the accident occurred, because the instrumentality was solely under the control of the defendant at the time of the accident. The problems that the plaintiff has in such cases have been given special treatment by the courts.

Where the accident is of the type that, in itself, speaks of negligence on the part of the defendant, the plaintiff is given the benefit of the **res ipsa loquitur** doctrine which creates a permissible inference of negligence on the part of the defendant. Res ipsa loquitur means that the thing (accident) itself speaks. The defendant has the opportunity to try to explain why he or she denies the negligence. The doctrine has its origin and justification in the probability that the accident was due solely to the defendant's negligence and the evidence concerning the occurrence is more readily available to the defendant, so he or she should come forward with an explanation. In most states the doctrine does not shift the burden of proof. The permissible inference, however, is sufficient in itself to carry the burden of proof even if the defendant has an explanation that exonerates him or her from any fault.

The following jury instruction on res ipsa loquitur is typical:

When an accident is such that ordinarily it would not have happened unless someone had been negligent, and if the instrumentality which caused the injury is shown to have been under the exclusive control of the defendant, you are permitted to infer from the accident itself and the circumstances surrounding it, that the defendant was negligent.

Before you are permitted to make this inference, you must find all of the following:

(1) that the accident is of the type that does not ordinarily occur in the absence of negligence;

(2) that the defendant was in *exclusive* control of the instrumentality which caused the injury (or property damage) claimed;

(3) that the accident did not result from any voluntary act or negligence on the part of the plaintiff or some third person for whom the defendant would not be responsible.

The doctrine has applicability in cases where a restaurant customer is injured by a foreign object in his or her food; where an airplane passenger is injured or killed due to an unexplained crash; where a passenger on a railroad train is injured when the train derails or crashes into another train operated by the same railroad; where a patient undergoes surgery and sustains injury to another part of his or her body during the operation; where a passenger is injured when an automobile leaves the highway and crashes for some unknown reason; where an elevator falls; where city gas escapes from utility pipes; where electricity escapes from an appliance under the defendant's control; where a dentist's drill slips causing injury to the patient's mouth; or a surgeon leaves a surgical instrument or sponge in the patient. In the last example, a jury would be allowed to infer that the physician was negligent for leaving a surgical sponge in the patient even though no physician testified on behalf of the plaintiff that a medical standard was violated. Most courts have concluded that laymen are capable of making that decision without the necessity of expert testimony.

There are numerous other situations in which the doctrine may have applicability. In all cases, however, it must be shown that the defendant was in exclusive control of the instrumentality at the time the alleged negligence occurred. For example, if the defendant's building collapsed, damaging the plaintiff's property and the defendant could show that the collapsed building was occupied by trespassing vandals at the time, the plaintiff would fail to establish the requisite of exclusive control by the defendant and, therefore, would not have the benefit of the doctrine. The doctrine may work in favor of the defendant against the plaintiff where the plaintiff has exclusive control of the instrumentality.

THE FEDERAL
RULES OF EVIDENCE

The ultimate objective of the Federal Rules of Civil Procedure is the determination of each case on a just basis. Justice is accomplished when the truth is ascertained and the law is correctly applied to those facts. Rule 102.

Most of the exclusionary rules of evidence are merely common sense rules which help to insure that the jury's verdict is based on evidence that is factual, probative, the best available, and that is not fabricated for purposes of the lawsuit. The exclusionary rules are premised in logic, practicability, human experience and human nature. Trial judges have a great deal of latitude or discretion in determining whether or not evidence should be excluded. When a judge has acted with discretion he or she will not be reversed. He or she may be reversed only for a clear abuse of discretion. The exclusionary rules cannot be applied with mathematical precision or certainty. The tendency is to rule in favor of admissibility, letting the jury decide what weight to give to the evidence.

If a party fails to object or neglects to move the court to strike evidence improperly received, he or she waives the right to complain. He or she is not permitted to use the error as a basis for seeking a new trial or reversal upon appeal. As always, there is an exception to the general rule. If the error was so manifest and so likely to have brought about an unjust result, the trial court or appellate court may take notice of "plain error" and grant relief in the form of a new trial, directed verdict or reversal. Rule 103(d).

If a lawyer believes that the court has erroneously excluded evidence which would be helpful to a client, he or she has a right to make an *offer of proof* outside the hearing of the jury. The offer of proof is nothing more than a statement by the lawyer or testimony of a witness showing the facts which would have been established if the evidence had been allowed. The lawyer's statement or witness's testimony is made part of the trial record and, therefore, may be considered by the appellate court in the event there is a subsequent appeal. Rule 103(a) (2).

Objections to evidence are supposed to be stated in a concise technical form without argument. For example, a lawyer may state: "The question is objected to on the grounds of hearsay." A lawyer is subject to criticism by the court and possibly receives a counter-objection if he or she argues: "The question is objected to because this witness doesn't have any personal knowledge about the subject matter and is only relying upon some highly questionable statement she heard or read." Lawyers are not supposed to argue the value, weight or effect of the evidence until the final arguments. Rule 103(c). The lawyers may seek leave of the court to argue their positions on the evidence outside of the hearing of the jury.

Materiality

Probably the most fundamental requirement of evidence is that it be **material.** Evidence is material if it has a bearing on the issues in the lawsuit. If one party attempts to inject facts into the case which do not relate to the issues as raised by the pleadings, the opposing lawyer should object on the grounds that the facts are immaterial. If there is no objection to evidence which is immaterial, that evidence may have the effect of amending the pleadings by implication. The pleadings are then construed to conform to the evidence, rather than vice versa. Rule 15(b). A judge may exclude immaterial evidence on his or her own motion to keep the parties from digressing and to avoid abuses of the court's time.

There is an unfortunate trend toward the use of the word "relevancy" instead of "materiality." The distinction should be maintained. They involve different concepts.

Relevancy

To be admissible, evidence must be relevant which means the evidence must be material *and* have probative value. Rule 401 defines relevancy as "evidence having any tendency to make the existence of any fact that is of consequence to the determination of the action more probable or less probable than it would be without the evidence." If the evidence does not logically tend to prove or disprove a controverted fact, the evidence is subject to exclusion on the grounds that it is irrelevant.

Relevancy may be determined by such factors as time and distance. For example, if a witness observed a motor vehicle traveling at a high rate of speed when it was ten miles away from the point where it was subsequently involved in an accident, the question arises whether the evidence of speed so distant would logically tend to prove how the accident occurred. Evidence which shows that the defendant motorist was an habitual drunk and drunk during the day preceeding the accident in question would not have any probative value if he was not under the influence of intoxicants at the time of the accident. Evidence that the defendant had been involved in a similar accident at the same place three years earlier does not tend to prove how or why the second accident occurred. Proof that the defenant was found liable on other contracts, which he denied, does not prove he is liable on the one in question. Evidence which shows that the defendant had a small quantity of alcohol before the accident should be excluded unless it can be shown that the party's conduct was actually affected by the alcohol. Irrelevant evidence tends to cloud and confuse the issues. It needlessly takes up the time of the court. Too often it has a prejudicial effect because it may raise innuendoes of wrongdoing without any factual basis.

Best Evidence

Courts require the parties to present the best evidence reasonably available. This means that a copy of a document should not be used if the *original document* is reasonably available. Rule 1002. Otherwise, copies of documents are subject to the objection that they are "not the best evidence." If the absence of the original can be explained, then a copy is the best evidence and may be used. For example, if it can be shown that the opponent was last to have custody of the original, or that the original is needed elsewhere, a copy may be used. Of course, parties may stipulate to the use of copies and that is often done in cases involving hospital and business records.

Hearsay

Hearsay evidence is any out of court statement, oral or written, which is offered to prove the truth of matters referred to in the statement. The rule excluding hearsay is logical and goes to the very heart of the adversary system. Facts should be established through witnesses who have firsthand knowledge about the facts. It is their powers of observation, memory, and truthfulness which the jury should assess and not that of another person who heard the observer's description of the facts. Hearsay evidence deprives the parties of the *right* of cross-examination. The basic rule against hearsay and its application are fairly easy to understand. The numerous important exceptions to the hearsay rule are what create the difficulties for lawyers and the courts. The exceptions are based upon the usual reliability of some kinds of hearsay evidence and the convenience of using it.

Historically, any statement made by an adverse party could be received into evidence against him or her as an "admission." Admissions by a party were received into evidence as an exception to the hearsay rule. Rule 801(d) (2) provides that such admissions shall be received into evidence on the basis that they are not hearsay. An admission may be made by the party or by the party's agent who had authority to make such statements. The admission by an agent, of course, must be made during the agency relationship. Rule 801(d) (1) also provides that prior out of court statements made by a witness may be received into evidence as substantive evidence, not merely impeachment, if the prior statement was under oath and subject to cross-examination. Such prior statements would have to be part of a deposition or testimony at a hearing or a trial. Again, the rule declares such statements not to be hearsay.

Parol Evidence

When the parties enter into a written contract which purports to contain the entire agreement, it would be unfair to have either party attempt, at trial, to change the terms of that agreement by oral testimony. Consequently, an exclusionary rule of evidence has evolved, known as the parol evidence rule, which precludes any evidence which attempts to vary or contradict the clear language of a writing that the parties have used to formalize their agreement. The rule applies to contracts, promissory notes, mortgages, deeds, wills, etc.

As is true of most rules, there are exceptions to the parol evidence rule. Parol evidence may be received to clarify ambiguities in the writing. But a judge must first determine that the writing is ambiguous, i.e., reasonably subject to more than one meaning. Also, parol evidence may be used to prove that the written document was induced or procured by fraud by the other party. A contract may be set aside (rescinded) where there is a mutual mistake by the parties going to the very heart of the contract. Fraud or mutual mistake may be proved by parol evidence. Proof of a mutual mistake must be established by *clear and convincing evidence* — not by a mere preponderance of the evidence. Parol evidence may be received to establish a subsequent change in the contract mutually agreed to by the parties. However, most formal written agreements or undertakings expressly provide that any modification must be in writing, signed by all parties.

Dead Man Statute

Some states have the so-called dead man statute which provides that a party to a lawsuit may not testify concerning any oral statements he or she heard another person make if, at the time of trial, the person who made the utterance is deceased. The statute is intended to reduce the possibility that parties may fabricate evidence. If a party fails to object to such testimony when presented, the evidence will be received, and a verdict may be based upon it. In other words, the exclusionary rule created by the statute must be asserted in a timely manner at trial or the statutory prohibition is waived. Note that the exclusionary rule applies only to prevent *parties* from testifying. It does not prevent independent witnesses from testifying about oral statements made by persons who died before trial. The dead man's statute has no application to writings; it applies only to oral statements.

The Federal Code of Evidence does not recognize the dead man statute. Rule 616.

Evidence and Public Policy

Some evidence is excluded because it would be contrary to public policy to allow its use at trial. A primary example is the rule which precludes parties from putting in evidence another party's statements made in the course of settlement negotiations. Rule 408. The courts want parties to discuss their differences and to settle their controversies without having to go through a trial if possible. Settlement negotiations are good! If parties had to labor under the fear that their efforts to compromise would be used against them, negotiations would be sharply curtailed, if not impossible. Therefore a jury is never told about the parties' negotiations. The danger is much too great that a jury would be unduly influenced by such knowledge.

Rule 409 goes on to provide that a party's offer to pay another's medical expenses may not be used against the offeror as an admission of liability for the accident. A typical situation is where a person falls down on premises where he or she is visiting. The owner of the premises may suggest, even urge, the guest to have a medical checkup, which the owner will pay for. The suggestion cannot be used against the offeror as an admission of fault. The offer may be proved, however, for the purpose of holding the offeror to his or her promise.

In a personal injury action where the accident was allegedly caused by a dangerous condition on land or in a building or where a defect in a prodcut caused injury, the plaintiff would undoubtedly be helped with his or her burden of proving that the condition or product was unreasonably dangerous by proving that the defendant made repairs or changes right after the accident. After all, such a change could well be interpreted as an admission that it was dangerous. However, if the courts were to allow evidence of remedial measures, defendants would be discouraged from making changes which may provide greater safety in the future. Again, public policy considerations have led the courts to exclude evidence of remedial measures. Furthermore, a party's standard of care should not be judged on the basis of hindsight. Repairs and changes are generally the result of hindsight. Rule 407.

Where changes have been made after an accident, the defendant's lawyer usually brings that fact to the attention of the court at the very beginning of the trial and requests the court to order the plaintiff and the plaintiff's witnesses to avoid any reference to the change. Evidence of the changes could be so predjudicial as to require a **mistrial.** Proof that the condition was dangerous will have to come from some other source or be accomplished in some other manner.

In cases where a dispute develops as to whether a product is unreasonably dangerous, one of the considerations may be the cost of making changes to make the product safe. If the cost is prohibitive, the manufacturer may be excused for not eliminating the hazard. In recent years, there has been a trend permitting evidence of subsequent improvements in products where the defendant claims that the proposed changes would have been too expensive. The fact that changes were made after the accident is very convincing evidence that the expense was not prohibitive. Evidence of remedial measures is permissible whenever a party contends that it was *not feasible* to make it safe. Rule 407. Evidence that the defendant made subsequent changes on his or her property may be admissible to prove ownership of the property at the time in question if ownership is disputed. Rule 407.

Evidence of Conduct

Admissions may be made by conduct or silence. These are sometimes called verbal acts. For example, immediately following an automobile accident, one driver might accuse the other of failing to signal or failing to stop for a stop sign. If the person accused of wrongdoing fails to respond by denying the accusation, his or her silence, under some circumstances, may be considered to be an admission that the accusation was true. The test is whether, under the circumstances, one would ordinarily expect a denial if the accusation were false. Perhaps the party was hard of hearing or incapacitated due to injuries, then silence could not be considered to be an admission of fault.

If a party's "admission" is offered into evidence against him or her and the admission came out of a written statement, deposition, oral conversation, etc., the party who made the admission has a right to introduce into evidence the entire conversation or entire statement insofar as it relates to the "admission" in dispute. The Rules of Evidence do not allow parties to take alleged "admissions" out of context.

Hearsay Exceptions

Rules 803 and 804 undertake to codify many of the exceptions to the hearsay rule. A detailed discussion of the exceptions goes beyond the scope of this book. They are quoted here for convenient reference.

RULE 801 *Definitions*

Important

The following definitions apply under this article:

assertion is not a question

(a) Statement. A "statement" is (1) an oral or written assertion or (2) nonverbal conduct of a person, if it is intended by him as an assertion.

(b) Declarant. A "declarant" is a person who makes a statement.

(c) Hearsay. "Hearsay" is a statement, other than one made by the declarant while testifying at the trial or hearing, offered in evidence to prove the truth of the matter asserted.

(d) Statements which are not hearsay. A statement is not hearsay if —

> **(1) Prior statement by witness.** The declarant tesifies at the trial or hearing and is subject to cross-examination concerning the statement, and the statement is (A) inconsistent with his testimony, and was given under oath subject to the penalty of perjury at a trial, hearing, or other proceeding, or in a deposition, or (B) consistent with his testimony and is offered to rebut an express or implied charge against him of recent fabrication or improper influence or motive, or

> **(2) Admission by party-opponent.** The statement is offered against a party and is (A) his own statement, in either his individual or a representative capacity of (B) a statement of which he has manifested his adoption or belief in its truth, or (C) a statement by a person authorized by him to make a statement concerning the subject, or (D) a statement by his agent or servant concerning a matter within the scope of his agency or employment, made during the existence of the relationship, or (E) a statement by a co-conspirator of a party during the course and in furtherance of the conspiracy.

RULE 802 *Hearsay Rule*

Hearsay is not admissible except as provided by these rules or by other rules prescribed by the Supreme Court pursuant to statutory authority or by Act of Congress.

RULE 803 *Hearsay Exceptions;*
Availability of Declarant Immaterial

The following are not excluded by the hearsay rule, even though the declarant is available as a witness:

> **(1) Present sense impression.** A statement describing or explaining an event or condition made while the declarant was perceiving the event or condition, or immediately thereafter.

(2) **Excited utterance.** A statement relating to a startling event or condition made while the declarant was under the stress of excitement caused by the event or condition.

(3) **Then existing mental, emotional, or physical condition.** A statement of the declarant's then existing state of mind, emotion, sensation, or physical condition (such as intent, plan, motive, design, mental feeling, pain, and bodily health), but not including a statement of memory or belief to prove the fact remembered or believed unless it relates to the execution, revocation, identification, or terms of declarant's will.

(4) **Statements for purposes of medical diagnosis or treatment.** Statements made for purposes of medical diagnosis or treatment and describing medical history, or past or present symptoms, pain, or sensations, or the inception or general character of the cause or external source thereof insofar as reasonably pertinent to diagnosis or treatment.

(5) **Recorded recollection.** A memorandum or record concerning a matter about which a witness once had knowledge but now has insufficient recollection to enable him to testify fully and accurately, shown to have been made or adopted by the witness when the matter was fresh in his or her memory and to reflect that knowledge correctly. If admitted, the memorandum or record may be read into evidence but may not itself be received as an exhibit unless offered by an adverse party.

(6) **Records of regularly conducted activity.** A memorandum, report, record, or data compilation, in any form, of acts, events, conditions, opinions, or diagnoses, made at or near the time by, or from information transmitted by, a person with knowledge, if kept in the course of a regularly conducted business activity, and if it was the regular practice of that business activity to make the memorandum, report, record, or data compilation, all as shown by the testimony of the custodian or other qualified witness, unless the source of information or the method or circumstances of preparation indicate lack of trustworthiness. The term "business" as used in this paragraph includes business, institution, association, profession, occupation, and calling of every kind, whether or not conducted for profit.

(7) **Absence of entry in records kept in accordance with the provisions of paragraph (6).** Evidence that a matter is not included in the memoranda, reports, records, or data compilations, in any form, kept in accordance with the provisions of paragraph (6), to prove the nonoccurrence or nonexistence of the matter, if the matter was of a kind of which a memorandum, report, record, or data compilation was regularly made and preserved, unless the sources of information or other circumstances indicate lack of trustworthiness.

(8) **Public records and reports.** Records, reports, statements, or data compilations, in any form, of public offices or agencies, setting forth (A) the activities of the office or agency, or (B) matters observed pursuant to duty imposed by law as to which matters there was a duty to

report, excluding, however, in criminal cases matters observed by police officers and other law enforcement personnel, or (C) in civil actions and proceedings and against the government in criminal cases, factual findings resulting from an investigation made pursuant to authority granted by law, unless the sources of information or other circumstances indicate lack of trustworthiness.

(9) Records of vital statistics. Records or data compilations, in any form, of births, fetal deaths, deaths, or marriages, if the report thereof was made to a public office pursuant to requirements of law.

(10) Absence of public record or entry. To prove the absence of a record, report, statement, or data compilation, in any form, or the nonoccurrence or nonexistence of a matter of which a record, report, statement, or data compilation, in any form, was regularly made and preserved by a public office or agency, evidence in the form of a certification in accordance with Rule 902, or testimony, that diligent search failed to disclose the record, report, statement, or data compilation, or entry.

(11) Records of religious organizations. Statements of births, marriages, divorces, deaths, legitimacy, ancestry, relationship by blood or marriage, or other similar facts of personal or family history, contained in a regularly kept record of a religious organization.

(12) Marriage, baptismal, and similar certificates. Statements of fact contained in a certificate that the maker performed a marriage or other ceremony or administered a sacrament, made by a clergyman, public official, or other person authorized by the rules or practices of a religious organization or by law to perform the act certified, and purporting to have been issued at the time of the act or within a reasonable time thereafter.

(13) Family records. Statements of fact concerning personal or family history contained in family Bibles, genealogies, charts, engravings on rings, inscriptions on family portraits, engravings on urns, crypts, or tombstones, or the like.

(14) Records of documents affecting an interest in property. The record of a document purporting to establish or affect an interest in property, as proof of the content of the original recorded document and its execution and delivery by each person by whom it purports to have been executed, if the record is a record of a public office and an applicable statute authorizes the recording of documents of that kind in that office.

(15) Statements in documents affecting an interest in property. A statement contained in a document purporting to establish or affect an interest in property if the matter stated was relevant to the purpose of the document, unless dealings with the property since the document was made have been inconsistent with the truth of the statement or the purport of the document.

(16) Statements in ancient documents. Statements in a document in existence twenty years or more the authenticity of which is established.

(17) Market reports, commercial publications. Market quotations, tabulations, lists, directories, or other published compilations, generally used and relied upon by the public or by persons in particular occupations.

(18) Learned treatises. To the extent called to the attention of an expert witness upon cross-examination or relied upon by him in direct examination, statements contained in published treatises, periodicals, or pamphlets on a subject of history, medicine, or other science or art, established as a reliable authority by the testimony or admission of the witness or by other expert testimony or by judicial notice. If admitted, the statements may be read into evidence but may not be received as exhibits.

(19) Reputation concerning personal or family history. Reputation among members of his family by blood, adoption, or marriage, or among his associates, or in the community, concerning a person's birth, adoption, marriage, divorce, death, legitimacy, relationship by blood, adoption, or marriage ancestry, or other similar fact of his personal or family history.

(20) Reputation concerning boundaries or general history. Reputation in a community, arising before the controversy, as to boundaries of or customs affecting lands in the community, and reputation as to events of general history important to the community or state or nation in which located.

(21) Reputation as to character. Reputation of a person's character among his associates or in the community.

(22) Judgment of previous conviction. Evidence of a final judgment, entered after a trial or upon a plea of guilty (but not upon a plea of nolo contendere), adjudging a person guilty of a crime punishable by death or imprisonment in excess of one year, to prove any fact essential to sustain the judgment, but not including, when offered by the government in a criminal prosecution for purposes other than impeachment, judgments against persons other than the accused. The pendency of an appeal may be shown but does not affect admissibility.

(23) Judgment as to personal family or general history, or boundaries. Judgments as proof of matters of personal, family or general history, or boundaries, essential to the judgment, if the same would be provable by evidence of reputation.

(24) Other exceptions. A statement not specifically covered by any of the foregoing exceptions but having equivalent circumstantial guarantees of trustworthiness, if the court determines that: (A) the statement is offered as evidence of a material fact; (B) the statement is more probative on the point for which it is offered than any other evidence which the proponent can procure through reasonable efforts; and (C) the general purposes of these rules and the interests of justice will best be served by admission of the statement into evidence. However, a statement may not be admitted under this exception unless the proponent of it makes known to the adverse party sufficiently in advance of the trial or hearing to provide the adverse party with a fair opportunity to prepare to meet it, his intention to offer the statement and the particulars of it, including the name and address of the declarant.

RULE 804 *Hearsay Exceptions: Declarant Unavailable.*

(a) Definition of unavailability. "Unavailability as a witness" includes situations in which the declarant —

Based on
necessity

(1) is exempted by ruling of the court on the ground of privilege from testifying concerning the subject matter of his statement; or

(2) persists in refusing to testify concerning the subject matter of his statement despite an order of the court to do so; or

(3) testifies to a lack of memory of the subject matter of his statement; or

(4) is unable to be present or to testify at the hearing because of death or then existing physical or mental illness or infirmity; or

(5) is absent from the hearing and the proponent of his statement has been unable to procure his attendance (or in the case of a hearsay exception under subdivison (b) (2), (3), or (4), his attendance or testimony) by process or other reasonable means.

A delcarant is not unavailable as a witness if his exemption, refusal, claim of lack of memory, inability, or absence is due to the procurement or wrongdoing of the proponent of his statement for the purpose of preventing the witness from attending or testifying.

(b) Hearsay exceptions. The following are not excluded by the hearsay rule if the declarant is unavailable as a witness:

(1) Former testimony. Testimony given as a witness at another hearing of the same or a different proceeding, or in a deposition taken in compliance with law in the course of the same or another proceeding, if the party against whom the testimony is now offered, or, in a civil action or proceeding, a predecessor in interest, had an opportunity and similar motive to develop the testimony by direct, cross, or redirect examination.

(2) Statement under belief of impending death. In a prosecution for homicide or in a civil action or proceeding, a statement made by a declarant while believing that his death was imminent, concerning the cause or circumstances of what he believed to be his impending death.

(3) Statement against interest. A statement which was at the time of its making so far contrary to the declarant's pecuniary or proprietary interest, or so far tended to subject him or her to civil or criminal liability, or to render invalid a claim by him or her against another, that a reasonable man in his position would not have made the statement unless he believed it to be true. A statement tending to expose the declarant to criminal liability and offered to exculpate the accused is not admissible unless corroborating circumstances clearly indicate the trustworthiness of the statement.

(4) Statement of personal or family history. (A) A statement concerning the declarant's own birth, adoption, marriage, divorce, legitimacy, relationship by blood, adoption, or marriage, ancestry, or other similar fact of personal or family history, even though declarant had no means of acquiring personal knowledge of the matter stated; or (B) a statement concerning the foregoing matters, and death also, of another person, if the declarant was related to the other by blood, adoption, or marriage or was so intimately associated with the other's family as to be likely to have accurate information concerning the matter declared.

(5) Other exceptions. A statement not specifically covered by any of the foregoing exceptions but having equivalent circumstantial guarantees of trustworthiness, if the court determines that (A) the statement is offered as evidence of a material fact; (B) the statement is more probative on the point for which it is offered than any other evidence which the proponent can procure through reasonable efforts; (C) the general purposes of these rules and the interests of justice will best be served by admission of the statement into evidence. However, a statement may not be admitted under this exception unless the proponent of it makes known to the adverse party sufficiently in advance of the trial or hearing to provide the adverse party with a fair opportunity to prepare to meet it, his intention to offer the statement and the particulars of it, including the name and address of the declarant.

RULE 805 *Hearsay Within Hearsay*

Hearsay included within hearsay is not excluded under the hearsay rule if each part of the combined statements conforms with an exception to the hearsay rule provided in these rules.

[handwritten margin note: catch all — judge can let in whatever he/she wants]

20

Trial Preparation

The parties and lawyers should be able to make an informed judgment about the merits of a case and the case's settlement value after completing their investigation and discovery procedures. If a party has fully and carefully used the discovery tools available, he or she should be able to compare the strengths of his or her case against the strengths of the opponent's case. He or she should be able to recognize the weaknesses on both sides. But for one reason or another, some cases cannot be settled, and a trial is necessary to resolve the parties' controversy.

Having concluded that the case cannot be settled, each party must develop a plan for presenting his or her case-in-chief* and to counter the opposition's case-in-chief. Many factors come into play. In some respects, planning trial strategy is like a chess game because the opposing parties' tactics may vary considerably. For example, a strong witness may be countered with strong circumstantial evidence or a rule of law that excludes the evidence or by impeachment. It is a matter of "punch and counter punch."

A party must plan his or her own case, prepare to meet the opponent's case *and* try to anticipate how the opponent will deal with his or her case. Trial preparation obviously requires a lot of careful thought and analysis. A party must not be beguiled by his or her own case. He or she must consciously strive for objectivity and thoroughness.

---

*Plaintiff's case-in-chief refers to all of the plaintiff's evidence, except for the rebuttal evdidence which is offered only after the defendant presents his or her case-in-chief.

The amount of time that a lawyer has available in which to prepare for trial varies from case to case and from court to court. The sooner the preparation can begin, the better. And yet, if the preparation begins too soon, it may become diluted, subject to changing circumstances and even subject to changes in the law. Some facets of the preparation are less affected by the passage of time so that there is less danger of an early effort being lost or diminished by subsequent developments. Gathering and analyzing the documentary and other tangible evidence come in this category. The final preparation of individual witnesses to testify must be done shortly before the witnesses take the stand. Deciding when to begin each phase of the preparation is a matter of judgment which should get better with experience.

As a paralegal gains experience, he or she should be able to initiate steps in the trial preparation, establish time tables, and make recommendations for the trial preparation. In most cases, the "preparation" continues even into the trial. Paralegals are often needed to locate new evidence and witnesses while the trial is in progress. They can provide significant help by lining up witnesses and the evidence as needed. There is no set formula to trial preparation. Nevertheless, there are some fundamental considerations that are applicable to most cases. A review of them should be helpful to an understanding of the process.

Ideally, the preparation begins by an analysis of the client's claim or defense. Does he or she have one? Should the case really be forced to trial? Can the client's case be presented through the evidence now available? Is the evidence admissible? Is the evidence credible? Is it persuasive? If the answers to these questions are in the affirmative, the same questions must be asked about the opponent's claim or defense. The answers to these questions come from the answers to interrogatories, oral depositions, responses to requests for admissions, witness statements, medical reports, investigation memorandums, photographs, records, etc. This analysis gives an overview which will help to keep the rest of the preparation on track and in perspective.

Lawyers are usually able to estimate the approximate time their cases will be scheduled for trial. Most courts periodically have *calendar calls* at which time a number of cases are scheduled for trial on some sort of a time table. There are various approaches to setting up a time table. A court may establish a priority for the cases, one beginning as soon as the preceding case is concluded or otherwise disposed of. In this way the parties always know their relative position on the calendar, but may not know the exact date on which their case will be reached. They must keep in close contact with the clerk of court and with the lawyers on the preceding cases to find out how the calendar is progressing. Sometimes cases are given *day certain* settings. This means that the case will begin on a specified date, and the court will clear its calendar of all other matters so that the case can begin at the time designated. Day certain settings are most often used when a case involves many parties, or many witnesses or when witnesses and/or parties must travel a long distance to attend the trial.

When a court holds a calendar call — often involving fifty or more cases — the judge asks the lawyers if they are ready for trial; if the pleadings require any amendments; if there are any special problems concerning the period during which the court expects to try the cases listed on the calendar. For example, a lawyer may already be scheduled for trial on another case in another court. The potential conflict can be avoided by the court and lawyers by working together.

On occasion, a court cannot reach all the cases set for trial during a given term of court. If a case is not reached, it is usually given a priority setting at the next calendar call or the next term of court. The court's failure to reach a case and try it at the time scheduled may cause the parties considerable expense and frustration. No one has been able to devise a system that completely solves the problem. The need to give the parties adequate notice and time to prepare must be compared against the need to keep the courts continuously busy. If all cases were given day certain settings, the courts would be idle much of the time because so many cases are settled, dismissed or postponed for some reason. Consequently, a judge wants and needs to have other cases ready to begin trial as soon as one is concluded.

If a case on the calendar is not ready for trial, the parties usually can stipulate that it should be stricken from the calendar and reinstated at a later date by stipulation of the parties or by motion of any one of the parties. However, if a party is not ready to go to trial because he or she has been dilatory, the court has the authority to set the case on for trial anyway. One party's neglect or "dilatory tactics" should not work to the prejudice of the other parties. Justice should not be delayed. A good case, whether for the plaintiff or defendant, tends to deteriorate with the passage of time. Of course, the opposite is also true: a poor case tends to get better with the passage of an excessive amount of time.

At some point before trial, the court may order a pretrial conference pursuant to Rule 16. Conferences may be scheduled in the particular court as a matter of routine or by special order. The presiding judge may conduct the conference or may delegate the responsibility to a magistrate. The court order setting the pretrial conference may direct the parties to submit "pretrial statements" through which various disclosures are made, including a list of all witnesses, exhibits and any other factors that might affect the trial.

The lawyers who will try the case should attend the conference, and some courts require it. However, occasionally it is necessary for an associate of the trial lawyer to appear for him or her due to conflicts in the schedule. Nevertheless, it is essential that the lawyer who attends the conference be fully acquainted with the file so that he or she can discuss it intelligently, and have authority to enter into stipulations concerning matters of evidence, law and procedure.

The purpose of pretrial conferences is to simplify the case. The factual and legal issues may be narrowed by court order or by stipulation of the parties. The court has authority to amend the pleadings at the conference without any prior motion. All admissions and stipulations made by the parties during the conference become part of the court's order issued after the conference. Frequently, courts use the pretrial conferences to move the case along toward trial by ordering that the parties complete discovery within a specified period. The order may also determine the trial date. If the parties have any unusual problems concerning the scheduling of witnesses or presentation of evidence, the pretrial conference is the time and place to make the problem known to the court, and to work out a solution.

Usually the parties have at least one or two weeks' time between the calendar call and commencement of the first trial on the current term. Once the series of trials begin, the parties may have no more than a half day's notice. When the assignment clerk calls during morning hours instructing counsel to appear at 1:30 o'clock that afternoon, a paralegal can be a tremendous help to get everything lined up and ready to go.

As soon as a lawyer receives a trial date, he or she must notify the clients and all of the witnesses he or she intends to call to testify at trial so they can arrange their schedules. Frequently, it is desirable to check on the availability of witnesses whom the opponent is expected to call. There is nothing unethical in doing so unless a privileged relationship is involved. For example, the Rules of Civil Procedure do not authorize a party to have direct discussions about the case with the opponent's expert witnesses. Rules 26 and 35. Witnesses who are not cooperative, but are needed for the client's case, should be subpoenaed promptly. The sooner subpoenas are served, the more certain a party is to have all the witnesses he or she needs.

A lawyer's preparation for trial should (1) make sure that he or she has collected all of the available evidence; (2) determine the admissibility of the evidence; (3) make sure that he or she is able to present a prima facie claim or defense; (4) make sure the evidence is persuasive; (5) preview the opponent's case in an objective, logical manner; (6) determine how the opponent's claims on the facts can be met and answered; (7) anticipate disputes on legal issues and resolve them satisfactorily before the trial. When lawyers begin to handle important litigation, they find it useful to prepare a formal, written trial brief forcing a *complete* analysis. The possibility of making false assumptions about the facts and law is greatly reduced by writing each step of the analysis. However, as lawyers become more experienced they rely upon a much less formal and less time-consuming approach.

The logical and usual place to begin trial preparation is a review of the office file which includes the pleadings, investigation materials, discovery documents, exhibits and correspondence. The initial review has several related purposes: (1) to insure the availability of proof for all essential elements of the cause of action or affirmative defenses; (2) to organize the evidence into a logical, understandable format for presentation at trial; (3) to locate any additional evidence that may not have been available previously; (4) to ascertain any apparent conflicts in the known evidence; (5) to prepare the client and witnesses to testify in court. Lawyers usually begin the analysis of the cases and evidence by using a hypothesis that supports the client's version of the transaction or occurrence. Then the hypothesis is tested by each item of evidence and each item of evidence is tested by the hypothesis. A lawyer strives to make sure that all of the evidence is consistent with his or her theory of the case. He or she wants the evidence to be not only credible but persuasive. By the time the case reaches trial, a lawyer should feel that the greater weight of the evidence supports his or her client's case. Otherwise, it is better to settle on the best terms he or she can get.

A trial is considered to be a search for truth. A lawyer must not fabricate evidence or permit a client to do so. He or she must not conceal evidence, and must not lead any witness into error. So what does a lawyer do when he or she finds contradictions or inconsistencies in the evidence? As a lawyer previews the evidence, a conscious effort must be made to be objective. If the evidence consistently contradicts his or her own client's version, he or she must advise the client about the realities of the case. Perhaps the claim or defense should be dropped. Perhaps new efforts should be directed toward a settlement. On the other hand, there may be just a few pieces of evidence which appear to be contradictory. The minor inconsistencies may not destroy the case but may confuse it or lead to embarrassment at trial. Every effort should be made to resolve the conflicts and problems.

A paralegal can provide invaluable help compiling and organizing the evidence. In the beginning, a supervising lawyer may specify the items of evidence he wants pinpointed in the depositions, exhibits and records. But with experience, paralegals would need less and less direction. A paralegal may be asked to prepare deposition outlines for the purpose of identifying and locating testimony and exhibits. Detailed preparation helps to insure that the trial will run smoothly. A paralegal should keep in mind that a lawyer needs to know the facts that can be developed out of each witness and exhibit, whether those facts are helpful or detrimental to the client's case. Exhibits are of no value unless an adequate foundation can be laid for their introduction. Someone must be able to identify each exhibit and establish its genuineness. Background information on each witness may be important to the lawyer to help him or her know how to deal with the witness.

Sometimes it is desirable to check on the availability of the "opponent's witnesses." Of course, no privileges can be violated. Those witnesses who are not cooperative but who, nevertheless, are needed at trial, should be subpoenaed to come to court at a specific time. The sooner subpoenas are obtained from the clerk of court and service is attempted, the more sure a lawyer is of effectuating service.

A subpoena directs and requires the witness, or even a party, to appear in court at a specified time. "Subpoena" means that the witness must appear "under penalty" of law. This is the only means a lawyer has of compelling attendance. If a person fails to comply with the subpoena, the party who served the subpoena is in a good position to claim surprise and move the court for a postponement (continuance) or delay of the trial. Otherwise, if no subpoena is served, a lawyer merely relies upon the witness's promise to come when needed and if the witness does not show up, the trial judge may well deny a motion for a delay. A subpoena shifts the onus from the lawyer to the witnesses themselves to make sure they are present when needed.

A witness who fails to comply with a subpoena is in contempt of court and subject to disciplinary action, including a fine or incarceration. Of course, some failures to comply may be excused or justified and no penalty will be assessed. But the burden is upon the individual witness, not the lawyer, to satisfy the judge that the excuse is meritorious.

There are times when some witnesses prefer to appear in court pursuant to a subpoena and not merely upon the request of a party or lawyer. For example, in some localities a policy exists requiring law enforcement officers and other public officials to appear in court only if subpoenaed. Another example is the treating physician who has a close relationship to the plaintiff, but whose testimony tends to favor the defendant. He or she may recognize the duty to appear in court, but wants everyone to know that he or she is appearing against his or her patient only by being compelled to do so by subpoena.

It is difficult to know just when the court will be ready for the witness to appear. Nevertheless, a specific time and place must be stated in the subpoena. The problem is often resolved by designating a time in the subpoena which is the earliest probable time that the court will be ready for the witness. The witness is told that if he or she will cooperate by keeping near a telephone so as to be reached on a moment's notice, he or she may wait at home or at work until needed. The alternative is for the witness to sit in the courtroom and wait for his or her turn. The wait could be days. A lawyer takes a little bit of a risk by accommodating witnesses in this manner because he or she is primarily responsible for any delay that might result. But a bigger risk is taken by not subpoenaing a witness who is unreliable.

Federal court subpoenas are usually served by a United States marshal. However, any person eighteen years of age or more, who is not a party to the suit, may serve a subpoena in a civil case. Rule 45(c). The process server must give the witness the established *witness fee* when he or she serves the subpoena. Also the witness must be paid a *mileage fee* based upon round trip milage from the place of service to the courthouse. In some cases, it would be appropriate to give the witness a mileage fee based upon the mileage from his or her home to the courthouse even though the witness may have been served at some other location, such as at work. If there is any doubt, the greater amount should be tendered. If a witness absolutely refuses to accept the tender of money suspecting he or she is being bribed, or for whatever reason, the process server's affidavit of service should show that a specified amount of money was tendered. The amount tendered and accepted must be stated in the affidavit of service. The affidavit of service should be promptly filed with the clerk of court.

If the witnesses cannot be reached by telephone, personal contact is necessary. The lawyers must have the witness's home and work telephone numbers so that every witness can be contacted on short notice. It is also well to obtain the telephone number of a close friend or relative who usually knows where the witness can be located when away from home.

A lawyer should meet with each witness to discuss the case and the witness's testimony before the witness takes the stand. Sometimes it is desirable to have a meeting with two or more witnesses at the same time so that they can help each other recall pertinent details. The witness conferences should be held close enough to the trial date that the witnesses do not forget the matters covered. This is not a time for discovery or investigation.

Each witness should be advised about the nature of the case and the basic issues in controversy, and should be told about his or her role in the case, i.e., the importance of his or her testimony and just where that testimony fits into the overall picture. This helps the witnesses to become reassured about the procedures and his or her own ability to handle the situation.

Assure each witness that it is entirely proper to preview their testimony. If a witness is asked on cross-examination whether or not he or she has met with either of the lawyers before trail, he or she should feel free to admit such. It is not only proper, it is expected.

If the witness is going to be compensated, he or she should be assured that it is proper in civil litigation for the parties to reimburse witnesses for time and expenses for appearing in court. Payments made or promised to a witness, however, must not be a profit for the witness. If a witness is asked whether he or she has been promised compensation for appearing in court, the witness should be prepared to respond that, indeed, he or she has been assured that expenses — such as mileage, parking and lost wages — will be paid by the party who has called him or her. The exact amount cannot be determined until after the witness has completed his or her part in the trial, and that is usually the best answer to any question about the amount.

A slightly different situation is presented where the witness is a hired expert who does expect to profit by testifying. He or she provides the employer — one of the parties — with a service, but that service should be paid for on some reasonable or standard basis. It is not uncommon for an expert witness to command a fee of several hundred dollars or more for appearing in court for only a few hours. On cross-examination he or she may be required to testify concerning the amount of the charges for this and other court appearances. If an expert witness indicates some reluctance to divulge the information, the reluctance may adversely affect the jury's opinion of him or her. Of course, an excessive fee is also damaging. If an expert witness has been foolish enough to agree to a contingent fee, his or her credibility will be severely damaged.

Witnesses such as engineers and physicians, who have records relating to the litigation, should be reminded to bring *all* of the records which pertain to the particular client or patient, transaction or occurrence. For example, a physician may be inclined to bring to court only those records which *he* considers relevant to the particular accident in question and to leave at his office other records pertaining to treatment accorded for some other accident or medical problem. However, the relevancy or irrelevancy of the records is not for him or her to determine. Failure to have all of the records available could result in the exclusion of the records he brought and possibly the exclusion of all his testimony. More than likely, he will be required to return to court with all of his records.

A problem arises whether or not to review with a witness his or her signed or recorded statement. If the witness uses the statement to *refresh his or her recollection,* he or she may be required to produce the statement on cross-examination. The statement is then available to the adverse party to determine whether or not the testimony has been consistent with the statement. Furthermore, the witness may be examined concerning any other relevant facts contained in the statement. Usually a witness can prepare adequately without reading the statement. There is no need for review of the statement and to "refresh his or her memory" from it if he or she has a present recollection of the pertinent facts. However, if the statement does refresh his or her recollection, he or she should use it and become thoroughly familiar with what it says.

If a witness's deposition has been taken, the transcript should be reviewed to be sure that his or her prior testimony is clearly in mind. Usually the few dollars that it costs to photocopy a deposition transcript for the witness's use is well justified. Since the deposition is part of the court file and is not considered part of the lawyer's work product, there is never a need to avoid "refreshing the witness's recollection" from the deposition transcript. The other lawyers have their copies and, presumably, know the contents.

Of course, witnesses and the client should examine the exhibits which may be used at trial, such as photographs, records, correspondence, plats and expert's reports. If an exhibit is to be offered into evidence through a witness, the procedure used in laying foundation for the exhibit should be explained to the witness. Again, it is desirable to actually go through the procedure in the office.

A careful review must be made of all the exhibits to be used in trial. It may be desirable to make photocopies of some of the documents that will be exhibits because once the documents are received into evidence, the court has custody. They may not be conveniently available for reference. Copies may be used for preparing a witness to testify or for preparing the final argument or other purposes. No mark should be made on original documents, photographs, or other things that may be used as exhibits. Underlining, notations in the margins, and "x's" used in photographs to pinpoint locations or provide other information might cause the exhibit to be inadmissible or reduce its authority. Markings should be made only *during* the trial. Markings made before the witness uses the document in court are considered to be similar to leading questions.

Courts may require the parties to appear before a magistrate, referee or judge to have all their exhibits identified and marked days before the trial is to begin. The parties are encouraged to stipulate to the necessary foundation for exhibits. Stipulations on foundation conserve the court's time. Any exhibit which is not disclosed and marked as part of the pretrial conference procedure is subject to exclusion for failure to comply with the court's order. The federal rules do not establish any particular system for identifying exhibits. However, local court rules may establish a mandatory procedure for uniformity.

As a lawyer begins reviewing the file for the purpose of preparing for trial, he or she has in mind that he or she must be able to present sufficient evidence to establish a prima facie claim or defense; otherwise, the case will be subject to a directed verdict against his or her client. Also, the quality of his or her evidence must be assessed. It must be convincing as well as admissible, or the jury will not be persuaded by it. The opponent's evidence will predominate. If the exhibits contradict his or her own witnesses, or if those witnesses are likely to contradict each other, the client will surely lose. A case that has inconsistencies is like the proverbial house which is divided against itself — it falls!

Through the investigation and discovery a lawyer obtains the facts that he or she must work with at trial. The trial preparation is geared to determining the best ways of presenting the facts and meeting the opponent's theory. A lawyer must present the truth at court. He or she must not fabricate or conceal evidence; must not suborn perjury; and must not lead a witness into error. So what does the lawyer do when he or she finds contradictions in the evidence? As a lawyer previews the evidence, in effect, he or she tries the case as both lawyers, the judge and jury. He must strive for objectivity. If the evidence consistently contradicts his or her own client's version of the matter, a lawyer must advise the client about the unhappy realities of the case. Perhaps the claim or defense should be dropped or perhaps a compromise should be negotiated promptly. Perhaps the client should be prepared to give more or demand less for settlement purposes.

A lawyer is often confronted with bits and pieces of contradictory evidence which do not destroy the case, merely confuse it. For some reason certain pieces of evidence don't quite fit together. The challenge is to ascertain where and why the errors crept into the facts as assembled. If a significant inconsistency cannot be explained, a party is gambling by going to trial.

The analysis of the evidence begins by using a hypothesis which supports the client's version of the transaction or occurrence. The weight of the evidence should confirm the validity of the hypothesis. Next, determine whether apparent conflicts are truly conflicts. There is always the possibility that an apparent conflict arises out of a misunderstanding of the evidence. We all have a tendency to make assumptions about facts. False assumptions create traps. A lawyer's analysis of the facts *must* be objective.

Facts may appear to be contradictory or inconsistent on their face, while actually they are not. For this reason, a lawyer and his legal assistants should obtain as much personal knowledge about the case as possible. They should meet the witnesses personally. They should inspect the instrumentalities involved. They should visit relevant locations. Personal knowledge provides a much better perspective. The personal contacts give a much better "feel" for the case. The apparent inconsistencies may disappear. For example, an inspection of the accident site may show why one witness could make an observation by sight or sound that another witness couldn't make in another location. A lawyer cannot successfully challenge a witness's testimony unless he or she has more knowledge or a better understanding of the matter in question.

Inconsistencies ought to be tested against the realities of physical fact and scientific knowledge. For example, suppose that in an automobile accident case a witness claims that the defendant was going "fast", "maybe 40 mph" when the defendant's truck struck the rear of the plaintiff's stopped automobile. However, photographs show only a small dent in each vehicle, only a couple feet of faint skidmarks were left by the defendant's front wheels and the plaintiff's automobile was admittedly moved only a foot by the contact according to the plaintiff's own version. Certainly the established physical facts are inconsistent with the eye witness's version of a high speed collision. If this witness were appearing for the plaintiff, the witness would be no real problem for the defendant's lawyer to cross-examine because the witness's testimony is not credible and will surely be rejected by the jury. But assume this witness has other evidence which is credible and which the defense lawyer needs — he or she does not want to destroy the witness's credibility. What can the lawyer do? How can he or she help the witness to avoid being incredible?

Common sense dictates that the witness should be approached in a manner that will avoid challenging and upsetting him or her. A disgruntled witness is particularly stubborn. There is always the danger that he or she may misinterpret attempted interviews as tampering with the truth. Please note that the Code of Professional Conduct requires lawyers and paralegals to avoid even the appearance of impropriety.

The first step in dealing with a difficult witness is to assure him or her that it is proper, even necessary, to talk with the lawyers about the case. Admittedly, he or she has no absolute obligation to do so, but everyone usually benefits including the court. Even a hostile witness is usually interested in seeing pertinent photographs, plats, official reports and other exhibits which will be used at trial. The exhibits can be used as the "bait" and an excuse for conferring in preparation for the trial. Initially, the emphasis must be upon those points wherein the witness's testimony is consistent with the other facts, especially those facts which are helpful to the client's case. An effort must be made to avoid discussing the "erroneous facts" until after the witness has been shown, step by step, how the facts, exhibits and his or her testimony fit into the whole picture. Once the witness senses that he or she is talking with a friendly person who appreciates his or her cooperation and importance, the witness is more likely to be in a frame of mind to listen to reason. Then facts can be brought to his or her attention which are contrary to that witness's "erroneous beliefs." The lawyer or paralegal must be careful not to demean the witness. If the witness is permitted to argue or even state the erroneous version at the outset of the interview, he or she is going to have more difficulty accepting the correct facts, and will be defensive. Hopefully, a witness who harbors erroneous beliefs will abandon them when shown the whole picture. If he or she doesn't abandon them entirely, he or she may, nevertheless, be less adamant about them at trial.

A case normally centers upon and revolves around the parties, i.e., the clients. But a lawyer *cannot* ask jurors to put themselves in the client's position and empathize with him or her. Nevertheless, every effort must be made by a lawyer and the client to establish rapport with the jury, to have them like, understand, and believe in him or her. These objectives should help direct the trial preparation. Unless the client has been schooled in public relations work, he or she is going to need a lot of help. He or she must be made to feel comfortable in court especially when on the witness stand. Sincerity and authority are the hallmarks of a good witness.

Help make the client feel comfortable in this new experience by outlining the trial procedure. By knowing what is happening and why, he or she will be much less nervous. Everyone tends to be nervous, even apprehensive, about the unknown. He or she should be told a little about each step of the trial, from the selection of the jury to the verdict. The client must understand the legal theory of the case, what the opposition contends and how his or her case is to be presented. Even if these matters have been discussed before, they should be reviewed immediately before trial. One side benefit from this kind of a briefing before trial is that the client may be more appreciative of his or her lawyer's efforts and problems.

A client's testimony needs to be authoritative. There are many facets to the appearance of authority. No list of considerations could be complete. The factors discussed in the chapter on preparing a witness for an oral deposition are some of the most important: guidelines for testifying. But a deposition differs in one very important respect: the jury does not see or hear the deposition testimony. Seeing and hearing the witness may add substantially to his or her authority or detract from it.

If the client's deposition was taken, he or she should be given a copy of the transcript to study even *before* meeting with him or her. Important points should be highlighted. A paralegal can help witnesses and clients prepare for trial by reviewing the depositions and statements with them. The client's thorough preview of the transcript will shorten the time needed for preparation. It will make him or her feel more confident about the rest of the preparation. He or she should be encouraged to *write down* any questions that come to mind as he or she studies the transcript. If not written down, they may be forgotten by the time he or she arrives at the office. Then the client wonders and worries about the questions he or she forgot.

The client should be cross-examined from his deposition. Test his or her memory. Remind him or her of the guidelines for testifying. Give trick questions that erroneously *assume* facts favorable to the opposition. Have *him or her* write down important facts and figures to reinforce memory and ability to recall. He or she must not use any such notes when testifying. Is there a danger that the client will know his or her "story" too well so that it appears fabricated and rehearsed? Not really. Any such appearance should be manifest during the mock examination in the office. If the client consistently reflects on each question before answering, then answers in a slow, deliberate manner while looking at the jury, and occasionally at the lawyers, his or her credibility should be strong.

Most of the guidelines for testifying in a deposition apply to testifying in court. However, there are some significant differences. At trial the objective is to advance the client's theory of the case and persuade the jury to accept it. The impact of testimony in a deposition may be different than at trial. Whereas the witness in a discovery deposition should not volunteer information or explain his or her testimony, testimony at trial should put forth his or her theory of the case. *The best answer at trial may not be the shortest answer.* Each question put to the client should be considered as a vehicle for advancing his or her claim or defense, regardless of who propounds the question. This does not mean that the witness should go beyond the questions with his or her answers nor be nonresponsive.

The following recommendations for appearing and testifying in court before a jury should be helpful.

1. Dress appropriately. Be well groomed and have shoes shined. Be polite in and out of the courtroom.

2. Visit the accident scene and study it. Compare it with the photographs and diagrams that may be used as exhibits.

3. Become acquainted with what the other witnesses will probably testify to.

4. Avoid discussing confidential matters in the presence of jurors, witnesses and strangers.

5. Make written notes about important developments in the case and about questions that occur.

6. Act interested and sincere whether on the stand or in the courthouse halls.

7. When a lawyer asks a question, look at him or her. When answering the question, look at the jury. Avoid looking at the ceiling, out the window or at the floor. Don't steal furtive glances at "your" lawyer as though, "I really made a good point there" or "please help me."

8. Explain your answer if necessary or when it seems appropriate. A witness has a right to give a complete answer — even if the opposing lawyer tries to cut short the answer.

9. If you realize that you have given a wrong answer, correct it right away.

10. Avoid expressions such as: "to tell the truth" or "to be honest" or "to the best of my knowledge." These phrases weaken the testimony. If the witness believes his or her answer is true, there is no reason to qualify it.

11. Avoid exaggeration and minimizing.

12. Never lose your temper. Regardless of what happens, be calm and deliberate. Try to relax. If you are getting irritated, tired, confused or physically uncomfortable, ask for a drink of water or a short recess if necessary.

13. Do not argue or fence with a lawyer. But you don't have to agree with the lawyer's questions. Statements of disagreement should not be made in a disagreeable manner.

14. If a lawyer tries to put you on the defensive by starting questions with "you *admit* that . . . " it may be appropriate to tell him you don't know what he or she means by "admit."

15. Don't deny that you prepared yourself to take the stand by reading the deposition transcript, viewing the accident scene, and conferring with your lawyer. But don't let him or her suggest or imply that you do not have an independent recollection of the facts.

16. Do not refer to insurance unless specifically advised by your lawyer before taking the stand that the matter of insurance is a proper subject in the case. The court, lawyers and other witnesses will carefully avoid the subject. An improper reference to insurance could cause a mistrial.

A helpful step in trial preparation is a mock cross-examination of the client to discover any weakness in his or her ability to remember and relate the facts.

The entire trial procedure should be outlined for the client so that he or she understands what is happening as it is happening. He or she should be told that the lawyers and judge will meet in the judge's chambers for a few minutes to discuss various matters including questions of law, the scheduling of witnesses, the possibilities of settlement and preliminary motions. He or she should listen very carefully to all opening statements, especially to that of the opposition, because the opposing lawyer usually explains in an opening statement just how he or she is going to prove the case. The client must be forewarned that, as a party, he or she may be called for cross-examination by the other party during the opponent's case-in-chief. Rule 43(b). The more familiar a client is with the procedures, the more comfortable and the more authoritative his or her testimony will be.

The final step in an attorney's preparation for trial is the preparation of written, requested jury instructions. Each attorney not only has the right but perhaps a duty to prepare requested instructions for the court to use. Some courts' rules expressly require it. However, in the routine case, that step is often neglected because an attorney knows that the trial judge has his or her own so-called boilerplate instructions to give regardless of how well drawn or stated the attorney's requested jury instructions are. Nevertheless, by submitting written, requested jury instructions, an attorney helps to "protect his or her record" in case the court errs by giving the wrong instructions.

21

Fact Brief

A fact brief is used to conduct a formal analysis of a case and to teach analysis of fact issues. Lawyers seldom take the time to prepare a fact brief. However, they must go through the same mental processes to determine the state of his or her preparation and the soundness of the evidence. The fact brief begins with a dissection of the pleadings and a determination of the remaining fact issues. The brief then itemizes and categorizes the fact issues. Finally, the brief discusses how each contested fact will be proved or disproved.

A fact brief is to be distinguished from a *trial brief* which is prepared for the information of the trial judge concerning matters of law. A trial brief ordinarily discusses facts but is not concerned with how those facts will be proved. A fact brief is for the benefit of the lawyer or paralegal who prepared it. Indeed, it is like a game plan which should be kept out of the hands of the opposition.

The sample fact brief in this chapter is concerned with an action to enforce a decedent's contract to make a will. The plaintiffs claim they had a contract with the testator-decedent by which he was going to bequeath his house to the plaintiffs if they would take care of him for the rest of his life. Unfortunately for the plaintiffs, the decedent's will left the house to the defendant. This fact brief is one prepared by the defendant's lawyer to guide his trial preparation. He wants to help the court sustain the will, thereby giving his client the house and defeating the plaintiffs' claim of a contract. The reader should note that the factual issues have been sharply delineated. The purpose of the brief is to compile, correlate, and analyze the evidence according to the legal issues.

ABSTRACT OF PLEADINGS

Complaint	Answer	Reply or no required reponsive pleading
On June 7, 1950, plaintiffs and decedent entered into an agreement whereby plaintiffs agreed to give up their home and to move into decedent's house, and to take care of decedent and his house until his death.	Denied—that the plaintiff agreed to care for the decedent.	
In consideration of the agreement, decedent promised to convey his house and lot at 74 Golf Terrace, Edison, Minnesota, to the plaintiffs.	Denied	
Plaintiffs gave up their home, moved in with William Brown, and fully performed their part of said agreement.	Denied—that plaintiffs performed their part of the agreement.	
Decedent devised his house to Edward Bordon in his will dated July 20, 1957, instead of devising his real property to the plaintiff as required by the agreement.	Denied—the existence of the agreement to devise decedent's property to the plaintiffs.	
Plaintiffs performed personal services valued at $30,000.	Denied—the performance of the services.	
	No cause of action exists.	
	Agreement is unenforceable because it is within the statute of frauds.	
	Plaintiffs have been fully compensated by the salary of 100 dollars per month, free rent and utilities, and the $2,000 bequest in the decedent's will.	

ISSUES

1. There was no agreement between the decedent and the plaintiffs whereby the decedent agreed to devise his real property at 74 Golf Terrace, Edison, to the plaintiffs in return for their services.

2. The services were not satisfactorily performed by the plaintiffs, and

therefore, they breached the contract, if there was one.

DEFENDANT'S CASE IN CHIEF

1. There was no agreement made between the plaintiffs and the decedent whereby the decedent promised to convey his real property at 74 Golf Terrace, Edison, Minnesota, in return for the performance of services by the plaintiffs, for the facts are:

a. The complaint states that there was only one arrangement made between the plaintiffs and the decedent.

b. This arrangement was initiated and consummated on June 7, 1950, during a dinner party at the decedent's home, given in honor of Dr. Olson.

c. Negotiations and statements concerning the arrangement were made during a card game in the presence of Dr. Carl Olson, William Mitchell, John Hughes, and William Brown, the decedent.

d. The terms of the alleged arrangements were substantially these: The Hugheses agreed to move into the upstairs apartment of the decedent's home, and to take care of the yard and walks and perform other external maintenance on the house; in return the decedent agreed to pay the Hugheses $100 per month, and to provide the apartment and utilities at no cost.

e. At no time during the negotiations or the ensuing arrangement was any reference to or mention made concerning the decedent's house, or any agreement to devise said house to the plaintiffs at decedent's death.

f. This proposal was made by the decedent to John Hughes, and after a short discussion with Mrs. Hughes, the plaintiffs accepted these terms.

g. No mention was made by either party that the plaintiffs would be personally caring for the decedent.

The law is:

Whether a contract was made is primarily a question of fact to be determined by the trial court. The burden is upon the plaintiff to prove the fact of the contract and its terms. The terms of the contract must be definite and certain, and the contract must be established by clear and convincing evidence. The oral contract is within the statute of frauds and may be enforced only through an action in equity.

2. The plaintiffs failed to satisfactorily care for the decedent's house and yard as provided by the contract.

a. The plaintiffs failed to rake the leaves as a result of which the yard usually appeared unkept in the fall and spring and aroused ill will among several of the neighbors.

b. The plaintiffs failed to mow the grass at reasonable intervals, causing large portions of the lawn to become infested with crabgrass and other noxious weeds.

c. The plaintiffs were normally several months late in changing the storm windows and screens, and failed entirely to change the storm windows in 1956.

d. The plaintiffs never shoveled the snow from the sidewalks.

e. The plaintiffs failed to remove an accumulation of ice from the front sidewalk, the accumulation having occurred from the runoff of an eaves spout. As a result, a passing neighbor fell and broke his ankle, and under threat of an action at law, decedent paid $750 to the claimant as a settlement.

f. The reason for the lack of care given to the maintenance of the yard and house, besides irresponsibility, can be attributed to the fact that the plaintiff was gainfully employed as a paint brush salesman, and in carrying on his business, had little time to devote to the property.

g. The decedent did some of the outside work himself, when it became apparent that it would not otherwise be done.

h. The plaintiffs sporadically helped the decedent clean the lower floor of the house, and the decedent normally did his cleaning himself.

i. The decedent did his own cooking, laundry, and other personal duties.

j. The plaintiffs, although friendly with the decedent, remained apart from the decedent both in their everyday life and social activities. Mrs. Hughes was often out with her friends and entertained often in the apartment.

k. Robert Burger, decedent's attorney, acted as decedent's financial advisor and kept all of his accounts.

l. As compensation for the arrangement, the plaintiffs received 100 dollars per month, free rent, and utilities. They also received a bequest of $2,000 in the decedent's will.

m. Decedent was at all times in good physical condition and capable of caring for himself.

The law is:

When an oral agreement is made unenforceable by the statute of frauds and does not merit specific performance, the plaintiff may recover only damages for services rendered under the agreement under the theory of quasi contract, and the measure of such recovery will be the value of the services rendered less the benefits the plaintiffs received under the contract. Nor can the plaintiff recover damages for breach of the oral contract. The value of the property to be devised is not a measure of recovery.

To recover specific performance, the terms of the contract must be definite and certain. The services must be performed under the terms of the contract. To merit specific performance, the services must be of a peculiar and personal nature. If the part performance of the contract is as beneficial to the plaintiff as to the deceased, specific performance will not be allowed.

ANTICIPATED CASE OF PLAINTIFF

1. There was an oral contract in which the decedent promised to devise his house and lot to the plaintiffs: "If you come live with me and care for me and my house until I die, I will devise you my house." Mr. Hughes, "I accept."

Meet this by disputing the terms of the alleged contract, and by contending that these terms do not specify that the plaintiffs were to assume a peculiar domestic relationship with the decedent.

2. That the plaintiffs are entitled to recover $30,000 for the value of the services that they performed.

Meet this by showing the services were not fully and adequately performed. Show what the proper measure of recovery is, and show that the plaintiffs have been fully compensated. Show the plaintiffs failure to present their claim in probate court. Also show the actual value of the services that the plaintiffs allegedly performed.

3. That decedent has made statements to neighbors to the effect that the plaintiffs were to receive the property when the decedent died.

Meet this by showing that the witness is a friend of the plaintiffs and is biased. Show that plaintiffs never objected to the will. Also show that the plaintiffs made statements adverse to their pecuniary interest.

4. Plaintiffs will testify as to their close relationship with the decedent.

Meet this by showing that the decedent addressed the plaintiffs by their last names and did not appear well acquainted at the party on June 7, 1950. Show that decedent was interested in activities with his own friends, that he was independent and capable, and that the relation was merely friendly. Show that Mr. Hughes worked a large number of hours per week, and that Mrs. Hughes was absorbed with her friends and community interests.

5. Plaintiffs will testify that they gave up a lease at a loss of $100, a $5,000 per year job, and friends in moving from Anoka.

Meet this by showing that plaintiffs moved into a $100 apartment, had many new friends, and that the plaintiff appeared to be fully employed.

MEMO OF TESTIMONY-IN-CHIEF FOR DEFENDANT

1. William Mitchell, witness

   a. *As to relationship with decedent —*
      Long time friend.
      Did work for same railroad. Now retired.
      Lives at 72 Golf Terrace.
      Hunting and fishing companion of decedent.
      Conversation with decedent about getting someone to help him.
      Suggested calling minister.
      Decedent told him of the minister's suggestion.

   b. *As to the oral agreement —*
      Was invited to the dinner party of the decedent on June 7, 1950.
      Purpose of the party.
      Was with decedent when Olson asked if he could bring plaintiff.
      Was a member of the card game and heard negotiations.
      Heard the terms: $100 per month, apartment and utilities for services.
      Was with decedent at all times during evening and helped straighten up.

   c. *As to the will —*
      Was present when drawn up.

Made on July 20, 1951, in evening.
Presence of the plaintiffs.

b. *Quality of the work performed —*
Always had seasonal work done much before plaintiffs.
William Brown did some of the yard work.
Plaintiffs repainted porch, but it had to be repainted.
Specific items of disrepair and unperformed or misperformed services.
Decedent did own cooking, and enjoyed it.
Decedent did his own housecleaning, and laundry professionally.

e. *As to decedent's health —*
Decedent's health was excellent for his age.
Accompanied decedent on hunting and fishing trips.
Decedent's illness of 1951 a mild heart attack.
Recovery in 1½ months — two week confinement to house.
Subsequent to illness, sound as before — fishing, officer in church.

f. *As to plaintiffs' living quarters —*
Complete apartment in second floor of decedent's house.
Originally furnished for Paul Smith and wife while going to University.
Outside entrance.

2. Robert Burger, witness

a. *As to the will of decedent —*
Called to hospital on July 20, 1951, to draw up will.
Reads the will to court after identifying signature.
That plaintiffs were present when will was made.
All persons in position to hear provisions — read provisions to decedent.
Plaintiffs did not object to provisions, and have not to date.
Decedent specific and clear on provisions he desired.

b. *As to decedent's financial matters —*
Decedent a client for ten years.
Took care of all monthly expenses as decedent did not wish to be bothered.
Paid taxes, utilities, and other monthly bills.
Paid the plaintiffs $100 per month by check.
Cancelled checks sent to decedent — does not know of their whereabouts.
Paid threatened claim in amount of $750 as a settlement.
Thought claim valid because unnatural condition.
Took over decedent's investments in 1952.
Told by decedent that plaintiff incompetent to invest and lost money.
Finally back into stable securities.

c. *As to the upstairs apartment in decedent's house —*
Knew of the previous occupancy by Smith and wife.
Had advised what kitchen equipment to buy.
Has gone thru it — five rooms and bath — all necessary facilities.
Expert in real estate — sells — buys — has made many leases.
Familiar with decedent's neighborhood and price of apartments.
Rental value $100 plus utilities.

d. *As to decedent's health —*
Saw him every month or two during the six years.
As alert and active after the illness as before.

3. Allen Anderson, witness

a. *As to the quality of work done by the plaintiffs —*
Went by decedent's house everyday on way to the bus.
Grass never cut on time — crab grass and noxious weed set in.
Storms and screens never changed on time.
Storms never removed in 1956.
Sidewalks never shoveled, except for a few times when decedent did it.
Leaves never raked unless decedent did it — heard neighbor complain.
Saw plaintiff painting porch, later saw another painter doing it.
Fell on sidewalk and fractured left ankle.
Off work for three weeks.
Told attorney to start action, but settled with decedent for $750.
Fall occurred from hump of ice which had accumulated from eaves spout.

b. *As to plaintiff's hours away from home —*
Many times saw plaintiff leaving house at 8:00 a.m.
Often noticed him driving into the yard at about 5:00 p.m.
Was given a ride to work by plaintiff several times.
Plaintiff told him business good and working long hours.
Business rushing during spring, summer, and fall according to plaintiff.

c. *As to plaintiff's statements adverse to his interest —*
During one ride, plaintiff said hated to leave house when old man died.
During another ride, said too bad the old man had relatives.
State that witness had nothing against plaintiff; thought him O.K.

MEMO OF ANTICIPATED TESTIMONY FOR PLAINTIFF

1. Raymond Quin, friend of decedent's, will probably be called to testify to the terms of the oral agreement.

a. See that he testifies only to facts within his own knowledge.
b. Determine his relation with the plaintiffs. Impeach by use of friendly witness by showing intimacy with the plaintiffs.
c. Test his certainty of the agreement.
d. Have him corroborate the purpose of the party.

2. John Hughes, plaintiff, will probably be called to testify to the extent of his services and also to the oral agreement.

a. See that he testifies only to facts within his own knowledge.
b. See that he does not testify to any part of the oral agreement.
c. Bring out the fact that he is an interested party.
d. Impeach on investments and personal services by friendly witnesses.

3. George Robb, friend of decedent's, will probably be called to testify to the quality of services performed by the plaintiffs, and subsequent statements of decedent indicating his obligation to plaintiffs.

   a. See that he testifies only to facts within his own knowledge.
   b. Determine how he observed the performance of the services.
   c. Counter subsequent admissions by plaintiffs' statements to Anderson.

   Lawyers ordinarily do not sit down and diagram issues or write fact briefs. Some cases are so simple or routine that a written fact brief would be of no value. However, every lawyer goes through the procedure in his or her mind when preparing a case for trial. Each lawyer must prepare a case in the manner which is most effective for him or her. For example, there are some lawyers who believe that putting together a good final argument is the place to begin. They feel that the argument will determine what evidence they need to develop and the manner in which the evidence should be presented.

   A legal assistant may be asked to prepare an analysis of the facts in light of legal issues stated by the lawyer who is preparing the case. The analysis method could be similar to the above. It is almost as important, in these exercises, to anticipate the opponent's case as to define and develop the client's case.

22

Summary Judgments

On occasion, it is possible for parties to avoid the time and expense of a trial by having a case determined on a motion for *summary judgment*. Rule 56. The procedure is appropriate and highly desirable when there is no dispute on the material (determinative) facts, and the only issues are questions of law. A party may seek a summary judgment concerning one or more or all of the legal issues in a case. Summary judgment motions cannot be used for resolving fact issues.

Motions for summary judgment have two principal values or applications. They are useful for submitting issues of law to the court for determination where there is no real dispute on the governing facts. And they are useful for determining how the law is to be applied to a given set of facts. Though motions for summary judgment are usually thought of as a defense tactic, they may be used effectively by plaintiffs to eliminate nonmeritorious affirmative defenses. Rule 56(a).

A court will entertain a motion for summary judgment only if it clearly appears that there is no dispute on the material facts. Therefore, it is common for the moving party to prepare a stipulation of facts for the court to show the absence of any dispute. If the nonmoving party can show, in good faith, that there is a dispute on the facts, a motion for summary judgment must be denied.

Some examples may be helpful to illustrate the use and limitations of summary judgment motions. Suppose that the plaintiff brought suit on a written contract in which the plaintiff claims the defendant agreed to sell a certain parcel of land to the plaintiff. Suppose further that a dispute exists concerning one of the terms of the contract. If the parties agree that the contract is binding on them and the only issue concerns the proper interpretation of the contract, the matter may be determined by summary judgment. However, if the court determines that the contract is ambiguous and that evidence outside the written document is necessary for a proper construction of the contract, there is an issue of fact which precludes the court from granting summary judgment.

Suppose that a plaintiff was injured as a result of malpractice on the part of a defendant physician, but the statute of limitations ran against the claim before the plaintiff commenced his action. If the defendant physician can show the court when she last treated the plaintiff, when the cause of action accrued, and when the action was commenced against her, she is in a position to move the summary judgment. If, in fact, all of the requisites exist for a successful statute of limitations defense, the court may order the claim dismissed as a matter of law. The statute of limitations is, in this instance, a determinative issue, i.e., dispositive of the entire case. So even though a dispute exists between the parties concerning the alleged malpractice, the plaintiff's contributory negligence, and the extent of the alleged injuries, the court may grant summary judgment. However, the material facts concerning the statute of limitations defense must not be in dispute. If the plaintiff could claim in good faith that the defendant acted to fraudulently conceal the malpractice and kept him from discovering the cause of action — thereby tolling the statute of limitations — a fact issue would exist precluding a summary judgment.

In any summary judgment proceeding, the court must be supplied with sufficient facts to be able to determine the questions of law. The facts must be supplied through writings such as the pleadings, affidavits, stipulations of fact, deposition transcripts, and records. Whatever facts are documented and are to be considered by the court must be admissible in evidence as in a trial. Rule 56(e). Facts presented by affidavits must be based upon personal knowledge. Affidavits must contain basic information showing that the witness is competent and otherwise qualifies to state the facts contained in his or her affidavit. Of course, affidavits and other supporting documents used in making a motion for summary judgment must be served with the motion. If any affidavits are filed in opposition to a motion for summary judgment, the affidavits must be served upon the other parties in good season before the motion is heard. Most state courts require *all* documents to be served and filed on or before the day preceding the hearing.

A motion for summary judgment is a major step in any case. Therefore, a party is required to give ten days notice of the motion before the hearing, rather than the mere five days which is applicable to most other motions. Rule 56(c).

The ten days allowed by Rule 56 may not be sufficient to enable a party to obtain all the information needed to oppose a motion for summary judgment. In that event, the party may obtain a continuance of the motion by filing one or more affidavits showing that certain facts are not presently available by affidavits or otherwise. The court may order a continuance of the motion, and that depositions be taken or other steps implemented to complete the preparation for the summary judgment hearing. Rule 56(f). Though the rule refers to affidavits of the parties, usually lawyers make their own affidavits to show why the needed evidence is not currently available.

Parties must not file any affidavits in bad faith for the purpose of delaying or avoiding a summary judgment. Rule 56(g). Any such misconduct may lead to imposition of costs, lawyer's fees and/or a contempt of court citation. Any opposition to a motion for summary judgment should be directed only at the merits of the motion or procedural defects.

Motions for summary judgment tend to be disfavored by the system because they have the affect of denying the losing party his or her day in court — a trial. It seems that if a judge can find any basis for denying a motion for summary judgment, he or she will. Nevertheless, summary judgment motions continue to be important to the judicial processes. They help to dispose of a lot of nonmeritorious claims and defenses without the necessity of a trial.

23

Juries

The parties to a civil action have a constitutional right to a trial by jury.* The right to a jury trial is preserved and implemented by Rule 38. The jury's sole function is to determine the *facts* so that the law, as determined by the judge, can be applied to the facts. A jury verdict results from the jury's conclusion about the facts and the jury's application of the rules of law to those facts.

If a party does not assert the right to a jury trial, he or she automatically waives it. Then the trial judge becomes the fact finder. A *demand for a jury* may be made by the plaintiff by noting the demand on his or her complaint. The defendant may make the demand on his or her answer. Or, either party may serve a *jury demand* in writing. But the written demand must be served within ten days after service of the last pleading. The demand for a jury trial may specify the fact issues to be tried by the jury leaving all nonspecified fact issues to be determined by the trial judge. However, an unlimited general demand for trial by jury has the effect of making all disputed fact issues subject to determination by the jury. If a party receives a demand for jury that is limited to a specific issue, he or she has ten days in which to serve a counter demand for jury specifying additional fact issues or making a general demand which is all inclusive. Usually a party makes a general demand because he or

*United States Constitution, 7th Amendment: In Suits at common law, where the value in controversy shall exceed twenty dollars, the right of trial by jury shall be preserved, and no fact tried by a jury shall be otherwise re-examined in any Court of the United States than according to the rules of the common law.

she can always waive the right to a jury at any time — assuming the other parties do not object. Rule 38(d).

If a demand for jury was not made by either party as required by the rules, the judge may, nevertheless, order a jury trial if he or she thinks that a jury trial would be preferable. The order may be made pursuant to a motion by one or more of the parties or upon the court's own initiative. Why would a judge encourage a jury trial? A judge may have to spend a considerable amount of time reviewing and weighing the evidence and making decisions concerning the disputed facts. After making his or her determination concerning all of the issues in the case, he or she must prepare documents called **Findings of Fact, Conclusions of Law,** and Order for Judgment which the clerk serves upon the parties. The clerk of court must enter judgment in accordance with the Order for Judgment. This is a time-consuming process. Juries help to expedite the court's business and litigation — contrary to a belief held by some people. A judge may elect to use an "advisory jury" even in those cases where the parties do not have a constitutional right to a jury trial. However, a judge cannot choose to have a jury hear cases in which the United States government is the defendant if the action against the government is pursuant to a statute which expressly provides that trial shall be without a jury. There is no denial of due process of law in such cases because the federal government is immune from suit. If a statute waives governmental immunity permitting an action without a jury, the plaintiff can hardly complain about the waiver being only partial.

Jurors are selected at random from voter registration lists in the district or division in which the court sits. Some courts use a combination of voter lists and driver license lists in an effort to get a broader cross-section. Each potential juror must fill out a juror qualification form. A person must meet certain minimum requirements to qualify for jury service in the federal courts. A juror must be a citizen of the United States, at least eighteen years of age, able to read and write, able to understand English, physically capable of participating and mentally competent to serve. A person *may* be disqualified from service if he or she has been convicted of a crime punishable by imprisonment for one year or more or have criminal charges pending against him or her for such a crime. A term of service does not exceed 30 days unless more time is needed to finish a trial already begun within the 30 day period. Jurors are not called for service more than once during a two year period.

When a jury panel is needed the court directs the clerk to issue subpoenas for qualified jurors. The subpoenas are served by registered mail or by the marshal. The subpoena states that failure to appear as directed subjects the venireman to a fine of $100.00 or three days imprisonment or both. A person may be excused from jury service only if he or she can show an "undue hardship" or "extreme inconvenience." If so, his or her term of service is only postponed. Jurors may be called upon to hear and decide either criminal cases or civil cases during a single term of service.

When the parties and lawyers arrive at the courtroom, ready to begin trial, they usually spend some time with the judge discussing the case, procedures, scheduling problems, and settlement. When it appears that the case is ready, the judge directs a deputy clerk or bailiff to bring a jury panel to the courtroom. The size of the panel depends upon the number of jurors needed to try the case. Historically, a civil action required twelve jurors plus one or more alternates if the case promised to be a long one. Most civil actions are now tried by a jury of six persons plus alternates. Each party is entitled to three **peremptory challenges.** The number of *challenges for cause* are unlimited. From the jury panel twelve or more jurors are called to sit in or near the jury box so that they can be asked questions concerning their qualifications to sit on the particular case. The **voir dire** examination may be conducted by the lawyers or by the judge or both. If court rules specify that the judge is to ask all voir dire questions, the lawyers have a right to submit written questions to the judge for him or her to ask. The judge has broad discretion in deciding what questions to ask the prospective jurors.

A trend toward having judges rather than lawyers conduct the voir dire examination is primarily grounded in the belief that trials are significantly shortened by keeping lawyers from having a discussion with each juror. A few judges feel that lawyers tend to take too long. However, it is respectfully suggested that the solution to the problem, if there is one, is for the judges to exercise their authority to control the proceedings by ordering counsel to avoid repetition and irrelevant questions. The trial judge does not need to wait for the opposing counsel to object. The lawyers should have primary responsibility for conducting the voir dire examination.

The judge begins the voir dire examination by telling the jury panel why they have been assembled and the purpose of the voir dire examination. He or she briefly explains the nature of the case, defines issues, identifies the parties, and introduces lawyers. The names and addresses of probable witnesses are read to the jury for the purpose of determining whether the jurors are acquainted with any of the persons who will testify. If it turns out that a juror does know a party, lawyer or a witness, the nature of the relationship must be disclosed.

The judge's introductory remarks may be similar to the following.

Members of the Jury Panel: You have been summoned to this courtroom so that of your number six may be selected to hear, try and determine this case. It may be that you would be an excellent juror in 99 out of 100 cases; however, because of the fact that you may be acquainted with one or more of the parties, the lawyers, the witnesses, or because you have a present leaning one way or another about *this* case or this type of case, you may be considered to be biased or prejudiced. What we seek are six persons from varying walks of life who will diligently seek the truth; who will fairly and impartially and without fear or favor try the issues of fact; and who will decide this case upon the evidence adduced here in the courtroom and upon the law that will be given to you by me.

In order that we may ascertain if you are a proper or qualified person to sit as a juror in this case, I first, then counsel, will ask you questions about your qualifications. In so doing, it is not the lawyers' intention to pry into your private life, but it is their duty to select a jury of the quality and character indicated. Please be open, frank and responsive to the questions put to you so that justice may be done between the parties.

So that you may intelligently respond to questions put to you testing your qualifications, I shall briefly state: the identity of the parties; the nature of the case as reflected by the pleadings; the identity of the lawyers; the names of possible witnesses; and, certain fundamental rules of law applicable to this and all cases of like character.

The judge and lawyers may ask questions of the veniremen concerning their:

1. Family
2. Education
3. Past and present occupations
4. Prior jury experience
5. Experience with similar occurrences or transactions
6. Experience with litigation as a party or witness
7. Attitude toward the judicial system or type of lawsuit in question
8. Attitude toward the parties or witnesses
9. Willingness to follow and apply the law

The questions may be put to veniremen in the order by which they were seated. Or, questions may be put to the panel as a whole, and each juror responds with a raised hand if a question applies to him or her. This, of course, is the faster method and tends to avoid unnecessary repetition. However, it is also the least satisfactory, for it fails to develop sufficient thought, discussion and commitment to the process on the part of the veniremen.

The defendant's lawyer questions the panel first. He or she usually concludes a voir dire examination by requesting the jurors to set aside their natural feelings of sympathy, to keep an open mind about what the evidence proves until they have heard *all* the evidence, and to follow the court's instructions on the law even if the jurors feel that the law should be different. The plaintiff's lawyer usually concludes his or her examination with a request that the jurors listen carefully to the evidence and that they give the case the same thoughtful consideration that they would want for their own important matters. The techniques employed by lawyers differ greatly, but always the primary objective is to weed out undesirable jurors from the panel without causing annoyance or embarrassment to anyone. The process works well.

A peremptory challenge permits a lawyer to excuse (strike) a potential juror without being required to give a reason. Whereas a juror who is excused "for cause" is stricken because there is, at least, the appearance of actual or implied bias. Actual bias exists when a juror acknowledges that he or she cannot be totally fair. His or her bias may be against or for a party. Or, a juror may be biased because of the type of case it is. If a venireman is related to one of the parties or to one of the lawyers or works for a party, there is implied bias, and will be excused by the court even if the person claims he or she *can* be fair.

In the typical case the plaintiff and defendant are each allowed three peremptory challenges. But if there is more than one defendant, they have to share the peremptory challenges unless adversity exists between them. Ordinarily the parties are considered adverse to each other only if the pleadings raise issues between them. For example, cross-claims make codefendants adverse. The same factors determine whether or not coplaintiffs must share the three peremptory challenges. The judge must try to keep veniremen from claiming bias for the purpose of evading service.

The most common procedure for conducting the voir dire examination in civil cases is for the defendant's lawyer to question the entire panel first. Then the plaintiff's lawyer conducts his or her examination. Veniremen who have actual or implied bias are stricken for cause before the examinations are concluded. After all the questioning is concluded, the defendant's lawyer is required to strike one juror from the jury list. Then the plaintiff's lawyer must strike one juror. The process continues until each side has exercised three peremptory challenges, and only six jurors are left plus any alternate jurors that are needed. The last venireman to enter the jury box and to survive the challenges is the alternate.

Some courts use a different voir dire procedure whereby each lawyer interrogates each venireman in the order seated. The venireman is challenged or accepted before the next venireman is questioned. The procedure is more cumbersome and does not give the lawyers an opportunity to compare all the veniremen before exercising their precious peremptive challenges. The procedure may cause a little more embarrassment because the peremptory challenges have to be exercised before going on to the next juror rather than striking all extra jurors from the jury list at the end of all the questioning. In the system first discussed, the jurors know that six of their number must be eliminated even though all of them may be perfectly acceptable; whereas, in the latter procedure, each juror is accepted or rejected personally by the parties before the lawyers have the opportunity to interview the remaining jurors.

Upon selection of the twelve or six jurors who will try the case, they take an oath to follow the court's orders and instructions. The following is typical of the juror's oath:

> You each do swear that you will impartially try the issues in this case and a true verdict give according to the law and the evidence given you in court; your own counsel and that of your fellows you will duly keep, you will say nothing concerning the case, nor suffer anyone to speak to you about it, and you will keep your verdict secret until you deliver it in court. So help you God.

The jurors are usually reminded at this point that they must act upon reason and good judgment, not feelings or emotion or speculation. Some preliminary instructions are usually given by the judge as follows:

> As to the law of this case, it will be given to you by me at the appropriate time. However, you are instructed that you must take that law exactly and precisely as I shall give it to you, that you apply such law to the facts as you find them to be from the evidence, and that you render your verdict accordingly, regardless of where the "chips may fall." The Court

(trial judge) does not make the law, but merely declares it in a given case. The law comes from federal and state constitutions, from federal and state statutes, and from declarations contained in judicial decisions stating the public standards of rights and duties in matters not covered by the constitutions and statutes. In this connection, you are instructed that if judges and juries were not bound by these tangible statements of the law, if in each lawsuit the judge or the jury could set up private and personal standards of rights and duties as a basis for deciding the case, one would never know in advance of a decision how he or she should have acted in a particular situation and no one would be safe.

Cases arising out of similar relationships or circumstances must be decided on settled principles of law and not on the notions of the trial judge or of a jury. Accordingly, it must be readily apparent to you that even though you may have an opinion as to what the law is or should be, you must set that aside; you must accept and apply the law exactly and precisely as I shall give it to you. I cannot at this time instruct you as to all rules of law applicable to this case because I have not, as yet, heard the evidence.

I have some general instructions which I think will be of assistance. Our hours are generally from 9:30 a.m. to 12:00 p.m., 2:00 p.m. to 5:00 p.m. Those hours may be modified or extended depending upon circumstances. For example, should a witness's testimony be near completion at the customary recess time, we would tend to continue so that the witness would not need to come back for the next session.

Promptness, of course, is extremely important, and I am sure I need say no more about that.

During the morning session, about midway, and the afternoon session, about midway, we will take a 15 minute recess. On those occasions, as well as during the noon hour and after hours, you will be among the public. Do not discuss this case or the subject matter of the case with anyone. Once the case is over and you have rendered your verdict and you have been discharged from the case, then you can speak as fully and freely as you wish. On the other hand, if anyone should inquire, it is up to you. You can say, "I've done my best; I'd rather not discuss it."

You know where the accident occurred. Please do not go out and view the premises. You are not investigators. You are to determine the facts from the evidence submitted here in the courtroom — so keep that in mind.

You must try to keep an open mind until all of the evidence has been presented and until you have been instructed, by me, concerning the applicable rules of law. The plaintiff will proceed with his or her case first, followed by the case-in-chief of each of the defendants. If new material is submitted, the plaintiff will have the right of rebuttal. If on rebuttal new material is submitted, then each of the defendants will have a right of rebuttal. In that way, all of the evidence that is proper and competent will be submitted to you without repetition. After all of the evidence has been presented, and the parties have rested their cases, you will have the opportunity to hear the attorneys' summations. The attorneys will review the evidence and draw conclusions from it. They will also discuss the rules of law as they apply to the evidence. Prior to those summations, I will have discussed with counsel the law which I have determined applies to the case and which I will give to you. The summations may be — and usually are — of assistance to you, but the responsibility of decision is yours — not that of the attorneys. When you enter the jury room, you will have all of the tools with which to determine the facts of the case and to apply the law in an appropriate manner. In the meantime, do not jump to conclusions as each witness takes the stand. You must keep an open and objective mind while the case is being presented. You should maintain that same objectivity when you commence your deliberations.

You may take notes if you wish. However, those notes are *your* own personal notes for refreshing *your* own memory. If your memory has then been refreshed so that you can say, "Now of my own knowledge, I know this was said," or whatever the case may be, then, of course, you can say that to your fellow jurors. But your fellow jurors *should not* use your notes to refresh their memories. Such notes are no more authoritative than another juror's memory. There is a danger that when writing notes, other important evidence will not be heard.

There may be, from time to time, conferences here at the bench. Those conferences with counsel are intended to be out of your hearing. They involve questions of law or procedure, not questions of fact. Do not attempt to overhear our conversation. Under no circumstances should you guess the subject of our conversations and permit that to bear upon your determination of facts or the ultimate issues of the case. If you were to do so, your decision or determination would not be on solid facts and the law, but would be based upon speculation and conjecture — which is repugnant to good judicial administration.

If at any time during the course of the trial something of a personal nature bothers you, you come to me about it. I am sure I can handle it so that it will not be detrimental to any party. But do not ask me what the evidence is, because that is solely within your province. That is your responsibility. As I indicated before, you should not consider or even know what I think of the evidence.

Sometimes, after the jury commences deliberations, there is a disagreement as to what a witness may have said — and it seems so simple to call the court and say, "May we come back and have the court reporter read a witness's testimony?" I do not permit that, except under unusual circumstances. In all probability, I will have started another trial. Counsel have perhaps gone their respective ways and may be trying another lawsuit — even in another county. In order to have you come back in and have portions of the testimony read to you, I would have to contact counsel, get them back, and recess my case. And then, after I have permitted the reading of that one witness's testimony, the attorneys may be constrained to point out that, in fairness, the testimony of other witnesses who touched upon that subject ought to be read; otherwise, there may be an overemphasis of one facet of the case. By the time I comply, we would be trying the case all over again.

If you fail to hear a question of an attorney or an answer of a witness, speak up, raise your hand, then I will make sure that it is read back at that time in its proper continuity and without any fear of possible overemphasis.

The jury performs its ultimate function by returning a verdict. The verdict which it uses will be of a type and form selected by the trial judge. The most common verdict form is a "general verdict." It is very short. The jury simply states that it finds for the plaintiff in $X.00 or it finds "for the defendant," which means the plaintiff recovers no money damages. If the defendant prevails on his or her counterclaim, the amount is noted. In federal courts, the verdict must be unanimous, and it is signed only by the foreman or forelady. In civil actions in some states, courts allow the jury to return a *five-sixths verdict* after six hours of deliberation. In other words, a verdict must be unanimous if rendered during the first six hours of deliberation. Thereafter, five of six or ten of twelve jurors may agree on the verdict. Each concurring juror must sign the verdict form. The foreman does not sign it unless he is a concurring juror. The concurring jurors must agree to all parts of the verdict. The United States Supreme Court has held that five-sixths verdicts in criminal cases deny the defendant due process of law and, therefore, are unconstitutional.

A case may be submitted to the jury on a special verdict which consists of specific questions pertaining to the facts in controversy. The jury must answer each question thereby resolving the basic issues of fact. The court then applies the law to the facts as determined by the jury and issues an order for judgment accordingly. The jury's answer to each question may be short; usually "yes" or "no." Example:

1. Did defendant sign the promissory note (Plaintiff's Exhibit A)? Yes or No:

_____

2. Was the defendant negligent? Yes or No: _____
3. If your answer to question 2 is "yes," was the defendant's negligence a direct cause of the accident? Yes or No: _____

When a case is submitted to the jury for its determination, it usually takes several hours for them to review the evidence and reach a verdict. Four to six hours seems to be an average length of time for deliberations in a typical civil case. While the jury is considering the case, the trial judge may begin trying another case. Or, he or she may conduct other essential business of the court. When the trial judge acts as the fact finder, he or she must conduct a similar careful review of the evidence, just as the jury does, then prepare writing Findings of Fact, Conclusions of Law, and Order for Judgment. The length of time required by the judge to go through this procedure well justifies the expense of the jury system. Just as important, it often takes the trial judge a long time to make his or her decision — sometimes months. During that period of time, it is said that the judge has the case "under advisement." The delay may cause the parties a great deal of anxiety as well as inconvenience. Yet, lawyers are very reluctant to pressure the judge for an earlier decision.

Jurors must not discuss the case with anyone while the case is in trial; they should not even discuss the case amongst themselves. Such discussion might cause them to reach a conclusion prematurely. There is also danger that a juror might express an unfortunate conclusion or opinion that he or she may be reluctant to give up. For the same reason, jurors are often urged to avoid making strong, irretractible statements at the beginning of their deliberations.

After the verdict is received by the judge in open court, the lawyers may ask to have the jury polled for the purpose of confirming that it is the true verdict of each juror. Usually the right to poll the jury is waived. Very often lawyers elect not to be present when the verdict is returned. This is because they do not want to waste time waiting at the courtroom. The judge or clerk will notify them of the verdict by telephone within minutes after the verdict is received.

Occasionally, jurors determine that they need clarification on some point of law or procedure, so they notify the judge through the bailiff that they need additional instructions. In that event, the lawyers must be summoned to the courtroom so that they can hear the jury's question or problem and try to assist the judge in resolving it. The responsibility, of course, belongs to the judge. Usually the problem can be solved merely by rereading the instructions already given. Sometimes the jury wants to know the effect of their special verdict before signing it. The ordinary answer is that they are not supposed to concern themselves with the effect of the verdict — just the truth. "Let the chips fall where they may." However, some states have laws permitting the judge and lawyers to inform the jury of the effect of their answers in a special verdict.

Jurors do not have to talk to anyone about their verdict, deliberations, or any other aspect of the trial after the case is concluded. On the other hand, there is no law against a juror talking to the parties, lawyers, reporters, or anyone else about the case if he or she wants to. If it should appear that the jury or any of its members was guilty of misconduct in the course of the trial, that could be a basis for setting aside the verdict. If either party learns of or suspects that there has been misconduct by the jury, he or she must inform the trial judge of the suspicion or information. The court, not the parties, must conduct an investigation of the alleged jury misconduct. Interviewing jurors after the verdict should not be used as a subterfuge for finding error and obtaining a new trial. Contact with jurors after the trial by the parties or their lawyers may result in a waiver of any right to complain of jury misconduct.

There is a dynamic quality to the jury system. Most litigants seem to prefer to have their cases decided by a jury rather than by a judge who may well be more intelligent and better educated. Litigants tend to be suspicious of decisions made by one person regardless of that person's qualifications. Litigants seem to be more concerned about being treated impartially than wisely. "Impartiality," in this sense, is *not* synonymous with "fairness" which suggests extrajudicial considerations and judgments as to what is the better result. The jury system, it is said, is for the losing litigant, because a verdict is usually more palatable to the loser than a judge's decision. The prevailing party is probably going to be satisfied with whatever system is used.

When jurors complete their term of service, they have been enriched by the experience of serving their government and community in a very important role. They have a better understanding and appreciation for the judicial system. They are soon able to set aside the worries which accompany a conscientious effort to do the job right.

24

Post-Trial Motions

Occasionally one of the parties, and once in a while all of the parties, are disappointed in the jury's verdict or the judge's Findings of Fact, Conclusions of Law, and Order for Judgment. The losing party's first consideration is to obtain a new trial. But mere disappointment in the result is not grounds for obtaining a new trial or for appealing. If the trial was conducted without any *prejudicial* error, there is no basis for changing the result. Error is considered prejudicial only if it appears that the error adversely affected the outcome of the case in a significant manner.

The losing party's lawyer may bring the errors to the trial court's attention by making a *motion for new trial* which must be served upon all parties within ten days after the entry of judgment. If the judgment was entered on Monday, the ten day period begins to run on Tuesday. The motion must specify the alleged errors.

There are many possibilities for error in the course of a trial. Errors may pertain to substantive points of law or to matters of procedure. Some of the more common grounds for a new trial are:

Misconduct on the part of one or more jurors.   If jurors should attempt to conduct their own investigation outside of the courtroom, that would constitute misconduct which could require a new trial. A juror's contact with one of the parties or witnesses before or during the trial could give the appearance of favoritism or worse. A juror's false statement in the voir dire examination could be the basis for a new trial.

Misconduct on the part of the prevailing party.   If the prevailing party concealed evidence, concealed witnesses, suborned perjury, presented false testimony, made an improper remark during final argument, etc., the trial court would be obligated to order a new trial in favor of the losing party. The misconduct must be substantial, prejudicial and not corrected during the trial.

Discovery of new evidence.   If the losing party can show that there is new, additional evidence which could well change the outcome of the case *and* that the evidence could not have been discovered and obtained by the exercise of due diligence before the trial was completed, a new trial may be ordered. Parties are required to be diligent in gathering their evidence for presentation at trial. If more time is needed to secure important evidence, additional time usually can be obtained, providing the parties have not been dilatory and provided that the delay will not cause substantial prejudice to other parties. It would be unfair for a party to avoid or neglect to present evidence and then use the omission to obtain a new trial. For that reason, the losing party must be able to convince the court that the newly discovered evidence was unavailable or could not have been discovered before the trial concluded.

Inappropriate award of damages.   The amount of compensation to be awarded is peculiarly a question of fact for the jury. However, courts have developed a sense of proportion about the adequacy or inadequacy of money damages for cases. If the award is one which does not shock the judge's conscience as being either too much or too little, the award will be allowed to stand. But an award which is manifestly unfair will be set aside and a new trial ordered. The new trial may be limited to the issue of damages only or to the issue of liability only. A motion for a new trial on the issue of damages is usually a blended motion in which the moving party asks for an *additur* to the verdict (assuming the award is too little), or a *remittitur* to the verdict (assuming the award is too much). The trial judge may determine that a certain amount of money added to or taken away from the verdict will do substantial justice, and that by ordering an award accordingly, the expense of a new trial may be avoided. He or she may issue an order providing that if the plaintiff will accept a remittitur, in an amount stated, he or she will deny the defendant's motion for a new trial due to the excessiveness of the verdict. On the other hand, he or she may issue an order granting an additur for the plaintiff and, unless the defendant agrees to pay the additional specified sum, over and above the verdict, the court will grant the plaintiff's motion for a new trial on the issue of damages. The order for an additur or remittitur does not have to be tied to an order for a new trial.

Occasionally, a case is presented where an injured plaintiff claims to have spent many thousands of dollars for medical treatment for injuries allegedly sustained in an accident, but the defendant is able to present considerable, believeable evidence to the effect tha the medical expenses were not due to the accident in question. A very small verdict may result. Weighing the evidence and equities of such a situation can be a very difficult responsiblity for the trial judge and the appellate court.

Unrectified errors of law at trial.   Throughout a trial, the presiding judge is confronted with questions of law. The judge has to rule on the admissibility of controverted evidence. He or she must rule on requested jury instructions and often prepares his or her own jury instructions. If any of the rulings are erroneous and the error was duly brought to his or her attention, the losing party is entitled to a new trial if he or she can show that the error probably adversely affected the outcome of the case. Rule 103. Technical errors of little substance are never the basis for securing a new trial.

A lawyer's objection to evidence is sufficient notice to the judge of the error concerning the evidence. There is no need for a lawyer to argue each evidentiary ruling or to make a specific exception to the judge's rulings. There may be a little problem, however, where a lawyer objects to certain improper evidence but states the wrong grounds for his or her objection.

If a lawyer believes that the court has misstated the law in the jury instructions, he or she is required to bring that error to the judge's attention before the jury commences its deliberations. Ordinarily, as soon as the judge is finished with the instructions, he or she turns to the lawyers and asks whether there have been any errors or omissions in the instructions. The lawyers must speak then or forever hold their peace. It is unnecessary to rehash errors in the instruction which were discussed on the record in chambers before the judge undertook to instruct the jury. Also, a lawyer has protected his or her record, in this regard, by filing proper written requested instructions.

Verdict not supported by the evidence.   If the losing party feels that he or she was entitled to a directed verdict on an issue because there was no evidence to support the particular claim or defense, and the motion for directed verdict was denied, he or she may make a motion for a new trial on that ground. Usually, it is very difficult to obtain a new trial on this ground because almost any believeable evidence on the issue is enough to carry the issue to the jury. The trial court, in effect, has a duty to try to sustain the verdict if that is reasonably possible. Every reasonable doubt is resolved in favor of the verdict. This motion is always accompanied by another motion called motion for judgment notwithstanding the verdict.

A motion for a new trial must state precisely the grounds for the motion. Proof of the error may be shown to the trial court by having a partial transcript of the proceedings prepared by the official court reporter. The motion may be supported by affidavits of persons who have knowledge of the claimed errors. Additionally, the motion is almost always based on the facts as recorded in the judge's minutes made during the trial.

The Rules provide that a trial judge may order a new trial within ten days after the entry of judgment even though neither party has made a motion for a new trial. The same power permits the trial judge to order a new trial on grounds which were not raised by the losing party's motion for a new trial.

The order for new trial must state the reasons or grounds for granting a new trial. However, an order denying the motion for a new trial needs no explanation.

A motion for new trial is considered the first step to an appeal. In some state courts, a motion for a new trial is practically a prerequisite to an appeal. It gives the trial judge an opportunity to consider and correct an alleged error. It also gives the judge an opportunity to explain the reasons for his or her decision. However, in federal court, the losing party may simply appeal from the judgment. The *scope* of review in certain appellate courts is broader if the appeal is from an order denying a new trial rather than an appeal from the judgement.

25

Judgments

A judgment is the court's final expression of the parties' legal rights and obligations. A judgment is entered in the court file and judgment docket after a full trial on the merits. Or it may be entered as the result of a party's default as shown by the court records. Most courts also allow judgments to be filed on the basis of a party's *confession of judgment.* The terms *judgment* and *decree* are frequently used interchangeably. Historically, a decree was the utlimate determination by a Court in **equity.** The court decreed what the parties were to do or not do. Whereas a judgment was rendered by a Court of Law and usually awarded a sum of money or disallowed the claim for a sum of money.

The judgment is a document that is usually prepared by the clerk of court. If the case was decided upon a general verdict and resulted in an award of money or a determination that no recovery should be had, the clerk of court is required to forthwith enter judgment according to the verdict. Rule 58. However, if the jury returned a special verdict or a general verdict with answers to interrogatories, the trial judge must prepare an Order for Judgment. The order directs the clerk of court how to prepare and state the terms of the judgment. The judge must approve the form of the judgment before it is officially filed. Approval is indicated by his or her signature.

A court's order for judgment may be similar to the following:

The above-entitled action came on for trial before the Court and a Jury, the Honorable Russell A. Smith, U.S. District Judge, presiding, and the issues having been duly tried and the Jury having duly rendered its verdict,

It is Ordered and Adjudged that plaintiff, Robert I. Miller, recover of the defendant, Thomas Jones, the sum of $25,000 and his costs of action. Dated at Chicago, Illinois, this _____ day of October, 1981.

/s/ Raymond A. Johnson
Clerk of Court.

The clerk of court notes on the *judgment docket* or *judgment roll* the fact that the judgment was entered on a particular date and in a particular amount. The judgment may conclude that the plaintiff is entitled to recover specific property or that he or she is the owner of certain property. As discussed in the section on remedies, there are various forms of relief which may be ordered by a court. Whatever the form of relief, it is stated in the judgment.

A judgment is, in itself, a valuable property right for a judgment creditor. When the judgment is filed, it becomes a lien against the judgment debtor's property, at least that property which is not exempt from seizure through a writ of execution or writ of attachment. A judgment for money may be assigned or transferred to another person. Of course, such transfers should be in writing and filed with the clerk of court. State law determines the length of time during which a judgment is enforceable. The federal courts follow and apply state law in this regard. A typical period of time for a judgment to remain effective is ten years. The judgment creditor may, however, renew the judgment before expiration by applying for a renewal and paying a nominal fee. Once the judgment expires, it becomes a nullity. It is no longer a lien or encumberance against the judgment debtor's property. It cannot be enforced against him or her.

Under the laws of most states, a judgment creditor is entitled to interest on the amount of the judgment. Interest begins to accumulate on the date the judgment is entered. It should be noted that in many jurisidictions interest accrues on the jury's verdict from the day the verdict is rendered. Where interest is allowed on the verdict, that amount should be incorporated into the amount of the judgment.

If the judgment had the effect of determining that property owned by the judgment debtor should be transferred to the judgment creditor by execution of a deed or other conveyance, and the defendant refuses to do so, the court may appoint a trustee to do the act for the judgment debtor. In some jurisdictions, the court is empowered to declare that that which the judgment debtor should have done, is done. The court order has the effect of the deed which the judgment debtor refused to perform. The judgment becomes a public record showing transfer of title and is accepted for filing by the local Register of Deeds.

If the judgment is for a sum of money and the debtor cannot or will not pay it, the court may issue a *writ of execution* which directs the executive branch of the government, usually a sheriff, to locate the defendant's property, seize it, and sell it in the manner prescribed by law. The usual procedure is to sell the property at a public auction with due notice given to the public and to those persons who have special interests in the property. Usually, the property is held for a designated period of time during which the judgment debtor has an opportunity to redeem the property by meeting his or her obligation. A judgment creditor may be required to post a bond protecting the judgment debtor against any errors or improprieties which might occur when the property is seized and sold. The sheriff probably does not know the exact location of the judgment debtor's property. Therefore, it behooves the judgment creditor to provide the sheriff with whatever information he or she can about the identity and location of nonexempt property to be seized. The sheriff charges the creditor for his or her time and expenses, but these expenses ultimately become the responsiblity of the judgment debtor.

Not infrequently, neither the judgment creditor nor the sheriff can locate any of the debtor's properties or monies. In that event, the judgment creditor is allowed to conduct *supplementary proceedings* for the purpose of trying to locate the debtor's monies and properties. Upon motion, the court will issue an order requiring the judgment debtor to appear at a specified time and place for a deposition in which the debtor may be questioned about his or her earnings, properties, past transfers of property and any expectancy of future acquisitions. The debtor may be asked about his or her current and recent employments, salary, mode of payment, checking accounts, savings accounts, accounts receivable, etc. The debtor's testimony is under oath, so he or she is subject to the penalties of perjury. If the debtor refuses to answer questions about the nature and extent of properties and financial condition, he or she is subject to a contempt of court order. Armed with the new information obtained in the supplementary proceedings, the judgment creditor is able to secure a new writ of execution directed to the sheriff who can try once more to locate, seize, and sell the debtor's monies and properties. If the sheriff is able to find cash, the money itself may be turned over to the judgment creditor. Again, the sheriff deducts his or her fees and expenses before the judgment creditor is paid. However, the judgment creditor's total recovery is not necessarily reduced by the amount of the sheriff's fees. If enough money or property is found, the judgment debtor ends up paying the additional costs incurred.

A judgment debtor should not be subject to harassment by supplementary proceedings. Therefore, judgment creditors are allowed to have only a certain number of depositions during a year. A court order is required for each deposition. The proceedings are governed by state law.

If a third person is indebted to the judgment debtor or holds monies or properties of the debtor, the judgment creditor may claim and recover such monies and properties through a garnishment proceeding. He or she does this by obtaining a *garnishment summons* which must be served on the third person who is designated as the *garnishee*. The summons advises the garnishee of the fact of the indebtedness and the amount of it. It directs the garnishee to disclose to the garnishor the amount of monies, if any, that is being held by the garnishee. The garnishee does this by serving and filing a *garnishment disclosure*. Garnishment procedures are frequently used to tie up bank accounts and wages earned. In most states, if not all, wages are given a partially exempt status so that only a fraction of the debtor's take home pay may be seized.

A judgment of one court may be transferred to a court in another jurisdiction for enforcement. The procedure is relatively simple. An authenticated, sometimes called "exemplified," copy of the original judgment must be filed with the second court. The judgment establishes the nature and extent of the debtor's obligation. As provided in the United States Constitution, the states are required to give full faith and credit to each other's judgments. The defendant — judgment debtor — may contest the judgment on the grounds that the original court lacked jurisidiction or that he or she has paid the judgment. Either of these defenses requires a trial to establish the truth. A defect in jurisdiction may occur because the trial court failed to obtain jurisdiction over the person of the defendant, or over the subject matter of the litigation. The trial court may lack jurisdiction because it went beyond its power in granting a particular remedy or it acted beyond its geographical limitations. The judgment debtor has the burden of showing that jurisdiction was lacking. The judgment is presumed to be valid, and the judgment debtor has the burden of proving facts in avoidance of the judgment.

When a judgment creditor transfers the judgment to another jurisdiction and brings an action on that judgment to enforce it against the debtor, the defendant cannot *collaterally attack* the judgment. That is to say, the judgment debtor cannot attempt to relitigate any of the issues which were decided in the first trial or issues which should have been determined in the first trial. He or she may not challenge the sufficiency of the evidence. He or she cannot even attempt to show that errors occurred in the first trial which caused the loss.

Courts are reluctant to allow the prevailing party to enforce a judgment before the losing party exhausts or waives his or her post trial remedies. Therefore, it is not uncommon for a judge to attach to the Order for Judgment a thirty day stay against entry of judgment or a ten day stay against execution on the judgment. Rule 62. If an appeal is taken and the proper bond is posted by the appellant, he or she is entitled to a court order staying any proceedings by which the judgment creditor may attempt to enforce the judgment.

26

Appeals

Only a small percentage of cases are appealed. Very often the amount in controversy simply does not justify the cost and effort that goes into an appeal. An appeal is usually more expensive than the trial. A majority of the cases appealed are affirmed. The system tends to favor the party who prevailed in the trial court.

The first step in an appeal is for the losing party to serve and file a *notice of appeal*. In federal court, the notice of appeal must be filed within thirty days of the date on which the judgment is entered. A notice of appeal may be similar to the following:

(Title of Cause)   Notice of Appeal

To: Plaintiff John Smith and Joe Brown, his attorney:

Please Take Notice that defendant will appeal to the Second Circuit Court of Appeals from the judgment entered in the above entitled action on

(date of judgment)

_____

Attorney for Defendant
Address

The party who initiates the appeal is called the *appellant*. The party against whom the appeal is taken is called the *appellee* in federal courts. Many state courts call the appellee a *respondent*.

When the notice of appeal is filed with the clerk of district court, the appellant must pay a twenty-five dollar filing fee. If there is a judgment for a sum of money against the appellant, he or she must file a *supersedeas* bond which protects the prevailing party for the amount of the judgment. In the event the appeal is denied, the bond guaranties that the prevailing party can collect the amount of the judgment docketed in the district court as well as taxable costs. If the plaintiff is the appellant and there has been no award of money in his or her favor, a cost bond may still be required that protects the defendant for the costs he or she will incur in connection with the appeal. It is not uncommon for the parties to enter into a stipulation waiving the appeal bonds. The respondent benefits by the waiver because if he or she loses the appeal, the cost of the bond is taxable against him or her in most cases.

The appellant must order a transcript of the proceedings from the official court reporter within ten days after filing his or her notice of appeal. The transcript and district court file — which makes up the record on appeal — must be sent to the clerk of the court of appeals within forty days after the filing of the notice of appeal. The record consists of all the pleadings and other documents filed with the clerk, plus all the exhibits and the original copy of the transcript of the trial. The transcript usually includes all of the testimony, motions at trial, and jury instructions. However, the lawyers may stipulate that certain parts of the record may be omitted. Frequently the opening statements and closing arguments are omitted. The original transcript must be filed with the clerk of court by the reporter. Each party is provided with one copy of the transcript.

The appellant must prepare a brief on the law and the "appendix to appellant's brief." The brief and appendix ordinarily are printed — not merely typewritten. Printed briefs help to insure ease of reading and care in preparation. Consequently court rules require printing. The appendix consists of the pleadings and other documents filed with the district court in connection with the case. It also contains pertinent portions of the transcript relating to the issues to be submitted to the appellate court. The appellant is supposed to notify the respondent of those portions of the transcript which he or she intends to include in the appendix. The respondent may request that other portions be included, and if the appellant refuses to include those additional portions, the respondent may arrange for a supplemental printing of them.

The appellant has only forty days in which to prepare the appendix and appellant's brief after the original record has been transmitted to the clerk of the appellate court. The record consists of the original copy of the trial transcript made from the court reporter's stenographic notes, and a certified copy of the clerk of court docket entries showing the dates on which each document was filed with the court. If more time is needed for preparing the brief and appendix, the appellant must make his or her request before the forty day period expires. The request is made to the district court — not to the appellate court.

The appellant's brief is divided into several sections and should be as concise as possible. It must contain a statement outlining the nature of the case; a chronological review of the case listing the date on which the action was commenced and each important procedural date thereafter. It must contain a concise, nonargumentative statement of the facts which were established through the pleadings and the evidence at trial. Preparation of the statement of facts is considered by most lawyers to be the most difficult part of good brief writing. Each important fact necessary to the appeal must be stated along with a page reference showing where that fact may be found in the record.

The appellant must formulate and state the legal issues to be decided by the appellate court. If the appellee disagrees with the legal issues as propounded by the appellant, the appellee may submit a statement of the issues in his or her brief. It is hoped that the parties will agree, at least, on the issues to be argued. But stating the precise legal issue is not always an easy task.

The body of the brief is an argument on the law. The appellant's lawyer attempts to convince the appellate court that errors occurred and that the errors prejudiced the outcome of the case. He or she argues the facts and cites legal authorities which support that position. But the appellant is not allowed to argue that the jury merely reached the wrong verdict. The appellate court assumes that the verdict is consistent with the evidence which favored the appellee. Any evidence favoring the appellee which is inconsistent with the verdict is presumed to have been rejected by the jury — if not necessary to the verdict. The fact that more witnesses and exhibits supported the appellant's theory of the evidence is of no importance on appeal. For example, suppose that the plaintiff claims to have sustained brain damage in an accident; that the evidence showed he was attended by six physicians; that one of the six was of the opinion that the accident caused the plaintiff's alleged brain damage; that one physician had no opinion on the issue; that four were emphatic that the accident did not cause any brain damage; and that one independent medical examiner chosen by the defendant testified that to a reasonable medical certainty the accident did not cause any injury. If the appellate court determined that the *one* physician supporting the plaintiff's claim of brain damage was competent to render such an opinion and that there was an adequate foundation for his opinion, the verdict would stand even though the greater number of witnesses testified to the contrary. The appellate court is not supposed to act as a super jury. Its function is to make sure that the law was correctly stated and applied, and that the trial procedures met the requirements of law and due process.

The legal authorities used in the appellate briefs may include published decisions of the appellate court in which the case is pending and decisions of other courts that have considered the issue. Decisions in other cases rendered by the appellate court in which the appeal is pending, are, of course, the most persuasive for determining the issues on appeal. Indeed, if the decisions are directly in point, they should be determinative of the case. A court should always follow the precedent of its own decisions. Such decisions are considered binding upon the court and are followed unless the appellate court chooses to *overrule* its prior decisions. The holdings by other courts on the issues raised are helpful because of the rationale of the opinions; courts ordinarily strive for uniformity concerning rules of law.

The last section of a legal brief is the conclusion. Customarily, the conclusion is used to state the legal issues in a positive way, indicating how the court should rule. The conclusion also specifies the type of relief sought by the appellant, i.e., new trial or judgment notwithstanding the verdict or a new trial on a single issue such as damages. A good conclusion is concise — not a reargument.

The appellee has thirty days from the date he or she receives the appellant's brief in which to prepare and file a brief. The appellee argues in support of the trial court's rulings and that any errors that did occur were not prejudicial. The format of the appellee's brief is very similar to the appellant's brief. In some appellate courts, the appellant may file a reply brief, which merely gives the appellant a chance to make a rebuttal argument against the appellee's brief.

Once in a while an appellate matter raises an issue that may have a substantial impact on persons or companies who are not parties to the suit, and they may want to participate in the appeal. Such persons may apply to the court for leave to file an *amicus curiae brief* — a brief by a "friend of the court." No one has an absolute right to file an amicus brief. The court considers the nature of the applicant's interest in determining whether or not to permit the appearance. Obviously, the parties have an interest in who will participate and to what extent. But the parties have no veto power over a motion for leave to file an amicus brief.

The circuit court of appeals clerk schedules the appeal for oral argument before three or more appellate judges. In state appellate courts and the United States Supreme Court, the appellate jurists are referred to as "Justices." The parties usually have at least thirty days notice of the hearing date. The court ordinarily hears three or four arguments during the course of a morning's session. Each case is allotted one hour or less. Therefore, each party has only thirty minutes or less, in which to present his or her argument. The appellant may be allowed to save some of the allotted time for replying to the appellee's argument. During the arguments the judges ask such questions as they deem necessary. The appellate judges almost never state what their decision will be. A lawyer is often able to make an educated guess about the probable outcome, however, by the nature of the judges' questions and by their apparent attitude toward the issues. The appellate court's decision is usually rendered within three or four months after the argument, sometimes sooner. Of course, the length of time for the court's decision depends upon many factors, and it could be even longer in coming.

Upon receiving the appellate court decision, the losing party may determine that some point has been neglected or overlooked by the appellate court. The remedy is to file a motion for a rehearing in which he or she sets forth the reasons why a rehearing is thought necessary. If the court is convinced by the written motion that a rehearing is justified, a rehearing is ordered. However, more often than not, motions for rehearing are denied without explanation.

Only a small percentage of the cases that go to the circuit courts of appeal are carried to the United States Supreme Court. Very few cases present issues that create an absolute right to appeal to the highest court in the land. Most cases are appealed to the Supreme Court pursuant to a writ of certiorari which is a writ (order) from the Supreme Court to a circuit court of appeals directing that a certified record of its proceedings in the particular case be sent up for review. A party applies to the Supreme Court for issuance of the writ. If it appears to the Supreme Court that there is a split of authority among the circuit courts of appeal concerning the particular issues and that an important issue is involved, the Justices are likely to allow the appeal so that the conflict can be resolved. Also, if the appeal raises significant constitutional questions or questions of general importance to the nation, the appeal probably will be allowed. The amount of money or property in question is not a major factor in determining whether or not the Supreme Court will elect to hear the case.

Appellate courts have inherent power to overrule their prior decisions and to propound new rules of law. To a large extent, however, the stability of our legal system depends upon the reluctance of appellate courts to change rules of law once decided. The principle is referred to as stare decisis. Most changes in the law should come through the legislatures. The appellate courts cannot change laws enacted by the legislature. However, the courts can change their "interpretations" of statutes, and that has almost the same effect. An appellate court may determine that a legislative law is invalid because the statue violates the Constitution or there was some defect in the procedures by which the statute was enacted. A statute may be too vague to be enforceable, thus violating due process requirements. Courts have the ultimate responsibility for interpreting the laws, and, obviously, there are times when courts recognize that they erred in the past. Then they must overrule their prior decisions.

An appellate court may reverse the decision of a trial court and order entry of judgment in favor of the appellant. In that event, the litigation is put to an end. Or the appellate court may determine that an error was committed in the course of the trial that prejudiced the outcome of the case and that the appellant is entitled only to a new trial. In that event, the appellate court *remands* the case to the district court for a new trial. A new trial may be awarded on all issues or on certain specified issues. For example, a court may determine that the error in question did not affect the jury's determination of liability in favor of the plaintiff against the defendant; however, the error could have affected the jury's determination of the amount of damages awarded to the plaintiff. Under those circumstances, the court could direct the trial court to have a new trial on only the issue of damages. In that event, the first trial was not a complete waste; the parties avoid the time and expense of presenting again evidence concerning liability. Having the issues narrowed in this way may help the parties to reach a settlement before the case is retried.

The appellate courts have broad discretion in determining what costs should be awarded to the parties in connection with the appeal. The order or decision specifies what costs, if any, are allowed and to whom the costs are awarded.

In the United States Circuit Courts of Appeal, most cases are heard by only three appellate judges. One of those judges writes the opinion of the court, and he or she signs the opinion. If the case has unique importance, all of the judges in the circuit may hear the arguments and participate in the decision-making. If one or more of the judges disagrees with the majority, he or she may write a *dissenting opinion* which is published along with the majority opinion. On occasion, a judge may agree with the result reached by the majority, but disagree with the reasons given for the majority decision. He may file a *concurring opinion* in which is stated separately the reason why he or she reached the conclusion that he or she did. Of course, a unanimous decision is usually considered to be more forceful authority for use as a precedent in the event the same issue is raised again in another case. If a court is closely divided in reaching a decision, it is quite possible that the decision will be overruled the next time it comes before the court.

A Personal Note

A career as a legal paraprofessional should be interesting and, at times, even exciting. A competent paralegal should be able to derive a good deal of satisfaction by fulfilling his or her assignments.

As you prepare to assume responsibilities heretofore reserved to lawyers, you should give some consideration to the attitude with which you will approach those responsibilities. I have a few suggestions which may help you to avoid mistakes, embarrassment and disappointment.

You should be proud of your association with the legal profession and judicial system. Conduct yourself as a professional person. Dress appropriately. Be courteous to all persons with whom you come into contact, especially when dealing with an adversary or his or her representatives. Be on time and keep appointments. A calendar should be used to schedule your appointments and deadlines. Operate on the premise that by being timely, you will do the best job possible. Use the language of the profession. It will help you to be more precise in your thinking and communications. Strive to develop a reputation for reliability and candor. Do not represent or imply that you are a lawyer.

Develop an appreciation that each matter you work on is very important to someone even though the work may seem routine to you. When you handle an assignment for a client, you should demonstrate the same interest and concern that you would want for your own important matters. Some matters are very personal in nature. All matters, whether of a business nature or otherwise, should be treated as confidential. Avoid the temptation to make "innocent" disclosures about the cases you are handling. Equally important, guard against making accidental disclosures.

You must not violate court rules or court orders or professional ethics. There is no question but that, on occasion, some temporary advantage may be gained by disregarding professional duties. Don't do it! Don't let anyone mislead you into a violation. There is no case, no client, no employer who is important enough to justify sacrificing your own integrity and professional standing for his or her convenience or benefit. Remember that litigation is an adversary process. The system works well because each party has the opportunity and responsibility for presenting his or her own case. The process would collapse overnight if it were not conducted by professionals in accordance with rules and standards that establish fair play. Do not do anything to upset the delicate balance.

Continue your education by attending seminars and reading professional articles relative to your work. Ask questions about assignments. Find out why you have been given assignments. Learn from your mistakes, and do not become defensive because of past mistakes. Accept responsibility for what you do and for what you know you should have done, but didn't. Accept corrections and suggestions graciously. There is usually more than one way to perform a task. The fact that the lawyers you work with prefer a different method than you learned or different than you prefer should not bother you.

Try to make helpful suggestions for accomplishing the work that needs to be done for clients. Be thoughtful and innovative. But be careful not to exceed your authority. Always be looking for ways of working more effectively and more efficiently. Keep copies of the documents (even letters) you prepare. They will help you when working on similar assignments to do the job better and faster than the first time. One of the surest ways to gain satisfaction, if not enjoyment, from your work is to strive to perform each task perfectly. There is always satisfaction in doing a job well — whether or not anyone else happens to notice.

Lawyers and the whole judicial process depend on effective communications, both oral and written. Develop an appreciation for use of good grammar. Strive to express yourself concisely. Be specific in your statements rather than relative or conclusionary. Try to avoid ambiguities. Be alert to the meaning of words you use in your letters and documents. When interrogating witnesses and clients, learn to use short, specific questions. Organize your thoughts before you write your letters, reports, statements, and memorandums.

Develop an appreciation for logical thinking. As you work on assignments, try to keep the whole picture in mind. Try to be objective in analyzing the facts and the case as a whole. It is all too easy to become oversold on a client's claim or defense. We tend to delude ourselves in an effort to help our clients. But a client is better served by objective advisors than fervent "yes persons."

APPENDIX CONTENTS ━━━━━━━━━━

V. Miscellaneous Forms

VI. Deposition Transcript   353

VII. Review   387

VIII. Glossary   393

IX. Third Party Practice   401

The Twelve Federal Judicial Circuits   404

Time Table for Civil Cases

This Time Table revised to September 1, 1980, indicates the time for each of the steps of a civil action as provided by the Federal Rules of Civil Procedure, the Federal Rules of Appellate Procedure, the 1970 Revised Rules of the Supreme Court and Title 28 of the United States Code Annotated. Usually the periods permitted for each of these steps may be enlarged by the court in its discretion. In some cases no enlargement is permitted. Civil Rule 6(b) and Appellate Rule 26(b) state when, and under what conditions, an enlargement may be allowed.

Service by mail is complete upon mailing. Civil Rule 5(b) and Appellate Rule 25(c). Whenever a period of time is computed from the service of a notice or other paper, and the service is made by mail, 3 days are added to the prescribed period of time. Civil Rule 6(e) and Appellate Rule 26(c). Variations which make impossible the application of any rigid limitation of time to all steps of the action are indicated in the Time Table. Citations are to supporting rules and are in the form "Civ.R. ——" for the Rules of Civil Procedure and "App.R. ——" for the Rules of Appellate Procedure. Citations to the 1970 Revised Rules of the Supreme Court are not abbreviated.

ADMISSIONS

Requests for admissions, service of	On plaintiff after commencement of action and on any other party with or after service of summons and complaint on him. Civ.R. 36(a).
Response to requested admissions	Answers or objections must be served within 30 days after service of the request, or such shorter or longer time as court may allow, but unless court shortens time, defendant need not serve before expiration of 45 days after service of the summons and complaint upon him. Civ.R. 36(a).

ANSWER
  To complaint

See also, "Responsive Pleadings", this table. Service within 20 days after service of summons and complaint unless otherwise ordered by the court or provided by an applicable state statute or rule when substituted service is made under Rule 4(e) upon a party not an inhabitant of or found within the state. Civ.R. 12(a).

Service within 60 days after service upon the United States Attorney, in action against the United States or an officer or agency thereof. Civ.R. 12(a).

The time for responsive pleading is altered by service of Civ.R. 12 motions. See "Responsive Pleadings", this table.

  To cross-claim

Service within 20 days after service of pleading stating cross-claim. Civ.R. 12(a).

60 days for United States. Civ.R. 12(a).

The time for responsive pleading is altered by service of Civ.R. 12(a) motions, see "Responsive Pleadings", this table.

  To third-party complaint

Same as answer to complaint. Civ.R. 14(a).

  To notice of condemnation

Service within 20 days after service of notice. Civ.R. 71A(e).

  Removed actions

20 days after receipt of pleading, or within 20 days after service of summons, or within 5 days after filing of removal petition, whichever is longest. Civ.R. 81(c).

  Proceedings to cancel certificates of citizenship under 8 U.S.C.A. § 1451

60 days after service of petition. Civ.R. 81(a) (6).

ANSWERS (or objections) to interrogatories to party

Service within 30 days after the service of the interrogatories, except that a defendant may serve answers or objections within 45 days after service of the summons and complaint upon him. Court may allow a shorter or longer time. Civ.R. 33(a).

CLASS actions	As soon as practicable after commencement court is to determine by order whether action is to be so maintained. Civ.R. 23(c) (1).
CLERICAL mistakes in judgments, orders, or record	May be corrected at any time; but during pendency of appeal, may be corrected before appeal is docketed in the appellate court, and thereafter while appeal pending may be corrected with leave of appellate court. Civ.R 60(a).
COMPLAINT	Filing commences action — must be served with summons. Civ.R. 3.
COMPUTATION of time	Exclude day from which period runs and include last day of period unless a Saturday, Sunday, or holiday, in which case period runs to the end of next day which is not a Saturday, Sunday, or holiday. Civ.R. 6(a); App.R. 26(a).
	Intermediate Saturdays, Sundays, and holidays are included except where the period is less than 7 days, in which case they are excluded. Civ.R. 6(a); App.R. 26(a).
	Service by mail is complete upon mailing. Civ.R. 5(b); App.R. 25(c).
	Service by mail adds three days to a period of time which is computed from such service. Civ.R. 6(e); App.R. 26(c).
	Legal holidays are defined by Civ.R. 6(a) and App.R. 26(a).
COSTS	Taxation on 1 day's notice. Motion to review taxation of costs 5 days after taxation. Civ.R. 54(d).
DEFAULT	
Entry by clerk	No time stated. Civ.R. 55(b).
Entry by court	If party against whom default is sought has appeared, he shall be served with written notice of application for default judgment at least 3 days prior to hearing on such application. Civ.R. 55(b).
DEFENSES and objections, presentation of	
By pleading	See "Answer", this table.

By motion	Motion shall be made before pleading if further pleading is permitted. Civ.R. 12(b).
At trial	Adverse party may assert at trial any defense in law or fact to claim for relief to which such party is not required to serve responsive pleading. Civ.R. 12(b).
Motion affects time for responsive pleading	Service of motion under Civ.R. 12 alters times for responsive pleading. See "Responsive Pleadings", this table.

DEPOSITIONS

See, also, "Interrogatories", and "Depositions on written questions", this table.

Notice of filing	Promptly. Civ.R. 30(f) (1), (3) and Civ.R. 31(b), (c).
Notice of taking	By either party after commencement of action except that plaintiff must obtain leave if he seeks to take a deposition prior to the expiration of 30 days after service of the summons and complaint upon any defendant or service made under Civ.R. 4(e), except that leave is not required (1) if defendant has served a notice of taking deposition or otherwise sought discovery, or (2) if the special notice provided by Civ.R. 30(b) (2) has been given. Civ.R. 30(a).
	Reasonable notice to every party. Civ.R. 30 (b).
Objections	As to admissibility, objection may be made at trial or hearing, but subject to Civ.R. 28(b) and 32(d) (3). Civ.R. 32(b).
	As to errors or irregularities in the notice, service promptly. Civ.R. 32(d) (1).
	As to disqualification of officer, objection made before deposition begins or as soon thereafter as disqualification becomes known or could be discovered. (Civ.R. 32(d) (2).
	As to competency of witness or competency, relevancy, or materiality of testimony — not waived by failure to make such objection before or during deposition unless the ground might have been obviated or removed if presented at that time. Civ.R. 32(d) (3) (A).

As to errors and irregularities at oral examination in manner of taking deposition, in the form of questions or answers, in the oath or affirmation, or in conduct of parties, and errors which might be obviated, removed, or cured if promptly presented — seasonable objection made at taking of deposition. Civ.R. 32(d) (3) (B).

As to form of written questions submitted under Civ.R. 31 — service within time allowed for serving succeeding cross or other questions and within 5 days after service of last questions authorized. Civ.R. 32(d) (3) (C).

As to completion and return (transcription, signing, certification, sealing, etc.) — motion to suppress made with reasonable promptness after defect is or might have been ascertained. Civ.R. 32(d) (4).

Orders of protection	No time stated. Civ.R. 26 (c).
Motion to terminate or limit examination	Any time during the taking of the deposition. Civ.R. 30(d).
Perpetuate testimony pending appeal	Motion in district court upon same notice and service thereof as if action was pending in district court. Civ.R. 27(b).
Perpetuate testimony before action	Service of notice and petition 20 days before date of hearing. Civ.R. 27(a) (2).
Taking	Time specified in the notice of taking unless enlarged or shortened by the Court. Civ.R. 30(b) (1), (3).
DEPOSITIONS on written questions	See also "Depositions", this table.
When taken	After commencement of action. Civ.R. 31(a).
Cross questions	Service within 30 days after service of the notice and questions. Civ.R. 31(a).

Redirect questions	Service within 10 days after being served with cross questions. Civ.R. 31(a).
Recross questions	Service within 10 days after service of redirect questions.
Notice of filing of deposition	Promptly. Civ.R. 31(c).
Objections to form	Service within the time allowed for serving the succeeding cross or other questions and within 5 days after service of last questions authorized. Civ.R. 32(d) (3) (C).
DISCOVERY	Orders for physical or mental examination of persons —

Time stated in order. Civ.R. 35(a).

See, also, "Admissions", "Depositions", "Depositions on written questions", "Interrogatories", "Production of Documents", this table. |
DISMISSAL for want of subject-matter jurisdiction	Any time. Civ.R. 12(h) (3).
DISMISSAL by plaintiff voluntarily without court order	Any time before service of answer or motion for summary judgment. Civ.R. 41(a) (1).
DISMISSAL of counterclaim, cross-claim or third-party claim, voluntary	Before service of responsive pleading, or if none, before introduction of evidence at trial or hearing. Civ.R. 41(c).
DOCUMENTS, Production of	See "Production of Documents", this table.

ENLARGEMENT of
    time
    generally

Act required or allowed at or within specified time by Civil Rule, notice thereunder, or court order	Court for cause shown may (1) with or without motion or notice order period enlarged if request therefor is made before expiration of period originally prescribed or as extended by previous order, or (2) upon motion made after expiration of the specified period permit act to be done where failure to act was result of excusable neglect; but court may not extend time for taking any action under Civ.R. 50(b), 52(b), 59(b), (d) and (c), and 60(b), except to extent and under conditions stated in them. Civ.R. 6(b).
On appeal	Court for good cause shown may upon motion enlarge time prescribed by App.Rules or by its order for doing any act or may permit act to be done after expiration of such time; but court may not enlarge time for filing notice of appeal, petition for allowance, or petition for permission to appeal; nor may the court enlarge time prescribed by law for filing petition to enjoin, set aside, suspend, modify, enforce or otherwise review, or a notice of appeal from, an order for an administrative agency, board, commission or officer of the United States, except as specifically authorized by law. App.R. 26(b).
Affidavits in opposition, service	Time may be extended by court. Civ.R. 6(d).
Taking deposition on oral examination	Court for cause may enlarge or shorten time. Civ.R. 30(b) (3).
Hearing of motions and defenses	May be deferred until trial. Civ.R. 12(d).
Mail, service by	Adds three days to a period that is computed from time of service. Civ.R 6(e); App.R. 26(c).
Injunction — temporary restraining order	May be extended 10 days by order of court or for a longer period by consent of party against whom order is directed. Civ.R. 65(b).

Response to   Time may be enlarged or shortened by court.
request for   Civ.R. 36(a).
admissions

EXECUTION
Stay   Automatically: No execution to issue, nor proceed-
                      ings for enforcement to be taken, until expiration
                      of 10 days after entry of judgment; exceptions —
                      injunctions, receiverships, and patent account-
                      ings. Civ.R. 62(a).

                      Stay according to state law. Civ.R. 62(f).

                      Motion for new trial or for judgment. Civ.R. 62(b).

                      Stay in favor of government. Civ.R. 62(e).

                      Supersedeas on appeal. Civ.R. 62(d).

                      Stay of judgment as to multiple claims or multiple
                      parties. Civ.R. 62(h).

FILING papers   Complaint must be filed at commencement of
                      action. Civ.R. 3.

                      All papers required to be filed must be filed with
                      clerk unless the judge permits them to be filed with
                      him. Civ.R. 5(e).

                      All papers after the complaint required to be
                      served must be filed either before service or within
                      reasonable time thereafter. Civ.R. 5(d).

FINDINGS
Motion to amend   10 days after entry of judgment. Civ.R. 52(b).
                      Exception from general rule relating to enlarge-
                      ment. Civ.R. 6(b).

FOREIGN law   Reasonable written notice required of party
                      intending to raise an issue concerning the law of a
                      foreign country. Civ.R. 44.1.

HEARING of   Unless local conditions make it impracticable,
motions   district court shall establish regular times and
                      places for hearing and disposition of motions
                      requiring notice and hearing; but judge may make
                      orders for the advancement, conduct, and hearing
                      of actions. Civ.R. 78.

                      Service of notice 5 days before time specified for
                      hearing unless otherwise provided by these rules
                      or order of court. Civ.R. 6(d).

Hearing of certain motions and defenses before trial on application of any party unless court orders deferral until trial. Civ.R. 12(d).

HOLIDAYS
New Year's Day, Washington's Birthday, Memorial Day, Independence Day, Labor Day, Columbus Day, Veterans Day, Thanksgiving Day, Christmas Day, and any other day appointed as a holiday by the President or the Congress of the United States or by the state in which the district court is held. Civ.R. 6(a); App.R. 26(a).

INJUNCTION (Temporary restraining order granted without notice)
Order shall be indorsed with date and hour of issuance, filed forthwith in clerk's office, and entered of record. Civ.R. 65(b).

Expiration within such time, not to exceed 10 days, as court fixes, unless within time so fixed the order is extended for like period or, with consent of party against whom order is directed, for longer period. Civ.R. 65(b).

Motion for preliminary injunction shall be set down for hearing at earliest possible time — takes precedence of all matters except older ones of same character. Civ.R. 65(b).

Motion for dissolution or modification on 2 days' notice or such shorter notice as court may prescribe; hear and determine motion as expeditiously as ends of justice require. Civ.R. 65(b).

INSTRUCTIONS
Requests
At close of evidence or such earlier time as court directs. Civ.R. 51.

Objections
Before jury retires to consider verdict. Civ.R. 51.

INTERROGATORIES to parties
Service on plaintiff any time after action is commenced. Service on any other party with or after service on him of summons and complaint. Civ.R. 33(a).

Answers or objections
Service within 30 days after the service of the interrogatories, except that a defendant may serve answers or objections within 45 days after service of the summons and complaint upon him. Civ.R. 33(a).

INTERVENTION	Upon timely application. Civ.R. 24(a), (b).
	Person desiring to intervene shall serve a motion to intervene upon the parties as provided in Civ.R. 5. Civ.R. 24(c).
JUDGMENT or order	
Alter or amend judgment, motion to	Shall be served not later than 10 days after entry of judgment. Civ.R. 59(e). Exception to general rule relating to enlargement. Civ.R. 6(b).
Clerical mistakes	May be corrected any time; but during pendency of appeal, may be corrected before appeal is docketed in the appellate court, and thereafter while appeal pending may be corrected with leave of appellate court. Civ.R. 60(a).
Default	See "Default", this table.
Directed verdict — motion for judgment in accord with motion for directed verdict	Within 10 days after entry of judgment or after jury has been discharged without verdict. Civ.R. 50(b). Exception from general rule relating to enlargement. Civ.R. 6(b).
Effectiveness	Judgment effective only when set forth on a separate document and when entered as provided in Civ.R. 79(a). Civ.R. 58.
Entry of judgment	Upon general verdict of jury or upon court decision that a party shall recover only a sum certain or costs or that all relief shall be denied, entry forthwith and without awaiting any direction by court (unless court otherwise orders). Upon court decision granting other relief or upon special verdict or general verdict accompanied by answers to interrogatories, entry upon prompt court approval of form. Entry shall not be delayed for taxing of costs. Civ.R. 58.
Entry, notice of	Immediately upon entry clerk shall serve notice thereof by mail in manner provided in Civ.R. 5 and make note in docket of the mailing. Such mailing is sufficient notice for all purposes for which notice of entry of order is required by these rules; but any party may in addition serve a notice of such entry in manner provided in Civ.R. 5 for service of papers. Civ.R. 77(d).

Lack of notice of entry by clerk does not affect time to appeal or relieve or authorize court to relieve party for failure to appeal within time allowed, except as permitted by App.R. 4(a). Civ.R 77(d).

Offer of judgment	Service more than 10 days before trial begins. Civ.R. 68.
	Acceptance, written notice of — service within 10 days after service of offer. Civ.R. 68.
On pleadings, motion for judgment	After pleadings are closed but within such time as not to delay the trial. Civ.R. 12(c).
Relief from, on grounds stated in Rule 60(b)	Motion within a reasonable time and not more than 1 year after judgment, order, or proceeding entered or taken, for following grounds: (1) mistake, inadvertence, surprise, or excusable neglect; (2) newly discovered evidence; (3) fraud, misrepresentation, or other misconduct. Civ.R. 60(b). Exception from general rule relating to enlargement. Civ.R. 60(b.
	Motion within a reasonable time, for following grounds: (1) judgment void, (2) judgment satisfied, released, or discharged, (3) prior underlying judgment reversed or otherwise vacated, (4) no longer equitable that judgment have prospective application, (5) any other reason justifying relief. Civ.R. 60(b). Exception from general rule relating to enlargment. Civ.R. 6(b).
Stay	See "Execution", this table.
Summary judgment	See "Summary Judgment", this table.
JURORS	Alternate jurors (in order in which called) replace jurors who, prior to jury's retiring to consider verdict, are found unable or disqualified to perform duties; alternates not replacing regular jurors shall be discharged after jury so retires. Civ.R. 47(b).
JURY trial Demand	Service any time after commencement of action and not later than 10 days after service of last pleading directed to the triable issue. Civ.R. 38(b).

Adverse party may serve demand for jury trial within 10 days after service of first demand or such lesser time as court fixes. Civ.R. 38(c).

Removed actions

If at the time of removal all necessary pleadings have been served, demand for jury trial may be served:

By petitioner, 10 days after the petition for removal is filed;

By any other party, within 10 days after service on him of the notice of filing the petition. Civ.R. 81(c).

Demand after removal not necessary in either of two instances: (1) prior to removal, party has made express demand in accordance with state law; (2) state law does not require express demands and court does not direct otherwise. Civ.R. 81(c).

LEGAL HOLIDAY

See "Holidays", this table.

MAIL

Service by mail adds 3 days to period computed from time of service. Civ.R. 6(e); App.R. 26(c).

MORE DEFINITE STATEMENT
Furnished

Must be furnished within 10 days after notice of order or other time fixed by court or court may strike pleading. Civ.R. 12(e).

Motion for

Must be made before responsive pleading is interposed. Civ.R. 12(e).

MOTIONS, notices, and affidavits

See, also, specific headings, this table.

In general

A written motion, supporting affidavits, and notice of hearing thereof — service not later than 5 days before time specified for hearing unless a different time is fixed by rule or by order of court. Civ. R. 6(d).

Opposing affidavits may be served not later than one day before hearing, unless court permits otherwise. Civ.R. 6(d).

NEW TRIAL

Motion and affidavits	Motion shall be served not later than 10 days after entry of judgment. Civ.R. 59(b). Exception from general rule relating to enlargement. Civ.R. 6(b). If motion based on affidavits, they shall be served with motion. Civ.R 59(c).
Opposing affidavits	Shall be served within 10 days of service of motion for new trial; period may be extended for additional period not exceeding 20 days either by court for good cause shown or by parties by written stipulation. Civ.R. 59(c).
Initiative of court	Not later than 10 days after entry of judgment, court may order new trial for any reason for which it might have granted new trial or motion. Civ.R. 59(d). Exception to general rule relating to enlargement. Civ.R 6(b).
	After giving parties notice and opportunity to be heard, court may grant motion for new trial, timely served, for reason not stated in the motion. Civ.R. 59(d). Exception to general rule relating to enlargement. Civ.R 6(b).
Judgment notwithstanding verdict, verdicts set aside on motion for	Party whose motion has been set aside may serve motion for new trial pursuant to Civ.R. 59 not later than 10 days after entry of such judgment. Civ.R. 50(c).

OBJECTIONS to orders or rulings of court

At time ruling or order of court is made or sought; if party has no opportunity to object to ruling or order at time it is made, absence of objection does not thereafter prejudice him. Civ.R. 46.

OFFER of judgment

Must be served more than 10 days before trial. Civ.R 68.

Acceptance must be served within 10 days after service of offer. Civ.R. 69.

ORDERS

See "Judgment or order", this table.

PARTICULARS, Bill of

Abolished. Civ.R. 12(e), as amended in 1948. See, however, "More Definite Statement", this table.

PLEADINGS
Amendment of

Once as matter of course before responsive pleading served or within 20 days if no response is permitted and action has not been placed on trial calendar. Civ.R. 15(a).

By leave of court or written consent of adverse parties, at any time. Civ.R. 15(a).

During trial or after judgment to conform to evidence or to raise issues not raised in pleadings but tried by express or implied consent of parties. Civ.R. 15(b).

Supplemental

Upon motion of party — court may upon reasonable notice permit service of supplemental pleading setting forth transactions, etc., since date of pleading to be supplemented. Civ.R. 15(d).

Adverse party pleading to supplemental pleading — if court deems advisable, it shall so order, specifying time therefor. Civ.R. 15(d).

Averments of time

Such averments are material and shall be considered like all other averments of material matter. Civ.R. 9(f).

Judgment on, motion for

After pleadings are closed but within such time as not to delay the trial. Civ.R. 12(c).

Striking of matter from

Motion made before responding to a pleading or, if no responsive pleading permitted, within 20 days after service of pleading. Civ.R. 12(f).

On court's own initiative at any time. Civ.R. 12(f).

PROCESS
Amendment

At any time, unless it clearly appears that material prejudice would result to substantial rights of party against whom process issued. Civ.R. 4(h).

Return

Person serving process shall make proof of service thereof to court promptly and in any event within time for response to process. Civ.R. 4(g).

PRODUCTION
of documents

Request for,
service of

On plaintiff any time after commencement of action. On any other party with or after service of summons and complaint upon him. Civ.R. 34(b).

May accompany notice of taking deposition. Civ.R. 30(b) (5).

Response to
request

Within 30 days after service of the request except that a defendant may serve response within 45 days after service of the summons and complaint upon him. Court may allow longer or shorter time. Civ.R. 34 (b).

Time of
inspection

The request shall specify a reasonable time. Civ.R. 34(b).

Subpoena

See "Subpoena", this table.

REFERENCES AND
Referees

Order of
reference

When reference is made, clerk shall forthwith furnish master with copy of order. Civ.R. 53(d) (1).

Hearings before
master

Time for beginning and closing the hearings, as fixed by order of reference. Civ.R. 53(c).

Meetings

First meeting of parties or attorneys to be held within 20 days after date of order of reference. Vic.R. 53(d) (1). Upon receipt of the order of reference, unless order otherwise provides, master shall forthwith set time and place for such meeting and notify parties or their attorneys. Civ.R 53(d) (1).

Speed — either party, on notice to parties and master, may apply to court for order requiring master to speed the proceedings and make his report. Civ.R 53(d) (1).

Failure of party to appear at appointed time and place — master may proceed ex parte or adjourn to future day, giving notice to absent party of adjournment. Civ.R. 53(d) (1).

Report of master

Filing of, time as fixed in order of reference. Civ.R. 53(c). Clerk shall forthwith mail notice of filing to all parties. Civ.R. 53(e) (1).

Objections (in non-jury actions) may be served within 10 days after being served with notice of filing of report. Civ.R. 53(e) (2).

Court action on report and objections thereto — application (in non-jury actions) for such action shall be by motion and upon notice as prescribed in Civ.R. 6(d). Civ.R. 53(e) (2).

Speed — either party, on notice to parties and master, may apply to court for order requiring master to speed the proceedings and make his report. Civ.R. 53(d) (1).

REMOVED actions

Answers and defenses

Within 20 days after the receipt through service or otherwise of a copy of the initial pleading setting forth the claim for relief upon which the action or proceeding is based, or within 20 days after the service of summons upon such initial pleading, then filed, or within 5 days after filing of the petition for removal, whichever period is longest. Civ.R. 81(c).

Demand for jury trial

Demand after removal not necessary in either of two instances: (1) prior to removal, party has made express demand in accordance with state law; (2) state law does not require express demands and court does not direct otherwise. Civ.R. 81(c).

Petition for removal

Within 30 days after receipt through service or otherwise of a copy of the initial pleading setting forth the claim for relief upon which the action or proceeding is based, or within 30 days after service of summons if such initial pleading has then been filed in court and is not required to be served on defendant, whichever period is shorter. 28 U.S. C.A. § 1446(b).

If the case stated by the initial pleading is not removable, a petition for removal may be filed within 30 days after receipt by the defendant, through service or otherwise, of a copy of an amended pleading, motion, order or other paper from which it may first be ascertained that the case is one which is or has become removable. 28 U.S.C.A. § 1446(b).

REPLY

See, also, "Responsive pleadings", this table.

To answer or third-party answer	Only if ordered by court. Civ.R. 7(a). Service within 20 days after service of order, unless order otherwise directs. Civ.R. 12(a).
To counterclaim	Service within 20 days after service of answer. Civ.R. 12(a). United States or agency or officer thereof shall serve reply within 60 days after service upon U.S. attorney. Civ.R. 12(a).
Alteration of time by service of Civ.R. 12 motion	See "Responsive pleadings", this table.

RESPONSIVE PLEADINGS

See, also "Answer", and "Reply", this table.

To amended pleading	Within 10 days after service of amended pleading or within time remaining for response to original pleading, whichever is longer, unless court otherwise orders. Civ.R. 15(a).
To supplemental pleading	As ordered by court. Civ.R. 15(d).
Alteration of time by service of Civ.R. 12 motion	Service of motion permitted under Civ.R. 12 alters times for responsive pleadings as follows unless different time fixed by court (see Civ.R. 12(a)):

   (1) if court denies motion, service of responsive pleading within 10 days after notice of denial;

   (2) if court postpones disposition until trial on merits, service of responsive pleading within 10 days after notice of postponement;

   (3) if court grants motion for more definite statement, service of responsive pleading within 10 days after service of the more definite statement.

RESTRAINING order, temporary, without notice

See "Injunction", this table.

RETURN   Amendment of process or proof of service at any
                              time unless it clearly appears that material
                              prejudice would result to substantial rights of
                              party against whom process is issued. Civ.R. 4(h).

                              Prompt proof of service required not later than
                              time fixed for response. Civ.R. 4(g).

SUBPOENA
   Discovery rule,   Objection (written) — service (by person to whom
   production of   subpoena directed) within 10 days after service of
   books etc., under   subpoena or on or before time specified in
                              subpoena for compliance if such time is less than
                              10 days after service. Civ.R. 45(d) (1).

                              If objection made, party serving subpoena may
                              move upon notice to deponent for order at any time
                              before or during deposition. Civ.R. 45(d) (1).

   Documentary   Motion to quash — made promptly and in any
   evidence,   event at or before time specified in subpoena for
   generally   compliance. Civ.R. 45(b).

   Witness   Subpoena specifies time for attendance and giving
                              of testimony. Civ.R. 45(a).

SUBSTITUTION of   In cases of death, incompetency, or transfer of
parties   interest — motion for substitution, together with
                              notice of hearing, served on parties as provided in
                              Civ.R. 5 and upon persons not parties in manner
                              provided in Civ.R. 4 for service of a summons.
                              Civ.R. 25(a), (b), (c).

                              Dismissal as to deceased party unless motion for
                              substitution is made not later than 90 days after
                              death is suggested upon the record. Civ.R. 25(a).

                              Successor of public officer substituted automati-
                              cally. Order of substitution may be entered at any
                              time. Civ.R. 25(d).

SUMMARY
  JUDGMENT,
  motion for
  Claimant   May move at any time after expiration of 20 days
                              from commencement of action or after service of
                              motion for summary judgment by adverse party.
                              Civ.R. 56(a).

  Defending party   May move at any time. Civ.R. 56(b).

Service	Service of motion at least 10 days before time fixed for hearing. Civ.R. 56(c).
	Service of opposing affidavits prior to day of hearing. Civ.R. 56(c).
SUMMONS	Issues forthwith. Civ.R. 4(a). No time prescribed for service but undue delay may permit statute of limitations to run or warrant dismissal for want of prosecution. Civ.R. 3.
	Proof of service — person serving process shall make proof of service thereof to court promptly and in any event within time for response to process. Civ.R. 4(g).
SUPPLEMENTAL pleadings	See "Pleadings", this table.
SUPERSEDEAS or stay	See "Execution", this table.
TERM	The district courts deemed always open. Civ.R. 77(a).
	Terms of court have been abolished. 28 U.S.C.A. §§ 138-141, as amended by Pub.L. 88-139, Oct. 16, 1963, 77 Stat. 248.
THIRD-PARTY practice	Third-party plaintiff need not obtain leave if he files third-party complaint not later than 10 days after he serves his original answer. Otherwise, must obtain leave on motion upon notice to all parties to the action. Civ.R. 14(a).
VERDICT Judgment in accordance with prior motion for directed verdict	Party who has moved for directed verdict: (1) not later than 10 days after entry of judgment may move to have verdict and any judgment entered thereon set aside and to have judgment entered in accordance with his motion for directed verdict, or (2) if verdict was not returned, such party within 10 days after jury has been discharged may move for judgment in accordance with his motion for directed verdict. Civ.R. 50(b).
	Exception from general rule relating to enlargement.

New trial after
verdict set aside

Party whose verdict set aside on motion for judgment notwithstanding verdict may serve motion for new trial pursuant to Civ.R. 59 not later than 10 days after entry of judgment notwithstanding verdict. Civ.R. 50(c) (2).

Sample Pleadings Used in Federal District Court in Products/Negligence Action

UNITED STATES DISTRICT COURT

DISTRICT OF (STATE)

——————— DIVISION

Wayne Brown,
            Plaintiff,
    vs.
Lamb Motoren, a foreign corporation;
Johnson Power, Inc., a Wisconsin corpo-
ration; and Eldon Motors, a division of
Tri-State Industries, a California corpo-
ration,
            Defendants.
	}	COMPLAINT

Plaintiff, for his Complaint and cause of action against the above-named defendants, and each of them, states and alleges as follows:

I

At all times material herein plaintiff was and still is a citizen of the State of Minnesota, and a resident of the County of Hennepin.

II

At all times material herein, defendant Lamb Motoren, was and still is a corporation organized under the laws of West Germany and was and still is a citizen of West Germany, having its principal place of business in the United States of America in a state other than the State of Minnesota.

III

At all times herein mentioned defendant Johnson Power, Inc. was and still is a corporation organized under the laws of the State of Wisconsin, and was and still is a citizen of said state and has its principal place of business in a state other than the State of Minnesota.

IV

At all times herein mentioned defendant Eldon Motors, a division of Tri-State Industries, Inc., was and still is a corporation organized under the laws of the State of California, and was and still is a citizen of said state and has its principal place of business in a state other than the State of Minnesota.

V

The amount in controversy between the parties exceeds the amount of Ten Thousand and no/100 Dollars ($10,000.00), exclusive of costs and interest.

VI

At all times herein mentioned defendant Lamb Motoren was engaged in the manufacture, distribution and sale of gasoline motors and engines, and prior to the date of the accident hereinafter mentioned, manufactured the gasoline engine involved herein, and caused the same to be distributed and sold in the State of Minnesota.

VII

At all times herein mentioned defendant Eldon Motors, a division of Tri-State Industries, Inc. was a corporation engaged in the handling, sale and distribution of gasoline motors and engines manufactured by the defendant Lamb Motoren and sold such gasoline motors and engines including a gasoline engine serial No. 658874 purchased by plaintiff, with the permission, consent and agreement and as agent for the defendant Lamb Motoren.

VIII

Prior to January 18, 1981 defendant Lamb Motoren manufactured a certain two cylinder engine, 650 c.c. displacement, serial No. 658874, which said engine was distributed and delivered into the State of Minnesota by the defendant Eldon Motors, a division of Tri-State Industries, Inc., and was sold to the plaintiff by the defendant Johnson Power, Inc.

IX

On January 18, 1981, while plaintiff Wayne Brown was using said engine for the purpose for which it was intended, and at which time plaintiff was unaware of any defect existing in said engine, the crankshaft thereof fractured causing injuries and damages as hereinafter set forth.

X

That said injuries and damages were a direct cause of the defective and dangerous condition of said engine which rendered the same hazardous and unsafe and which exposed persons using said engine for the purpose for which it was intended to an unreasonable risk of serious bodily harm; that said accident and the resulting injuries and damages sustained by the plaintiff were further caused by the negligent and defective design and manufacture of said gasoline engine in the following respects: (a) said engine was defective because of the design and manufacture of crankshaft mechanism; (b) because of the failure of the defendants, and each of them, to properly inspect said engine for defects; (c) because of the failure of the defendants, and each of them, to adequately test said engine for defects; (d) because of the failure of the defendants, and each of them, to provide necessary and proper warnings and instructions with respect to the use and operation of said engine and potential hazards relative to its use.

XI

Defendants, and each of them, were guilty of breaches of implied warranty of fitness and purpose and breaches of warranty of merchantability of said engine and defendant Johnson Power, Inc. is liable in addition thereto for breaches of express and implied warranties of suitability for the particular purpose for which plaintiff purchased and used said engine.

XII

As a result of the accident above described, plaintiff Wayne Brown was injured; has suffered pain in the past and may suffer pain in the future; has been caused to incur expenses for medical care and treatment and may be caused to incur further and like expense in the future; has been prevented from carrying on his usual occupation and activities and may have suffered a diminution of his earning capacity all to his damage in the sum of One Hundred Fifty Thousand and no/100 Dollars ($150,000.00).

Wherefore, plaintiff prays for judgment against defendants, and each of them, in the sum of One Hundred Fifty Thousand ($150,000.00) Dollars, together with his costs and disbursements herein.

_____
                    Attorneys for Plaintiff

Plaintiff Demands Trial by Jury.

UNITED STATES DISTRICT COURT

DISTRICT OF (STATE)

_____ DIVISION

Wayne Brown,
 	
                    Plaintiff,
 	
vs.
 	
Lamb Motoren, a foreign corporation;
Johnson Power, Inc., a Wisconsin corpo-
ration; and Eldon Motors, a division of
Tri-State Industries, a California corpo-
ration,
 	
                    Defendants.
	SEPARATE ANSWER
	AND CROSS-CLAIM OF
	ELDON MOTORS, A
	DIVISION OF
	TRI-STATE
	INDUSTRIES, INC., A
	CALIFORNIA
	CORPORATION

Comes now this answering defendant, and for its separate answer to plaintiff's complaint:

I

Denies each and every allegation, statement, matter and thing in said complaint contained, except as hereinafter expressly admitted or alleged.

II

Admits the allegations of Paragraphs I, II, III, IV, and VI of plaintiff's complaint, and further admits that during the time mentioned this answering defendant was a corporation engaged in the distribution of gasoline motors and engines manufactured by the defendant Lamb Motoren, a foreign corporation.

III

Specifically denies any negligence, breaches of warranty or any other unlawful or improper conduct on the part of this answering defendant, which would cause it to be legally liable to the plaintiff whether as alleged in the complaint or otherwise.

IV

Alleges that if the plaintiff sustained injuries and damages, whether as alleged in the complaint or otherwise, that said damages were caused in whole or in major part by plaintiff's contributory negligence, or resulted from the improper use of said machine by the plaintiff.

V

Alleges that such damages as plaintiff may have sustained if they were not caused solely and exclusively by the negligence and want of due care of the plaintiff, were the result of negligence and breaches of warranties on the part of others for whom this answering defendant is not responsible.

CROSS-CLAIM

Further answering and for the cross-claim of the defendant Eldon Motors, a division of Tri-State Industries, Inc. against Lamb Motoren, a foreign corporation, alleges:

I

That at all times material herein the defendant Eldon Motors, a division of Tri-State Industries, Inc., served solely as a distributor of engines such as that described in plaintiff's complaint for the defendant Lamb Motoren; that is to say, that it purchased said engines from Lamb Motoren for the purpose of resale to others at the wholesale level; that defendant Eldon received said engines from the manufacturer Lamb Motoren in a packaged condition and resold them at the wholesale level to others in the same condition and packaging in which they were received from the manufacturer with no additions or changes in the product being undertaken or executed during the period of handling of said product by the distributor Eldon Motors, a division of Tri-State Industries, Inc.

II

That if it should be determined and adjudged that the motor described in plaintiff's complaint was distributed from manufacturer to consumer in the fashion described and the motor did in fact pass through the distributive corporate hands of Eldon Motors, and if it further be adjudged that there is some liability on the defendant Eldon Motors and in favor of the plaintiff, under the facts as alleged in Paragraph I above, then Eldon Motors is entitled to be fully indemnified and held harmless by Lamb Motoren for all such liability to the plaintiff together with attorneys' fees and other defense costs incurred by Eldon Motors in the defense of this action.

Wherefore, this answering defendant prays that plaintiff take nothing by his pretended cause of action, and, alternatively, prays that in the event there is liability adjudged against this defendant in favor of the plaintiff, then in that event Eldon Motors, a division of Tri-State Industries, Inc., be granted judgment of indemnity or contribution, as the case may be, against Lamb Motoren, together with its costs and disbursements herein.

———————————————————
Attorneys for Defendant
Eldon Motors

Jury Trial Demanded

UNITED STATES DISTRICT COURT

DISTRICT OF (STATE)

_____ DIVISION

Wayne Brown,

                Plaintiff,

    vs.

Lamb Motoren, a foreign corporation;
Johnson Power, Inc., a Wisconsin corporation; and Eldon Motors, a division of
Tri-State Industries, a California corporation,

                Defendants.

**ANSWER TO
CROSS-CLAIM**

Lamb Motoren, for its Answer to the Cross-Claim of Eldon Motors,
alleges:

I

Denies each and every allegation in said Cross-Claim contained, except
as hereinafter admitted, qualified, or otherwise duly answered or explained.

II

Admits those paragraphs numbered I and II of the Cross-Claim.

Wherefore, Lamb Motoren prays that the Cross-Claim of defendant
Eldon Motors be dismissed, and that this defendant have judgment as prayed
for in its Separate Answer to Amended Complaint and Cross-Claim, together
with its costs and disbursements herein.

_____

                Attorneys for Defendant
                Lamb Mortoren

UNITED STATES DISTRICT COURT

DISTRICT OF (STATE)

_____ DIVISION

Wayne Brown,

                Plaintiff,

   vs.

Lamb Motoren, a foreign corporation;
Johnson Power, Inc., a Wisconsin corporation; and Eldon Motors, a division of
Tri-State Industries, A California corporation.

                Defendants.

CROSS-CLAIM

Comes now defendant Eldon Motors and for its Cross-Claim against defendant Johnson Power, Inc.:

I

Alleges that plaintiff in the above-entitled action has caused a Summons and Complaint to be served upon each of the above-named defendants, and that plaintiff alleges in said complaint that all defendants are liable to plaintiff for money damages, as set forth more fully in said complaint.

II

Alleges that defendant Eldon Motors has interposed an Answer to the Complaint and has denied liability to plaintiff, all as set forth more fully in said Answer, a copy of which has been served on all parties.

III

Alleges that if plaintiff sustained injuries and losses as alleged in the complaint, or otherwise, said losses and injuries were proximately caused by the negligence and breaches of warranty by defendant Johnson Power, Inc., as set forth more fully in plaintiff's complaint.

IV

Alleges that if Eldon Motors Corporation is determined to be liable to plaintiffs for money damages, it is entitled to indemnity or contribution, as the case may be, from defendant Johnson Power, Inc.

Wherefore, defendant Eldon Motors prays for judgment of indemnity or contribution, as the case may be, from defendant Johnson Power, Inc. to such sums as are awarded to plaintiff against defendant Eldon Motors together with its costs and disbursements herein.

_____

Attorneys for Eldon Motors

Defendant Eldon Motors Demands
a Trial by Jury.

UNITED STATES DISTRICT COURT

DISTRICT OF (STATE)

——————— DIVISION

Wayne Brown,

Plaintiff,

vs.

Lamb Motoren, a foreign corporation;
Johnson Power, Inc., a Wisconsin corporation; and Eldon Motors, a division of
Tri-State Industries, a California corporation,

Defendants.

**ANSWER TO
CROSS-CLAIM**

Now comes the defendant, Johnson Power, Inc., and for its answer to the
Cross-Claim of Defendant, Eldon Motors, Inc., states:

I

Specifically denies each and every allegation in said Cross-Claim
contained.

Wherefore, defendant Johnson Power, Inc. prays that the Cross-Claim of
defendant, Eldon Motors, Inc. be dismissed, and that this answering
defendant have judgment for its costs and disbursements herein.

—————————————————————
Attorneys for Defendant
Johnson Power, Inc.

UNITED STATES DISTRICT COURT

DISTRICT OF (STATE)

_____ DIVISION

Wayne Brown,

      Plaintiff,

  vs.

Lamb Motoren, a foreign corporation;   **SEPARATE ANSWER**
Johnson Power, Inc., a Wisconsin corpo-   **TO COMPLAINT AND**
ration; and Eldon Motors, a division of   **CROSS-CLAIM**
Tri-State Industries, a California corpo-
ration,

      Defendants.

Now comes the defendant Johnson Power, Inc., a Wisconsin corporation, and for its separate Answer to the Complaint of the plaintiff herein:

I

Denies each and every allegation, matter and thing contained in said Complaint as to this defendant, save and except as is hereinafter admitted, qualified or otherwise explained.

II

Admits the allegations of paragraphs III, VI, VII and VIII except as paragraph VIII refers to the engine in question being sold to the plaintiff by the defendant Johnson Power, Inc., which this defendant specifically denies.

III

As to paragraphs I, II, IV, V and IX of the plaintiff's complaint, alleges that it has insufficient knowledge and information upon which to form a belief as to those allegations, and, accordingly, denies same and puts plaintiff to his proof.

IV

As and for a defense this answering defendant alleges that the accident described in plaintiff's Complaint and resulting injuries and damages to the plaintiff, if any, were caused by the contributory negligence of the plaintiff.

V

As and for a further defense this answering defendant alleges that if the plaintiff was injured and suffered damage as a result of the negligence, breach of warranty, defective design or manufacture or through fault of any other party named herein, then said injuries and damage were caused by the negligence, breach of warranty, defective design or manufacture or through fault of defendant Lamb Motoren and Eldon Motors, Inc.

CROSS-CLAIM

Now comes the defendant Johnson Power, Inc., a Wisconsin corporation, and for its cross-claim against the defendants Lamb Motoren, and Eldon Motors, Inc.

I

Alleges that if there was any injury or damage to the plaintiff due to negligence, breaches of warranty, defective design or manufacture, failure to properly inspect or test, failure to provide necessary and proper warnings and instructions, or otherwise, of any person other than the plaintiff, then said injury and damage were caused by defendants Lamb Motoren and Eldon Motors, Inc.

II

Alleges that in the event this answering defendant is determined to be liable to the plaintiff, this answering defendant should have judgment against defendants Lamb Motoren, and Eldon Motors, Inc. for such amount by way of indemnity or contribution as the Court should find just and proper.

Wherefore, Johnson Power, Inc. prays that plaintiff's pretended cause of action be dismissed as to this defendant, and that it have judgment for its costs and disbursements herein; and further this answering and cross-claiming defendant prays that in the event it is adjudged that the plaintiff recover against this defendant, that it have judgment against defendants Lamb Motoren and Eldon Motors, Inc. for the amount of such recovery by way of indemnity or contribution, together with its costs and disbursements herein.

_____

Attorneys for Defendant
Johnson Power, Inc.

UNITED STATES DISTRICT COURT

DISTRICT OF (STATE)

_____ DIVISION

Wayne Brown,
 	
            Plaintiff,
 	
   vs.
 	
Lamb Motoren, a foreign corporation;
Johnson Power, Inc., a Wisconsin corpo-
ration; and Eldon Motors, a division of
Tri-State Industries, a California corpo-
ration,
 	
            Defendants.
	**ANSWER TO
	CROSS-CLAIM**

Comes now defendant Eldon Motors, Inc. and for its Answer to the Cross-Claim of defendant Johnson Power, Inc.:

I

Denies each and every allegation, statement, matter and thing in said Cross-Claim contained, except as previously admitted or alleged in this answering defendant's Answer and Cross-Claim heretofore served on the parties.

Wherefore, defendant Eldon Motors, Inc. prays that defendant Johnson Power, Inc., take nothing by reason of its pretended Cross-Claim, and that this answering defendant have judgment for its costs and disbursements herein.

_____

Attorneys for Eldon Motors

Defendant Eldon Motors, Inc.
Demands Trial by Jury.

Sample Forms Used In Declaratory Judgment Action For Construction of Contract

UNITED STATES DISTRICT COURT

DISTRICT OF (STATE)

———— DIVISION

Linda A. Smith, a minor, by Clyde A.
Smith, her father and natural guardian,
                    Plaintiffs,

    vs.

Mutual Insurance Company, a corporation and David T. Black,
                    Defendants.

COMPLAINT*

Come now plaintiffs above-named, and for their cause of action allege:

1. That defendant Mutual Insurance Company is an insurance corporation which has its principal place of business in the State of Georgia.

2. That Linda A. Smith is the minor daughter of Clyde A. Smith, having been born on July 29, 1964, and lives in the latter's household at 3043 Hayes Street N.E., Madison, Wisconsin.

3. That at all times material herein the Hayden Automobile Leasing Corporation was the owner of a certain 1980 Dodge Automobile bearing 1980 (State) license number 3SG737.

4. That at all times material herein said Dodge automobile was leased by the Hayden Automobile Leasing Corporation to Rent A Car System, Inc., for the purpose of subleasing to the general public.

5. That at all times material herein defendant Mutual Insurance Company had in full force and effect a certain automobile liability insurance

*This complaint is for a declaratory judgment as authorized by Rule 57.

policy issued to Rent A Car System, Inc. and Hayden Automobile Leasing Corporation, a copy of said policy is attached hereto as Exhibit A.

6. That on or about June 15, 1980, Clyde A. Smith leased said Dodge automobile from Rent A Car System, Inc. for his own use and the use of the members of his family, including Linda A. Smith. That said lease agreement was entered into at the City of Madison, Dane County, Wisconsin, and a true copy of said lease is attached hereto as Exhibit B.

7. That on or about June 18, 1980 while plaintiff Linda A. Smith was driving said Dodge automobile with the permission and consent of the Hayden Automobile Leasing Corporation and Rent A Car System, Inc. she was involved in a motor vehicle collision with defendant David T. Black at the intersection of Fairview Avenue and Ryan in Madison, Wisconsin.

8. That said David T. Black has made a claim against Linda A. Smith for money damages as compensation for certain alleged injuries and property damage said to have resulted from the accident.

9. That plaintiff Linda A. Smith is an additional insured under said insurance policy issued by defendant Mutual Insurance Company, and is entitled to the full benefits provided by said policy.

10. That plaintiffs have made demand upon defendant Mutual Insurance Company to provide Linda A. Smith with a defense to the claim of David T. Black or settle the claim, as is appropriate; however, defendant Mutual Insurance Company denies any obligation to plaintiffs and David T. Black under said insurance policy.

Wherefore, plaintiffs pray for a judgment and decree of this Court determining the rights, liabilities, duties and legal relationships between the parties hereto; that, specifically, it be determined and declared that defendant Mutual Insurance Company insures plaintiff Linda A. Smith under said policy; and that plaintiffs have judgment for their costs and disbursements herein.

_____

Attorneys for Plaintiffs

Plaintiffs Demand Trail by Jury.

UNITED STATES DISTRICT COURT

DISTRICT OF (STATE)

_____ DIVISION

Linda A. Smith, a minor, by Clyde A.
Smith, her father and natural guardian,
                    Plaintiffs,

    vs.   ANSWER

Mutual Insurance Company a corporation and David T. Black,
                    Defendants.

Comes now defendant Mutual Insurance Company, and for its Answer to the Complaint of plaintiffs herein:

I

Admits that at all times material herein this answering defendant was a duly organized insurance company authorized to conduct a general insurance business in the State of Wisconsin with its principal place of business in the State of Georgia; and, further, that Linda A. Smith is the minor daughter of Clyde A. Smith, having been born July 29, 1964, and resides in the latter's household at 3043 Hayes Street Northeast, Madison, Wisconsin.

II

Admits further that this answering defendant issued a certain policy of insurance to Rent A Car System, Inc. and Hayden Automobile Leasing Corporation, a copy of which is attached to the Complaint, marked Exhibit A.

III

Specifically denies that Clyde A. Smith leased said Dodge Automobile from Rent A Car System, Inc. for his own use and the use of the members of his family, including Linda A. Smith.

IV

Specifically denies that plaintiffs have made a demand upon defendant Mutual Insurance Company to provide Linda A. Smith with a defense to the claim of David T. Black or settle his claim, as alleged in plaintiffs' Complaint or in any other manner.

V

Specifically denies that plaintiffs were insured pursuant to the terms and provisions of the policy of insurance issued by this answering defendant to Rent A Car System, Inc. and Hayden Automobile Leasing Corporation pursuant to the terms and provisions of the lease agreement entered into by Clyde A. Smith with Rent A Car System Inc., a copy of which is attached to plaintiffs' Complaint and marked Exhibit B.

VI

Except as hereinbefore admitted, qualified or otherwise answered, this answering defendant denies each and every allegation, matter and thing in said Complaint contained, and each and every part thereof, as though more fully set forth herein at length and denied in particular.

Wherefore, this answering defendant prays that plaintiffs take nothing by reason of their pretended cause of action, and that judgment be entered on behalf of this answering defendant for its costs and disbursements incurred herein.

_____

Attorneys for Defendant
Mutual Insurance Company

UNITED STATES DISTRICT COURT

DISTRICT OF (STATE)

—————— DIVISION

Linda A. Smith, a minor, by Clyde A.
Smith, her father and natural guardian,
Plaintiffs,

vs.

Mutual Insurance Company, a corporation and David T. Black,
Defendants.

ANSWER OF
DAVID T. BLACK

Defendant, David T. Black, for his Answer to plaintiffs' Complaint herein states and alleges:

I

Unless otherwise admitted, qualified or explained herein, said Defendant denies each and every thing, matter or allegation contained in Plaintiffs' Complaint herein.

II

Said Defendant does not have sufficient knowledge or information to form a belief as to the truth or falsity of the allegations contained in Paragraphs I, II, III, IV, V, VI, IX, or X and puts Plaintiffs to their strict proof thereof.

III

Defendant Black admits Paragraphs VII and VIII of Plaintiffs' Complaint herein.

IV

That said Defendant has also and will in the future make claim against all interested parties for his personal injuries and his property damage.

Wherefore, David T. Black prays for a judgment and decree of this Court determining the rights, liabilities, duties and legal relationships between parties hereto and awarding unto said Defendant his costs and disbursements.

————————————————————

Attorneys for Defendant Black

UNITED STATES DISTRICT COURT

DISTRICT OF (STATE)

_____ DIVISION

Linda A. Smith, a minor, by Clyde A.
Smith, her father and natural guardian,
               Plaintiffs,

   vs.

Mutual Insurance Company, a corporation, and David T. Black,
               Defendants.

**NOTICE OF MOTION
AND MOTION**

To: Linda A. Smith, a minor, by Clyde A. Smith, her father and natural guardian, and their attorneys, _____ , and David Black and his attorney, _____ .

PLEASE TAKE NOTICE that the defendant Mutual Insurance Company will move the Court sitting at Special Term on Wednesday, the 7th day of June, 1981, at 9:30 a.m., or as soon thereafter as counsel can be heard, for an Order of the above-named Court, allowing defendant Mutual Insurance Company to serve a Third Party Summons and Complaint on Clyde A. Smith and Federal Farm Insurance Company, in order to join all of the interested parties in the above-captioned declaratory judgment action.

Said Motion is to be based upon the files and records of the above-captioned Court, together with the attached Affidavit.

_____

Attorneys for Defendant
Mutual Insurance Company

UNITED STATES DISTRICT COURT

DISTRICT OF (STATE)

—————— DIVISION

Linda A. Smith, a minor, by Clyde A.
Smith, her father and natural guardian,
                    Plaintiffs,
         vs.   AFFIDAVIT
Mutual Insurance Company, a corpora-
tion, and David T. Black,
                    Defendants.

STATE OF WISCONSIN
                              ss
COUNTY OF DANE

David R. Lewis, being first duly sworn on oath, deposes and says that he is one of the attorneys representing the defendant Mutual Insurance Company in the above-captioned declaratory judgment action.

That on or about March 14, 1981, defendant Mutual Insurance Company was served with a Summons and Complaint, a copy of which is hereto attached and marked Exhibit "A". That said Summons and Complaint among other things, seeks declaratory relief determining that defendant Mutual Insurance Company provides coverage for plaintiff Linda A. Smith as a result of a motor vehicle accident which took place on June 18, 1980, between a motor vehicle owned by Hayden Automobile Leasing Corporation and Rent A Car System, Inc., which had been rented by plaintiff's father, Clyde A. Smith and which was being driven at the time by plaintiff Linda A. Smith, and a car driven by defendant David T. Black.

That plaintiff's father, Clyde A. Smith, and Federal Farm Insurance Company have an interest in the above-captioned declaratory judgment action and would be affected by the declaration.

That in order for the above-named Court to grant complete relief in the above-captioned matter, that it is necessary for Clyde A. Smith and Federal Farm Insurance Company be joined as third-party defendants so that their rights may be determined along with the rights of Linda A. Smith and Mutual Insurance Company.

That any declaration by the above-captioned Court in this declaratory judgment action would affect the rights of Clyde A. Smith and Federal Farm Insurance Company and that Clyde A. Smith and Federal Farm Insurance Company should be joined as third-party defendants in order that any declaration by the above-captioned Court regarding insurance coverage of Linda A. Smith would be binding upon all interested parties, including Clyde A. Smith and Federal Farm Insurance Company.

A copy of the proposed Third-Party Summons and Complaint is attached hereto and marked Exhibit "B".

Further, Affiant sayeth not, except that this Affidavit is made in support of defendant Mutual Insurance Company's Motion to join Clyde A. Smith and Federal Farm Insurance Company as third-party defendants in the above-captioned matter.

_____

David R. Lewis

Subscribed and sworn to before
me this 26th day of May, 1981.

_____

Notary Public

UNITED STATES DISTRICT COURT

DISTRICT OF (STATE)

_____ DIVISION

Linda A. Smith, a minor, by Clyde A.
Smith, her father and natural guardian,
     Plaintiffs,
  vs.
Mutual Insurance Company, a corporation and David T. Black,
          Defendants.

_____

Mutual Insurance Company, a corporation,
     Third-Party Plaintiff,
  vs.
Clyde A. Smith and Federal Farm
Insurance Company,
     Third-Party Defendants.

**(EXHIBIT B)
THIRD-PARTY
COMPLAINT**

Comes now defendant and third-party plaintiff above named and for its cause of action against third-party defendants herein:

I

Alleges that at all times material herein defendant and third-party plaintiff Mutual Insurance Company was a duly organized and existing corporation authorized to conduct a general insurance business in the State of Wisconsin.

II

Alleges that third-party defendant Federal Farm Insurance Company was a duly organized and existing corporation authorized to conduct a general insurance business in the State of Wisconsin at all times material herein.

III

Alleges that Clyde A. Smith, third-party defendant herein, entered into a lease agreement with Rent A Car System, Inc. on June 15, 1980, and that said lease agreement was entered into in the City of Madison, County of Dane, State of Wisconsin.

IV

That on or about the 8th day of March, 1981, a lawsuit was commenced against defendant and third-party plaintiff Mutual Insurance Company by Linda A. Smith, a minor, by Clyde A. Smith, her father and natural guardian, in which plaintiff Linda A. Smith, a minor, seeks to determine her rights, if any, upon a policy of insurance issued by defendant and third-party plaintiff Mutual Insurance Company to Rent a Car System Inc.; that third-party defendants, Clyde A. Smith and Federal Farm Insurance Company, a corporation, ware the real parties in interest in any determination of the rights of Linda A. Smith pursuant to the terms and provisions of the Mutual Insurance Company policy or the lease agreement entered into between Clyde A. Smith and Rent A Car System, Inc.

V

That third-party defendant, Federal Farm Insurance Company, a corporation, at all times material herein had in full force and effect a policy of automobile insurance issued to third-party defendant Clyde A. Smith; that by the terms and provisions of said policy of insurance third-party defendant Federal Farm Insurance Company agreed to indemnify Clyde A. Smith and Linda A. Smith, in addition to defending Clyde A. Smith and Linda A. Smith against any suits or claims arising out of the operation of a motor vehicle by Clyde A. Smith or Linda A. Smith, including but not limited to the claim presented by defendant David T. Black.

Wherefore, defendant and third-party plaintiff Mutual Insurance Company prays that the Court determine the rights of Clyde A. Smith and Linda A. Smith, plaintiffs, to coverage under the Federal Farm Insurance policy issued to Clyde A. Smith; and that the Court enter judgment in favor of third-party plaintiff Mutual Insurance Company in accordance with the request set forth in its Answer; and that judgment be entered on behalf of plaintiff Linda A. Smith and third-party defendant Clyde A. Smith, holding that said plaintiff and third-party defendant are entitled to insurance coverage pursuant to the terms and provisions of third-party defendant Federal Farm Insurance Company's policy, together with costs and disbursements incurred herein.

_____

Attorneys for Third-Party
Plaintiff

UNITED STATES DISTRICT COURT
DISTRICT OF (STATE)
_____ DIVISION

Linda A. Smith, a minor by Clyde A.
Smith, her father and natural guardian,
Plaintiffs,

vs.

Mutual Insurance Company, a corporation and David T. Black,
Defendants.

ORDER

The above-entitled matter came before the Court on the motion of defendant Mutual Insurance Company for leave to serve and file a third-party complaint in the form attached to the motion. Thomas Jones, Esq., appeared on behalf of plaintiffs in opposition to the motion. David Lewis, Esq., appeared on behalf of defendant Mutual Insurance Company in support of the motion.

The Court having heard and considered the proposed third-party complaint, and having heard the arguments of counsel and being fully advised in the premises,

IT IS HEREBY ORDERED that defendant Mutual Insurance Company's motion for leave to serve and file a third-party complaint is denied.

This order is without prejudice to Mutual Insurance Company or the Federal Farm Insurance Company to litigate issues between them through a third-party section or otherwise. Specifically, counsel for Mutual indicated the possibility of a dispute as to which Insurance Company has the primary coverage. That issue was not resolved by the above Order.

By the Court:

_____

Judge of District Court

(date)

UNITED STATES DISTRICT COURT

DISTRICT OF (STATE)

_____ DIVISION

Linda A. Smith, a minor, by Clyde A.
Smith, her father and natural guardian,
                 Plaintiffs,

   vs.

Mutual Insurance Company, a corporation and David T. Black,
                Defendants.

**NOTICE OF MOTION
AND MOTION**

To: Defendant Mutual Insurance Company and its attorneys; and, Defendant David T. Black and his attorneys.

PLEASE TAKE NOTICE that the above-named plaintiffs, through their undersigned attorneys, will bring the attached motion on for hearing at a special term of the above-named Court to be held at the courthouse in the City of Madison, Wisconsin on the 24th day of August, 1981, at 9:00 a.m., or as soon thereafter as counsel can be heard.

MOTION

Plaintiff Linda Smith hereby moves the Court, through her undersigned attorneys, for an Order accelerating the above entitled action on the active trial calendar for trial by jury as soon as the Court's business will permit. This Motion is made on the grounds that the case involves a determination as to whether the Mutual Insurance Company affords liability coverage for an automobile accident that occurred on June 18, 1980, which allegedly resulted in injuries to defendant David T. Black. Mr. Black has made claim against plaintiff Linda Smith for compensatory damages. It is to the benefit of all parties to know as soon as possible whether or not Linda A. Smith does have liability coverage under the Mutual Insurance Policy. That an acceleration of the case on the active trial calendar should not cause prejudice to any of the parties herein.

_____

Attorneys for Plaintiff

UNITED STATES DISTRICT COURT
DISTRICT OF (STATE)
_____ DIVISION

Linda A. Smith, a minor, by Clyde A. Smith, her father and natural guardian, Plaintiffs, vs. Mutual Insurance Company, a corporation and David T. Black, Defendants.	FINDINGS OF FACT, CONCLUSIONS OF LAW AND ORDER FOR JUDGMENT

The above-entitled declaratory judgment action came before the Court for trial without jury on (date). Plaintiffs appeared in person and by their attorney _____ . Attorney _____ , appeared on behalf of defendant.

The Court having heard the evidence presented by the parties and having considered the arguments of counsel and all the files, records and proceedings herein, makes its:

FINDINGS OF FACT

1. Linda Smith is a minor daughter of Clyde A. Smith, and at all times material herein resided in his household at 3043 Hayes Street North East, Madison, Wisconsin.

2. That defendant Mutual Insurance Company is an insurance corporation authorized to conduct its insurance business in the State of Wisconsin, including the issuance of automobile liability insurance policies.

3. That the Hayden Automobile Leasing Corporation owned a certain 1980 Dodge automobile which, at all times material herein, was leased by Hayden Automobile Leasing Corporation to the Rent A Car System, Inc., for the purpose of subleasing to the general public.

4. That at all times material herein defendant Mutual Insurance Company had in full force and effect the automobile liability insurance policy in question (Exhibit A) in which the Rent A Car System and the Hayden Automobile Leasing Corporation were named insureds; that said policy provides, among other things, that persons under the policy include:

> "Any other person while using an owned automobile with the permission of the named insured, provided his actual operation * * * is within the scope of such permission * * *."

5. That on June 15, 1980 Clyde A. Smith leased the said Dodge automobile from Rent A Car System, Inc. to replace his automobile which was used by his family and which had been damaged in an accident on or about June 11, 1980; that he specifically informed the Rent A Car System clerk, June Wilkerson, that he needed to lease the automobile to temporarily

replace a family automobile which had been damaged in an accident while his daughter was driving it.

6. That Clyde A. Smith signed a "Rental Agreement" (Exhibit B) before taking possession of the Dodge Automobile, but he did not read the terms and conditions stated on the back thereof, including:

> "Further said vehicle will be operated only by renter or * * * (2) Any member of renter's immediate family provided that renter's permission first be obtained and all such operators shall be at least 21 years of age and duly qualified and licensed."

That said provisions were not otherwise brought to the attention of Smiths before the motor vehicle accident of June 18, 1980; that Clyde A. Smith truthfully and fully answered the clerk's questions pertaining to the Rental Agreement so that she could complete the form.

7. That on or about June 18, 1980 Clyde A. Smith authorized Linda A. Smith to operate the Dodge automobile, and while operating said Dodge automobile Linda A. Smith was involved in a motor vehicle collision with defendant David T. Black at the intersection of Fairview Avenue and Ryan Street in Madison, Wisconsin; that defendant David T. Black has made a claim against Linda A. Smith for money damages for injuries and property damage he alleges resulted from said accident.

8. That at the time of said June 18, 1980 accident, plaintiff Linda A. Smith was driving the Dodge automobile with the permission and consent of the Hayden Automobile Leasing Corporation and Rent A Car System, Inc.

CONCLUSIONS OF LAW

1. That plaintiff Linda A. Smith was operating the Dodge automobile with the permission and consent of the Hayden Automobile Leasing Corporation and the Rent A Car System, Inc.

2. That plaintiff Linda A. Smith is an additional insured under the terms and provisions of defendant Mutual Insurance Company automobile liability insurance policy.

3. That defendant Mutual Insurance Company is obligated to assume defense of the claim by David T. Black against plaintiff Linda A. Smith and pay on behalf of Linda A. Smith all sums which she may become legally obligated to pay as damages for the claim of David T. Black up to the limit of the policy.

4. That plaintiffs are entitled to recover their costs and disbursements herein.

ORDER FOR JUDGEMENT

Let Judgment be Entered Accordingly.

By the Court:

_____
Judge of District Court

Dated: _____

MEMORANDUM

The facts in the above case cannot be distinguished from those in Taylor v. Allstate, 286 Minn. 449, 176 N.W.2d 266 (1970). The "Rental Agreement" does contain a limitation or prohibition to the effect that no one under 21 years of age is authorized to operate the leased automobile, and plaintiff Linda Smith was under age. However, the evidence clearly shows that the prohibition was not brought to the attention of the Lessee, Clyde A. Smith, nor to the attention of his subpermittee Linda Smith.

As noted in the *Taylor* case, the lessor should know and appreciate that when an automobile is leased for the purpose of temporarily replacing a family automobile, it will probably be used by members of the lessee's family, including minor children. The burden is upon the owner to make clear to his permittees or subpermittees any limitations which he desires to impose on the scope of the permittee's use of a leased automobile. An uncommunicated intent to limit the scope of consent is not effective.

In Taylor v. Allstate, supra, the lease agreement contained a similar prohibition to that in the present case, and the lessee signed the lease agreement. Nevertheless, it was not effective to preclude permission and consent to the lessee's minor son. The same is true in the present case.

This memorandum is part of the attached order.

/s/ _____
(District Judge)

Sample Forms Used For

Concluding Litigation

STATE OF MINNESOTA	DISTRICT COURT
COUNTY OF _____	_____ JUDICIAL DISTRICT
Georgia Watson,	
Plaintiff,	STIPULATION FOR
vs.	DISMISSAL
Alvin Johanson,	
Defendant,	

The above-entitled action, having been fully compromised and settled,

NOW THEREFORE, it is stipulated and agreed, by and between the parties hereto, through their respective counsel, that said action may be and hereby is dismissed with prejudice and on the merits, but without further costs to any of the parties.

IT IS FURTHER STIPULATED AND AGREED that either party, without notice to the other, may cause judgment of dismissal with predjudice and on the merits to be entered herein.

_____
Attorneys for Plaintiff

_____
Attorneys for Defendant

STATE OF _____ }   DISTRICT COURT

COUNTY OF _____ }   _____ JUDICIAL DISTRICT

Anderson Fish Company, }   DISMISSAL
        Plaintiff,   }   WITHOUT PREJUDICE

  vs.   }
Alan B. Fredericks,   }   File No. _____
        Defendant.

The above-entitled action may be and is hereby dismissed without prejudice and without further costs to either party.

_____

                           Attorneys for Plaintiff

_____

                         Attorneys for Defendant

Dated: _____

RELEASE OF ALL CLAIMS

FOR AND IN CONSIDERATION of the payment to me/us at this time of the sum of _____ Dollars ($ _____), the receipt of which is hereby acknowledged, I/we, being of lawful age, do hereby release, acquit and forever discharge _____ of and from any and all actions, causes of action, claims, demands, damages, costs, loss of services, expenses and compensation, on account of, or in any way growing out of, any and all known and unknown personal injuries, developed or undeveloped, and property damage resulting or to result from the accident that occurred on or about the _____ day of _____ , 19 ____ , at or near _____ .

I/we hereby declare and represent that the injuries sustained may be permanent and progressive and that recovery therefrom is uncertain and indefinite, and in making this release and agreement it is understood and agreed that I/we rely wholly upon my/our own judgment, belief and knowledge of the nature, extent and duration of said injuries, and that I/we have not been influenced to any extent whatever in making this release by any representations or statements regarding said injuries, or regarding any other matters, made by the persons, firms or corporations who are hereby released, or by any person or persons representing him or them, or by any physician or surgeon by him or them employed.

I/we clearly understand that I/we are releasing _____ and that this release includes all injuries now known to me/us and also all injuries now unknown, and I/we clearly understand that this release also includes all disabilities or results which may develop in the future from injuries now known or unknown to me/us.

It is further understood and agreed that this settlement is the compromise of a doubtful and disputed claim, and that the payment is not to be construed as an admission of liability on the part of _____ by whom liability is expressly denied.

This release contains the ENTIRE AGREEMENT between the parties hereto, and the terms of this release are contractual and not a mere recital.

I/we further state that I/we have carefully read the foregoing release and know the contents thereof, and I/we sign the same as my/our own free act.

WITNESS _____ hand and seal this _____ day of _____ , 19 __ .

In presence of

CAUTION! READ BEFORE SIGNING

_____

_____   _____ (Seal)

_____   _____ (Seal)

_____

RELEASE AND INDEMNITY AGREEMENT

KNOW ALL MEN BY THESE PRESENTS: That we, Robert William Grant and Gloria Jean Grant, husband and wife, of _____ County, State of _____ in consideration of the sum of Nine Thousand Five Hundred and No/100 Dollars ($9,500.00), and other valuable consideration, to us duly paid, receipt whereof is hereby acknowledged, do hereby for ourselves, our heirs, executors, administrators, successors, and assigns, release, acquit and forever discharge Patrick Mathias Ryan, Mutual Insurance Company, Richard Martin Halvorson, and Federal Farm Insurance Company of and from any and all actions, causes of action, claims, demands, damages, costs, loss of services, expenses and compensation, on account of, or in any way growing out of, any and all known and unknown personal injuries, developed or undeveloped, and property damage resulting or to result from an accident that occurred on or about June 24, 1981, at or on Highway 35W at the turn-off onto County Road No. 42 in the County of _____ , State of _____ .

We hereby declare and represent that the injuries sustained may be permanent and progressive and that recovery therefrom is uncertain and indefinite, and in making this release and agreement it is understood and agreed that we rely wholly upon our own judgment, belief and knowledge of the nature, extent and duration of said injuries, and that we have not been influenced to any extent whatever in making this release by any representations or statements regarding said injuries, or regarding any other matters, made by the persons, firms or corporations who are hereby released, or by any person or persons representing him or them, or by any physician or surgeon by him or them employed.

We clearly understand that we are releasing Patrick Mathias Ryan, Mutual Insurance Company, Richard Martin Halvorson, and Federal Farm Insurance Company and that this release includes all injuries now known to us and also all injuries now unknown, and we clearly understand that this release also includes all disabilities or results which may develop in the future from injuries now known or unknown to us.

It is further understood and agreed that this settlement is the compromise of a doubtful and disputed claim, and that the payment is not to be construed as an admission of liability on the part of Patrick Mathias Ryan, Mutual Insurance Company, Richard Martin Halvorson, and Federal Farm Insurance Company by whom liability is expressly denied.

In and as a further consideration of the receipt of the above amount, the undersigned hereby agree, except for attorney fees and direct suit costs, to indemnify and to reimburse or make good any loss or damage or costs that the said Patrick Mathias Ryan, Mutual Insurance Company, Richard Martin Halvorson, and Federal Farm Insurance Company may have to pay, and to hold them harmless from and against any and all demands, liabilities and charges which any of them may incur by reason of their being made a party to any lawsuit arising out of the aforementioned accident which occurred on June 24, 1981, and particularly, but not limited to any claim for contribution or indemnity made by any individual, person, persons or party against whom the undersigned made or may make any claim, claims, commence litigation or institute legal proceedings; and this release and indemnity agreement in the event of a breach thereof, may be pleaded as a defense and the said Patrick Mathias Ryan, Mutual Insurance Company, Richard Martin Halvorson, and Federal Farm Insurance Company, their heirs, executors, administrators, successors, assigns or their estate will not be required to respond in damages to us in any action whatsoever and any other proceedings of every kind, nature and description which may be brought, instituted, or taken by us and others against the said Patrick Mathias Ryan, Mutual Insurance Company, Richard Martin Halvorson, and Federal Farm Insurance Company, their heirs, executors, administrators, successors, assigns or their estate.

This release and indemnity agreement contains the entire agreement between the parties hereto, and the terms of this release are contractual and not a mere recital.

We further state that we have carefully read the foregoing release and indemnity agreement and know the contents thereof, and we sign the same as our own free act.

Date: _____ , 19 __ .

In The Presence of:

_____

_____

          _____
          Robert William Grant

          _____
          Gloria Jean Grant

COVENANT NOT TO SUE

KNOW ALL MEN BY THESE PRESENTS, that Daniel Trost, Paul Trost and Thomas E. Trost, hereinafter referred to as plaintiffs, for and in consideration of the sum of Four Hundred Dollars and no cents ($400.00), the receipt of which is hereby acknowledged, do hereby convenant and expressly agree with The Griff Company and Mutual Insurance Company, their successors and assigns (all of whom are hereafter referred to as "Settling Parties") not to further prosecute the suit for damages by plaintiffs pending against The Griff Company in the _____ Municipal Court, County of _____ , State of _____ , and agree to execute a Stipulation for Dismissal with prejudice in said action insofar as The Griff Company is concerned.

Plaintiffs further covenant and expressly agree with the Settling Parties to forever refrain from instituting any other action or making any other demand or claims of any kind against said settling parties for damages sustained by them as a result of an accident which occurred on June 22, 19__ in the Village of _____ , _____ .

The aforesaid consideration is not intended as full compensation for damages claimed by plaintiffs arising from said accident. However, by this covenant, plaintiffs do hereby credit and satisfy that portion of the total amount of their damages from said accident which has been caused by the negligence, if any, of such Settling Parties hereto as many hereafter be determined to be the case in the further trial or other disposition of this or any other action. Plaintiffs do hereby release and discharge that fraction and portion and percentage of their total cause of action and claim for damages against all parties resulting from said accident which shall hereafter, by further trial or other disposition of this or any other action, be determined to be the sum of the portions or fractions or percentages of causal negligence for which any or all of the Settling Parties hereto are found to be liable.

By this settling agreement the Settling Parties are hereby discharged of their liability for contribution with respect to the claim for damages of plaintiffs resulting from said accident.

Plaintiffs reserve to themselves the balance of the whole cause of action which they may have against Lloyd Koesling as a result of said accident. This covenant is not entered into nor in any way intended to release any claim or cause of action by plaintiffs against Lloyd Koesling as a result of said accident.

Plaintiffs specifically agree to hold the Settling Parties harmless and specifically agree to indemnify them from any claim, demand or cause of action by Lloyd Koesling for apportionment by way of contribution, whether such claim for contribution is alleged to arise by reason of judgment, settlement or otherwise.

Plaintiffs will effect compliance with the provision of the last paragraph by settling and compromising any recovery which they might later obtain from Lloyd Koesling, whether or not arising from judgment, so that such recovery does not exceed the amount determined by application to total damages of plaintiffs of that proportion or fraction or percentage of causal negligence for which Lloyd Koesling may be found to be or considered to be liable and thereby eliminating any claim by Lloyd Koesling and his subrogees, insurers, assigns or successors for equalizing contributions from the Settling Parties.

The Settling Parties in whose favor this convenant not to sue is executed, reserve and retain all claims and causes of action which they or any of them might have against others and, including, without limiting the generality of the foregoing, any claim for contribution which they might have against Lloyd Koesling.

The payment of the consideration for this convenant is not to be construed as an admission, on the part of any of the Settling Parties, of any liability whatsoever in consequence of said accident, to plaintiffs or to any other party.

This covenant is intended to release any claim for contribution against the Settling Parties in connection with said accident in the same manner and mode as the covenant and/or release before the court in the case of Pierringer v. Hoger, 21 Wis.2d 182, 124 N.W.2d 106 (1963).

IN WITNESS WHEREOF I have hereunto set my hand and seal this _____ day of May, 19 __ .

In presence of

_____

_____

_____
Daniel Trost

_____
Paul Trost

_____
Thomas E. Trost

STATE OF _____ ⎫
                                 ⎬ ss
COUNTY OF _____ ⎭

On this _____ day of May, 19 __ before me personally appeared _____ to me known to be the persons described herein, and who executed the foregoing instrument and _____ acknowledged that _____ voluntarily executed the same.

_____
Notary Public

My term expires _____ , 19 __ .

RELEASE AND COVENANT NOT TO SUE

AS TO AUTO LISTINGS, INC.

AND JOHN RIDER

FOR THE SOLE CONSIDERATION of Six Thousand Five Hundred and no/100 Dollars ($6,500.00), the receipt of which is hereby acknowledged, I hereby fully and forever release and discharge Auto Listings, Inc. and John Rider and The Mutual Insurance Co., their heirs, administrators, executors, successors and assigns from all claims, demands, damages, actions, rights of action of whatever kind or nature whether statutory, based on contract or otherwise, which I now have or may hereafter have arising out of, in consequence of or on account of all injuries to me, including any latent injuries and all developments and results therefrom, known and unknown injuries, whether developed or undeveloped, and anticipated and unanticipated consequences of all such injuries, and damages to property resulting to me in any way from an accident which occurred on or about the 27th day of March, 1981, at or near County Road 15 and Orchard Road in _____ , _____ County, _____ . In accepting said sum I hereby release and discharge that fraction, portion or percentage of the total cause of action, or claim for damages I now have or may hereafter possess against all parties responsible for my damages which shall by trial or other disposition, be determined to be the sum of the fractions, portions or percentages of causal negligence for which the parties herein released are found to be liable to me as a consequence of the above accident.

I hereby accept said sum as a compromise and settlement of all claims on account of the dispute between the parties hereto as to whether the above named parties are liable to me or not, and also as to the nature, extent and permanency of the injuries sustained by me.

I agree that in making this release, I am relying on my own judgment, belief and knowledge as to all phases of my claims and that I am not relying on representations or statements made by any of the persons hereby released or anyone representing them or physicians or surgeons employed by them.

I agree that the payment of the above sum is not to be construed as an admission of any liability whatsoever by or on behalf of the above named parties, by whom liability is expressly denied.

I further agree that any claim of whatever kind or nature the above named parties might have or hereafter have growing out of the above accident, is hereby expressly reserved to them.

This release is intended to release only the parties specifically named. The undersigned expressly reserves the balance of the whole cause of action or any other claim of whatever kind or nature not released hereby which I may have or hereafter have against any other person or persons arising out of the above accident.

As a further consideration for this release I agree to indemnify the parties released hereby and save them harmless from any claims for contribution or indemnity made by any other person, firm or corporation adjudged liable with or in addition to the parties released hereby; and the undersigned agrees to satisfy any judgment which may be rendered in favor of the undersigned, satisfying such fraction, portion or percentage of the judgment as the causal negligence of the parties released is adjudged to be of all causal negligence of all adjudged tort-feasors. In the event the undersigned fails to immediately satisfy any such judgment to the extent of the fraction, portion or percentage of the negligence as found against the parties released, the undersigned hereby consents and agrees that upon filing a copy of this agreement, without further notice, an order may be entered by the court in which said judgment is entered directing the Clerk thereof to satisfy said judgment to the extent of such fraction, portion or percentage of the negligence as found against the parties released and discharged under this release.

The undersigned acknowledges that as a result of the injuries sustained in the accident of March 27, 1981, he has incurred medical expenses with _____ Memorial Hospital of the reasonable value of $1,419.00 and that a hospital lien has been filed on behalf of said hospital and that out of the amount being paid as consideration for this release he will satisfy said lien and furnish the parties released herein a satisfaction of said lien as to said parties.

The undersigned further acknowledges that he has as an inducement to the parties released hereby represented and warranted to them that at the time and place of the accident out of which his claim arose and for which this settlement has been made, he was not in the course and scope of his employment with Auto Listings, Inc. and that he is not entitled to recover benefits under the Workmen's Compensation Law of (State) therefor. The undersigned agrees that the payments made hereunder are received in lieu of any benefits that he may be entitled to recover under the Workmen's Compensation Law of (State); for the injuries sustained on March 27, 1981. That in the event it is ever determined that he was in the course and scope of his employment with Auto Listings, Inc. at the time of the accident here involved and is entitled to benefits under the (State) Workmen's Compensation Law therefor that Auto Listings, Inc. and The Mutual Insurance Co. as their Workmen's Compensation insurer are entitled to a full credit to the extent of the payment made for the release herein given on any liability that may be determined against them under the Workmen's Compensation Law for the injuries and damages sustained by the undersigned as a result of said accident.

The undersigned further acknowledges that it is his intention to proceed with a claim and action for damages against Gary Ford, the owner of the automobile in which he was riding at the time of the accident here involved to recover such damages as he may be able to prove against said Ford and that an action has been instituted in the District Court of Hennepin County,

Minnesota therefor. That in the event it is determined in said action against Ford either directly or indirectly, or as a consequence thereof or as an adjunct thereto that Ford is entitled to be indemnified for any liability that he may have as a result of said accident by any of the parties released hereby, then and in that event the undersigned agrees to satisfy and release any such claim to the entire extent thereof in consideration of the payment that has been made as set forth herein.

It is further understood and agreed, and within the contemplation of the undersigned and the parties released hereby, that the undersigned intends to pursue an action against Patrick Vickner, individually, and doing business as Vick's to recover damages as provided by (dram shop statute) for the recovery of such loss and damages as he may have sustained as a result of this accident. That the undersigned hereby agrees that the parties released hereby may have a cause of action for contribution or indemnity against Patrick Vickner individually, and doing business as Vick's under (dram shop statute) and that he will do nothing to prejudice that claim and will cooperate and assist the parties hereby released in pursuing, and perfecting that claim, and shall attend hearings and trials and assist in securing and giving evidence and obtaining the attendance of witnesses therefor.

The undersigned further agrees to dismiss the action which has been instituted in the District Court of _____ County in the _____ Judicial District on his behalf against Auto Listings, Inc., on the merits and with prejudice as to said defendant.

Signed and sealed at Minneapolis, Minnesota, this 18th day of June, 19 __ .

CAUTION: READ BEFORE SIGNING.

_____
                                        James Kendall

In the presence of:

_____

_____

Miscellaneous Forms

UNITED STATES DISTRICT COURT

DISTRICT OF _____

_____ DIVISION

Mary Smith,

        Plaintiff,

   vs.

Robert Jones,

        Defendant.

NOTICE OF TAKING
ORAL DEPOSITION

To: Robert Jones and Clay Johnson, his attorney.

    YOU WILL PLEASE TAKE NOTICE that the oral deposition of Robert Jones will be taken on the 7th day of May, 1982, at 10:00 o'clock A.M. at 2205 Parkway South, Chicago, Illinois, by and before a notary public, or some other officer qualified by law, and that the said Robert Jones shall present himself at said time and place for the purpose of his oral deposition.

_____

Attorneys for plaintiff

UNITED STATES DISTRICT COURT

DISTRICT OF _____

_____ DIVISION

William Smith,

<table>
<tr><td></td><td>Plaintiff,</td><td rowspan="3">MOTION FOR PRODUCTION
OF DOCUMENTS
File No. _____</td></tr>
<tr><td>vs.</td><td></td></tr>
<tr><td>R. E. Miller Corporation,</td><td>Defendant.</td></tr>
</table>

MOTION

Plaintiff, William Smith, moves the Court for an Order requiring defendant R. E. Miller Corporation to produce and to permit plaintiff to inspect and copy the following documents:

Release dated June 1, 1981, signed by plaintiff for a consideration of Five Hundred ($500.00) Dollars paid by defendant and referred to in defendant's Answer.

Statement signed by William Smith on May 3, 1981, and given by him to R. E. Miller Corporation.

Defendant, R. E. Miller Corporation has possession, custody or control of each of the foregoing documents. Each of them constitutes or contains evidence relevant to the subject matter of this action as is more fully shown in affidavit attached hereto.

_____
Attorney for Plaintiff

(date)

NOTICE OF MOTION

To: R. E. Miller Corporation and Richard Jones, its attorney:

YOU WILL PLEASE TAKE NOTICE that the undersigned will bring the above motion on for hearing at a Special Term of the above-named Court to be held in the City of Los Angeles on the third day of May, 1981 at 10:00 A.M. or as soon thereafter as counsel can be heard.

_____
Attorney for Plaintiff

UNITED STATES DISTRICT COURT
DISTRICT OF _____
_____ DIVISION

William Smith,

        Plaintiff,

vs.

R. E. Miller Corporation,

        Defendant.

AFFIDAVIT

STATE OF _____

COUNTY OF _____

} ss

William Smith, being first duly sworn on oath, says:

1. That defendant, by and through its liability insurance company, received from plaintiff on or about June 1, 1980, the Release referred to in the Answer and said Release is now in the files of said insurance company.

2. That on or about June 3, 1980, said insurer on behalf of defendant, visited plaintiff while plaintiff was in Memorial Hospital and at that time talked to plaintiff and recorded the answers in writing and had plaintiff sign the same. Plaintiff was not at that time, nor at any time subsequent thereto, given a copy of said statement. Said statement is now in the files of defendant's liability insurer.

3. That each of said documents are relevant to the subject matter of this action. Defendant has pleaded the Release as an affirmative defense. Plaintiff, at one time received a copy of said Release, but it is now lost and cannot, after diligent search, be found. Said statement taken in writing from plaintiff on June 3, 1980, contains statements made by plaintiff while in the hospital and under the influence of drugs and relates directly to the occurrence involved in this law suit.

_____

William Smith

Subscribed and sworn to before
me this 30th day of April, 1980.

_____

Notary Public

UNITED STATES DISTRICT COURT

DISTRICT OF _____

_____ DIVISION

William Smith,

               Plaintiff,   ORDER REQUIRING

  vs.   PRODUCTION OF

R. E. Miller Corporation,   DOCUMENTS

               Defendant.

The above matter was heard by the Court at Special Term on the third day of May, 1980, on plaintiff's motion for production of certain documents. John Doe, Esq. appeared in support of said motion, and Richard Roe, Esq. appeared in opposition thereto.

It appears that defendant has possession and control of the documents in question and said documents contain or constitute evidence material to the subject matter of this action and good cause being shown,

IT IS ORDERED, that defendant produce and permit plaintiff's attorney to inspect, copy and photograph the following documents:

Release, dated June 1, 1979, signed by plaintiff and releasing claims against defendant.

Statement, dated June 3, 1979, signed by plaintiff and pertaining to the facts involved in this case.

Said documents are to be delivered to plaintiff's attorney within five days hereof and returned by plaintiff to defendant promptly upon completion of the photocopying.

_____

Judge of District Court

Dated: _____

UNITED STATES DISTRICT COURT

DISTRICT OF _____

_____ DIVISION

APPLICATION FOR APPOINTMENT OF

GUARDIAN AD LITEM

To the Above-Named Court:

William Johnson, a minor, applies to the Court and states:

1. Applicant's full name is William Johnson; he is fifteen (15) years old, and resides at 264 Elm, in the City of Fairfield, County of _____ , State of _____ .

2. Applicant's father is deceased; applicant's mother is Mrs. Sarah Johnson, residing at 23 South Front Street, Denver, Colorado; that applicant has no custodian or testamentary or other guardian.

3. Applicant is not married.

4. Applicant has, as he is advised by _____ , an attorney of this Court, a good cause of action against Leo Hatfield for personal injury, which action your applicant is desirous of commencing forthwith in this Court.

5. Thomas Murphy, age 47, residing at 6754 A Street, Fairfield, _____ , and a salesman by occupation, is a responsible person competent to act as guardian ad litem for applicant in said action.

Wherefore, your applicant prays said Thomas Murphy, or some other competent person, be appointed guardian ad litem of applicant to commence and prosecute said action for applicant.

_____

William Johnson

STATE OF _____

ss

COUNTY OF _____

William Johnson, being duly sworn, deposes and says that he has read the foregoing Petition subscribed by him, and knows the contents thereof, and that the same is true of his own knowledge, except as to those matters stated therein on information and belief, and as to those matters he believes it to be true.

_____

William Johnson

Subscribed and sworn to before me
this 2nd day of January, 19 ___ .

_____
Notary Public

CONSENT OF GUARDIAN

I hereby consent to act as guardian ad litem of William Johnson, for the purposes stated in the foregoing Petition.

_____
                                    Thomas Murphy

(date)

UNITED STATES DISTRICT COURT

DISTRICT OF _____

_____ DIVISION

ORDER APPOINTING GUARDIAN AD LITEM

On the foregoing attached Application and Consent, and on motion of _____ , Esq. attorney for the petitioner,

IT IS ORDERED, that Thomas Murphy, be and hereby is, appointed guardian ad litem of William Johnson, for the purpose of prosecuting one Leo Hatfield as requested in the petition.

By the Court:

_____
                                    Judge of District Court

Dated: _____

UNITED STATES DISTRICT COURT

DISTRICT OF _____

_____ DIVISION

OATH OF GUARDIAN

I, Thomas Murphy, do swear that I will faithfully and justly perform all the duties of the office and trust which I now assume as guardian ad litem for William Johnson, to the best of my ability. So help me God.

_____
Thomas Murphy

Subscribed and sworn to before me
this 2nd day of January, 19 __ .

_____
Notary Public

UNITED STATES DISTRICT COURT

DISTRICT OF _____

_____ DIVISION

(Title of Case)   **INTERROGATORIES**

(Commonly directed to plaintiff
in wrongful death action.)

Defendants respectfully submit to the plaintiffs for answer by them under oath as provided for by the Rules of Civil Procedure the following interrogatories:

1. State decedent's date and place of birth.

2. State decedent's residential addresses for the past ten years preceding his death, indicating the period of time he was at each address, respectively.

3. Describe fully all disabilities that decedent had immediately prior to the accident, including any disability for which he had received medical care or that affected his employability or otherwise limited his activities.

4. Describe fully the extent of decedent's formal education, including the schools attended, degrees obtained and dates of completions.

5. State the amount of income decedent reported as income in his United States federal tax returns for each of the years 1979, 1980 and 1981, respectively.

6. Describe decedent's employments during the five years preceding his death including the name of each employer, period of time for each employment, his job title, and a description of the work he performed in each job.

7. As to each personal injury accident the decedent had ever had state:

   (a) the date of the accident

   (b) the location of the accident

   (c) the type of accident

   (d) the nature and extent of injuries sustained

   (e) the names and addresses of physicians who attended him

   (f) the names and addresses of hospitals at which he received treatment

   (g) the nature and extent of any consequential disability

   (h) the name and address of all persons against whom claims were made due to the accident

8. State the name, address, age and relationship to decedent of each next of kin for whom claim is being made in this action.

9. Describe fully the pecuniary contribution made by decedent to each next of kin for whom claim is being made in this action.

10. Specify each item of special damages claimed by the trustee by showing the source of each expense, the amount of money owed or paid, and the dates of payments.

11. Describe in detail the occurrence of the accident referred to in the complaint.

12. State the alleged immediate cause of decedent's death.

13. If decedent had ever been convicted of a crime, identify the court where the judgment was entered, the date of conviction and describe the nature of the offense for which he was convicted.

14. State the names and addresses of all witnesses who have any knowledge or information about the alleged accident.

15. Identify by name, address, and occupation each person who has custody of photographs relevant to the alleged accident.

16. Identify each photograph by its subject matter and the date on which it was taken.

17. State the names and addresses of all persons from whom statements have been obtained, and indicate the date on which each statement was made.

_____

Attorney for Defendant

(date)

UNITED STATES DISTRICT COURT

DISTRICT OF _____

_____ DIVISION

(Title of Case)   **INTERROGATORIES**

(Commonly directed to plaintiff
in personal injury action.)

To: Plaintiff Above-Named and _____ His Attorney.

PLEASE TAKE NOTICE that defendant demands answers to the following continuing interrogatories under oath, pursuant to the provisions of Rule 33 of the Federal Rules of Civil Procedure:

1. State the names and addresses of all persons you claim have any knowledge or information concerning the accident described in the complaint.

2. State the names and addresses of all persons you claim have any knowledge or information about the injuries alleged in the complaint.

3. List all expenses and losses you claim you incurred by reason of the alleged accident.

4. List the dates on which you were examined or treated at any hospital whether as an in-patient or out-patient.

5. List the dates on which you received any medical treatments and medical examinations at a physician's office, giving the name and address of such physician.

6. Describe fully how the alleged accident occurred.

7. List all other accidents of any kind whatsoever in which you have been involved by answering the following:

   (a) dates and places;

   (b) type of accident such as automobile, work or otherwise;

   (c) names and addresses of all persons involved;

   (d) nature of injuries;

   (e) doctors and hospitals rendering care and treatment;

   (f) names of all persons, corporations, employers and insurance companies against whom claims were made.

8. State the names and addresses of all persons, including parties, from whom you have obtained statements or reports concerning the above entitled matter; give the date on which the respective statements and reports were obtained.

9. If you have any insurance which covers any of the expenses or losses you claim resulted from the accident in question, state the name of the insurer and the amount of the coverage afforded.

10. State the date and place of your birth.

11. State your social security number.

12. Describe the nature and extent of your alleged injuries.

_____

Attorneys for Defendant

(date)

UNITED STATES DISTRICT COURT

DISTRICT OF _____

_____ DIVISION

(Title of Case)   INTERROGATORIES

(Commonly directed to defendant in accident cases.)

To: The Above Named Defendants and To _____ Their Attorney.

Plaintiff in the above entitled matter requests answers to the following interrogatories in compliance with Rules 26 and 33 of The Federal Rules of Civil Procedure:

1. State the name, address, age, employer and occupation of all eye witnesses to the accident referred to in the complaint herein known to you, your counsel or their associates, investigators, employees or agents, whether obtained in the course of the investigation, preparation for trial or otherwise.

2. State the name, address, age, employer and occupation of all persons being or arriving at the scene of the accident referred to in the complaint on file herein known to you, your counsel or their associates, investigators, employees or agents, whether obtained in the course of investigation, preparation for trial or otherwise.

3. State the name, address, age, employer and occupation of all persons who have any knowledge or information relating to the accident referred to in the complaint on file herein, including expert witnesses, known to you, your counsel or their associates, investigators, employees or agents, whether obtained in the course of investigation, preparation for trial or otherwise.

4. State the name, address, age, employer and occupation of all persons who have any knowledge or information relating to the personal, social, vocational, avocational, educational or other background of the plaintiff in the above entitled action known to you, your counsel or their associates, investigators, employees or agents, whether obtained in the course of investigation, preparation for trial or otherwise.

5. List the names of any of the persons referred to in your answers to interrogatories 1, 2, 3 and 4 whom you have interviewed, stating the date, time and location of each such interview, the name, address, employer and occupation of each person present at the time of each such interview, and the name, address, employer and occupation of the party conducting the interview.

6. With regard to each person listed in your answers to interrogatories 1, 2, 3 and 4 from whom you have obtained a statement, state:

a. The date and time each such statement was taken.

b. The location at which each such statement was taken.

c. The name, address, employer and occupation of the person taking such statement.

d. Whether each such statement was oral, written, court-reported or otherwise preserved (specifying).

e. Whether the party from whom each such statement was taken was provided with a copy thereof.

7. If you have secured any photographs, slides, motion pictures or other photographic or non-photographic visual representations relating in any manner to the subject matter of the complaint herein, state:

a. The type of visual representation secured.

b. The subject matter of each such visual representation (specifying such in detail).

c. The date each was taken, or made.

d. By whom each was taken, or made.

e. Who is currently in possession of the negatives and prints, or other representations.

8. Excluding matters already referred to in your answer to interrogatory 6, do you have knowledge of any other physical evidence of any type or nature whatsoever relating in any manner to the subject of this litigation? If so, state:

a. In detail, a description of the nature of all such physical evidence.

b. Who is currently in possession of, or has custody over, such evidence.

9. State the name of the insurance company or companies that carry your liability insurance covering the occurrence or accident involved herein, and state the amount of coverage under said policy or policies.

10. State whether or not you have insurance coverage applicable in this case which involves co-insurance or any excess insurance. If so, state:

a. The names of the companies carrying such insurance.

b. The limits of such coverage(s).

11. If you have any knowledge of the plaintiff having ever sustained any injuries prior or subsequent to the occurrence which is the subject matter of this litigation, state:

a. The precise nature of each such injury.

b. The date each such injury was sustained.

c. The location where each such injury was sustained.

d. The names and addresses of the persons involved in the occurrence surrounding such injury.

e. The names and addresses of the physicians or other healing-arts practitioners rendering medical treatment for such injury.

12. If you have any knowledge of the plaintiff having every suffered from any illnesses, diseases or disabilities at any time prior or subsequent to the occurrence which is the subject matter of this litigation, state:

a. The precise nature of each such illness, disease or disability.

b. The date each such illness, disease or disability was incurred, contracted or otherwise endured.

c. The location where each such illness, disease or disability was incurred, contracted or otherwise endured.

d. The names and addresses of all persons having knowledge of each such illness, disease or disability.

e. The names and addresses of each doctor rendering medical treatment for each such illness, disease or disability.

13. Describe in detail the manner in which the accident alleged in the complaint herein occurred.

14. At the time of the accident, where were you coming from and where were you intending to go?

15. If you consumed (i) any liquor, beer or other alcoholic beverage of any sort whatsoever, or (ii) any drug, narcotic, pills or any medication of any sort whatsoever, within the twenty-four hour period preceding such accident, state:

a. What precisely was consumed.

b. The quantity consumed.

c. The time and place of each such consumption.

d. The name and address of each person observing you at each such time and place.

16. Describe in detail all conversations which took place at the time of, or following, the accident and list the names and addresses of the persons involved in such conversations and the names and addresses of all persons who overheard or may have overheard such conversations.

17. With regard to all medical reports or medical records of any type or nature examined by or in the possession of you, your attorney, your insurers, or any of their agents or employees relating to the plaintiff in this action, state:

a. A description of each such report or record being specific as to the date and author.

b. The method by which said report or record was obtained by you.

c. Will you attach a copy of each such report or record to these interrogatories without the necessity of a motion to produce?

18. With regard to each employment, payroll, or personnel record or file examined by or in the possession of you, your attorney, your insurers, or any of their agents or employees relating to the plaintiff in this action, state:

a. A description of each such record or file being specific as to the date and author.

b. The method by which said record or file was obtained by you.

c. Will you attach a copy of each such record on file to these interrogatories without the necessity of a motion to produce?

19. With regard to each expert witness that you expect to call to trial, state:

a. The subject matter in which the expert is expected to testify.

b. The substance of the facts and opinions to which the expert is expected to testify and a summary of the grounds for each opinion.

These interrogatories are continuing in nature and it is specifically requested and demanded that all information coming to your attention subsequent to the completion of your answers to these interrogatories which is in any manner relevant to such interrogatories be promptly made available to plaintiff's counsel.

_____
Attorney for Plaintiff

(date)

AUTHORIZATION FOR RELEASE OF
MEDICAL INFORMATION

Patient _____ Address _____

Birthdate _____   _____

This will authorize _____Hospital/Clinic to release

to: _____
(name/title of person/organization and address)

information from the medical records maintained while I was a

patient at _____ Hospital/Clinic during _____
(dates)

The information to be disclosed is:

_____ Discharge Summary   _____ Operative Reports

_____ Consultation Reports   _____ Pathology Reports

_____ History and Physical Exam _____ X-ray Reports

_____ Laboratory Reports   _____ Other (specify)

                                   _____

The information is needed for the following purpose(s): _____

_____

_____

I understand that I may revoke this consent at any time and that upon
fulfillment of the above-stated purpose(s), this consent will automatically
expire without any express revocation. I do not authorize further release to
any other third party.

                          _____
                          (signature of patient/guardian)

_____
(Witness)

                          _____
                          (relationship to patient if signed
                          by guardian)

                          _____
                          (reason patient is unable to sign)

FEDERAL TAX
RETURN AUTHORIZATION

To: Internal Revenue
      Ogden, Utah

Please be advised that you are hereby authorized to disclose and make available to (Law Firm Name), and any member thereof, copies, which may or may not be certified, of the undersigned _____ 's Federal Income Tax Returns for the year(s) _____ - _____ .

Dated: _____

_____

Social Security No. _____

STATE OF _____   DISTRICT COURT
COUNTY OF _____   _____ JUDICIAL DISTRICT

(Title of Case)   **REQUEST FOR PRODUCTION
                             OF WITNESS STATEMENTS**

                         *   *   *

To: The Above-Named Defendants and to _____ , their attorney.

In Accordance with Rules of Civil Procedure, plaintiff requests that copies of the following be made available within ten (10) days:

All statements made by parties or non-parties concerning the above action or its subject matter.

For the purpose of this request, a statement is (a) a written statement signed or otherwise adopted or approved by the person making it, or (b) a stenographic, mechanical, electrical, or other recording, or a transcription thereof, which is a substantially verbatim recital of an oral statement by the person making it and contemporaneously recorded.

_____

Attorney for Plaintiff

(date)

FILE NO. _____

WITNESS REPORT OF ACCIDENT

—AM

DATE OF ACCIDENT_____19___TIME_____PM PLACE_____

CITY_____ COUNTY_____ STATE_____

CAR A _____ _____ _____ _____
                Make   Color   Direction Moving   Driver's Name

CAR B _____ _____ _____ _____
                Make   Color   Direction Moving   Driver's Name

CAR C _____ _____ _____ _____
                Make   Color   Direction Moving   Driver's Name

WHERE WERE YOU WHEN THE ACCIDENT HAPPENED?_____

IF YOU WERE IN ONE OF THE CARS INVOLVED, WHICH ONE?_____SEATED WHERE?   _____

DID YOU SEE THE ACCIDENT HAPPEN?_____ SEE THE CARS AFTERWARDS?_____

COMPLETE DIAGRAM

Illustrate position of cars at time of collision:

INDICATE DIRECTIONS

SHOW STOP SIGNS AND TRAFFIC LIGHTS

SHOW CARS THUS

LABEL EACH STREET

A B C

STATE BRIEFLY HOW ACCIDENT HAPPENED_____

_____

_____

_____

_____

_____

_____

WERE THERE ANY STOP SIGNS OR TRAFFIC LIGHTS FACING CAR A?_____CAR B? _____CAR C? _____

WERE ANY STOP-AND-GO LIGHTS VIOLATED BY CAR A?_____CAR B?_____CAR C? _____

WERE ANY STOP SIGNS VIOLATED BY CAR A?_____CAR B?_____CAR C? _____

WHAT IF ANY TRAFFIC VIOLATIONS DID YOU SEE BY CAR A? _____

        CAR B?_____ CAR C? _____

PLEASE ANSWER ALL QUESTIONS ON BOTH SIDES

WERE ALL LIGHTS BURNING ON CAR A?_____CAR B?_____CAR C?_____

WHAT, IF ANY, SIGNALS WERE GIVEN BY CAR A?_____CAR B?_____CAR C?_____

WHAT WAS THE SPEED OF CAR A?_____CAR B?_____CAR C?_____

WHAT WAS THE SPEED LIMIT?_____

WAS VISIBILITY RESTRICTED FOR DRIVER OF CAR A?_____CAR B?_____CAR C?_____
   (Indicate whether rain, snow, fog, dust, trees, shrubs, buildings, parked cars)

CONDITION OF ROAD OR STREET: DRY_____ICE_____SNOW_____WET_____MUDDY_____

WHERE WAS POINT OF IMPACT ON CAR A?_____

   CAR B?_____CAR C?_____

WHAT DEFECTS DID YOU SEE IN THE CONDITION OF CAR A?_____

   CAR B?_____CAR C?_____

WHAT MARKS OR DEBRIS DID YOU SEE ON THE ROAD?_____

WHERE WERE THEY WITH REFERENCE TO THE CENTER OF THE STREET AND WITH REFERENCE TO THE CARS INVOLVED?

_____

_____

LENGTH OF SKID MARKS, IF ANY, FROM CAR A?_____CAR B?_____CAR C?_____

WHAT WAS THERE ABOUT THE POSITION OF THE CARS, OR THE MARKS ON THE ROAD, OR OTHER FACTS THAT YOU

OBSERVED, TO INDICATE WHO WAS TO BLAME FOR THE ACCIDENT?_____

_____

WAS EITHER CAR ON THE WRONG SIDE OF THE ROAD?_____

WHAT DID YOU HEAR THE DRIVERS SAY AFTER THE ACCIDENT?_____

_____

WERE YOU INJURED?_____DID ANYONE ELSE APPEAR TO BE INJURED?_____IF SO, IN WHAT CAR?_____

WHO ELSE WAS A WITNESS TO THIS ACCIDENT?

   NAME _____ ADDRESS _____

   NAME _____ ADDRESS _____

      YOUR NAME HERE: _____ AGE: _____

         ADDRESS: _____

         TELEPHONE: RESIDENCE _____ BUSINESS: _____

            DATE: _____

UNITED STATES DISTRICT COURT

DISTRICT OF (STATE)

——————— DIVISION

Anderson Construction Company, Inc.,

Plaintiff

vs.

Smith Industries, Inc.,

Defendant

BILL OF COSTS

Judgment having been entered in the above entitled action on the 14th day of September, 1982, against defendant, the clerk is requested to tax the following as costs:

Fees of the clerk	$ 60.00
Fees of the marshal	21.36
Fees of the court reporter for all or any part of the transcript necessarily obtained for use in the case	N/A
Fees and disbursements for printing	N/A
Fees for witnesses	1087.15
Fees for exemplification and copies of papers necessarily obtained for use in case	N/A
Docket fees under 28 U.S.C. 1923	20.00
Costs incident to taking of depositions	N/A
Costs as shown on Mandate of Court of Appeals	N/A
Other costs (please itemize):	
Photographer's fee for blow-up of picture of grain elevator used at trial	124.11
Photographic copying fee for photographs of failed structure used at trial	107.95
TOTAL	$1,420.57

STATE OF NORTH DAKOTA

COUNTY OF BURLEIGH } ss

I certify under penalty of perjury that the foregoing costs are correct and were necessarily incurred in this action and that the services for which fees have been charged were actually and necessarily performed. A copy hereof was this day mailed to counsel for Defendant with postage fully prepaid thereon. Executed on October 4, 1982.

——————————————————

Attorney for Plaintiff

Please take notice that I will appear before the Clerk who will tax said costs on October 18, 1982 at 9:00 a.m.

_____

Attorney for Plaintiff

Costs are hereby taxed in the amount of $ _____ this _____ day of October, 1982, and that amount included in the judgment.

_____

Clerk

_____

Deputy Clerk

NOTICE

Sec. 1920. Taxation of costs.

"A judge or clerk of any court of the United States may tax as costs the following:

(1) Fees of the clerk and marshal;

(2) Fees of the court reporter for all or any part of the stenographic transcript necessarily obtained for use in the case;

(3) Fees and disbursements for printing and witnesses;

(4) Fees for exemplification and copies of papers necessarily obtained for use in the case;

(5) Docket fees under section 1923 of this title;

(6) Compensation of court appointed experts, compensation of interpreters, and salaries, fees, expenses, and costs of special interpretation services under section 1828 of this title."

Sec. 1924. Verification of bill of costs.

"Before any bill of costs is taxed, the party claiming any item of cost of disbursement shall attach thereto an affidavit, made by himself or by his duly authorized attorney or agent having knowledge of the facts, that such item is correct and has been necessarily incurred in the case and that the services for which fees have been charged were actually and necessarily performed."

The Federal Rules of Civil Procedure contain the following provisions:

Rule 54(d). "Except when express provision therefor is made either in a statute of the United States or in these rules, costs shall be allowed as of course to the prevailing party unless the court otherwise directs; but costs against the United States, its officers, and agencies shall be imposed only to the extent permitted by law. Costs may be taxed by the clerk on one day's notice. On motion served within 5 days thereafter, the action of the clerk may be reviewed by the court."

Rule 6(e) "Whenever a party has the right or is required to do some act or take some proceedings within a prescribed period after the service of a notice or other paper upon him and the notice or paper is served upon him by mail, 3 days shall be added to the prescribed period."

Rule 58 (in part). "Entry of the judgment shall not be delayed for the taxing of costs."

Deposition Transcript

This is an actual deposition taken in connection with a personal injury claim which resulted from an automobile accident. The transcript illustrates the necessity of being persistent and detailed. Four major areas are covered, though the areas are not separated in any obvious manner: (1) deponent's background, (2) deponent's previous health and accidents, (3) the accident in question, (4) the consequential injuries and expenses. Paralegals may be asked to prepare summaries of investigations, interrogatories, and depositions. Of particular interest is the obvious lack of preparation that the deponent had for the deposition. The transcript should be read in light of the various guidelines suggested for preparing a witness to testify. As an epilogue, the defendant's insurer was able to obtain a dismissal of the case with only a nominal settlement.

Duane Johnson,
                     Plaintiff,
     vs.
Clarence A. Smith,
                     Defendant and
               Third-Party Plaintiff,   DEPOSITION
                                               TRANSCRIPT
     vs.
Carolyn Jones,
               Third-Party Defendant.

APPEARANCES

Thomas Clarke, Esq., appeared in behalf of the plaintiff.

John Fredricks, Esq., appeared in behalf of the defendant and third-party plaintiff.

Lang & Spencer, by Robert L. Lang, Esq., appeared in behalf of the third-party defendant.

DISCOVERY DEPOSITION OF DUANE JOHNSON, taken under the Federal Rules of Civil Procedure for the District Courts, at 700 Titan Building, Detroit, Michigan, on August 13, 1981, before John R. Nash, a notary public, commencing at approximately 11:10 o'clock a.m.

DUANE JOHNSON,

plaintiff, called in behalf of the defendant and third-party plaintiff, having been first duly sworn, testified on his oath as follows:

EXAMINATION

By Mr. Fredricks:

Q. Will you state your full name, please?

A. Duane Anthony Johnson.

Q. What is your birthdate?

A. One — twenty-two — sixty.

Q. Where were your born?

A. Kansas City, Kansas.

Q. Where?

A. Kansas City, Kansas.

Q. Where do you currently reside?

A. You mean in Detroit.

Q. Yes.

A. South Detroit.

Q. What is your address?

A. 1530 East 40th and a half street.

Q. East 40th and a half?

A. Yes. South Detroit.

Q. How long have you lived there?

A. About nine months.

Q. Are you married?

A. No, single.

Q. Have you ever been married?

A. No, I haven't.

Q. Do you live with anyone at that address?

A. Friend.

Q. Who?

A. Catherine Baker.

Q. What's the name again?

A. Catherine Baker.

Q. You say you are friends.

A. Well, just two-bedroom apartment.

Q. I mean you are not related in any way.

A. No.

Q. How long has she been there?

A. About a year or two. About a year.

Q. Where did you reside before moving to your current address?

A. 16th Avenue. I forgot that apartment number. It was on 20 — 26th and 16th Avenue.

Q. How long did you live at that address?

A. About two months, three months.

Q. Where do your parents reside?

A. At the present time 4245 Park Avenue South.

Q. And your father's name is what?

A. Donald Johnson.

Q. Are you presently employed?

A. Part time.

Q. Where do you work?

A. Hearns Auditorium.

Q. I'm having a hard time hearing you.

A. Hearns Auditorium. That's on the Detroit campus.

Q. What do you do there?

A. Work in the office. Office work.

Q. How long have you worked there?

A. This summer. Started this summer. Summer work. That's for Model City.

Q. Who is your immediate supervisor?

A. Henry Hyslop.

Q. Will you spell the last name?

A. H-y-l—H-y-s-l-o-p.

Q. Do you intend to continue working there indefinitely?

A. No. That's just summer work, you know.

Q. Will that job end then in September?

A. It ends this month some time.

Q. What other jobs have you had since August of 1979?

A. I was working at Honeywell on an assembly line, I think that was in '79.

Q. You work at Honeywell where?

A. In Detroit, Honeywell.

Q. What kind of work did you do for Honeywell?

A. Was just small work, just on an assembly line like thing. It wasn't no kind of strenuous work.

Q. For what period of time did you work there?

A. That was summer work too.

Q. What was your pay rate while at Honeywell?

A. Two dollars.

    Mr. Clarke: You are going to have to yell a little bit louder, because I'm having a little bit of trouble hearing you, too.

    The Witness: About two dollars an hour.

Q. (By Mr. Fredricks) Did you take an employment physical, exam—

A. No, I didn't.

Q. — before going to work for Honeywell —

A. No.

Q. — while working at Honeywell?

A. No.

Q. Did you make out an application for that employment?

A. Yes, I did.

Q. And was there any inquiry about the status of your health or physical condition in that application?

A. No, there wasn't.

Q. Okay. What was your condition, your physical condition, when you made your application to work at Honeywell. Were you having any problems?

A. The application wasn't like that, you know, as far as your health. The application wasn't — you know, it didn't ask about your health, you know, your background, nothing like that.

Q. I'm asking you now what was your condition when you made out that application.

A. Back trouble and neck.

Q. Back and leg trouble.

A. Back and neck.

Q. And neck. Anything else?

A. That was the most — main thing at that time.

Q. Did you have to make out an appliction for your work when you started working for Hearns Auditorium?

A. No.

Q. Have you had any other employment since August of 1979?

A. No. I was working — last year I was working at the Children's Theatre and —

Q. Where?

A. Detroit, South Detroit. That was at — at the Mann. No, not the Mann, it's on 3rd Avenue, the Art Institute, Detroit Art Institute, and I was working for the Children's Theatre. That's combined together.

Q. How long did you work there?

A. That was summer work also.

Q. What was your pay rate at the time?

A. Two dollars an hour.

Q. You worked forty hours a week, did you?

A. Yes.

Q. When you were at Honeywell, did you work forty hours a week?

A. Yes, it was.

Q. Did you work regularly at all of these jobs during the summer months? Did you work regularly, or did you have to miss a lot of time?

A. Well, I was getting hot pack treatments at Dr. Peterson's office.

Q. You mean after work?

A. Well, sometimes I have to go on work because his office is only open in the afternoon.

Q. Other than the times you went for back treatments, did you have to miss any time from work?

A. Yes. A little sometimes, yes.

Q. Do you have a record of what time you missed from work?

A. At home when I started I did, yes.

Q. Do you have that with you?

A. I don't have it with me, no.

Q. What chiropractor were you seeing?

A. Dr. Peterson.

Q. Thomas Peterson?

A. Thomas Peterson.

Q. I understand he is a chiropractor?

A. I beg your pardon.

Q. Do you understand that he is a chiropractor?

A. He was my doctor, I don't know what he was.

Q. I thought you said you were seeing a chiropractor. Did I misunderstand?

Mr. Lang: (nods head.)

Mr. Clarke: Maybe he was talking about therapist. Were you talking about the guy that gave you the heat and all that stuff?

The Witness: I don't know his name.

Q. (By Mr. Fredricks) Bill Freeman?

A. Yes, something like that.

Q. William Freeman or something like that.

A. Yes, I believe so. You see, when I was going to Wahlstrom I was getting treatment too before I seen him.

Q. You completed high school?

A. Yes.

Q. What high school did you attend?

A. Central, Detroit Central.

Q. When were you graduated?

A. Seventy-nine.

Q. Did you participate in sports in any school?

A. That was '78, I'm sorry. Sometimes, yes.

Q. What sports?

A. Basketball and just any — really any intramural thing. I didn't go out for —

Q. Were you ever injured in any sports?

A. No.

Q. Have you been involved in any other motor vehicle accidents other than the one of August 17th, 1979?

A. No.

Q. At any time?

A. No.

Q. Have you ever been in a car when it has collided with another car, or object, or —

A. No. No.

Q. Even if you weren't hurt.

A. No.

Q. This is the only motor vehicle accident you have ever been in?

A. Yes, it was.

Q. All right. Have you been injured in any other accidents of any kind at any time?

A. No, I haven't. Any other automobile accidents?

Q. No, no, any other accidents of any kind —

A. No.

Q. — at any time where you hurt yourself any way.

A. Well, I was just in an accident —

Q. All right.

A. — about two weeks ago, maybe a month ago.

Q. Where did the accident happen and —

A. On Traverse.

Q. What?

A. Traverse. Exact address I don't know. It was somewhere down Traverse Avenue.

Q. What happened?

A. Crossed the center line.

Q. Was this an automobile accident?

A. Yes.

Q. Oh. Well, you tell me, describe for me what — were you a driver?

A. Yes, I was.

Q. And what happened?

A. I was fixing a calendar watch and I was — the passenger was fixing my calendar watch, and she turned it — messed it up, and I looked down at it and went in the other lane.

Q. Was this a head-on type collision?

A. Yes.

Q. Did the police investigate?

A. Yes, they did.

Q. What time of the day did it happen?

A. In the afternoon, about twelve o'clock, one o'clock.

Q. It was daylight at that time?

A. Yes, it was.

Q. Who was your passenger?

A. Rebecca Parsons.

Q. Where does she live?

A. Cleveland.

Q. Cleveland?

A. North Cleveland.

Q. Where in North Cleveland?

A. I forget the address.

Q. Will you get that for me or get it to your attorney?

  Mr. Clarke: No, I'm not going to get — why don't you find out if he got hurt. If he got hurt, then I will get you what you want, but you are dinging around on a fender-bender, I suspect, and if that's where you are going —

Q. (By Mr. Fredricks) Were you hurt at all in the accident?

A. Just stitches on my lip.

Q. You struck your face against something inside the car?

A. Yes.

Q. Where did you get the stitches?

A. In the lip and also chin.

Q. Lip and chin.

A. Yes.

Q. Any other injuries in the accident?

A. And teeth, my teeth.

Q. What happened to your teeth?

A. They were all out, just about. Oh, they are all loose, you know.

Q. Lower front teeth were lossened?

A. Lower and upper.

Q. Any other injuries?

A. That was about all. I just hit the steering wheel.

Q. Have any headaches following the accident?

A. No.

Q. You haven't had any headaches since that accident a month ago?

A. No, I haven't.

Q. What doctors did you go to, for example?

A. General Hospital.

Q. Where else?

A. That was it.

Q. All of the treatment you have received was at General Hospital?

A. Yes.

Q. Have you been to Dr. Thomas Peterson since that accident?

A. No.

Q. Earlier I asked you about any other automobile accidents —

A. Yes.

Q. — and you didn't mention this.

A. Well, I didn't — you know, I really forgot about the accident. It didn't, you know, mean nothing.

Q. All right. Now, you search your mind; are there any other automobile accidents?

A. No.

Q. Do you have a driver's license?

A. Yes, I do.

Q. What's the number on it? Would you get it out and check it for me? Now, have you been involved in any other accidents of any kind? I'm not referring —

A. You mean a passenger — no, I haven't, nothing.

Q. In no sports — you have never fallen down and hurt yourself, you have never burned yourself, you have never cut yourself, you have never had any other trouble?

A. No.

Q. All right. Have you been hospitalized at any time in your life other than for childbirth?

A. Just for asthma.

Q. When was that?

A. That was — I was born with it.

Q. When were you hospitalized for it?

A. I don't remember the exact date. Last year some time. Two years before that. I stayed in the hospital with asthma.

Q. What hospital did you go to?

A. General Hospital.

Q. Have you ever made a claim against anyone for injuries other than this accident?

A. No.

Q. After completing high school you went to college.

A. Yes.

Q. What colleges have you attended?

A. Wahlstrom in Uhler, Michigan.

Q. What years did you attend?

A. Seventy-nine, '80.

Q. Did you have a physical examination at that college?

A. Yes.

Q. Did you have any treatment for your back condition?

A. Yes, I did.

Q. What course of study did you pursue there? Liberal Arts?

A. Liberal Arts.

Q. All right. Did you complete one academic year at Wahlstrom?

A. It was more or less a program like for people who aren't capable of going to college but may, you know, learn something at college, you know, if they have the opportunity to go. Do you understand?

Q. Is there a name for that program?

A. It was called Demos.

Q. What?

A. Demos. D-e-m-o something. Demos. I don't know how to spell that.

Q. What month did you start then, September?

A. Yes.

Q. And —

A. Seventy-nine, '80.

Q. What month did you complete the course?

A. I went the whole — full two years.

Q. Okay. Have you gone to another institution, college?

A. I'm going to the University at the present time.

Q. Well, you mean you have actually registered for class?

A. Yes.

Q. Will you be starting as a freshman?

A. Sophomore and junior, half and half now.

Q. Didn't you attend at Chicago?

A. No, I haven't. I seen it in the thing but I changed it. It was at Wahlstrom.

Q. I see. Did you live on campus when you were at Wahlstrom?

A. Yes, I did.

Q. Have you had your physical examination for the University?

A. Last year I did.

Q. When was that?

A. I don't know. It was at the beginning of the school year.

Q. Have you received any treatment for any physical condition or problems at the University Health Service?

A. No, I haven't.

Q. Or Hospital?

A. No.

Q. All right. Now, referring to the accident of August 17th, 1979, that happened early on a Sunday morning, didn't it?

A. Sunday morning?

Q. Saturday night or Sunday morning.

A. Yes.

Q. Do you recall what time it happened?

A. No, I can't. It was — I think it was about one, one o'clock.

Q. Okay. It was dark out at the time, wasn't it?

A. Yes, it was.

Q. And would it be consistent with your recollection that it was about 1:35 in the morning?

A. Probably so.

Q. Who were you with that night?

A. Carolyn Jones. She was driving. And a Ruby Watts, another girl, was in the back seat.

Q. Who was the other girl?

A. Ruby Watts.

Q. Ruby what?

A. Watts, W-a-t-t-s.

Q. W-a-t-t-s? Where does she live?

A. I have no idea.

Q. Where were you going at the time?

A. Probably home.

Q. Probably?

A. Yes.

Q. Don't you remember?

A. It was probably my house. I'm pretty sure it was. See, I live about four blocks from the accident, and we were going in the direction. I believe we were. She was taking me home, I'm pretty sure.

Q. Where had you been?

A. Probably at some dance or something. At a dance.

Q. Where?

A. Downtown. I forget the name of the club. I believe we went, you know, here and there. Let's see —

Q. Did you have anything —

A. No, no, no, this was a house party. I'm sorry. It was a house party, a get-together.

Q. Did you have anything alcoholic to drink?

A. No. They didn't have anything, I'm sure they didn't. No.

Q. How about Miss Jones?

A. No, she doesn't drink.

Q. Were you dating that night? Was this a date with either of the two girls?

A. Well, I knew Carolyn from — we grew up together, just about. Well, we went to school together, high school, grade school. She just stopped and picked me up.

Q. All right. At the time of the accident, you were riding in a Buick automobile?

A. (nods head.)

Q. And you were traveling in an easterly direction on 38th Street.

A. Yes.

Q. And the other car was in a northerly direction on 2nd Avenue.

A. Yes.

Q. Do you recall whether Miss Jones put on her turn signals as she approached this intersection?

A. We were going straight. We were going straight.

Q. Did she put on her turn signals, or don't you know?

A. I'm sure she didn't. I'm sure she didn't, because wasn't no sense in turning, you know, that way.

Q. How far were you going to continue going straight ahead?

A. Oh, I would say we were going to my house, and I live about four blocks away on Park Avenue, and I believe it happened on 2nd Avenue. Well, I was staying at 38th and Park at that time.

Q. Well, all right. What happened? How did the cars come together, do you know?

A. No. I was hit on my side, on the right side of the car.

Q. Did you see the Smith car at any time before the collision?

A. No.

Q. How fast was Miss Jones driving?

A. I didn't look at the speedometer. We weren't speeding or in a rush to go anywhere, you know. She normally drives slow anyways, the speed limit.

Q. Did anyone say anything before the collision occurred? Any exclamations?

A. No. Just hit. Surprised everybody.

Q. How would you describe the collision?

A. Sudden. Just happened, you know. I didn't — you know, surprised me.

Q. All right. What happened to the car in which you were riding, the Buick, when the collision did occur?

A. Seemed like it just pushed the car around in a circle, seemed like. Seemed like it just went around, you know.

Q. Are you saying the car was pushed sideways?

A. Yes. Like when it hit, seemed like I was — seemed like pain was just in my body, and I was just in pain, you know, for a second or two, and the car was just moving around.

Q. What was its position when the car came to rest?

A. It was in this way (indicating), turned like that all the way around.

Q. Well, the car had been traveling east, easterly?

A. (Nods head.)

Q. What way was it facing when it came to rest?

A. South. It might even have spun the whole time, you know, one whole time. Seemed like it was spinning a long time and sliding.

Q. Now, the other car stopped right at the point of impact, didn't it?

A. I — I thought it was down — across the intersection, I'm sure. I'm pretty sure it did.

Q. Did Miss Jones's car come to a stop outside of the intersection? Did it continue through the intersection and —

A. It was knocked past the intersection. Spun down, you know, like, towards west, east, went down. Like it spun and sort of pushed it forward down the street in a way and spun it too. Seemed like it happened — it did happen like that. Then it came to a stop.

Q. East of the intersection.

A. Yes.

Q. Is that your testimony?

A. It went past the intersection, a little way past it, I think.

Q. So that would be east of the intersection.

A. Yes. Going towards the river, that's — yes, right.

Q. All right. So that we are clear on this, you say that the Jones car came to rest east of the east curb line of 2nd Avenue.

A. It what? Pardon me.

Q. You say that the car came to rest east of the east curb line of 2nd Avenue.

A. Yes.

Q. Okay. Now, what happened to you when the collision occurred?

A. As soon as it hit?

Q. Right.

A. Seemed like I was in pain, and seemed like I was — seemed like I was just in pain for a short time, about a second or two, and like everything had blacked out for a second or two as I was in pain.

Q. Well, did you strike yourself against anything in the car, against the windshield?

A. Against the door, that side door I believe, or probably in the corner.

Q. You what?

A. Or probably in the corner of the — not the windshield. You know, like towards — kitty korner over.

Q. Do you remember that clearly?

A. It was — I know it was on the side, what I'm saying. It wasn't the windshield. I didn't hit the windshield at all.

Q. Did you have any accident markings on your person, any cuts, bruises, bumps?

A. Yes.

Q. What?

A. Legs — well, like everything was sore, but it was — you know, like — seemed like this side (indicating), and my legs were sore, like they were bruised and stuff.

Q. Well, Mr. Johnson, you have told me you were sore, but I want to know if there were any bumps or bruises, anything that someone else could see or feel.

A. I think it was just skinned, more or less.

Q. Skinned?

A. Skinned like.

Q. An abrasion?

A. Pardon.

Q. You mean an abrasion or rubbing of the skin?

A. Yes, abrasion.

Q. Where the skin wasn't actually broken, but it was just an abrasion of the skin, is that what you are saying?

A. Yes, I guess abrasion, I don't know. It was like — you know, it was skinned.

Q. And you are indicating that this was some place on your right arm.

A. It was on my — down here (indicating) on my chin.

Q. Now you are indicating your right chin.

A. Yes. Seemed like most of the pain was up here. Seemed like I hit the door, but my legs was hurting too.

Q. You are now indicating your right arm near your right elbow.

A. Well, seemed like my whole side was hurting, and my leg somehow was hurting too.

Q. Now you are indicating your whole right side was hurting.

A. Yes. Seemed it was a lot — I really don't know exactly — all I remember is something like my legs were hurting, too.

Q. Both legs. Is that what you are telling us?

A. I really don't remember. Just seems like it was hurting. My legs, they didn't — I didn't write it down or nothing what was hurting. It was a long time ago, and I don't remember exactly what was scratched or nothing like this.

Q. All right. You didn't notice any pain in your back or your neck immediately following the accident, did you?

A. No.

Q. The police came and investigated, didn't they?

A. Yes.

Q. And what did you tell the police about your condition?

A. Nothing. When I was walking around I thought I was all right.

Q. Did you seek any medical examinations or treatments right after the accident?

A. No.

Q. Well, didn't you go to General Hospital?

A. Yes. Well, like they were — they were busy like always, and they just took my temperature and told me to leave and — I could leave.

Q. Well, now you must listen to my questions carefully. I asked you if you sought any medical examinations. Well, you did —

A. The doctor — yes, I did —

Q. You went to General Hospital.

A. Yes.

Q. All right.

A. But I mean — go ahead.

Q. But they didn't do anything for you other than take your temperature, is that what you say?

A. No. Right.

Q. When did you next seek any medical examinations or treatment?

A. About a month or two after.

Q. Who did you see?

A. Dr. Peterson.

Q. How did you happen to go to Dr. Peterson?

A. Well, he is the only doctor that I knew over North, and I believe Carolyn told me about him because she was going there too.

Q. Who?

A. Carolyn Jones, the driver of the car.

Q. Okay. Had you ever been to Peterson before?

A. No.

Q. When did you first have any symptoms of neck problems, pains or discomfort?

A. About a month or two after when I went to see Dr. Peterson.

Q. Okay. That's when you first really noticed any pain or problem in your neck.

A. Yes.

Q. Okay. All right. When did you first notice any pain or discomfort or any problem in your back?

A. About the time when I went to see him.

Mr. Clarke: You mean you went for thirty days and you didn't have any trouble, and all of a sudden one day you had trouble with your back?

The Witness: Seemed like that.

Mr. Clarke: I don't believe that.

Mr. Fredricks: Pardon me.

Mr. Clarke: You mean you didn't have any trouble the day of the accident or the day afterwards?

The Witness: No.

Mr. Lang: Objected to as leading and suggestive.

Mr. Fredricks: Tom —

Mr. Clarke: Well, fantastic. I don't believe him.

Mr. Lang: Whether you believe him or not, that's what he said.

Mr. Clarke: I don't think he understands the question.

Mr. Lang: It's clear that he does.

The Witness: I mean it didn't hurt just one month later. It was such a long time ago, like it — problems.

Mr. Clarke: Well, they are trapping you. The way you have answered these questions, that's the end of your lawsuit. That's basically what they have trapped you into here. Now, if you understand —

Mr. Fredricks: Now, that isn't true.

Mr. Clarke: That's true.

Mr. Fredricks: The word "trap" is not at all appropriate here, Tom.

Mr. Clarke: Well, it is when it's obvious to me he doesn't understand your question, that's all.

And if you understand what you are doing, then you can answer any way you want, but I want you to understand what you are saying here. That's why I'm here, to make sure you understand your questions.

The Witness: See, it was —

Mr. Fredricks: Let's see if we can't clarify this.

Mr. Clarke: Why don't you let him answer.

Q. (By Mr. Fredricks) About the time that you first had difficulties with your neck and low back is when you went to see Dr. Peterson. Whether that was a week after or a month after, that's when you started having difficulty, and you went to see him at that time because you did notice that you were having difficulty.

A. Well, let me say — like I probably had some pain first. It was a long time ago, and I don't exactly remember how — how many days or what it was when I went to see Dr. Peterson after the accident or nothing like this. Like the pain probably came a week after, and I probably didn't think nothing of it, you know —

Q. All right.

A. — and it was probably there. I mean if a pain is just there, you don't go the same day, you see. I mean this is the way I looked at it. And from the questions you asked, you know, it was probably a month when I seen a doctor, a month or two months after when I went to see him to —

Q. But I'm asking you not when you went to see Dr. Peterson but when you first became aware of any discomfort in your neck or back, and you have said it was about a month, and now —

A. I mean I seen Dr. Peterson about a month or two after.

Q. That's what you meant.

A. I really don't even know exactly how long that was, exactly.

Q. But now it is your recollection that it was about a week or more after the accident before you first had any difficulty with your neck or your back, is that correct?

A. It was probably a week or so after I had trouble with my back?

Q. Yes.

A. I don't know exactly the — I really don't know. It probably was a week when I first felt pain somewhere.

Q. Now, do you recall if you were doing something particular, you were engaged in some activity when you first noticed this back pain where you were walking up a stairs, or lifting something, or driving a car, or —

A. I really don't remember.

Q. By the way, when you had this accident about a month ago, were you driving your own automobile?

A. No, I wasn't.

Q. Whose car were you driving?

A. The girl's car.

Q. Ruby's?

A. No.

Q. What was her name?

A. Rebecca Ann Parsons.

Q. Rebecca. It was her car.

A. Yes.

Q. Do you know who she had her insurance with?

A. No, I don't.

Q. Well, you must have talked with some insurance man —

A. Yes.

Q. — since the accident.

A. I don't remember his name though.

Q. Did he give you a card or —

A. He called on the phone.

Q. Okay.

Tom, do you have a copy of that — did the police investigate that accident?

Mr. Clarke: No, but if you have any authorization you want signed at all, why don't you give them to him now and I will have him check them.

Mr. Lang: What was the name of the person you had the accident with?

The Witness: I beg your pardon.

Mr. Lang: What was the name of the person you had the accident with?

The Witness: The other person. I forget her name. She was an elderly lady.

Mr. Lang: Do you know where she lives?

The Witness: South Detroit.

Q. (By Mr. Fredricks) All right. When you first noticed this pain in your back, or when you first noticed pain in your neck, what did it feel like. Describe it for me.

A. Just seemed like a sharp pain.

Q. Where was it located?

A. It was just a pain all over, seemed like. Seemed like I was paralyzed maybe — if that's the right term to use. Seemed like it was just — I can't even explain it.

Q. All right. Was this pain localized at any particular place in your back?

Mr. Clarke: You better explain what localized means, you know.

Q. (By Mr. Fredricks) You know —

A. I don't — I really couldn't tell you.

Q. Was the pain in your neck localized or at any particular spot in your back? Was it on one side or the other?

Mr. Clarke: What he is trying to say is what part of your neck — when you talk about your back, he wants to know whether it's in the middle of your back, or in the low back, or upper back. He wants to know what part of your neck or your back you are talking about.

The Witness: When I was going to say pain, it seems like a pain all over, I — you know, I didn't stop and think of where it was at, no, or nothing like this, because at the time I was being shook around at the same time.

Q. (By Mr. Fredricks) At the time you were being what?

A. At the time of the accident, you know. There was pain, and I was being shaken around at the same time, and I couldn't tell you exactly, you know, where the pain was. It was just a pain in the head all over.

Q. You have indicated that there was some period of time elapsed after the accident before —

A. Yes.

Q. — you became aware of pain in your neck and your back. Now I want to know when you did become aware of your neck pain or your back pain, where was it located?

A. Oh, you mean when I — after the accident.

Q. Yes.

A. Yes.

Q. It was a week or more after the accident, as I understand your testimony. Tell me what you felt.

A. It was in the lower back, pain in the lower back.

Q. All right. And was it on one side or the other? Was it on your left side or right side?

A. It was down the center of my back, the spinal cord.

Q. Right in the middle.

A. Yes.

Q. Was it below your belt?

A. It was down in the lower back.

Q. Below your belt line.

A. Lower part of my back.

Q. Was it below your belt line or above it?

A. Is this (indicating) below my belt line?

Q. This (indicating) is your belt.

A. Is this my belt (indicating), below my belt, or what?

Q. Yes, that's your — you have placed your hand well below your belt line.

A. That's where it was. That's where it was.

Q. All right, fine.

A. And my neck right here (indicating).

Q. Now, was there any particular activity, or were you doing something when you first noticed this pain in your low back?

A. I don't remember.

Q. All right. When you first noticed this pain in your low back, did it limit you in any way? Were your activities limited? Were your movements limited?

A. What do you mean, limited? What do you mean, was I limited? Could I walk?

Q. Did you have to go to bed because of the back pain, or did you have to stop swimming, or did you — is there anything that it did affect you in any way?

A. Like when it hurt, I just — well, it was — it would hurt. Like when I'm sitting at school. For instance, when I first noticed it I was in school or sitting in the chair.

Q. All right.

A. And it was just uncomfortable to sit in a chair.

Q. All right. Now, this would have been at Wahlstrom.

A. Yes, it was — well, like — it couldn't have been, because I seen Dr. Peterson before I went to Wahlstrom, and he said — let's see — I don't know how — I seen Dr. Peterson before I went to Wahlstrom, I was getting therapy at the clinic before I went to Wahlstrom, and now that — when I noticed it how it acted. Then I couldn't tell, but like when I was at school when I was sitting down at the chair, I remember that, you know, because I was always turning and stuff.

Q. How does your low back feel right now?

A. Uncomfortable.

Q. Well, is there pain in it?

A. Just seemed like a slight — slight pain.

Q. Slight pain.

A. (Nods head.)

Q. Does that keep you from doing anything?

A. No. I go — I still do what I do.

Q. How about your neck, how is that?

A. It's fair. It's all right.

Q. It's okay.

A. (Nods head.)

Q. All right. You are not having any trouble with it now?

A. No.

Q. When is the last time you had any trouble with your neck?

A. I was in the hospital about last month or month — about two months ago, month and a half ago, for treatment.

Q. Which hospital?

A. Mt. Sinai.

Q. And you did have trouble with your neck at that time?

A. Yes. My neck and back.

Q. And is that Mr. William Freeman again who gave you therapy?

A. This was in the hospital.

Q. Yes. He worked at — or he — at least he did work at Mt. Sinai.

A. No, I was in traction, they put me in traction.

Q. All right. The heat packs and traction seemed to help.

A. It was all right. Like after I got out of the hospital well, last — about a week ago I drove — well, rode down to Missouri, and it was uncomfortable sitting in the car.

Q. You were what?

A. It was uncomfortable sitting in the car, you know, long distance. Like, you know, drove to Missouri.

Q. Where in Missouri?

A. Monroe.

Q. Monroe.

A. Monroe.

Q. What did you go to Missouri for?

A. To see some people.

Q. Who?

A. Some people, some friends.

Q. Who did you go to see?

A. Some friends.

Q. What's their names?

A. I forget their last name.

Q. Who did you go with?

A. Some friends. Friend of mine and his family. See, they were — I just went for the ride just to go, just to go out of town, and it was their cousins and things.

Q. Whose car?

A. Their car.

Q. And what is their name?

A. Cross. Cross.

Q. First name.

A. I forget their first name, lady's first name. I went with a family and a friend of mine my age.

Q. And what's his name?

A. Brian Cross.

Q. What?

A. Brian Cross.

Does that make any difference who I go down there with?

Mr. Clarke: You tell him exactly what it was, that's all. You just tell him the truth, that's all I care about.

Q. (By Mr. Fredricks) Was it on that trip then — that was the last time you had any discomfort in your neck?

Mr. Clarke: I think he is talking about his back.

The Witness: My back. See, I —

Q. (By Mr. Fredricks) I thought you told me it was a month ago that you last had any problem with your low back.

A. No. It was my neck.

Q. Your neck.

A. My neck is pretty much better now, but my back I still have some pain. Like I feel a slight pain now in my lower back.

Q. All right.

A. And during the trip down to Monroe, Missouri, I felt discomfort in my back on the way down and on the way back, and —

Q. And what month did you make that trip, July of 1981?

A. It was this month.

Q. August of 1981.

A. Yes.

Q. Did you seek any treatment for your back?

A. After this?

Q. While on that trip.

A. No.

Q. Did you take —

A. I was just taking hot baths and stuff.

Q. I see.

A. And I got a massage a couple times.

Q. You did?

A. Well, from, you know, his mother. She rubbed it down with Ben Gay and stuff like that.

Q. After the trip.

A. Well, when I went down, got down to Monore.

Q. Did you say your mother?

A. No, this — the dude's mother massaged my back when I was down there.

Q. Okay.

A. Mrs. Cross massaged my back.

Q. Have you had any military service?

A. No.

Q. Have you had a physical exam for military service?

A. No. See, I was going to school and they just gave me a deferment for going to school.

Q. Do you have a military classification?

A. No, I don't.

Q. You don't have a military identification card or anything.

A. No.

Q. Have you ever been convicted of a crime?

A. No.

Q. Did you ever see or talk to this Smith after the night of the accident?

A. No.

Q. Did you talk to Mr. Smith at the scene of the accident?

A. No.

Q. Was there anyone in the car, Miss Jones' car, besides you and Ruby?

Q. No, just the three of us. Three of us.

Q. Do you have any plans to see Dr. Thomas Peterson again?

A. Well, I called him the other day, but he wasn't in, and I just wanted to talk to him because I haven't talked to him after I came out of the hospital. See, like when I came out of the hospital then I — he went into the hospital.

Q. He himself went in?

Q. Yes. And like I sort of tried to avoid going over to — I have just been sitting in a hot bath, hot water.

Q. You can move your neck, and your back is all right now, as I understand your testimony.

A. Yes.

Q. And it's your low back at this moment, you have slight pain in your low back.

A. Yes.

Q. Does that get worse at times?

A. At night.

Q. At night.

A. Yes.

Q. What happens at night that causes your back to bother you?

A. Seems like there is a pain all down my back.

Q. Well, what are you doing, or what position causes your back problem?

A. I got a water bed, and it still hurts.

Q. You have a water bed?

Q. Yes.

Q. How long have you had that?

A. About two months.

Q. Did it seem to help at all?

A. Not really. See, first I was sleeping on a mattress with a board up under, and that didn't seem to help it either.

Q. Did someone suggest that you try a water bed?

A. No.

Q. It was your own idea.

A. Yes.

Q. Does the water bed seem to hurt your back?

A. Not really. See, it hurts once in a while at night. It didn't hurt every night.

Q. I see. So usually your back feels better during the day than it does at night.

A. Sometimes I don't notice it during the day, sometimes I notice it during the day, sometimes at nights —

Q. What are you doing during the daytime that causes you to have back problems?

A. See, I sit down, I will be working in the office in Hearns Auditorium, and that's a lot of sitting, but I still walk around, you know, to — just to walk around, move my back around and stuff.

Q. The walking around seems to help.

A. Well, it's just moving around, if it —

Q. It does help.

A. It probably helps a little bit just to get up and move around.

Q. Does it?

A. Yes, it does. But when I sit down again for about five minutes, half hour again, I can feel the pain again.

Q. The pain in your legs cleared up quite soon after the accident?

A. Seemed like that came back little bit later too, pain in the other side of the leg.

Q. Your legs don't bother you now.

A. Not right now, no.

Q. When is the last time either of your legs bothered you? Been a long time?

A. Yes. About when I was seeing Dr. Peterson, getting therapy along in that time. Not the last — it probably was the last one. I haven't seen him —

Q. For about a year?

A. No, it hasn't been that long. About three — three or four months.

Q. Have you taken any drug store medicines or —

A. Prescriptions?

Q. Prescription, medicines?

A. Yes.

Q. When is the last time?

A. About four months ago.

Q. What drug store do you get your medicine at?

A. I didn't get the medicine, this girl got it for me. It was just pain pills.

Q. Miss Jones?

A. Yes.

Q. The girl —

A. The one I'm staying with now, she went to the drug store and got it. It was a pain pill though.

Q. Is it her prescription or yours?

A. Prescription Dr. Peterson wrote me.

Q. And when you had taken this medicine, why did you take it?

A. Why did I take it?

Q. Why?

A. For the pain.

Q. Where in?

A. My back pain.

Q. All right. Not your legs, not your neck, not for any headaches.

A. It was just — just a pain pill, Darvon. It's just for the pain. If you have pain in your leg, you know, supposed to knock it all out.

Q. The reason you have taken the Darvon is for your low back.

A. Yes, sir.

Q. All right. And that's all.

A. Yes, sir.

Q. Okay. You haven't had any particular problem with headaches following this accident, have you?

A. Yes.

Q. You have.

A. Yes.

Q. For what period of time did you have headaches?

A. Some time I had it all evening. Well —

Q. I mean for — was it a month following the accident, two months, three months?

A. I couldn't — I couldn't tell you exactly. It's — it should be in Dr. —

Q. I'm not asking for an exact period of time, I'm asking for some —

A. I really couldn't tell you. It should be in Dr. Peterson's record, because I let him know when it happened.

Q. When is the last time you recall being bothered by a headache, long, long time ago, over a year ago?

A. I still have them. Well, like when I went on that trip I had headaches going on the way down, something like a migraine headache. I remember the last time I had a terrible headache. Then again it was three, four months ago I was getting headaches, a headache, too.

Q. When?

A. About two or three months ago I was getting a headache.

Q. Did you have headaches while you were at Wahlstrom College?

A. I believe — I believe so.

Q. You don't recall now.

A. I'm pretty sure I did, because I remember getting a headache, you know, once in a while, serious headache.

Q. Like once a week?

A. No. I couldn't say exactly when — once a week or every two weeks. It was just a headache, you know, have a — a bad headache, you know, pain, headache.

Q. How often?

A. How often? What do you mean, how often?

Q. How often, when you were in college at Wahlstrom did you have a bad headache?

A. Well, I can't answer that, you know, too perfect.

Q. Do you have any photographs about the accident, connected with the accident?

A. Do I have any pictures?

Q. Yes.

A. No.

Q. Do you claim that you have lost any income as a result of the accident?

A. Work?

Q. (Nods head.)

A. Well, working, and taking the bus over there.

Q. Pardon me.

A. Taking the bus over from wherever I was at, taking a bus over to Dr. Peterson's office. And going too from Wahlstrom I was getting treatment, I had to —

Q. All right. You are claiming that you have lost some income.

A. Income and schooling too.

Q. Well, I'm not concerned about school time, I'm concerned about income right now. Do you file a tax return?

A. Did I this past one?

Q. Yes. Have you filed a tax return at any time since the August —

A. Yes.

Q. — accident?

A. Yes.

Q. Federal tax returns? You have.

A. (Nods head.)

Q. All right.

Tom, I will prepare authorizations for tax returns, and also an authorization for the accident report, and I will send them to you.

Mr. Clarke: Why don't you have him sign them now. Just sign any blank authorizations you have for any reason, because I would like to know about these things too. You can fill them in.

While you are looking, my notes show you were at the hospital for four hours.

The Witness: At General?

Mr. Clarke: Yes.

The Witness: I was there a long time just sitting.

Mr. Clarke: My notes also show you saw a doctor the next day. Who did you see the next day?

The Witness: A doctor.

Mr. Clarke: Yes, that's what this shows.

The Witness: I don't know. If it was anybody, it was Dr. Peterson, but I don't remember. I didn't see nobody at General.

(Whereupon a discussion was had off the record.)

Q. (By Mr. Fredricks) Have you ever had any injections in your neck or shoulders with a needle administered by any doctors?

A. No. No, I haven't.

Q. Pardon me.

A. No, I haven't.

Q. Have you ever had any electromyogram tests where they put a needle in your muscles and —

A. Just in the head, scalp.

Q. You have had that in your scalp?

A. Yes.

Q. And when was that done?

A. When I went to the doctor.

Q. For what?

A. When I went to the hospital for Dr. Peterson, at Mt. Sinai Hospital.

Q. And was that soon after the accident then, or when?

A. No, this was recently when I just went to the hospital about two months ago, month and a half ago, for treatment, treatments in the hospital.

Q. That was at Mt. Sinai.

A. Yes, it was.

Q. And that's the only place you have had any such tests.

A. Yes.

Mr. Clarke: I notice there is a bill here for injection something into your neck muscles; what's that for?

The Witness: What is it? What is it?

Mr. Clarke: Did it in the hospital, apparently.

The Witness: Which hospital?

Mr. Clarke: June 21st. It says injection, superior angles. Apparently into your neck.

The Witness: That was at Mt. Sinai.

Mr. Clarke: Yes.

The Witness: That's what it was then, at Mt. Sinai.

Mr. Clarke: You just told him you never had any injections. I want to know what you are talking about.

The Witness: I just seen it in the head and up here (indicating), but I don't know what he stuck down here (indicating).

Q. (By Mr. Fredricks) Do you know what I mean by a hypodermic needle, where you get a —

A. Blood thing?

Q. Yes. Needle that goes into your arm and they inject something under the skin or into the muscle.

A. All I remember is when they put pins all in the head and stuff, and —

Q. You don't remember Dr. Peterson ever injecting any needles into your neck or back?

A. No, I don't.

Q. Okay.

A. That one right there — they might have put some up here (indicating), but I don't remember.

Q. Sometimes he doesn't do it, Tom, and he records it in his records, so I'm not surprised.

Mr. Clarke: He charged twenty bucks for doing it.

Mr. Fredricks: Yes.

Mr. Clarke: I got to know, if he didn't do it, I want to know about it.

The Witness: Where was it I said those pins were at?

Mr. Clarke: I don't have to tell. We are asking you the questions. You were there, I wasn't.

The Witness: I had pins up here (indicating). Probably if they had some here (indicating), you know, I didn't feel it too much.

Q. (By Mr. Fredricks) You never had any problems and any discomfort in your throat area of your neck, have you? You didn't ever develop any pain in the front portion of your neck, did you?

A. Not that I recall.

Q. Okay.

A. Well, it was just —

Q. Just in the back of the neck.

A. You mean as far as strep throat or anything like this?

Q. No, I mean following the accident. Any injury to the front portion of your neck?

A. No, I can't — if it was, it was slight. It was just — what Dr. Peterson said it was, I don't know if it was here — you mean did I feel pain exactly right here (indicating) somewhere up in here (indicating).

Q. Yes.

A. No.

Q. Have you had strep throat or some problem like that?

A. One time, long time ago.

Q. Dr. Peterson didn't treat you for that?

A. No.

Q. You have been treated with some physical therapy at Mt. Sinai Hospital, and traction.

A. Yes.

Q. Have you had therapy or traction anywhere else?

A. At his office, at his clinic, and at Wahlstrom, downtown clinic.

Q. What clinic downtown? Was that Kennan's?

A. No. This was in Uhler, Michigan.

Q. Oh. What clinic?

A. It was at the hospital, at the Uhler Hospital down in Uhler, Michigan.

Q. But you said there was a clinic downtown in Uhler.

A. I meant Uhler Hospital, and there is a clinic there.

Q. At the hospital.

A. I believe so, yes.

Q. You saw some private doctors in Uhler.

A. Yes.

Q. Do you remember their names?

A. No, I don't.

    Mr. Fredricks: Do you have that, Tom?

    Mr. Clarke: No, except it's on the — I sent your adjuster the bill for some X rays down there, and I assume from that you can get a lead as to who ordered the X rays. I don't even know that.

Q. (By Mr. Fredricks) Right. At the present time you are engaging in all of the activities that you used to participate in and enjoy before this accident.

A. Yes.

Q. You are not claiming that you are now handicapped or prevented from doing things that you would otherwise do due to this accident?

A. Well, I — you know, I know my back is hurting, I won't be picking up something that's heavy or something. I try to use some common sense what to do and what not to do with my back.

Q. All right. But you can throw a soft ball and you can —

A. Yes.

Q. If you enjoyed ice skating, you would go ice skating, or if you bowled you would go bowling, and if you want to take a trip like to Missouri, you go ahead and do it.

A. Yes.

Q. Okay. Have you made any other trips —

A. No.

Q. — out of the state or out of town since?

A. Yes. Yes.

Q. Where?

A. San Antonio.

Q. Texas?

A. Yes.

Q. When?

A. Right after school was out.

Q. And what was the purpose for that trip?

A. Just going down to San Antonio, Texas.

Q. Did you make this trip by car?

A. Yes.

Q. Who did you go with?

A. Some friend of mine. It was three in the car.

Q. Well, who were the friends?

A. Some friends I went to school with.

Q. I'm interested in names.

A. They were no kin or nothing like —

Q. Pardon me.

A. They were no kin to me or nothing like that.

Q. All right. But what were their names? Was it Miss Jones? Was it Ruby?

A. No.

Q. Who?

A. Cooley. Cooley. They are from out of town. They are from out of town, from Des Moines.

Q. Oh, okay. Anyone else or any other trips?

A. No.

Q. How long were you gone to San Antonio?

A. Just down and back.

    Mr. Fredricks: I believe that's all the questions I have.

EXAMINATION

By Mr. Lang:

Q. Have you ever worn any kind of belt, or brace, or collar?

A. Yes. Like when I went for my — on the trip to Monroe I wore a back brace.

Q. Where did you get that?

A. At Mt. Sinai. Well, see, it was a traction belt and I just cut the things off of it and used it, just used it as a belt.

Q. How wide is that?

A. This wide (indicating).

Q. About six inches wide?

A. Yes.

Q. How many times have you been hospitalized since this accident of August of 79?

A. Just that once.

Q. And how long a time was that?

A. A week.

Q. Did the hospitalization help you?

A. Not really. Not really.

Q. How long have you lived in the Detroit area?

A. About eleven or twelve years.

Q. Did you have headaches before this accident?

A. Not that I can recall, no.

Q. You referred to migraine headaches; now, have you been bothered with migraine headaches?

A. Not like that. Not no headaches like this one. I used to have just plain headaches, you know, like cold headaches, but like these headaches is something else.

Q. How often do you get those?

A. Once in a while.

Q. How often is that? Once a month?

A. Once a month, twice a month. You know, it isn't —

Q. How long do they last?

A. A long time; about three or four hours.

Q. Do you take anything for them?

A. Yes.

Q. What do you take?

A. Aspirins.

Q. Does that relieve them?

A. No.

   Mr. Lang: I have no further questions.

   Mr. Clarke: We will waive the reading and signing and the notice of filing of the deposition.

                              *   *   *

STATE OF MICHIGAN } SS.
COUNTY OF WAYNE }

Be it known that I took the deposition of Duane Johnson, pursuant to agreement of counsel; that I was then and there a notary public in and for said county and state; that I exercised the power of that office in taking said deposition; that by virtue thereof I was then and there authorized to administer an oath; that said witness, before testifying, was duly sworn to testify to the truth, the whole truth and nothing but the truth relative to the cause specified above; that the deposition is a true record of the testimony given by the witness; that the reading and signing of the deposition was waived by the witness and pursuant to agreement of counsel; that I am neither attorney or counsel for, nor related to or employed by, any of the parties to the action in which this deposition was taken, and further that I am not a relative or employee of any attorney or counsel employed by the parties hereto or financially interested in the action.

WITNESS MY HAND AND SEAL this 22nd day of September, 1981.

John R. Nash

Notary Public, Wayne County, Michigan
My Commission Expires November 25, 1984.

Review

1. Who may serve a summons and complaint in a civil action?

2. Describe the various methods available for serving a summons and complaint upon a corporation.

3. Within how many days after service of the complaint upon the defendant may he start a third-party action without leave of the court?

4. When may a deposition be used at trial in lieu of the live testimony of the deponent?

5. If a party wants to inspect certain written documents which are in the possession of another party who refuses to permit the inspection, what, if any, remedy does he or she have?

6. What factors must be considered in determining whether the Court has jurisdiction of a particular case?

7. What consequences may result from a party's false answer to an interrogatory?

8. Define "res ipsa loquitur."

9. Define "negligence."

10. How many days notice must be given for the hearing of a motion?

11. As a practical matter, what guidelines should be followed in the preparation of interrogatories?

12. Is it ethical (proper) for an attorney to interview a witness after the witness's deposition has been noticed but before the deposition is taken?

13. May the parties stipulate to take a deposition without serving a notice for taking the deposition?

14. How soon after an action is commenced may the *defendant* serve a notice of taking deposition?

15. What are the distinctions between jurisdiction and venue?

16. What are the limitations on adverse medical examinations?

17. What is meant by general jurisdiction when referring to a Court?

18. Are a parties' income tax records (reports) subject to discovery? What procedures would be employed? What would have to be shown to justify obtaining the tax returns?

19. What are the prerequisites to obtaining an adverse medical examination?

20. How does a Request for Admissions differ from Written Interrogatories?

21. When may a Request for Admissions be served on a *non-party* and enforced against him?

22. What is "impeachment" as that term is used in civil litigation?

23. What considerations determine whether a party will use an oral deposition or written interrogatories for discovery?

24. Describe the proper and adequate preparation of a party for his deposition which is to be taken by the opposing attorney.

25. Describe at least four purposes or uses of oral depositions.

26. What is an affirmative defense, and how is it raised?

27. Define "Stare Decisis."

28. Define "special damages."

29. What is the function of the jury in a civil trial?

30. If a client consults a lawyer about a proposed illegal scheme which is later pursued by the client, to what extent will the communications be privileged or non-discoverable in a civil suit by a third-party against the former client and why?

31. How many peremptory challenges does a party have in a civil case? How many challenges for cause does a party have?

32. What are the consequences if plaintiff fails to prove a prima facie case? Discuss the procedures which the parties would follow.

33. When should pleadings and other papers, used in litigation, be filed with the Clerk of Court?

34. When a document used in litigation is served by mail, when is the service complete, i. e., effective?

35. What is an ex parte motion?

36. If the answer fails to either admit or deny an averment contained in the complaint, what is the status of the averment?

37. What are "special damages?"

38. What is an affirmative defense?

39. What happens to an affirmative defense if it is not set forth in a responsive pleading?

40. · What is meant by the term "compulsory counterclaim?"

41. What is a pretrial conference, and what are the purposes of such conferences?

42. What general information should be contained in all written motions?

43. What is the purpose or function of the notice of motion which is attached to and served with all written motions?

44. What sources of information may the court consider when ruling upon a motion for summary judgment pursuant to Rule 56?

45. Why is the plaintiff precluded from inquiring into defendant's financial worth when deposing the defendant?

46. What is a "cause of action" in civil litigation?

47. How does a "declaratory judgment" action differ from an action for money damages?

48. What is meant by "res judicata?"

49. What is meant by "splitting a cause of action?"

50. What factors must exist for communications with a lawyer to be considered privileged?

51. What is a contingent fee; and are such fees ethical?

52. Describe the extent of a lawyer's implied authority in the handling of his client's litigation.

53. On what grounds or for what reasons may a client discharge his attorney?

54. Describe the territorial jurisdiction of the federal district courts.

55. What is "proximate cause?"

56. What is "strict liability in tort?"

57. When is a civil action commenced, i. e., started?

58. If a notice of motion and motion are deposited in a U.S. mailbox on Saturday for service on the adverse party, but the mail is not picked up until Monday, and they are not delivered to the opposing attorney until Wednesday, what is the day from which one begins counting to determine whether adequate time for service was given?

59. If a party fails to appear at (attend) the deposition of a witness, can that deposition be used *for* or *against* the absent party when the case reaches trial? Does it make a difference whether the absent party was served with a "Notice of taking Deposition"?

60. What is a "dismissal without prejudice"?

61. If a party duly makes an admission in response to requests for admissions, when may that "admission" be used against him in any other proceedings?

62. What is the purpose and what are the limitations on opening statements by counsel?

63. What is an evidentiary "offer of proof" and how is it made?

64. After the jury returns a special verdict, what is the procedure for having judgment entered for the prevailing party?

65. Define "judgment."

66. What is an offer of judgment? Why is it used? How is the offer of judgment made? What are the time limitations as to when it can be made?

67. What is a special appearance?

68. What is meant by fair preponderance of the evidence in connection with a party's burden of proof?

69. What procedure would an attorney follow if he or she wanted to obtain separate trials on the issues of liability and damages?

70. What are the grounds for consolidating two or more action (cases) for the purpose of trial?

71. In a civil action, may a plaintiff force the defendant to take the stand to testify? If so, what procedure is followed?

72. How does a special verdict differ from a general verdict in its form, purpose, effect, and procedures?

73. What is an additur? When is it used? How is it obtained?

74. What are four grounds for ordering a new trial?

75. What is an affidavit of prejudice? Who signs it? What are the grounds for it?

76. What is the procedure for obtaining a restraining order, and what are the grounds for such an order?

77. What party has the right to final argument in a civil action?

78. What is the parol evidence rule?

79. What is meant by the "ultimate question of fact?"

80. Describe in general terms the procedure for prosecuting an appeal following an adverse jury verdict.

81. Who would have occasion to file an amicus curiae brief?

82. How many interrogatories may a party serve in a federal court action?

83. Is there any situation in which it is not necessary to pay a witness a subpoena fee?

84. Explain the difference, if any, between "admissions" made in answer to interrogatories, and "admissions" made during the course of a deposition, and "admissions" made in response to requests for admissions.

85. How is a substitution of parties accomplished in a civil lawsuit? (Rule 25)

86. Are insurance coverages discoverable? Why?

87. List at least four types of protective orders that a court may issue to limit discovery.

88. When does a party have a duty to supplement his oral deposition answers or written answers to interrogatories?

89. What is a subpoena duces tecum?

90. What grounds will permit the plaintiff to obtain the defendant's deposition in the thirty day period immediately following service of the summons and complaint on the defendant?

91. How is a case placed on the active trial calendar in federal court?

92. If a lawyer believes that his client's recollection of the accident in question is in error, explain the extent to which a lawyer may correct the client's version in preparing for a deposition or trial.

93. What is the voir dire examination?

94. Explain the function of a "findings of fact, conclusions of law and order for judgment."

95. Define hearsay evidence.

96. What is an "advisory jury?"

97. What factors determine whether evidence is relevant to a civil action?

98. To what extent may one party require the disclosure of opinions and conclusions developed by another party's hired expert? (This question pertains to non-medical expert opinion.)

99. What special arrangements must be made in a civil action for the deposition of a person who is confined to a prison?

100. If the parties and deponent cannot agree on the place of the deponent's

deposition and subpoena is necessary to compel the witness's attendance, what are the geographical limits on where the deposition may be taken? (Rule 45)

Glossary

Action at law. A claim which is recognized and enforceable at law. The claimant must have sustained some injury, damage or loss due to conduct on the part of the defendant which is prohibited by law.

Affirmative defense. New matter constituting a defense; new matter which, assuming the complaint to be true, constitutes a defense to it. The defendant has the burden of proof to establish the defense.

Certiorari. The name of a writ of review or inquiry. A higher court directs the lower court to deliver the court records and files so that the higher court may review the proceedings.

Comparative Negligence. A doctrine which requires the fact finder (jury) in a negligence action to determine the percentages of causal negligence attributable to each person involved in the occurrence. The plaintiff's causal negligence is not a bar to a recovery of compensatory money damages. If the plaintiff is found to be causally negligent, the amount of money damages recoverable is reduced by the amount of his or her causal negligence. However, if the plaintiff is more negligent than the defendant, some states hold plaintiff is barred from making any recovery against the defendant. If two or more defendants are found to be causally negligent, they must share the liability for money damages in proportion to their percentages of causal negligence.

Conclusion of law. A determination by the court of the issue in a civil suit. The application of rules of law to the established facts. The conclusions of law reached by the trial court which are the bases for entering judgment in a civil action.

Contingent. Dependency upon the occurrence of a condition or the existence of a set of circumstances.

Contribution.   The sharing of a loss or payment among two or more parties. A party may sue another to obtain contribution for a debt or obligation which they jointly owe to a third person.

Counterclaim.   A claim presented by a defendant in opposition to or deduction from the claim of the plaintiff. A claim made by the defendant against the plaintiff in the same action.

Court of record.   Courts whose acts and judicial proceedings are recorded for a perpetual memory.

Criminal.   (adj.)   That which pertains to or is connected with the law of crimes, or the administration of penal justice, or which relates to or has the character of crime.

Cross-claim.   A "cross-claim" is one brought by a defendant against a co-defendant concerning matters in question in the original action. Its purpose is to obtain some affirmative relief concerning matters in issue, to obtain full relief for all parties and a complete determination of all controversies arising out of matters alleged in original complaints, and to have affirmative relief against the co-defendant in the nature of an original action.

Damages.   A pecuniary compensation or indemnity, which may be recovered in the courts by any person who has suffered loss, detriment, or injury, whether to his person, property, or rights, through the unlawful act or omission or negligence of another.

Declaratory judgment.   One which simply declares the rights of the parties or expresses the opinion of the court on a question of law, without ordering anything to be done. Its distinctive characteristics are that no executory process follows as a matter of course, nor is it necessary that an actual wrong, giving rise to action for damages, should have been done, or be immediately threatened.

Demonstrative evidence.   Physical evidence which either is evidence, or contains evidence, or is illustrative of facts in controversy.

Deposition.   (1) The testimony of a witness taken not in open court, but in pursuance of a commission to take testimony as provided by court order or rule, and reduced to writing and duly authenticated, and intended to be used upon the trial of an action in court. It is sometimes used as synonymous with "affidavit" or "oath", but its technical meaning does not include such terms.

(2) A written declaration under oath, made upon notice to the adverse party for the purpose of enabling him to attend and cross-examine; or upon written interrogatories. The term sometimes is used in a special

sense to denote a statement made orally by a person on oath before an examiner, commissioner, or officer of the court, (but not in open court), and taken down in writing by the examiner or under his direction.

Directed verdict. A decision and order by the trial court by which the judge determines that a claim or defense lacks sufficient support in the evidence to let the claim or defense go to the jury for consideration. A directed verdict is usually granted against the party who has the burden of proof. It may be directed in favor of a party who has the burden of proof only if the evidence is conclusively in his favor. Judgment will be entered by the clerk according to the directed verdict.

Dismissal with prejudice. An adjudication on the merits, and final disposition, barring the right to bring or maintain an action on the same claim or cause.

Dismissal without prejudice. Dismissal without prejudice to the right of the complainant to sue again on the same cause of action. The effect of the words "without prejudice" is to prevent the decree of dismissal from operating as a bar to a subsequent suit.

Equity. In its broadest and most general signification, this term denotes the spirit and the habit of fairness, justness, and right dealing which would regulate the intercourse of men with men, — the rule of doing to all others as we desire them to do to us; or, as it is expressed by Justinian, "to live honestly, to harm nobody, to render to every man his due." It is therefore the synonym of natural right or justice. But in this sense its obligation is ethical rather than jural, and its discussion belongs to the sphere of morals. It is grounded in the precepts of the conscience, not in any sanction of positive law. In a restricted sense, the word denotes equal and impartial justice as between two persons whose rights or claims are in conflict; justice, that is, as ascertained by natural reason or ethical insight, but independent of the formulated body of law. This is not a technical meaning of the term, except in so far as courts which administer equity seek to discover it by the agencies above mentioned, or apply it beyond the strict lines of positive law. In a still more restricted sense, it is a system of jurisprudence, or branch of remedial justice, administered by certain tribunals, distinct from the common-law courts and empowered to decree "equity" in the sense last above given. Here it becomes a complex of well-settled and well-understood rules, principles, and precedents.

Ex parte. On one side only; by or for one party; done for, in behalf of, or on the application of, one party only. Ex parte motions are motions heard by the court with only one party in attendance.

Fiduciary. A fiduciary is a person or corporation who has assumed a special relationship to another person or another person's property such as a trustee, administrator, executor, lawyer, or guardian. The fiduciary must exercise the highest degree of care to maintain and preserve the person's rights and/or property which are within his charge. A fiduciary must place the interests of his charge ahead of his own. A lawyer is a fiduciary concerning any secrets, documents, and money given to him by the client for safekeeping during the professional relationship. A lawyer is not a fiduciary in the handling of the client's litigation.

Finding of fact. A determination of a fact by the court, averred by one party and denied by the other, and founded on evidence in case.

Foundation. A necessary showing of underlying facts or conditions to the admissibility of opinions and exhibits into evidence.

General jurisdiction. Such as extends to all controversies that may be brought before a court within the legal bounds of rights and remedies; as opposed to special or limited jurisdiction, which covers only a particular class of cases, or cases where the amount in controversy is below a prescribed sum, or which is subject to specific exceptions.

Grand jury. A jury of inquiry who are summoned and returned by the sheriff to each session of the criminal courts, and whose duty is to receive complaints and accusations in criminal cases, hear the evidence adduced on the part of the state, and find bills of indictment in cases where they are satisfied a trial ought to be had. They are first sworn, and instructed by the court.

Guardian ad litem. A guardian appointed by a court of justice to prosecute or defend for an infant in any suit, to which that infant may be a party. The infant may be a plaintiff or defendant.

Hearsay. Evidence not proceeding from the personal knowledge of the witness, but from the mere repetition of what he has heard others say. That which does not derive its value solely from the credit of the witness, but rests mainly on the veracity and competency of other persons. The very nature of the evidence shows its weakness, and it is admitted only in limited situations due to necessity.

Impeachment. To cast doubt on the credibility of a witness or exhibits by showing inconsistencies.

Impeachment evidence. Evidence offered solely for the purpose of casting doubt on other evidence received by the court. It is evidence which will not support a verdict. Some impeachment evidence may also be substantive evidence which will support a verdict.

Indemnity. A collateral payment or right to payment in favor of one person who has secured another against the latter's obligation to a third person.

The payment or right to a complete reimbursement for monies payed or owned to another. Indemnity results in a complete reimbursement. Whereas, contribution results in only a partial reimbursement.

Injunction. A prohibitive writ issued by a court of equity against a defendant forbidding the latter to do some act which he is threatening or attempting to commit, or restraining him in the continuance thereof. A court may issue an injunction if defendant's conduct is injurious to the plaintiff, and not such as can be adquately redressed by an action at law with money damages.

Joint and severable liability. Two or more parties may be liable to another party for the entire claim even though, as between the parties who are liable, they are entitled to a proportionate contribution.

Judgment. The official and authentic decision of a court of justice upon the respective rights and claims of the parties to an action or suit therein litigated and submitted to its determination.

Jurisdiction. It is the power and authority of a court and its office. A court's jurisdiction depends upon the court following due process of law. It may be limited to a specific territory and to certain types of actions or certain types of controversies, or certain classes of parties.

Letters Rogatory. A formal communication in writing, sent by a court in which an action is pending to a court or judge of a foreign country or state, requesting that the testimony of a witness resident within the jurisdiction of the latter court may be there formally taken under its direction and transmitted to the first court for use in the pending action.

Liability. A legal obligation to make restitution or pay compensation. Liability may be contingent or absolute.

Mandamus. This is the name of a writ which issues from a court of superior jurisdiction, and is directed to a private or municipal corporation, or any of its officers, or to an executive, administrative or judicial officer, or to an inferior court, commanding the performance of a particular act therein specified, and belonging to his or their public, official, or ministerial duty, or directing the restoration of the complainant to rights or privileges of which he has been illegally deprived.

Material. Important; more or less necessary; going to the merits; having to do with matter, as distinguished from form. In a civil action evidence is material if it relates to the issues raised by the pleadings.

Mistrial. An erroneous, invalid, or nugatory trial; a trial of an action which cannot stand in law because of want of jurisdiction, or a wrong drawing of jurors, or disregard of some other fundamental requisite.

Motion.   An application for a ruling or order made to a court or judge. The term is generally employed with reference to all such applications, whether written or oral.

Negligence.   The omission to do something which a reasonable man, guided by those ordinary considerations which ordinarily regulate human affairs, would do, or the doing of something which a reasonable and prudent man would not do.

Negligence per se.   Conduct, whether of action or omission, which may be declared and treated as negligence without any argument or proof as to the particular surrounding circumstances, either because it is in violation of a statute or valid municipal ordinance, or because it is so palpably opposed to the dictates of common prudence that it can be said without hesitation or doubt that no careful person would have been guilty of it.

Peremptory challenge.   By law and court rule each party to a civil action has a right to strike a specified number of jurors, usually two or three, from the panel during the voir dire examination without explaining or justifying removal of the jurors. Such strikes are called peremptory challenges.

Prima facie case.   A party has presented a prima facie case if he or she has presented sufficient evidence to establish all the elements of the cause of action or all the elements of an affirmative defense. The evidence must be sufficient to support a verdict or finding on the issue. A prima facie case may exist even though the evidence is in conflict or disputed.

Prima facie evidence.   On its face the evidence is presumed to be true unless disproved by some other evidence.

Prima facie negligence.   Proof of an act or omission that is specifically prohibited by law thereby establishing that the applicable standard of due care has been violated. The act of omission is, on its face, an act or omission of negligence. A party is permitted the right to explain and justify the violation. However, in the absence of some compelling excuse or justification the fact finder (jury) must find that the conduct was negligent. Whereas, an act or omission that is "negligent per se" may not be explained or justified.

Relevant.   Applying to the matter in question; affording something to the purpose. Evidence is relevant when it has probative value; when it tends to establish or negate a controverted fact.

Res ipsa loquitur.   A legal doctrine by which one party may establish an inference of negligence on the part of another party. The inference of negligence comes from a showing that the accident in question is of a kind that ordinarily does not occur in the absence of negligence; that the accident was caused by an instrumentality which was in the exclusive control of the defendant; that the accident was not caused by any act of the plaintiff or some third person.

Res judicata. A matter adjudged; a thing judicially acted upon or decided; a thing or matter settled by judgment.

Rule 35 medical examination. A medical examination of a party to an action conducted by a physician selected by an adverse party for the purpose of evaluating the person's physical, mental or blood condition. The medical examination is not in itself an adversary proceeding. The physician is expected to follow professional practices and procedures in conducting the examination and in making his evaluation.

Settlement. An adjustment between persons concerning their disputes. An agreement by which parties to a dispute ascertain what is coming from one to the other. A compromise between parties which is arrived at without a judicial order or decree.

Stare decisis. To abide by, or adhere to decided cases.

Stipulation. An agreement voluntarily entered into between the parties concerning some aspect of their litigation. An agreement between the parties which the court will recognize and accept to facilitate judicial proceedings. Stipulations may go to matters of procedure or substance.

Subpoena. A process to cause a witness to appear and give testimony, commanding him to lay aside all pretenses and excuses, and appear before a court or magistrate therein named at a time therein mentioned, to testify for the party named. Failure to comply places the person under penalty by the court.

Subrogation. The substitution of one person in the place of another with reference to a lawful claim, demand or right, so that he who is substituted succeeds to the rights of the other in relation to the debt or claim, and its rights, remedies, or securities.

Substantive evidence. That adduced for the purpose of proving a fact in issue, as opposed to evidence given for the purpose of discrediting a witness, showing that he is unworthy of belief.

Tort. A private or civil wrong or injury. A wrong independent of contract. A violation of a duty imposed by general law or otherwise upon all persons occupying the relation to each other which is involved in a given transaction or occurrence. There must always be a violation of some duty owing to plaintiff, and generally such duty must arise by operation of law and not by mere agreement of the parties.

Transitory cause of action.   A cause of action which follows the defendant and, therefore, may be commenced in any jurisdiction where the defendant can be found.

Ultimate question of fact.   The conclusions to be drawn by the jury from all the evidence which are dispositive of the claims and defenses of the parties. It is the fact to which the rules of law are applied so that a judgment can be rendered by the court.

Unilateral mistake.   A mistake as to the terms or effect of a contract made or entertained by one of the parties to it but not by the other.

Venue.   The place or county in which an injury is declared to have been done, or fact declared to have happened. The county or district in which an action is brought for trial, and which is to furnish the panel of jurors.

Voidable.   A contract is voidable when the contract's purpose is not contrary to law but making of the contract is technically defective due to the wrongful conduct or inadvertence of one of the contracting parties. The party or parties to the contract who did comply with all legal requirements has the option of enforcing the contract or avoiding it. On the other hand, a contract which is *void* cannot be enforced by any party.

Voir dire.   To speak the truth. This phrase denotes the preliminary examination by the court and attorneys of jurors where their competency, interest, etc., is tested.

Wrongful death action.   An action at law, created by statute that permits the heirs and next of kin to recover money damages from the decedent's tortfeasor for the pecuniary losses resulting from the decedent's death. The elements of the cause of action are established by statute in each state. State statutes also declare what pecuniary losses are compensable and the limitation, if any, on the total amount of damages recoverable.

Third-party Practice

The same facts which give rise to plaintiff's cause of action against the defendant may also create rights in favor of the defendant against some third person who has not been sued. For example, if a plaintiff consumer was injured due to some defect in a product he purchased, the consumer has a cause of action against the retailer and against the manufacturer. If the plaintiff chooses to sue only the retailer, the retailer may commence a third-party action against the manufacturer for contribution and/or indemnity. Frequently the manufacturer has the ultimate responsibility for the injury. If the retailer succeeds in showing that the manufacturer was responsible for the defect and injury, the retailer may obtain full reimbursement from the manufacturer for any money damages the retailer is obligated to pay to the plaintiff consumer. Another example: when an employee acts within the scope of his employment to carry out his employer's business purposes, the employer is vicariously liable to any person injured by reason of the negligent acts of the employee. This is true whether the employer is an individual or a corporation. If an injured party brings an action against the employer, the employer may have a cause of action against his employee or agent for indemnity. So if the employer is held liable to the plaintiff, the employer may be able to recover the same amount of money damages from his negligent employee, together with the employer's costs incurred in defending against the plaintiff's action. The employer may bring a third-party action against the employee for indemnity if the employee was not sued directly by the plaintiff.

Joint tortfeasors are entitled to contribution between them. For example, if two negligent motorists collide causing injury to a passenger and the passenger sues only one driver, that defendant driver may sue the other driver for contribution through a third-party action. This situation frequently arises when a wife is injured in an accident while her husband is driving. She may elect to sue only the other driver. But the defendant driver may bring a third-party action against the husband for contribution — assuming that the husband was negligent and assuming there is no family immunity.

The defendant commences a third-party action by serving a summons and complaint upon the third-party defendant. Service is made in the same manner as service of an original summons and complaint. Rule 4. The defendant has a right to commence a third-party action any time within ten days after serving his answer to the complaint. Rule 14(a). Otherwise, he must apply to the court for leave to commence the third-party action. Of course, the reason for limiting the time in which the third-party action may be started is that the defendant must not cause the plaintiff's case to be delayed. A substantial delay may seriously prejudice the plaintiff's rights so the Rules discourage any delay. The third-party action unavoidably complicates the litigation some. However, that fact alone does not preclude the right to a third-party action.

The ten day period for starting a third-party action begins to run the day after service of the answer. The defendant may move the court for an extension of time. If the motion for an extension of time is made within the ten day period, notice of the motion need not be given to the plaintiff. Rule 6(b). That is to say, the motion may be made "ex parte". But if the ten day period has expired, the defendant must make the motion by giving due notice to the plaintiff. Rule 6(d). A motion made after expiration of the ten day period should show there was excusable neglect for failing to act within the ten day period prescribed by Rule 14; that plaintiff will not be unduly prejudiced by the joinder; and that there is reason to believe that the proposed third-party defendant is liable to the defendant for indemnity or contribution. Frequently, such motions are accompanied by a proposed third-party complaint which states the cause of action for indemnity or contribution. If the plaintiff does not oppose a defendant's motion for an order extending the time for commencement of the third-party action, the court usually grants the motion as a matter of course.

The third-party defendant has twenty days in which to serve his answer. The third-party answer must be served upon the plaintiff and upon the *defendant and third-party plaintiff*. In turn, the third-party defendant may commence a fourth-party action for indemnity or contribution against anyone who is liable to him because of the transaction or occurrence in question. The third-party defendant then has the additional title of *fourth-party plaintiff*. Theoretically, there is no limit to the number of parties who may be joined in a lawsuit in this manner.

Third-party actions are not compulsory, as most counterclaims are. Any party may move the court to sever the third-party action from the main action. There are numerous reasons and grounds for obtaining a severance. Rule 42. However, consolidations are generally favored.

If the defendant is unsuccessful in his belated efforts to obtain leave to commence a third-party action, he may, nevertheless, start a separate lawsuit against the would-be third-party defendant for the same purpose of obtaining contribution or indemnity. But by having a separate lawsuit, he runs a risk that he, the defendant, will be found liable to the plaintiff and yet, he will be unsuccessful in proving a right to indemnity or contribution in the second action. The losing defendant has the burden of proving the plaintiff's damages when seeking indemnity or contribution in a subsequent trial. Of course, a second trial also increases the expenses.

A third-party defendant may serve a claim against the plaintiff if that claim arises out of the same transaction or occurrence. The plaintiff may also serve a claim upon the third-party defendant. When that is done, the third-party defendant is then treated as a direct defendant. The two or more defendants are referred to as co-defendants.

If there is more than one third-party defendant, each may serve a cross-claim against the other, just as co-defendants may do. Rules 13(g), 14(a). A third-party cross-claim requires an *answer to cross-claim*.

The third-party defendant's answer must assert whatever defenses the third-party defendant has to the third-party plaintiff's claim. In addition, the third-party defendant may allege defenses which the third-party plaintiff has against the plaintiff's claim. For example, if the defendant has a defense to plaintiff's claim, such as contributory negligence or assumption of risk or release or immunity or statute of limitations, the third-party defendant may raise that defense in his answer, regardless of whether that defense was raised in the defendant's answer. This is important because the third-party action is, by its nature, predicated entirely upon the defendant's liability to plaintiff. If the defendant is not liable to the plaintiff, there can be no liability on the part of the third-party defendant for indemnity or contribution. If the third-party defendant succeeds in keeping the plaintiff from recovering against the defendant, the third-party action automatically falls.

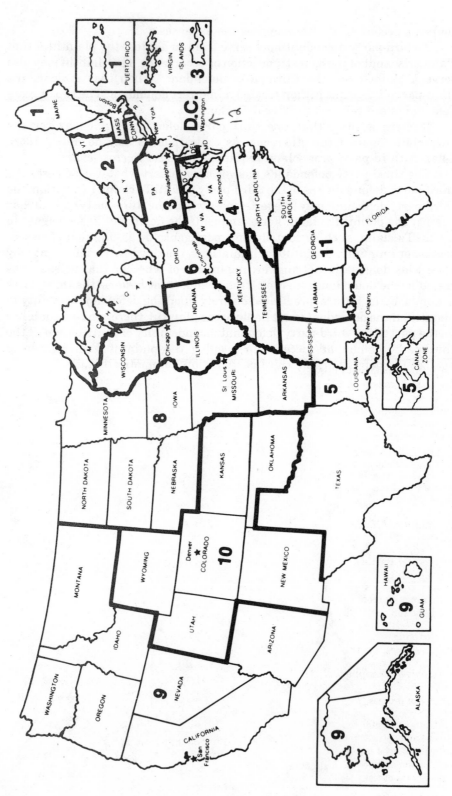

The Twelve Federal Judicial Circuits

Index ▬▬▬▬

†